fashion marketing

Palgrave Master Series

Accounting
Accounting Skills
Advanced English Language
Advanced Pure Mathematics
Arabic
Basic Management
Biology
British Politics
Business Communication
Business Environment
C Programming
C++ Programming
Chemistry
COBOL Programming
Communication
Computing
Counselling Skills
Counselling Theory
Customer Relations
Database Design
Delphi Programming
Desktop Publishing
e-Business
Economic and Social History
Economics
Electrical Engineering
Electronics
Employee Development
English Grammar
English Language
English Literature
Fashion Buying and Merchandising Management
Fashion Marketing
Fashion Styling
Financial Management
Geography
Global Information Systems
Globalization of Business

Human Resource Management
International Trade
Internet
Java
Language of Literature
Management Skills
Marketing Management
Mathematics
Microsoft Office
Microsoft Windows, Novell NetWare and UNIX
Modern British History
Modern European History
Modern German History
Modern United States History
Modern World History
The Novels of Jane Austen
Organisational Behaviour
Pascal and Delphi Programming
Personal Finance
Philosophy
Physics
Poetry
Practical Criticism
Psychology
Public Relations
Shakespeare
Social Welfare
Sociology
Statistics
Strategic Management
Systems Analysis and Design
Team Leadership
Theology
Twentieth-Century Russian History
Visual Basic
World Religions

www.palgravemasterseries.com

Palgrave Master Series
Series Standing Order ISBN 0–333–69343–4
(outside North America only)

You can receive future titles in this series as they are published by placing a standing order. Please contact your bookseller or, in case of difficulty, write to us at the address below with your name and address, the title of the series and the ISBN quoted above.

Customer Services Department, Macmillan Distribution Ltd
Houndmills, Basingstoke, Hampshire RG21 6XS, England

MASTERING

fashion marketing

Tim Jackson
and
David Shaw

palgrave
macmillan

First published 2009 by
PALGRAVE MACMILLAN

Palgrave Macmillan in the UK is an imprint of Macmillan Publishers Limited,
registered in England, company number 785998, of Houndmills, Basingstoke,
Hampshire RG21 6XS.

Palgrave Macmillan in the US is a division of St Martin's Press LLC,
175 Fifth Avenue, New York, NY 10010.

Palgrave Macmillan is the global academic imprint of the above companies
and has companies and representatives throughout the world.

Palgrave® and Macmillan® are registered trademarks in the United States,
the United Kingdom, Europe and other countries.

ISBN-13: 978–1–4039–1902–1
ISBN-10: 1–4039–1902–X

This book is printed on paper suitable for recycling and made from fully managed and sustained forest sources. Logging, pulping and manufacturing
processes are expected to conform to the environmental regulations of the
country of origin.

A catalogue record for this book is available from the British Library.

A catalog record for this book is available from the Library of Congress.

10   9   8   7   6   5
18   17   16   15   14   13   12   11

Printed and bound in Great Britain by
CPI Antony Rowe, Chippenham and Eastbourne

Contents

list of tables

list of figures

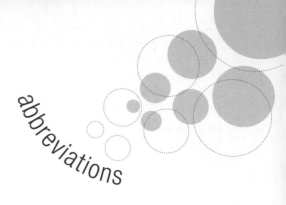

ACID	Anti Copying In Design
ACORN	A Classification of Residential Neighbourhoods
ASOS	As Seen on Screen
B2B	business-to-business
B2C	business-to-consumer
BBC	British Broadcasting Corporation
BCG	Boston Consulting Group
BMI	body mass index
BOGOF	buy one get one free
BRAD	British Rates and Data
C2C	customer-to-customer
CAPI	computer-aided personal interviewing
CATI	computer-aided telephone interviewing
CAWI	computer-aided web interviewing
CCR	customer conversion rate
CMT	cut, make and trim
CP	cost price
CPI	Consumer Prices Index
CSO	Central Statistical Office (UK)
CSR	corporate social responsibility
DC	distribution centre
DOS	directly operated store
EPOS	electronic point of sale
ESOMAR	European Society for Opinion and Marketing Research
ETI	Ethical Trading Initiative
FC	French Connection
FMCG	fast-moving consumer goods
GATT	General Agreement on Tariffs and Trade
Gen-C	Generation C
Gen-X	Generation X
Gen-Y	Generation Y

GINETEX	Groupement International d'Étiquetage pour l'Entretien des Textiles
HDTV	high-definition television
IMC	integrated marketing communications
IPR	Institute of Public Relations
LFW	London Fashion Week
LVMH	Moët Hennessy Louis Vuitton
MDA	mobile digital assistant
MFA	Multi-Fibre Arrangement
MMOPG	massive multiplayer online role-playing game
M&S	Marks & Spencer
MRS	Marketing Research Society
NGO	non-governmental organisation
NPD	new product development
NS-SEC	National Statistics Socio-Economic Classification
PDA	personal digital assistant
PEST	Political, Economic, Social and Technological
PETA	People for the Ethical Treatment of Animals
PLC	product life cycle
POS	point of sale
PR	Public Relations
RAJAR	Radio Joint Audience Research
RFID	radio-frequency identification
RSP	retail selling price
RTW	ready-to-wear
SBU	strategic business unit
SKU	stock-keeping unit
SL	Second Life
SMS	short message service
STP	segmentation, targeting and positioning
SWOT	strengths, weaknesses, opportunities and threats
TGI	Target Group Index
TNS	Taylor Nelson Sofres
TRAID	Textile Recycling for Aid and International Development
UDS	United Drapery Stores
URL	universal resource locator
USP	unique selling proposition
VAT	value added tax
WF	Worldpanel Fashion
WGSN	Worth Global Style Network
WTO	World Trade Organisation
WWD	Women's Wear Daily

acknowledgements

Garry Aspden	Adidas
Vanessa Belleau	TNS Worldpanel Fashion
Clare Boulton	London College of Fashion
Carl and Rachel Bromley	Sienna Couture
Val Buchanan	London College of Fashion
Ian Cartwright	Base London
Peter Christofi	Laura Fashions
Dr Frances Corner	London College of Fashion
Anika Davies	TNS World Panel Fashion
Sarah Dixon	Austin Reed
Caren Downie	ASOS
John Eastwood	University and College Union (retired)
Kathrin Freier	S. Oliver Group
David French	London College of Fashion
Nicola Griffin	Modus PR
Carmen Haid	Tommy Hilfiger
Charles Harrison-Wallace	London College of Fashion (retired)
Brenda Hegarty	*International Herald Tribune*
Stephen Henly	SAP
Sian Hession	Long Tall Sally
James Hobbs	TNS Worldpanel Fashion
Nick Hollingworth	Austin Reed
Fritz Homer	Woolford
Deirdre Hopkin	Rootstein Hopkins Foundation
Mathew Jeatt	Promostyl
The Joel Family	Joel & Sons
Bob Jolley	Mapleleaf
Mrs Kim	Sung Joo Group
Lekha Klouda	The Association of Charity Shops
François Lavergne	ESMOD
June Lawlor	House of Fraser

Kim Mannino	Promostyl
Suzy Menkes	*International Herald Tribune*
Prof Christopher Moore	Heriot-Watt University
Clare Morgan	Jaeger
Karen Mörsch	The Hasley Group
Martin Parker	Urban Outfitters (Europe)
Jodi Pritchard	Mercedes Australian Fashion Week
Rosemin Ratanshi	Patrick Cox
Ben Richards	Naked Communication
David Riddiford	Arnotts of Dublin
Angela Rumsey	WGSN
Alison Sachs	Swarovski
Steve Sharp	Marks & Spencer
Sally Smitherman	Retail Human Resources
Peter Swinscoe	Debenhams (retired)
Alison Thorne	Exley Hervey Executive Search
Dr Neil Towers	Heriot-Watt University
Roger Tredre	fashion journalist
Josina von dem Bussche-Kessell	Boucheron
Professor David Walters	Sydney Graduate School of Management
Simon Wilson	Hasley Group
Clare Woods	Club 21 (Armani)

introduction

The purpose of this book is to provide readers with insights into the diverse role of marketing within the fashion industry. It also aims to fill a gap in knowledge relating to the activities of the fashion marketing function in fashion companies and analyse the relationship between marketing theory and practice in the fashion industry.

For many years industry practitioners and those who study fashion marketing have depended on generic marketing theory to help them understand and operate effectively within the fashion business. However, the unique nature of fashion places limitations on the application of some generic marketing theory and models to fashion. Unlike most other industries, fashion companies experience volatile fluctuations in consumer preferences arising from uncontrollable factors that include the weather, the influence of taste-makers, and fast-evolving fads communicated through and influenced by the media. Fashion volatility makes demand for clothing and accessories very unpredictable compared with other sectors such as groceries where steady consumer demand patterns exist. As such, the 'one size fits all' theory including standard linear models of consumer decision-making does not always fit in with the reality of much contemporary fashion consumer purchasing behaviour. Similarly, generic market research methods are insufficient to describe and explain the information-gathering and analyses that underpin wider fashion marketing activity.

There is an expectation that fashions will change at regular points throughout the year. These periods of change are normally described as seasons and have their roots in the need to wear different types, styles and weights of clothing in line with varying weather patterns (summer, winter, etc). As global climate change has left many Western countries, the UK in particular, with warmer winters, the seasons now show a less significant distinction in the weather. Further, people's travelling habits are such that many will go to warmer countries at Christmas to benefit from sunny climates. Consequently many fashion retailers have responded to these variations of 'seasonal' demand with microseasonal ranges, which change monthly in many businesses. At the extreme end of the fashion market are the fast-fashion brands that change what is on offer even more frequently, with Zara being the most extreme, typically changing its stock 17 times in a year.

One could argue that such significant and frequent changes to fashion create a problem for consumers, who need to buy more products and buy them more often in order to remain fashionable. The problem is further compounded for consumers, as the strong social pressure to display specific brands conspicuously is manipulated by fashion companies to generate higher sales. It is easy to understand how complex the problem of fashion is for many people.

Interestingly, the concept of problem creation and solution is central to marketing activity. The very influential marketing academic Theodore Levitt (a previous editor of the *Harvard Business Review*) wrote that products were tools bought by consumers to solve problems. He famously wrote that when consumers buy a drill, it is in fact a hole that they need. Levitt went on to point out that businesses which understood consumers' problems were in a better position to satisfy them than those which only understood the 'tools'. In many respects this is correct, as fashion designers and manufacturers are more successful when they understand the importance of knowing their customers and apply marketing to their businesses in addition to the skills needed to design and manufacture.

The notion of consumers buying products and services to 'solve' problems, which they perceive to exist, suggests that the problems can be created or generated by marketers to sell products and services. In fact there is not much of a difference between the identification of a need and a problem. Much marketing is a fine line between identifying a genuine consumer need and creating a problem that ends up being a need for the consumer. For example in the 1980s the toothpaste brand Clinomyn used to run a slogan on TV adverts: 'No stains. No problem'. It is highly debatable whether consumers genuinely believed that a degree of staining on teeth (which is normally controlled by regular visits to dentists) was in fact a problem. However, the clear message was that people should reflect on how white their teeth were. From this example one can argue that marketing creates problems for consumers and then supplies the products to solve them. Another term for 'spotting a gap in the market' could be problem identification and creation. Although one could argue that there is nothing immoral about positioning a product around a concern, worry or insecurity that a consumer may have, the authors believe that marketing to children in such a way is inappropriate. This also applies to the recurring debate about size zero models and anorexia.

The term 'marketing' has a very specific context within fashion as it is more commonly used to describe a communications function linked to the promotion of products and services and the creation and maintenance of brand identity. The operational function called fashion marketing therefore has a narrowly defined role in the industry compared with the scope of marketing theory. Some might argue that this is a weakness of companies which choose to define marketing in the more limited communications role.

As the marketing function or department in a fashion company is typically a promotion and communications one, strategic and tactical marketing decisions are made about products by other retailer and brand functions. The functions normally involved are design, buying, merchandising and retail management, i.e. designing and creating fashion products, pricing them and also making decisions about where, when and how they should be sold. Readers should appreciate that many people are employed in fashion jobs that may not be considered to be a marketing function. However, the jobs are likely to be very important marketing roles, where the work is concerned with developing and distributing products and/or dealing directly with customers. In such cases it is important for fashion companies to understand the importance of marketing training (as opposed to promotional or communications training) to its sales and profitability. It is interesting to note that it is generally not a requirement for any of the functions to employ individuals who have marketing training or qualifications. The way in which different types of fashion business structure their marketing departments and activities varies from nothing to the large, formally structured in-house team.

So the term 'marketing' refers to both a generic academic subject and a specific fashion business function that has a much wider remit in non-fashion companies. In its widest interpretation it refers to the business activities associated with understanding needs, identifying and defining demand and developing, promoting and selling products to customers. There are many well-articulated definitions of marketing which talk about a process of identifying and satisfying customers' needs through the profitable supply of products and services. More recently definitions have broadened, referring to a social and managerial process through which organisations create and exchange value with their customers. Tucked beneath these various attempts to summarise the scope and role of marketing in as few words as possible are a number of key activities.

The identification of customers and their needs is a specialist role that involves the use of market research and an understanding of consumer buying behaviour. The development of new products and services requires an understanding of the benefits that are sought by consumers to satisfy particular needs. Through seeing products as packages of benefits which address particular needs, it is easier for marketers to develop products that will sell. Thus the knowledge and skills required to develop products are deeper than merely the technical knowledge of how to design and make a product. In fact, a fundamental premise of marketing is that marketers make what they can sell as opposed to attempting to sell what they make. The profitable supply of products and services to customers requires marketers to deliver effective marketing mixes that supply superior value compared with competitors.

In Levitt's drill example, the need that the consumer is addressing is a hole in a surface. The drill is merely a tool that can deliver the principal benefit of a hole. However, the drill itself may be endowed with a variety of other benefits provided by product features that include the fact that it is light (flexibility and comfort), the fact that it is cordless (convenience), a long battery life (convenience) and a variety of drill bits (wide range of jobs). Each of the benefits contributes to the use of a particular manufacturer's (or brand's) product, making it more or less competitive.

In the vast majority of cases marketing theory and practice assumes a sort of benevolent customer-centric view of the world. Many companies reverently cite corporate mantras extolling their customer service and a belief that the customer is always right. It appears, however, that many fashion companies regard customer service as an extension of store management, instead of a core marketing activity and increasingly important basis of differentiation.

This book intends to describe, explain and analyse how the holistic subject of marketing underpins successful fashion business. It also provides practitioners and academics with conceptual fashion contexts for the subject of marketing and explains the subject's relationship to the specialist fashion marketing function operating in the industry.

Chapter 1 (the customer and fashion consumption) investigates and explains the notion of what a customer is. It explains the subtle differences between consumers and business-to-business (b2b) customers and examines the importance of consumer profiling using contemporary examples. The chapter also reviews and evaluates relevant consumer behaviour theory.

Chapter 2 (marketing research and information for fashion) explains the whole scope and scale of marketing research and how it works in reality for fashion businesses. It explains the unique problems faced by fashion researchers and gives a clear pragmatic explanation of research techniques and how to apply them. It acts as a guide for finding relevant fashion information sources, which are often overlooked even by large fashion businesses. Case studies from Worth Global Style Network (WGSN) and Worldpanel Fashion (WF) illustrate the distinctive and important roles of qualitative and quantitative primary research to the fashion industry. Market research techniques such as sampling are explained and clear guidance is given upon such important qualitative research tools as the focus group and observational methods. It finally summarises the limitations of marketing research within the fashion context.

Chapter 3 (fashion segmentation, targeting and positioning) explains how markets are segmented by fashion companies and the important role of market positioning in achieving a competitive differentiation. The chapter gives clear pragmatic guidance as to how these fundamental marketing activities work in the context of fashion. The latest geo-demographic modelling tools are discussed and their potential uses explained. The chapter also explains how to use the ever-important technique of perceptual mapping.

Chapter 4 (the fashion product) clearly focuses on the unique and unforgiving nature of fashion products, examining in detail the way in which the fashion product is subdivided into both manageable and understandable categories. The problems of range width and depth are explained in the context of product-mix decision-making. The sources of product ideas are outlined in detail. Fashion product life cycles (PLCs) and their significance to successful fashion marketing management are clearly explained. The chapter concludes with a review of the implications of product for international fashion marketers.

Chapter 5 (pricing) explains the relationship between price, cost and perceived value. It goes on to review pricing theories and analyse their application to the fashion industry. The issues of profit product margin control and its management are clearly explained and analysed. The importance of mark-down management is also explained.

Chapter 6 (promotion and marketing communications) explains and analyses the unique way in which fashion is both communicated and promoted by the varying types of fashion business. Specific fashion communication tools are reviewed, with a particular emphasis on the key role of Public Relations (PR). The operational role of PR within the fashion calendar is explained. The chapter also provides details of roles and job descriptions for PR and marketing positions. The vastly underrated, yet increasingly important personal selling tool is given high importance, whilst the authors challenge previous linear consumer reaction to marketing stimuli in the unique context of fast-moving and disposable fashion.

Chapter 7 (channels of distribution and service) focuses on the channels of distribution used in the fashion industry and discusses each specific channel method in detail. The chapter also explains the trend towards multi-channel retailing and the critically important roles of service and relationship marketing.

Chapter 8 (branding in fashion and luxury) explains and analyses a variety of branding theory and models. Notions of brands and branding are discussed in the context of contemporary fashion in both the mass and luxury markets.

Chapter 9 (new approaches to fashion marketing) reviews, explains and analyses how various new marketing disciplines are evolving around new technologies and new media. It provides two models that illustrate how new marketing techniques such as guerrilla marketing work more closely with the consumer to achieve traditional objectives. Various new approaches to the subject are reviewed, including emotional branding, brand hijacking and avatar marketing.

Chapter 10 (strategic marketing for fashion organisations) provides an explanation of how marketing strategy and tactics are applied to the fashion industry. Many conventional strategic and tactical marketing models are explained and analysed. A new holistic model is provided to illustrate how the various corporate and strategic marketing models and theories relate to each other and the tactical application of the marketing mix. This chapter aims to explain the interface between marketing theory and fashion industry practice.

the customer and fashion consumption

Effective fashion marketing is about using customer insight to excite.

Steven Sharp – Marketing, Store Design and e-Commerce Director, Marks & Spencer

Introduction

The purpose of this chapter is to discuss a range of issues that are central to the focus of all marketing activity – the customer. The customer should be the first consideration for any marketer and is the embodiment of demand for all fashion products and/or services. The majority of books on marketing theory refer to customers within the parameters of segmentation or consumer behaviour. However, it is our belief that there is sufficient to say about customers to justify a discrete chapter that augments a separate section on segmentation in chapter 3.

A fundamental concept of marketing is that a business should make what it can sell, as opposed to attempting to sell what it has made. The assumption in the first part of this statement is that a business identifies a gap in the market based on customer demand and then provides products to satisfy it. The statement also alludes to different commercial approaches to business, one of which is marketing-led and another which is product-led. A marketing-led approach, also known as a customer-centric approach, has the customer at the centre of marketing activity, whereas a product-led approach focuses on developing products to sell.

Arguably the balance of power has now shifted more towards consumers and away from businesses. Today's consumer is well-informed about brands, products and prices, and has a sophisticated and continually evolving set of complex needs and wants which can be satisfied by a range of competing alternatives. The shift in power has also resulted in many consumers feeling that they 'own' or have a strong emotional attachment to a brand. For example, in 2005, Marks and Spencer rebranded around the slogan 'Your M&S'. This acknowledged research which reflected the strong views and personal associations that so many of their customers have with the brand. A number of marketers argue that brands now belong to consumers and are no longer the sole preserve of their parent company. Fashion adds a further complex dimension to understanding consumers and predicting their wants and behaviours since it changes so quickly.

Customer and consumer

The two words 'customer' and 'consumer' are often interchangeable but do not always refer to the same thing. The term 'consumer' is normally used to refer to someone who personally consumes a product or service and is, therefore, the end-user of that product or service. The consumer may or may not have bought the product himself/herself (for example it may have been a present), but will be the person experiencing its benefits. In fashion the most obvious category of consumer is someone who buys, then wears, the fashion products sold by brands. An individual who wears an item of fashion clothing is said to be consuming that fashion product according to economic and business theory.

Goods sold by brands (in the widest sense of the word) are normally referred to as consumer goods and the vast range of goods and services that a household would use fall into this category. The term 'consumer' is used in various ways to distinguish the individual from a business customer, such as a fashion retailer buying fabric from a textile manufacturer. The Consumer Prices Index (CPI) is a government measure of inflation that is calculated each month. It takes a sample of goods and services that a typical (consumer) household might buy, including food, heating, household goods and travel costs. The clear assumption therefore is that a consumer is the individual who uses the product or service for its intended end purpose. The terms 'business-to-business' (B2B) and 'business-to-consumer' (B2C) also draw a distinction between business customers and end-user consumers.

The term 'customer' is broader and refers to an individual or organisation who or which buys a product or service from a business or other organisation. As such, a customer may be either an end-user consumer or a B2B customer. In fashion there are many B2B customers as any brands selling products to consumers will themselves be customers of other businesses with whom they trade in a supply chain. For example the fashion brand Gap is a customer of the merchandise- identification (tags and labels) business Shore-to-Shore. Shore-to-Shore sells a range of merchandise-identification products including RFID (radio-frequency identification) and barcode tickets, woven brand labels and garment care labels which are important to Gap's fashion products (Gap being their customer but obviously not the end-user consumer of the product).

It is important to distinguish between the term 'consumer', who is the end-user of a product and the word 'customer', which may refer to a business. This is because the consumer will possess attitudes and opinions based on his/her experience of the benefits delivered by the fashion brand and its products.

Marketers need to understand the difference between the two terms, as each refers to a separate commercial scenario and each requires a fundamentally different marketing approach. Much research exists on purchase decision making and other related behaviours (during and after purchase) that specifically relate to the consumer.

Brands may also need to articulate the benefits of fashion products to their consumers in a more detailed and sophisticated way than other businesses in the supply chain that also contribute to that product, such as the label and RFID supplier. Some businesses in a fashion supply chain are not as focused on final product benefits of the fashion product which the consumer buys and uses. This is because they manufacture and sell component parts that combine to deliver the end product, for example fabric, trims, services and transportation. Their customer is in fact the brand (retailer or other). The complexity of the fashion supply chain varies widely depending upon the size, product type and market level of a business – each business must be certain to whom it is addressing any marketing activity or marketing communication. Every fashion consumer and customer has a unique set of needs, wants and demands. Failure to understand these requirements will automatically lead to wasted marketing effort.

Categories of fashion customer

1 Business to consumer (B2C)

In the context of fashion, B2C refers to the commercial relationship that exists between a fashion brand and the end-user consumer of the products supplied by that brand. In this case the consumer is a customer of a fashion brand retailing any fashion products and services. Brands retail their products and services to consumers through a variety of channels, including their own directly operated stores (including concessions), mail order and transactional websites.

2 Business to business (B2B)

B2B refers to the commercial relationship that exists between businesses in a fashion supply chain. Some typical examples include:

- a textile supplier selling fabric to a clothing manufacturer;
- a contract manufacturer selling fashion clothing and related products to fashion buyers for their stores;
- a PR agency selling its services to a fashion brand;
- a trend-prediction company selling its service to a fashion brand.

Readers should note, though, that the term 'customer' can apply in both a B2B context and B2C context. In addition, there is now another category, referred to as Consumer to Consumer (C to C), which has emerged from internet auction-based trading.

The fashion context

To a large extent, the fashion industry is product-led or design-led, depending on the type and market positioning of a fashion business. Many middle-market and niche fashion brands (including retailers) rely on differentiation in fashion design, styling and image to justify their market and price positioning. This approach effectively means that brands dictate fashion choices to consumers each season.

Further, since fashion is disposable and most fashion products do not endure much beyond a few seasons, consumers frequently start each season with a 'blank canvas'. In fact most consumers do not know what product they are going to end up buying. When shopping for fashion products, consumers will generally have an idea of the type of product they want (e.g. coat, pair of jeans, top) and a selection of brands, but will rarely have an accurate idea of the exact version they will select. This is because the wide choice available to them and the impact of point of sale (POS) marketing has a significant influence on decisions at the point of sale.

This uncertainty in the selection process is different for many non-fashion products, such as food and household items, where consumers' decisions are far more reliable and predictable. The uncertainty and the last-minute or impulse decision-making that are inherent to fashion shopping make it difficult for brands to plan with any degree of certainty how consumers will behave and respond to new seasons' ranges.

Practising marketers and those studying the subject of fashion marketing can benefit from an understanding of how consumers make purchasing decisions. The field of consumer buying behaviour is well established and contains a variety of useful concepts and models, which explain different aspects of consumers' purchasing. The following is a selection of those that the authors believe to be most useful. Readers should remember, though, that all generic theory and models require critical evaluation before being applied to fashion.

Consumer behaviour

It is generally accepted in marketing literature that a consumer's purchase decision is the result of an array of internal and external influences. Influences internal to a consumer are those relating to personality, motivation, perception and self-image. They are specific to the individual. External influences are much broader in range and include the macro environment in which the consumer lives, as well as specific group influences such as peers, family and other reference groups.

Maslow's hierarchy of needs

A key internal stimulus for behaviour is need. Abraham Maslow (1943) famously classified human needs into a hierarchy of different categories (see figure 1.1). His belief was that people satisfy their basic needs first, the most basic being associated with sustaining one's physiology. They include hunger, thirst and health. The hierarchy is based on the premise that people satisfy their basic needs before those higher up the hierarchy. For example, Maslow might argue that a consumer would ensure that his/her hunger is satisfied before worrying

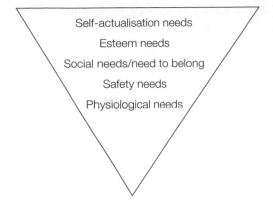

figure **1.1**   **Maslow's hierarchy of needs (adapted)**

about social or esteem needs. In a general sense this is true, although there are plenty of examples in fashion of consumers prioritising spending on fashion clothing and accessories over a healthy diet.

At an extreme level some individuals suffering from poor self-esteem may also suffer eating disorders, which could see them spending more money on trying to resolve their esteem issues through fitting in with a group or addressing a status problem at the expense of eating and their health. Consequently a fashion context may require marketers to re-evaluate the hierarchy and its application to some consumers' behaviour.

The theory is that individuals are motivated to satisfy their needs in order of priority. At the basic level of physiological need, people are concerned with satisfying the basic drives of thirst, hunger and, to more varying degrees, sex. Modern lifestyles are such that an individual may well satisfy multiple needs simultaneously. For example, a young person may conspicuously consume an isotonic sports drink (physiological and safety needs) from a branded container (social and status needs) following a sports competition. In this example the isotonic drink helps protect the person by including essential salts and sugars. The brand is on show to reinforce social membership among like-minded peers and provides the individual with a degree of status according to the brand.

In most cases fashion clothing and accessories are going to be addressing the top three levels of social needs, esteem needs and self-actualisation needs. Social and self-esteem needs are fairly obviously linked to the use by consumers of brands that conspicuously display group/tribe membership, status and identity. However, some designer and luxury brands also attempt to satisfy consumers' self-actualisation needs through the communication of a set of attitudes, beliefs and brand values that are esoteric and appeal to a consumer's perceived spiritual well-being. This is often achieved through conveying messages about inner-directed simplicity, serenity, independence from the mainstream, and a sense of a confident individual 'having arrived' at peace with himself/herself. Such needs may collectively be grouped under marketing terms such as 'well-being', which is an enhanced state achieved through the use of exotic and culturally interesting potions, treatments and esoteric value systems. In such cases a consumer is often investing a great deal of faith and belief in the marketing message and image of a product or service compared with its content.

Further influences on behaviour which are internal to the consumer include personality and other psychological factors involving motivation, learning, perception and beliefs and attitudes.

Personality

Personality is a unique combination of psychological traits which combine to direct an individual's response to stimuli. Typically the stimuli that marketers are concerned with are products, brands, prices, communications, distribution channels and the customer interface. The response sought by marketers is ultimately sales, although securing consumers' attention, interest, enquiries and trials (of products) are also important steps leading to a sale. Interest in consumers' personalities arises as brands endeavour to design and manufacture products, prices, communications and shopping environments that are consistent with target consumers' personalities. Consequently, a young (in terms of attitude) fashion retailer brand aims to reflect the personality of 'young at heart' and trend-aware fashion consumers within a wide (demographic) age spectrum. The distinction between Gucci and Yves Saint Laurent luxury fashion brands in the late 1990s was articulated by Tom Ford's summary statements of the target consumer profiles rock chick for Gucci and film star for YSL. Since then Gucci has evolved under different management and more recently summarised the same two brands as Gucci – seductive, powerful, accomplished; Yves Saint Laurent – contemporary chic.

Motivation

Motivation refers to the reason for an action. In the context of fashion consumption, motivation is the drive to be fashionable each season. Human motivation can be determined by both physiological and psychological needs. In a consumer society, needs inevitably turn into wants as consumers avail themselves of a wide choice of products and services to satisfy a particular need. Consumers normally end up 'wanting' a particular brand for the augmented benefits that a product often provides, such as brand image and status. Some argue that the process of purchasing or shopping has itself become an addictive experience for many consumers. The old saying 'It is better to travel hopefully than to arrive' suggests that the journey is often more exciting for some than the destination reached. This is true for many shopaholics for whom the process and experience of shopping and spending money is more pleasurable than owning the products purchased. Consumers who are motivated are ready to act.

Perception

To perceive something is to grasp it with the mind and to place a degree of interpretation upon it. The way in which consumers respond to marketing very much depends on how they perceive the marketing mix of the product in question. People living in developed consumer societies are bombarded with a mass of general marketing messages every waking hour. Such an onslaught of information requires individuals to screen out most of the information in order to remain sane. Shock tactics may help some brands to cut through the noise of competitors' marketing and grab consumers' attention. For example, FCUK's ambiguous brand name and Puma's limited edition Bonnie and Clyde sneakers (generating controversial PR) both succeeded in creating some of the world's most memorable marketing campaigns.

However, effective targeting, based on current and reliable research, enables marketers to use language, imagery and cultural references to influence customers' perceptions. In this way marketers hope to overcome the selective way in which individuals receive and interpret information.

Learning

In human development there is a continuing debate about the relative impact of nature versus nurture. However in terms of consumer preference, brands are learned. Individuals' actions result in experiences from which they learn. Learning may also occur from the vicarious experiences of reference group figures that have an influence on an individual. The learning process has been modelled in a simple way below.

Drive refers to a need, problem or other internal stimulus that motivates a person to act in a particular way, for example a child who wants to be part of a social group of peers. Stimulus refers to an object that is the focus of the drive. In the example a pair of sneakers may be regarded by a child as a vehicle for demonstrating shared values and common ground with peers. Cue is an indicator guiding when, where and how the individual will act. In the example a specific sneaker brand will be a cue that the child and his/her peers may associate with identity and status. If the response from the group of peers to the brand is positive, then there will be reinforcement of the sneaker brand's value as a tool to solve that particular problem.

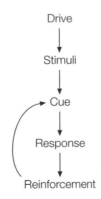

figure **1.2** **the learning process**

Self-concept/self-image

In many developed societies where social structures have become more fragmented and less cohesive, greater attention is placed on the self. Trend experts and cool-hunters reference significantly changed consumer attitudes towards being single, as marriage plays a less influential role in society than it has in the past. Weddings in the UK in 2007 were at an all-time low. Notions of personal freedom and me-focused lifestyles and brands help micro-segment the increasingly large number of individuals who are unmarried.

Self-concept (also referred to by marketers as self-image) is used to understand individuals' motivations, preferences and actions. Theory tells us that individuals have different self-images in different situations. Consumers are likely to buy products that support their self-image. The actual self-image is how the person really sees himself/herself. For example, an individual may consider himself/herself to be trendy, a free spirit and environmentally 'green', all of which may guide the purchasing behaviour of products. People also have an 'ideal self-image' (how they would like to see themselves, for example as successful) and a 'social self-image' (how they think others see them). Individuals may need to compromise their self-image in some situations to conform to recognised and required types. For example, working environments often impose a dress code and promotion may require individuals to project an image through their appearance, which is consistent with what they believe others to regard as successful.

Group theory

Theory concerning group influence on consumers' buying behaviour states that consumers refer to individuals from various groups to assist in the formation of attitudes, opinions and behaviours relating to the selection and purchase of products and brands. Marketers tend to categorise consumers into membership and reference groups, according to the level of contact and influence of the group on the individual. The interest in groups is concerned with the extent to which marketers can use the influence of group members in marketing to an individual.

The family is considered to be a very significant influence on an individual member in the selection of products and brands. Marketers are concerned with the roles and influence of the wife, husband and children on the selection and purchase of many fast-moving consumer goods (FMCGs). Many people still cling to the brands they used when growing up after having left the family unit and established their own household. However, the notion of what the family is has changed significantly since the 1950s. Attitudes to marriage and divorce, greater economic wealth, birth rates and increased life expectancy have contributed to many more single-person households. In many single-person households, family may refer not to a biological connection but to a group of close friends. Other groups including friends and work colleagues can also act as important influencers on awareness of, advocacy for and motivation to purchase products and brands.

Diffusions of innovation

Rogers's 1962 model (see figure 1.3) is still used today as a broad guide to classifying individuals' propensity to adopt new products (Rogers, 2003). The model has five simple classifications that are spread across a bell curve, illustrating the array of tendencies across a population:

- innovators;
- early adopters;
- early majority;
- late majority;
- laggards.

As with any generic model there are difficulties in application to a specialist area. For example, fashion is a phenomenon which is open to broad interpretation across a range of products from new technologies such as iPods/iPhones to simple T-shirts. The term 'innovator' may refer to the first few individuals to own an iPhone when applied to the consumption of technologies such as mobile phones/personal digital assistants (PDAs). The user has no involvement in the creation of the new product but is a conspicuous user of it. However, a fashion innovator refers to an individual who creates and conspicuously displays a style that later becomes fashionable. The two scenarios are different in terms of creativity, originality and influence. In many cases innovators will move away from, adapt or evolve a style to suit themselves.

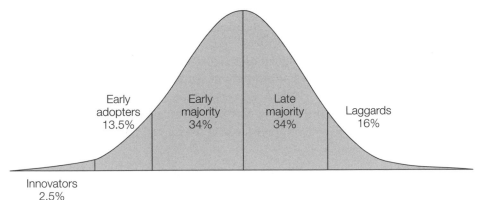

figure **1.3** **categories of innovativeness**

Knowing your customer

The term 'customer insight' refers to a deep level of understanding about customers' needs and wants. Market research studies are important sources of information about how consumers behave (in terms of their shopping activities) and their values, attitudes, lifestyles and opinions. However, fashion brands lose potentially valuable information on a daily basis as consumers exit shops without buying anything. Although some of this can be explained as consumers browsing, other causes inevitably relate to product or pricing problems. Product problems may be concerned with inappropriate designs, quality, poor fit and the lack of available sizes or product styles. Similarly, price points may be too high or price architectures inappropriate or confusing. A customer who spends time in a retail outlet and does not buy represents a potential missed sale and lost marketing opportunity. Common approaches to resolving stock problems normally involve the merchandising function in a fashion business. However, brands may also gain crucial insights into the causes of overstocking and poor sales by talking directly to their customers. Sometimes this may take the form of ad hoc qualitative research or quantitative surveys, although the best information is obtained from a continuous dialogue with regular customers who are known to staff in stores. In reality missed sales form an important part of the total sales equation: **actual sales + missed sales = potential sales**.

Consumer profiling

Chapter 3 explains consumer profiling as part of the segmentation and targeting process in fashion marketing. However, readers need to be aware that fashion brands should, as a matter of course, create profiles, or pen portraits, of their customers in order to help create a focus for marketing activity. A pen portrait is a written description of the typical customer of a fashion brand and includes the following details:

- demographics – a typical name, e.g. a stereotypical association with Shaz = low, Clarissa = high (recognising the important association of names with social groups), age, disposable income, family life stage, education, job;
- lifestyle – weekly activities relating to work and social lives;
- attitudes, interests and opinions – about contemporary life and popular culture;
- fashion adoption level – innovator, leader, follower, laggard;
- user occasions – situations when consumers have a need for a particular product.

Although this is an effective way of narrowing a target market and helps marketers to visualise a typical person, it is still only a written description that is devoid of any sense of life. The authors recommend using photographic images of actual consumers, to add a real visualisation that can supplement the written pen-portrait description. A photographic gallery of consumers can provide real insights into who a brand's consumers really are. Such visual data can also be analysed to identify other brands that the consumer is 'wearing' (such as clothing, accessories, shopping bags, baby buggies, key fobs, jewellery and mobile phones).

Interestingly, Gobé (2001) makes the point that the consumer is often viewed as the enemy in the aggressive marketing strategies and tactics employed and the language adopted to 'target' consumers and 'decode' their language. Consumers should be seen as real people. A further note of caution is that over-reliance by a brand on a narrowly defined target customer, who cannot possibly reflect the full spectrum of their consumers, may overlook the important individuals within micro-markets.

Generation gaps?

Each generation is different from the previous one. The distinctions used to be clear. Young people tended to be rebellious and older people more conservative. However, segmentation by generation type reveals marketing opportunities for fashion businesses, as the once-young generations become older and attempt to retain aspects of their youth. This enables marketers to segment consumers by attitude instead of age.

Generation categories

Baby boomers, Generation X (Gen-X) and Generation Y (Gen-Y) are further classifications of consumers that differentiate the characteristics specific to each generation. Although the terms more commonly apply to markets in the US, the characteristics defining each generation translate into most Westernised societies:

- Baby boomers: Born 1946–64, they are motivated by achievement and performance, interested in image and status and have experienced significant social change. They are now generally one of the wealthiest consumer segments.
- Gen-X: born 1965–76, they have grown up in a reshaped society (multicultural, different family structures), are focused on self and others with shared values (tribes) and are creative and independent.
- Gen-Y: born 1977–94, they are experiencing a much faster society in which multi-media communications and technology are central. They are more commercially aware at a younger age, but have a low level of interest in politics and religion.

Baby boomers are considered to be marketing literate, but are also influenced by marketing and advertising. They are redefining attitudes and behaviours at milestone ages and life stages, as their youthful mindset is different from previous generations of the same age. This segment may be the last to enjoy generous pensions and to benefit from the high appreciation in the value of the homes that they own. Gen-X consumers are believed to be cynical of marketing and much more individual in their fashion styling. Gen-Y consumers have been referred to as 'prosumers', reflecting their autonomy over purchasing decisions. They are 'marketing-smart', do not respond well to conventional brand communications and have a wide choice of products and brands available to them. Other more colloquial generational references include the 'Pepsi generation' that refers to a particular market creating youth lifestyle, and Trendwatching's Generation C (meaning content) (Gen-C) that refers to the large numbers of people contributing to user-generated content on various websites. This phenomenon is most commonly associated with social networking and is examined in more detail in chapter 9.

Views from current marketing research into those with whom people have *most* or *least in common* indicates that individuals have *least in common* with family members and neighbours and *most in common* with close friends and others with whom they share interests. These categories are likely to cut across classes and income levels. Today a womenswear fashion consumer is as likely to be wearing an item of clothing from the supermarket brand George as she is to own a Tiffany bracelet or a Burberry scarf. In a new culture of democratised fashion and accessible luxury, the demands of aspirational consumers are fully met by aspirational brands.

Social grade

Social grades, or socio-economic groups, are still used by market researchers to classify consumers into segments, but play a minor role in modern fashion segmentation. This is because mass-market fashion is no longer a homogenous market, but a highly fragmented one, in which consumers' tastes are more likely to be driven by niche reference groups and fashion 'tribes' than by social class. Furthermore, 'value retailers', such as Primark, and supermarket fashion (dubbed 'consumer couture'), from Tesco and Asda, have helped shift consumers' opinions about the credibility of such fashion products. There is no longer a stigma associated with owning value fashion products and, if anything, there is an inverted snobbery from many fashionistas and opinion leaders about wearing low-priced fashion. The success of charity-shop retailing and the recent big trend in vintage and retro fashion, much of which could be bought from charity shops and second-hand stalls, has helped to reinforce the 'low price is cool' message. It is interesting to note that, despite the recent upsurge in enthusiasm about the sustainability of fashion, low-priced value fashion still has a major following.

Marketers have recognised the importance of identifying and grouping

table **1.1** **common acronyms for target customer groups**

Yuppies	Young Urban Professionals
Dinkies	Double Income No Kids Yet
Sinkies	Single Income No Kids Yet
Bobos	Burnt-Out But Opulent People
Woopies	Well-Off Older People
Jollies	Jet-Setting Oldsters With Lots Of Loot
Glams	Greying Leisure-Affluent Middle-Aged People
Wags	Wives and Girlfriends (of footballers)
Mads	Mums and Dads (of footballers)

segments of consumers for many years. The communication of specific types through the media helps give some groups a personality which people can recognise and with which individuals relate. Table 1.1 includes some of the better known acronyms for target customer groups.

Frequently marketers will use acronyms, buzz words or other memorable terminology to identify new or significant consumer groups. 'Prada and Primark' is a simple illustration of how brand names may be put together to describe a particular shopper – in this case a consumer who mixes expensive and cheap fashion products and is personally wealthy but likes to find bargains. In addition to the names that are in fact acronyms, other important fashion consumer groups of the late 1990s and this millennium include:

- ladette: female equivalent of lads;
- metrosexual male: stylish urban man 'in touch' with his feminine side;
- tweeny: style and fashion conscious pre-teen (normally girl but also boy).

Marketing researchers often create their own typologies to describe meaningful groups of target consumers. This may involve the application of one or more demographic or lifestyle characteristics to define a group. For example, age and family status add further information to develop gradations in profiling consumers.

For example, a leading UK high-street retailer brand uses the following interpretation of life stages for internal classification of its consumers. The gradations in family life stages help it understand the direction, shopping priorities and habits of its customers:

- carefree;
- kids are us;
- family ties;
- freedom finders;
- golden years.

Similarly, table 1.2 shows the typologies used in a large TGI Europa and BMRB survey (23, 874 British adults aged 15+) conducted in 2004 (Mintel 2004).

table **1.2 fashion consumer typologies**

Big spenders	'I spend a lot on clothes'
Label seekers	'A designer label improves a person's image'
Stylish	'I have a very good sense of style'
Fashion-conscious	'I like to keep up with the latest fashions'
Well-dressed	'It is important to me to look well dressed'
Shopaholics	'I really enjoy shopping for clothes'
Practical	'I buy clothes for comfort, not style'
Sporty	'I do some form of sport or exercise at least once a week'
Individualists	'I like to stand out in a crowd'

source: Clothing Retailing Europe, Mintel (October 2006).

In 2004 the phenomenon of the Chav as a category of conspicuous consumer became the focus of considerable media attention in the UK. The attention broadened to include the international media as luxury fashion brands Burberry and Prada became associated with a Chav subculture. The popular media portrayal of a Chav is one of a young, white, underachieving, poorly educated and brand-obsessed individual. There are various explanations of how the word Chav originated, some based on acronyms and others linked to specific subcultures. Some commentators, including journalist and popular culture commentator Julie Burchill, point out that the derisory focus on Chavs is little more than a middle-class attack on a working-class sub-group. There is no doubt that discussion of the precise derivation of the word is sport for the media, but this is less relevant to business than the impact Chavs have had on fashion branding. Both Burberry, and to a lesser extent, Prada are believed to have suffered in the UK market as a result of the Chav association. Burberry has a particular problem with subculture associations because of the prominence of its highly recognisable trademark check, which featured on many of its 'low-entry-price' products. Lower-priced products, which typically include accessories such as bags, scarves and caps, enable aspirational consumers, who would not normally be able to afford to buy into a brand, to do so. Premium and luxury fashion companies are often victims of their own success, having created a highly desirable consumer brand whilst attracting a new but different market. To some extent a trade-off exists for a brand like Burberry between huge sales growth and brand dilution as less relevant consumers buy into their products. Burberry has achieved growth and a rejuvenated brand positioning but at the 'expense' of a link to Chavs and other problematic subgroups. The downside of such success is the lack of control over those who buy and associate themselves with the brand. However, Rose Marie Bravo, former CEO of Burberry, is reported to have viewed the Chav issue as a trend that would pass and not influence the brand's strategy or affect its long-term survival.

The identification of Chav culture with the bling cultural phenomenon has enabled the media to characterise trashy celebrity behaviour, lifestyles and appearance as 'Chav-like'. This has broadened the scope of Chav cultural references and fuelled interest in the subject. Celebrities who have been associated with the Chav phenomenon range from minor national celebrities to global stars including Britney Spears. The media reporting of Britney Spears's second wedding in 2004 focused on aspects of the event that were perceived to be deliberately 'trashy'. This included the fact that the bride, groom and guests all wore white shell suits, bearing the slogan 'Pimps', and enjoyed a wedding breakfast consisting of cheeseburgers.

More recently Chav symbolism has been linked with the wearing of fashion garments and accessories that conspicuously display price tags. Price tags are left on the products following purchase in order to display the high price and even sometimes the price reduction. One can speculate as to the motivation behind a perceived need to demonstrate what appears to be savvy shopping and the owner's affluent purchasing behaviour.

Burberry has also suffered a negative impact on its brand positioning from its adoption by football hooligans. Organised hooliganism in football is often associated with particular brands of clothing that have a strong English heritage, including Aquascutum, Hackett, Stone Island and Burberry.

The next generation

A big issue for all businesses to consider in the near future is how the next generation of consumers will differ from those of the past. Marketers need to consider how future consumers may differ, especially in respect of the media they interact with, the channels used to shop and the means of payment available to them. There is much debate about the development of technology and its impact on commercial activity. For example, the print media (newspapers and magazines) are already under pressure from online substitutes or equivalents and are internationally seeing circulation and readership numbers fall. Certainly, audience figures for the main five TV channels in the UK are dropping, as satellite and cable channels have taken audience shares away. However, many younger consumers are defaulting to computer- and web-based media for news and entertainment. Computer games, increasingly accessed and played communally online, specialist sites such as www.sneakerfreaker.com and blogs are simple examples of digital activities that compete with conventional media and entertainment for young adults' time and attention. Charles and Maurice Saatchi have made a distinction in society between those who are fully engaged with new technologies and media and those who are not, dubbing people as either digital natives or digital immigrants. These issues are explored more fully in chapter 9.

The customer is king (?)

This is a popular saying which, along with 'the customer is always right', is a reminder to businesses that the priority is to satisfy customers' needs in order to retain their business. Clearly neither statement is to be taken literally but should reflect a customer-centric attitude within an organisation. This means genuinely believing that the customer is the most important asset to an organisation and acting accordingly through proper attention to research, quality, service delivery and staff training. In fact, it is probably more accurate to say that those fashion companies which possess up-to-date customer information and insights are the kings. This is because insights into customers' attitudes and opinions can help direct and target marketing activity more effectively than the slavish adoption of a general mantra. Fashion businesses need to see their customers as real living people with whom they can connect, rather than a brief marketing-loaded description on a piece of paper that is formed from detached market research data. A key question that any senior fashion manager might ask himself/herself is, 'How often do I meet, talk with and listen to my customers?'

Not all customers are kings. Most markets are no longer homogenous and comprise individuals with different sets of values, attitudes and beliefs. This means that businesses can no longer afford to take a generalised, 'rose-tinted' view of their customers. The reality for mass-market fashion businesses is that customers are fickle and will switch to an alternative brand that offers what they perceive to be a superior package of benefits. Ironically, the introduction of so-called 'loyalty' schemes by supermarkets in the 1990s provided customers with incentives to shop around at competing retailers to take advantage of the different offers operating on different occasions. Many modern consumers have learnt to hold back spending near the end of a season, in order to benefit from the mid-season or end-of-season sales and secure a bargain. Reaction against unreasonable and overly demanding customers is the principal theme of the US website, www.customerssuck.com.

There is a shift away from regarding all customers as desirable clients and a move towards the selective relationship management of customers who represent greater profit potential. This is especially true in the financial services sector. Fashion-brand store cards and other means of transactional data collection can provide fashion brands with similar discriminating perspectives. Cherry-picking and targeting more affluent customers is standard marketing practice by fashion marketers.

Very selected targeting has resulted in the emergence of the 'smart' customer. Government legislation has clarified consumers' rights; individuals are more aware of those rights through greater access to information and the reporting of bad practice by consumer watchdogs and a variety of broadcast and print media. There is also a feeling in the UK that large businesses are fair game for the various guerrilla shopping tactics that customers might employ in reaction to the perception of Rip-off Britain.

Some major factors influencing fashion consumers

Macro trends are the broader trends which are external to a fashion brand but which impact on its business, markets and consumers. The following trends refer to the UK market although many are common to Western societies. Such trends are likely to impact on the mindsets of fashion consumers in terms of their values, perceptions, motivations and capabilities. Western fashion markets are extremely competitive and quite different from ten years ago. Some of the factors that have combined to change consumers are described below.

Wider availability of and access to fashion products

Shopping habits have changed over the last ten years and so have the ways in which consumers access fashion products. Many high streets, the traditional location for shopping, are congested, with local authorities restricting access by private cars. Shopping centres/malls and out-of-town retail parks have provided consumers with wider choice and simpler access. This access to a broader choice of retailers' stores and branded products has broadened consumers' awareness and purchasing of fashion brands and their products.

Additionally, e-commerce has recovered as a credible alternative to 'bricks-and-mortar' shopping since its emergence in the late 1990s and the subsequent dotcom crash in 2000. The latter knocked confidence in online shopping as many online brands collapsed or severely curtailed their activities. Boo.com is often cited as an online fashion business that failed owing to its inability to fulfil the orders it received from customers.

Since 2002 many retailers have invested in their online provision following the greater adoption of broadband by consumers and increased confidence in e-commerce generally. Hugely successful online retailers such as Amazon.com and the auction site eBay have contributed to making shopping online a mainstream activity. The success of Net-A-Porter.com in winning best fashion 'shop' at the 2004 British Fashion Awards is indicative of the enthusiasm for and potential of online shopping.

New entrants from Europe and America in particular have increased choice and sophistication in the fashion offered to consumers, for example fast fashion – Zara and H&M. The diversification of supermarkets into fashion, following the success of ASDA's George brand, presents a serious challenge to both clothing retailers and fashion brands. Increased usage of the Internet by consumers experienced in using eBay and shopping on Amazon is encouraging more fashion brands to revisit e-commerce as a credible distribution channel. Consumers are now spending more time each week interrogating the Internet than watching television – browsing and interrogating the Internet for fun is now an important leisure pastime.

Implications

Fashion brands must be aware that the accessibility of fashion products is a discriminating factor for some consumers in the selection of where and how to shop.

Each new generation of consumers is progressively more IT-competent. The Internet is likely to be the principal method of shopping for many Gen-Y and Gen-C consumers in the future.

Access to a wider range of media

The UK market has seen a large growth in all kinds of media, including a raft of new consumer magazines. Interest in celebrities has generated demand for magazines such as *Now* and *Closer* to rival *Heat, OK!* and *Hello!* Changed magazine formats such as the handbag size *Glamour* and *Teen Vogue* and the first weekly glossy magazine *Grazia* add to the wide choice available to consumers. The Internet, satellite and cable TV, terrestrial TV freeview channels, and numerous niche commercial radio stations provide consumers with choice on how they access entertainment and the news. For some, online media has already replaced traditional broadcast media as their major source of entertainment and daily information.

Implication

Advertisers face a complex problem in targeting consumers and communicating their messages effectively across so many niche media.

Demographic and social changes

There are a number of demographic and social changes that have had an impact on fashion consumption:

- An ageing population: In common with many European countries and America, the UK population is ageing. However, people are staying younger for longer in the sense that their values, attitudes and lifestyles are more youthful than those of previous generations at the same age. Women in their 40s and 50s are now the focus of great media and marketing interest, as opposed to being 'on the shelf'. The advertising campaign by soap brand Dove challenged the notion that being 40 is much different from being 20 and the slogan 'look the age you feel inside' is typical of the messages being communicated by many cosmetics brands. The successful US television series *Desperate Housewives* promises to do for the fortysomething woman what *Sex in the City* did for the thirtysomething segment. The term 'yummy mummy' has been coined to reference a mother whose outlook, attitude and appearance are youthful, having shed the burdens of child-rearing. The American equivalent is the term 'MILF'.
- The increasing numbers of individuals over thirty years of age who have never married: The trend towards a single life is increasing and has implications for the consumption of fashion. User occasions are likely to be different for single individuals than for those who are married.
- The 30% (approximately) of UK households who are 'singles' who have actively chosen to live alone.
- The increasing numbers of women in employment with the trend continuing over the next ten years.
- The increased wealth and disposable income (in real terms) for the asset-owning population.
- The increasing numbers of part-time workers.
- The increasingly diverse ethnic mix.

UK fashion consumption

Consumer spending on clothing in the UK amounted to £35.5 billion (€51.5 billion) in 2003 (Mintel). Tables 1.3 and 1.4 show where consumers are choosing to shop for women's clothing and accessories in the UK. Data are drawn from FashionTrak. FashionTrak is a market research division of Taylor Nelson Sofres (TNS) (see chapter 2 for further details) which specialises in the fashion market. Market shares are recorded by sales expenditure (i.e. the retail value of products sold) and unit volume (the numbers of products sold).

table **1.3** retail share – women's clothing and accessories (% expenditure)

Category	2002	2004	2005	2006
Clothing multiples	30.5	32.1	33.4	33.6
Clothing independents	8.6	8.5	9.1	8.3
General stores	20.2	19.5	18.3	17.6
Department stores	9.7	9.3	9.1	9.2
Mail order	9.0	8.4	7.7	7.2
Discounters/cash & carry	10.0	10.4	10.6	11.6
Sports shops	3.1	2.7	2.9	2.6
Supermarkets	4.2	4.9	5.1	6.0
Market stalls	1.2	1.1	0.9	1.0

source: WF (March 2006)

table **1.4** retail share – women's clothing and accessories (% volume in units)

Category	2002	2004	2005	2006
Clothing multiples	19.0	20.2	20.4	19.8
Clothing independents	4.3	4.2	4.2	4.1
General stores	20.6	19.3	18.1	17.8
Department stores	5.7	5.2	5.2	5.0
Mail order	6.3	5.7	5.3	4.9
Discounters/cash & carry	21.0	21.6	22.1	22.7
Sports shops	1.7	1.8	2.0	2.0
Supermarkets	13.7	15.4	17.2	18.3
Market stalls	2.6	2.4	1.9	1.9

source: WF (March 2006)

The clothing multiples category includes all Arcadia retailer brands and other retailer brands such as Next, Monsoon, River Island, H&M, Zara, Gap and New Look. Arcadia Group alone represents 8.1% of the market by expenditure and 5.0% by volume within the clothing multiples category in 2006. The general stores category includes BhS and Marks & Spencer (M&S). M&S alone accounted for 13.5% of the market by expenditure and 12.7% by volume in 2006.

This data indicates that although the value of M&S clothing sales is falling, the numbers of units sold is increasing, implying a change to its price positioning.

table **1.5** M&S womenswear market shares 2004 – 2006

	2004	2005	2006
Expenditure	14.5	13.8	13.5
Volume	12.8	12.3	12.7

source: WF (March 2006)

It is most likely the result of a strategy to target entry-level price points at very competitive levels across key product categories.

Clothing multiples account for approximately a third of womenswear clothing and accessories expenditure, but only one fifth of unit sales. By contrast, the combined expenditure on women's clothing and accessories through discounters/cash & carry and supermarkets is 15.5%. However their combined unit volume is over 39% of the market with supermarkets, including ASDA (George) and Tesco, showing the greatest increases in unit volume.

The clothing multiples face strong competition from supermarket brands and discount retailers. As fashion continues to reflect a more casual attitude to dress, consumers are able to buy simply made, low-priced and disposable commodity fashion from supermarkets. The type of distribution channel appears to be having an effect on the type of fashion being bought.

Conclusions

Fashion businesses face a variety of challenges in marketing products and brands to consumers. Markets are no longer homogenous in the way they used to be but are fragmented as consumers react to wider choice, cheaper prices, faster-changing fashions, accessible luxury, changing lifestyles, more information and different methods of shopping. Add to this radical changes in communications and entertainment technologies and it is easy to understand how difficult it is for brands to keep up with changing consumer demands. Many non-fashion industries ranging from financial services to luxury goods look towards fashion in order to gain insights into how to be competitive in fast-changing markets.

Fast fashion has contributed to a 'wear-now' demand for the latest fashion styles, which are communicated through various media following fashion shows and celebrity endorsement of products and brands. The 1990s represented a decade of growth and expansion for many global fashion brands. However, the anti-globalisation backlash against large corporations and some fashion brands such as Gap, Levi's and Nike reflects a trend for individualism and niche brands. In fashion there is a move away from the trend of following particular lifestyles towards 'self-affirmation' and being different. It is all the more vital, then, that any definition of marketing adopted by businesses has the word 'customer' as a focus.

Ultimately customers are a brand's biggest asset. Ironically the trend towards greater consumer influence may mean that 'Marketing managers are not in charge anymore. Consumers are' (Wipperfürth, 2006).

marketing research and information for fashion

Market research isn't about giving a designer a pass or fail report card but providing them with an innate understanding of how luxury consumers think. Inspiration, built on a complete understanding of the target customer's dreams, fears, values and opinions, will allow the creation of beautifully designed goods which will also be commercially successful.

Karen Mörsch, Director – Hasley Group

Introduction

The aim of this chapter is to review the theory of marketing research and explain how it can be applied to fashion businesses. Many marketing books cover marketing research content in a generic way, with an assumption that it can be applied universally. However, although it is important for the reader to understand conventional marketing research theory, such as sampling and data-collection methods, there are aspects of fashion that require the subject to be contextualised and applied. For example, there are many specialist sources of information which would probably not be relevant in a generic context but which are crucial to research within the context of the fashion industry. Some of these are discussed later in the chapter.

The term 'marketing research' refers to the process of gathering and analysing a wide range of different types of information in order to assist decision-making. In the context of this book, decision-making refers to commercial decisions that relate to the fashion industry. These are normally concerned with understanding customers and markets and ensuring that fashion products are suitable for target consumers. Marketing research also includes the more specific process of market research, which is used to collect new information about specific markets (customers and companies), and products or services. It is important for readers to understand that marketing research spans a wide variety of different types of information, ranging from the truly objective and empirical through to the more subjective.

It is worth remembering, though, that for most fashion brands a great deal of information might already exist, which could remove the need to undertake new market research. This might be from within the business and include information about products, such as regional sales data, or customers' store-card purchase data. Further research potentially accessible to fashion brands might also include market research reports (already acqired by the fashion company) and subscription to research information services such as WGSN, Target Group Index (TGI) and TNS WF. Although such specialist services entail a cost, there are often multiple uses for the information across their businesses.

Mintel, Verdict and TNS are market research companies that provide customised research services to clients and also produce regular market research reports about markets and consumer trends. TNS also has a specialist fashion research division called WF which supplies very detailed quantitative data about fashion-branded markets, including data about consumers and their spending. The scope and scale of WF (formerly known as FashionTrak) is discussed later on in this chapter. A useful tip for any fashion marketer is to establish what relevant information already exists before embarking upon costly new research.

What is marketing research?

Marketing research refers to that part of the marketing function concerned with developing insights into customers' needs, wants and preferences. Kotler et al. (2001) define it as 'the function linking the consumer, customer and public to the marketer through information – information used: to identify and define marketing opportunities and problems; to generate, refine and evaluate marketing actions; to monitor marketing performance; and to improve understanding of the marketing process'. This may appear to be a convoluted explanation, but it clearly identifies the interdependences between consumers and marketers in the process of satisfying customers' needs. It involves the systematic collection, recording and analysis of primary and secondary data used in the effective marketing of products and services. Its scope is generally considered to be broader than that of market research, referring to research into all aspects of the marketing mix and competition. The extremely competitive nature of the fashion industry means that brands need to ensure that their marketing mixes are relevant to their target market. The clichéd image of a person standing in a street undertaking a survey of passers-by has very little to do with the real world of commercial fashion information. While street surveys have their place, valuable fashion research comes from a variety of sources and formats, including visual aspects of fashion promotion such as visual merchandising. The influence of the fast-fashion concept is such that fashion brands operating in the young women's market need access to complex sales data and need to make fast tactical decisions on a weekly or even daily basis.

The Market Research Society (MRS) refers to 'market, social or opinion research' in outlining the scope of the content listed under market research on its website (www.mrs.org.uk). Most definitions of market research refer to the more specific process of collecting and analysing data about markets to inform marketing decisions. This appears to be a common interpretation that differs from the broader marketing research process, which encompasses a wide range of types and methods of gathering information: 'Market research is the systematic collection from external sources of any information about markets, and the analysis of this information for market planning and business decisions generally' (Talmage, 2008). The issues concerned with market research are covered later in this chapter under 'primary research'.

Market research may also be employed by fashion businesses to achieve publicity. In such cases the research findings are normally of secondary consequence. A clever, factual and well-timed survey, which offers a fresh and fun perspective on a subject, can succeed as a PR vehicle for a brand by getting news coverage in the media. For example a well-known lingerie brand might undertake a simple survey of men's gift-buying habits for Valentine's Day. Survey details released to news agencies in time for Valentine's Day will be very likely to result in the story being covered in the media, along with the name of a sponsoring brand.

There are a number of commercial selling organisations which operate in such a way that people believe them to be market research companies. They are companies which aim to sell products or raise funds under the guise of market research. The companies normally employ face-to-face or telephone-survey techniques, but are not interested in gathering research data as a main objective. Those that aim to sell to target consumers under the guise of marketing research are referred to as 'suggers', whereas those that aim to raise funds similarly are referred to as 'fruggers'. These practices are inconsistent with the ethical standards adopted by genuine market research companies. Gathering names and contact details under the guise of bogus marketing research with a view to selling to the individual later on is sometimes called 'data mugging'.

Accredited marketing research bodies

MRS and the European Society for Opinion and Marketing Research (ESOMAR) are two of the most influential bodies that provide a wealth of research information and services to support fashion marketers. They also have strict ethical codes relating to the gathering, use and dissemination of data and information gathered from both businesses and consumers.

ESOMAR is the leading global market research association and is recognised as the premier international industry advocate. Founded in 1948 (as the European Society for Opinion and Marketing Research), ESOMAR unites 4,000 members, both clients and providers of market research, in more than a hundred countries. Members come from all industry sectors, from advertising and media agencies, universities and business schools as well as public institutions and government authorities.

Why is marketing research necessary?

The main purpose of marketing research is to deliver accurate information that will enable a fashion business to make appropriate strategic and tactical decisions. The fashion industry is very competitive and fast-moving, which means that for fashion companies to be effective they need quick access to current and accurate information about products, customers and competitors. In simple terms all fashion businesses need continuous information about:

- **product sales** – both qualitative (e.g. why products are selling or not, what are future trends?) and quantitative (e.g. how much, which SKUs (stock-keeping units) and price points).
- **customers** – who is buying from them and why? How do the customers perceive the company compared with competitors?
- **market trends and opportunities** – which markets are growing, stagnating or in decline? Where are market growth and new opportunities expected to come from? What are the market share opportunities?
- **competition** – which are the direct and indirect competitors? Which do customers perceive to be substitutes for brand-switching? What is/will be the threat of new entrants?

Some key reasons for a fashion business to undertake marketing research are:

- to inform planning and decision-making (e.g. product or market development);
- to remain competitive and relevant to customers;
- to gain insights into new and existing customers (e.g. attitudes towards a fashion brand);
- to monitor and evaluate competitors;
- to evaluate all aspects of the fashion marketing mix (especially performance against declared marketing and marketing communications objectives).

Strategic decisions are normally related to long-term product and market plans, such as launching a new product or brand or repositioning a brand in an existing market. In either situation a fashion brand will need knowledge of the competition and an understanding about target customers' perceptions of the brand and its products. It is important for companies to decide what information they might need in order to make separate strategic and tactical decisions. The sort of information required to make tactical decisions is likely to be different from that used to inform strategic decisions. For example, visual information on denim trends from the west coast of America, available from WGSN's 'Trend Flash' service, is an example of information used to support tactical design decisions. The information is likely to influence a fashion brand's denim product design and styling decisions both pre- and in-season. Other examples of information used to support tactical decisions include research on competitors' current pricing structures. It is important, therefore, for readers to be aware of both the strategic and the tactical significance of marketing research to any fashion business.

Customer focus

Arguably the most important research focus for a fashion business is its customers. Fashion retailers and brands have access to a wide variety of information about customers via their stores and websites. They are able to research quantitative information about levels of customer flow into and around their outlets and track activity on websites. Store-card data can also provide retailers with useful data about customers' shopping behaviour and help target specific consumers and plan in-store sales promotions more effectively, although currently fashion retailers are not using such information as systematically as supermarkets. The potential for fashion databases to target consumers with new trends, preferred brands and fringe sizes, etc., still remains largely unexploited.

Fashion brands also need to know a great deal about the consumers they are selling their products to. Information gathered about target segments is analysed as part of the Segmentation, Targeting and Positioning (STP) process, which is outlined in chapter 3. In simple terms, though, a fashion brand needs to identify specific Characteristics about target consumers based on common segmentation criteria that include the following:

- demographics – age, gender, family status and stage, occupation, education, income;
- location – urban/rural, region, city/town, postcode;
- personality – adventurous, introverted;
- brand – awareness/beliefs;
- shopping habits – frequency/drive time/user status;
- lifestyle/values;
- fashion attitude and level of innovation.

These criteria merely identify broad types of consumer. Fashion brands need to understand more clearly what customers think of their brand and its products. Most brands are geared up to analyse sales information about products and can draw off many different kinds of sophisticated analyses about actual sales and future trends.

However, an over-reliance on electronic sales data alone does not provide insights into the important attitudes, beliefs and motivations of consumers towards brands. Sales data can only tell a fashion brand what has sold from the stock made available to consumers. Sales data alone cannot inform a fashion brand about what customers would have bought if their size were available and about a range of other missed sales opportunities.

Many fashion brands rely on electronic data to inform them about customers' buying behaviour, believing that so long as sales are on target there is no need to engage in costly market research about customers' attitudes and opinions to their brand. Perreault et al. (2008) make the point, 'the marketing concept says that businesses should meet the needs of their customers. Yet today, many businesses are isolated in company offices, far from potential customers.'

This 'customer closeness' is a term used to refer to the level of contact between company executives and customers/consumers. 'We have data coming out of our ears about customer transactions and we conduct thorough research insights about our customers. But there is nothing like meeting customers face-to-face to create a sense of reality about them. It is harder for the managers to avoid customers' concerns if they have met some of them. It is a way of bringing the insights to life' (Benady, 2004). However, some would argue that you need to know why people act in a certain way rather than simply knowing what they are doing.

Understanding customers better

More businesses are using ethnographic research to gain a better understanding of their customers, and to get to know more about their lives, attitudes, concerns and values. Ethnography is a type of research that focuses on the sociology of meaning through the close field observation of socio-cultural phenomena. Typically, the ethnographer focuses on a community and selects respondents who are known to have an overview and understanding of the community's activities. These respondents identify other informants who are representative of the community by using chain sampling to obtain a saturation of response in all empirical areas of investigation. Informants are normally interviewed a number of times to elicit further clarification and more detailed responses. The process reveals common cultural understandings which relate to the subject of the study. Ethnography is a qualitative research approach and is suited to understanding aspects of consumer behaviour that relate to symbolism and meaning in subcultures, which might be part of branding.

Accompanied shopping is another valuable qualitative research technique and is increasingly being used by retailers and brands.

The unique problems of fashion marketing research

It is fair to argue that fashion companies have been less rigorous in their use of market research to understand customers than have FMCG brands in other areas such as the grocery sector. This is probably because most fashion brands are design- or product-led rather than marketing-led, meaning that they produce what they think their customers will buy instead of involving consumers in the 'product development' process. This is a key area of difference between the approach of fashion brands and FMCG brands.

A new FMCG brand, developing a food or toiletry product, will typically seek the views of consumers in developing it. The research will include consumers' opinions on a wide range of factors including product design and quality through to packaging. However, mass-market fashion products are normally conceived by a designer and a buyer, who then make judgements about the product design according to expected fashion trends. The complexity of fashion trend development and the subsequent market adoption of particular trends in a season make it impractical to research consumers' views on the subject in advance.

Fashion buyers and designers do not ask consumers what style or colour they would like to wear next season, because most consumers do not know. Some of the contributing reasons for this unique problem are explained below.

Most consumers are fashion followers

Fashion requires mass adoption for it to exist, hence the terms 'in fashion' (recognised by a majority) and fashionable (accepted by the majority). The vast majority of fashion consumers are happy to wear what they believe to be fashionable (or at least relevant within a season) and want to convey an individual style without 'standing out'. In order to avoid standing out, they need the security of contemporary fashion products bought from credible brands (according to market segment), which are endorsed by the fashion press. This makes it difficult to research consumers' views on their adoption of a particular fashion ahead of a season. This is of course the ultimate dichotomy of fashion – the desire simultaneously to fit in but also to stand out from the crowd.

Sudden appearance and disappearance of trends

Powerful trends can emerge quickly and require the mass-market fashion follower to adopt a particular product (e.g. the poncho in 2004). In fast-fashion businesses such as Zara and Topshop, sudden fads emerge, which can come and go in a matter of two to four weeks.

Similarly, a significant trend lasting a number of seasons, such as the ostentatious display of brand logos associated with the bling subculture, can suddenly become unfashionable in a segment. Fashion brands now have to incorporate ways of addressing the new trend in individualism, which requires a 'don't flaunt it' message of brand association. The sudden emergence of fads and medium-term trends is also something that a fashion brand has to respond to. However, it is not easy to judge how consumers will react to a new trend in advance of its arrival. Classic market research methods are not likely to be useful tools in predicting such responses. Nevertheless, some continuous market research programmes can be used for post-event diagnosis and monitor attitudes and trend shifts as they are happening, for example the WF continuous research programme.

Seasonal cycles of trade fairs and fashion shows

There is an established series of events which include trade fairs and fashion weeks and which contribute to an evolving theme and 'look' of a fashion season. This is unique to fashion and means that the shared fundamentals of yarn types and colours, fabric prints and garment styling will have an impact on design trends in a season. Eventually the key and most commercial trends find their way to the mass market, and then the brands will attempt to exploit the particular look for all it is worth. The speed and power of these trends varies considerably, depending upon the market segment targeted and the consumer groups involved. Trends find their roots firmly implanted in these fairs and shows.

The press fashion calendar

The fashion press exert a great deal of influence over the reporting of fashion trends immediately prior to and throughout a season. The glossies (magazines) and dailies (newspapers) carry regular features that fit within a fairly standard schedule of what is covered when. For example, a glossy fashion magazine such as *Elle* will typically include a report on the spring/summer ready-to-wear runway trends in its February issue. It may interpret what it thinks the important trends are in a way that will be of interest to its readers. A daily such as the *Daily Mail* will also report on spring/summer at various points between January and August and focus on specific looks or products, such as 'the top ten summer dresses'. In both cases the media concerned are influencing trend perceptions 'in-season'. This makes it very difficult for any brand to know in advance of the season exactly which designs are sure to sell best. As fast fashion dominates much of the UK high street, brands have to respond to demand from consumers very quickly.

Common events and stages occur prior to and throughout a fashion season, impacting on consumers' fashion needs and behaviour. Some are linked to an entrenched system of social attitudes and behaviour about what to wear at certain times of the year: for example, party wear at Christmas, and other common 'user occasions' relating to work, holidays and a variety of other social occasions.

National and international media events such as awards ceremonies have emerged as part of a changing and evolving national culture in which fashion and celebrity are connected. The awards ceremonies then become opportunities to promote products, designers and fashion trends.

The focus on getting a seasonal look right used to be critical for all fashion businesses in the 1970s and 1980s. Clichés that are now embedded in our social jargon, such as 'brown is the new black', illustrate a structural idiosyncrasy that fashion retailers were expected to sell the 'right' looks for a season. Such looks used to be mandatory and manifested themselves in terms of colour (including specific shades), silhouette (e.g. skirt length) and fabric (e.g. corduroy). The 1990s saw a shift in the rigidity and importance of a specific look for a season and certainly now a fashion brand can sell skirts of different lengths, jeans with different leg styles and an array of colours and fabrics within the same season. However, fashion businesses still need to feature the select few styles in their ranges that the fashion press believe represent the zeitgeist of a season: 'In the world of fashion, if you don't follow the trends the press can ignore you. You are supposed to be yourself, yet at the same time follow the trends' (Armani).

These vagaries of the fashion business mean that many of the traditional market research techniques that are used in other industries are inappropriate to address issues of consumer demand for fashion products.

Stages in marketing research – in the fashion context

Marketing research refers to the broad process of collecting and analysing data that will be of use in making decisions relating to fashion products and markets. It includes information from both secondary and primary sources and in many cases brands already have access to a large amount of information. Figure 2.1 outlines the logical and sequential steps commonly involved in the marketing research process. It is important to be aware, though, that much product research is continuous and does not follow such a prescriptive process.

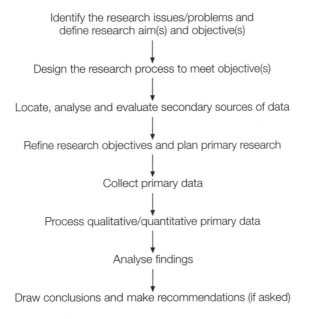

Identify the research issues/problems and
define research aim(s) and objective(s)

↓

Design the research process to meet objective(s)

↓

Locate, analyse and evaluate secondary sources of data

↓

Refine research objectives and plan primary research

↓

Collect primary data

↓

Process qualitative/quantitative primary data

↓

Analyse findings

↓

Draw conclusions and make recommendations (if asked)

figure **2.1**   **the typical marketing research process**

Defining research issues and problems

Before undertaking any fashion marketing research, it is important for any fashion business to define the key problems and issues that more information or research data will help resolve. For example, if a brand aims to enter a new market it will need a range of information that may be collected from both secondary and primary sources. Such information will include:

▸ the size of the market – e.g. potential sales, numbers and profile of consumers, average spend;
▸ the competitive structure of the new market – e.g. major competitors and their strengths and weaknesses;

- the attitudes of consumers to fashion and brands;
- the levels of brand awareness of the new company;
- the product range opportunities and price/margin levels;
- the optimum channel strategy (retail, wholesale, franchise, license, C to C).

This is by no means an exhaustive list and is only intended to identify the scope of knowledge that might be required. Alternatively the research problem might be more focused on evaluating the effectiveness of an advertising, PR or guerrilla marketing campaign.

Research design

The design of the research process will depend upon the research objective(s). Some objectives may be easily achieved through the use of secondary sources of information, including a variety of internal data (e.g. sales data, store-/loyalty-card data), whereas others will require new research. New research is referred to as 'primary research' and will normally involve the use of specialist market researchers. An example of primary research would be the recording and evaluation of customers' levels of awareness or of changing attitudes towards a particular brand or product following a marketing communications campaign. A critical part of the research design is the selection of a sample that can accurately represent the views of the wider market or population.

The need to think carefully about what has to be researched, why and to what potential effect is critical at the start of the research design process. It is easy, as a result of poor planning and design, to ask unnecessary, illogical and ultimately useless questions. Marketing research is an expensive process and resources must be used effectively and efficiently.

Secondary sources

Secondary sources of information are those that already exist and can be used in the context of a newly defined research problem. Secondary information is that which has originally been gathered for some other purpose. This does not mean, however, that the information is less relevant or necessarily less current. There are many categories of information which fall outside the boundaries of specific 'market research', such as company sales data, and yet still inform marketing decision-making.

Geo-demographic information and its uses within fashion marketing

The UK has a long history of researching its population, mainly for governmental taxation purposes, with the first major recorded census being the Domesday Book in 1063. The UK census of population is carried out every ten years, collecting a great deal of information about every household on topics ranging from education to ethnicity and host of other changing parameters. This basic information would, for example, help a fashion retailer to understand the age profile of a town in which it was proposing to open a store.

Commercial research organisations such as CACI maintain detailed post-code information about the different types of houses and the grouping of house types – this system is known as ACORN (A Classification Of Residential Neighbourhoods). Their classification system divides the UK's housing stock into around sixty different types, ranging from poorer council houses and estates to the wealthy suburbs. The type and value of housing stock is increasingly seen as a key indicator of an individual's wealth level and therefore his/her likely propensity to purchase goods and services. Whilst not foolproof, people in expensive areas tend to spend more on clothes than those in poorer neighbourhoods.

Another commercially available neighbourhood research tool is *Mosaic* developed by *Experian*. This system classifies residential postcodes by combining the electoral roll, housing and financial data (approximately 80 variables in all) and then puts UK households in 12 lifestyle groups, which in turn are broken down into around fifty sub-groups. By providing an understanding of the constitution of an area and its population and potential lifestyles, such information can easily be used to profile, for example, the price levels of clothing product ranges in that town, suburb or city.

All these geo-demographic modellers can customise their information for clients in order to ensure that the information provided can be used effectively and efficiently for marketing decision-making processes. Whilst such classification systems and data sources vary over time (as they develop clever ways to analyse their data sources), in essence they all provide similar research sources for the fashion marketer.

Other secondary sources of fashion information

Before embarking upon any fashion research programme, marketers should undertake an extensive trawl of all publicly available data and information held in libraries and on the Internet. It is pointless to keep reinventing the wheel when the metaphorical wheel you need is readily available with a little searching. The Internet contains many guides to help marketers find free information (a good example in 2006 was b2binternational.com/whitepaper1). Never spend money on primary research until you are certain that the information is not already available.

The following are important sources of secondary information for fashion brands. Some are available at little or no cost, although some more specialist information is also available – often at a much higher price:

▸ internal data on product sales by store – captured via electronic point of sale (EPOS);
▸ internal data on customers' shopping behaviour – captured via store cards;
▸ a market research report owned by the company but originally commissioned by another person – for example, Topshop commissioned a report into lingerie used by Miss Selfridge (both Arcadia Group brands);

- generic market research reports (e.g. Mintel 'Health and Beauty Retailing 2004') – these are usually available 'off the shelf', although they can be retrospectively tailored for specific purposes;
- online trend information (e.g. wgsn.com) – very useful for general and specific fashion product, market and consumer information;
- continuous market data (WF);
- press information (e.g. evaluating the effectiveness of PR activity).

Most fashion brands use market research reports or subscribe to specialist market and trend information companies such as WF and WGSN. Both companies are discussed later in this chapter. WGSN is an online provider of qualitative fashion data about fashion trends relating to products and global markets. It can provide very detailed visual information about what fashion and style trends are important in global markets. WF is focused on the British market (not Ireland) and provides critical insights into consumers' spending on fashion and their attitudes towards fashion clothing, footwear and accessories. Other market researchers such as Mintel and Verdict produce 'off-the-shelf' market research reports, available at a cost, on specific markets. For example, such annual reports as 'Fashion Retailing 2006' provide data about the size and structure of markets including sector (clothing), segment (women's wear) and value (total sales). Researching the availability of and regularly reviewing published secondary fashion research is an essential task for all fashion marketers.

Information available to fashion retailer brands within their own businesses

Most fashion retailers gather detailed product sales, stock data and information via their own merchandise planning and control systems. Such systems are usually based around proprietary merchandise-planning software.

The scope, scale and capabilities of these systems are very wide, with many being able to provide customised information suited to the specific needs of any fashion retail business. All of these systems receive sales information from electronic cash terminals in stores, regularly updating buyers and marketers with sales and stock information. Increasingly, this is integrated with e-commerce operations. Such data provide vital marketing research information used for fast, up-to-the-minute decision-making. They are also essential in controlling the overall buying profitability, as well as the control of price reductions or mark-downs, required to move slow-moving lines. It is estimated that the average high-street retailer may have well over ten thousand SKUs to control at any one time; the power of modern IT has been the driver behind the development of increasingly efficient modern merchandising and marketing planning techniques.

It is important for readers to appreciate that in most fashion businesses there is a huge amount of merchandise sales and stock information being generated on a daily basis. This is a rich source of secondary research information that is directly relevant to marketing decisions about fashion products.

Most sales data are captured using a laser to scan the barcoded ticket attached to the product. The barcode typically contains information about the product category, style, colour, size, season and price. Although currently used by a majority of fashion retailers, the optical-read barcodes are now being replaced by RFID tags, which emit a radio-frequency message containing all the key product data. RFID tags use miniature microchips, embedded in goods or packaging, to transmit product serial numbers and associated data to a scanner, without the need for batteries or human intervention. They can be used to track customer habits and reactions to special offers or certain goods in-store. Potentially, they may also be used in the future to collect data about specific customer's shopping preferences (in much the same way as loyalty-card schemes) and to give stores greater marketing opportunities to offer consumers more choices from their latest products. These new RFID tagging systems have many research advantages, and are also expected to help combat shop theft: newer versions of these tags are invisible to consumers, making it almost impossible for shoplifters to detect them. These tags easily trigger alarm systems unless removed/ deactivated at the time of purchase.

Merchandise planning systems are at the heart of the day-to-day business control of fashion retailers but their significance as a tactical marketing tool is sometimes underestimated. They are a vital source of marketing information that is mainly used for tactical decision-making, although over time they can gather and analyse data and information of more strategic significance.

Using available information sources

The type of research planning and data collection required will vary according to the activities of a fashion business. There is a tendency for people to think that fashion is all about fashion brands and retailing. However, suppliers and manufacturers also need information. It is worth considering how marketing research information may be accessed by them as well as by brands. For example, a cut, make and trim (CMT) manufacturer which sells products to fashion retail buyers (B2B) will need information about the retailer's business as well as about consumers.

Many of the larger fashion retail groups allow suppliers access to their business intranet in order for them to interrogate rates of sales and stock levels on the lines that have been supplied. Within the grocery sector, some retailers will (at a price) sell information to suppliers about the rates of sale of other competitor suppliers. The logic of giving out such sensitive marketing information to suppliers is to ensure that the supply chain is aligned effectively with demand and also to make suppliers more competitive in terms of the product and price proposition being offered to the retailer.

Fashion business	Customer	Information sources
Manufacturer	Retailer	Retailers' stores, competitors' stores, other suppliers, specialist market research and information services, national and international trade fairs, the trade and business press, company reports and websites
Retailer	Consumer	Sales data, store employees, loyalty-card data, personal shopping, accompanied shopping, specialist market research and information services, preview evenings, focus groups, consumer panels, mystery shopping

Information from stores

In addition to the electronically gathered data that retailers access from their outlets, sales staff working within a store can also be a rich source of information about the consumer. This is especially the case with fashion retailer brands that employ staff to sell products to consumers, as opposed to simply assisting sales in a passive way. Selling staff, as opposed to sales assistants, are generally sales-trained and on a commission scheme which acts as an incentive for them to achieve defined targets.

Knowledgeable, well-trained and motivated sales staff are usually the best judges of customer satisfaction levels at the POS. This is a perspective that is difficult to measure electronically. The regular and logical surveying of selling staff about customer issues is an underplayed marketing research activity for most fashion retailers. (*Note*: Fashion marketers are always advised to undertake regular sales-floor visits, to learn from trained selling staff – assuming they exist – about what the customers really need and want.)

Mystery shopping for fashion marketing

Although regular shop/store visits are an essential part of all fashion marketers' ongoing marketing research schedule, visits to shops by (usually known) head-office staff can often yield a false view of the actual day-to-day commercial situation. It is common in many larger fashion chains, when a director or senior manager visits one outlet or a small group of outlets, for the visit to yield a false impression of the total business's actual staffing and stock situation. This is because prearranged visits usually lead to more stock and staff being made available in anticipation of the visit (in order to avoid later criticism). Set-piece management visits rarely reveal the reality of the current trading situation.

The use of the mystery shopper can, however, provide a reality check on any fashion retail business. Mystery shopping companies can undertake objective and clandestine research by regularly visiting a sample of outlets, acting as customers to research and record the critical elements of service and product availability at the customer interface. The type of information researched and recorded varies according to the brief and/or any potential problems or issues predetermined ahead of the research programme. Areas of interest to a mystery shopper might include:

- sales service levels received compared with the service expected;
- sales staff levels of product knowledge;
- competitive comparison of own and competitors' service levels;
- in-store product colour and size availability;
- general level of retail standards – especially neatness and cleanliness;
- transaction efficiency – speed of queuing and transaction pace;
- general levels of selling-staff communication and friendliness.

Most large fashion retailers undertake longitudinal mystery shopping surveys to ensure that staff at the customer interface are actually delivering a consistent service level across the chain. Despite being an expensive research process, the value of continually understanding the service being experienced by the customer is invaluable marketing information. Mystery shopping is therefore a vital ingredient of the total fashion marketing research process.

Primary research

When relevant secondary data is not available, a company undertakes market research to gather primary data. Commonly recognised methods of collecting primary data include surveys and interviews, whether face-to-face or over the telephone. Unlike secondary information, primary data are collected for a specific purpose to answer a particular research question. The first stage of all primary research activity is accurately defining the research questions and objectives. It is normal for primary research objectives to be defined following a review of secondary sources of information.

Qualitative and quantitative data

Qualitative data are normally descriptive and quantitative data are normally numerical. Both kinds of data can be collected using secondary and primary research methods. Mintel market share statistics and sales figures featured in a WGSN news report would both be examples of secondary quantitative information. A respondent's answers to a series of closed questions as part of a street survey would be an example of quantitative primary research. By contrast, qualitative secondary information could refer to a factual narrative about a fashion brand's product range and qualitative primary inforamtion could be data recorded from an in-depth interview with a leading fashion designer.

Over time fashion companies need both qualitative and quantitative information to help them make informed marketing decisions. A critical part of fashion is keeping up with global trends and understanding how to interpret them for a season. To do this effectively a fashion brand requires information from a diverse range of sources that might include trade fairs, fashion-week runway shows, youth culture in key international cities, newly influential fashion markets and a host of other qualitative information. Frequently such information will need to be visual in order for brands to understand how to interpret it in the design of new products.

WGSN (WORTH Global Style Network)

WGSN is the world's leading online research, trend analysis and news service for the fashion and style industries. It is provides a unique blend of visual fashion information and text-based industry reportage and analysis. WGSN is intended to be a one-stop shop for its clients, combining elements of fashion, trend prediction, design and style information, news and business journalism and fashion market data. The company provides mostly qualitative data through their unique online subscription service. Launched in 1998 and originally a graphic design business, it is frequently referred to as a trend-prediction service, since it provides a vast array of information normally used in predicting future fashion looks. This includes the direction of designs, colour palettes, and fabrics for up to two seasons ahead of the industry.

All major yarn, textile, product and designer fashion shows are covered in detail through a blend of written analysis and comprehensive photographic coverage. In common with many traditional fashion-forecasting businesses such as Promostyl, Perclers and Trend Union, it provides a view of the future thorough the 'Think Tank' area of its site. This is a standardised facility in contrast to the more customised facilities that other 'forecasting' companies typically provide for their clients.

WGSN employs about a hundred and fifty people at the London head office, with further offices in New York and Hong Kong. However, it is only the London office that generates creative content as the other offices are concerned with reporting. The company is unique as it employs both designers and journalists (about eighty of its employees work on site content – thirty in design and fifty in journalism/research). Its team of creative and editorial staff travels extensively on behalf of subscribers and works with a network of experienced writers, photographers, researchers, analysts and trend scouts in cities around the world, tracking the latest stores, designers, brands, trends and business innovations.

Categories of information provided by WGSN include:

- **Catwalks** – detailed reviews of runway shows from global fashion weeks;
- **Trade shows** – reviews;
- **Trends Information** – reviews of major product and consumer trends;
- **City by City** – guides and visual coverage of store windows in key locations;
- **Think Tank** – prediction of future macro and product-specific trends;
- **News** – current events in the global fashion business.

Further content includes **Youth Market**, **What's in Store**, **Business Resource**, **Retail Talk**, **The Magazine**, **Beauty**, **Active Market** and **Graphics**.

A valuable aspect of the show reviews is the blend of factual reporting and expert analysis of show content through written analysis and photographs. However, a critically important benefit is the site's updating of information on a daily basis. Its network of trend scouts, photographers, journalists and designers continuously feed information through to the site, enabling clients to access the latest possible information from around the world. On the one hand WGSN is taking a view of the future, in common with contemporaries in the trend prediction businesses; on the other hand it acts as a portal to the living world of global fashion events, recording information as it occurs. It is able to do this because it operates online, allowing new information to be captured and communicated in a matter of seconds from anywhere in the world. Consequently WGSN is able to update its information faster than the more commonly available 'trend books' that many forecasting companies provide.

With a very broad client base that ranges from international designers such as Giorgio Armani to cars, including Daimler-Chrysler, WGSN is seen as providing a 'core' fashion and style message for a season. Other clients include Zara, Gap, Arcadia Group, Selfridges, Lane Crawford, Calvin Klein, Disney, Procter & Gamble and Motorola, indicating the diverse and global demand for its information.

Client-user analysis of the site reveals that runway shows are the most popular feature, receiving around four million hits per month. Although a number of other sites offer up-to-the-minute coverage of the designer collections from international runway shows, WGSN provides in-depth coverage, which includes focuses on accessories worn by models (e.g. all shoes worn by models at a particular fashion week).

The huge global usage of WGSN by many of the world's leading fashion businesses has led some observers to suggest that it might lead to the homogenisation of global fashion, as result of the mass sharing of fashion style and trend information. To date this fear has been largely unfounded since it is the way that the information and analysis is interpreted by a designer that is key. However, the digital nature and electronic screen delivery of fashion information also lacks the touchy-feely advantage of style and trend agencies, which provide printed trend books for their clientele. The trend book also has the advantage of having fabric swatches included that provide touch sensuality and true colour register. Ultimately a designer will compare and trade off the relative benefits of each type of information service. Many fashion brands use both types together! (*Note*: colours delivered electronically on a screen are normally not in true colour register and so are not always suitable for matching or comparison purposes.)

Sampling

What is a sample?

All marketers, including fashion marketers, often need to make marketing decisions about a whole market or potential group of consumers by researching a small group within a total population. Ultimately the best research into any fashion issue would involve the researcher talking to all actual and potential customers before taking any marketing decision. Time and financial considerations normally make this impossible, requiring research using a small representative group or sample of a total population. In essence, a cook does not need to eat an entire cake to decide what it tastes like – a small slice will do.

A sample, therefore, is a small group of people whose views are believed to reflect those of a wider population. In market research and statistical terms the word 'population' refers to those people about whom the market research is generalising. It does not refer to the entire population of a country.

Major types of sampling method

Probability sampling

A probability sample is a sample where all units in the population of interest have a known and 'non-zero' chance of being selected. Examples of probability samples include simple random, stratified and cluster.

Simple random sample

This refers to a sample which is drawn from a population where all members are listed and each has an equal chance of being selected. This kind of sampling approach is based on a statistical probability that as each member has an equal chance of being selected then the extent to which it is representative can be measured/quantified. The accuracy of a simple random sample is referred to as the significance level or level of confidence and is a statement about how likely the sample is accurately to represent the whole population. As samples become larger and more representative, they generally produce more significant and accurate results – the most accurate research occurring when the whole population is surveyed – this is, of course, generally totally impractical.

Stratified random sample

This is a type of probability sample where the units in a population of interest are divided into mutually exclusive and collectively exhaustive strata and a (proportionate or disproportionate) random sample is drawn from each stratum.

A systematic sample is a type of probability sample where every nth unit is included in the sample from a list of the population of interest. The value of n is calculated by dividing the number of units in the population of interest by the required sample size.

Cluster sample

This is a type of probability sample where a population of interest is divided into mutually exclusive and collectively exhaustive sub-groups (or clusters) and a sample of clusters is selected. From the selected clusters, a sample of units is drawn.

Non-probability sampling

This is widely used in fashion marketing research, since it is cost-effective, mainly as result of the lower number of respondents required compared with probability sampling. However, as it is not based on random chance, it is impossible to quantify the statistical sampling error. Although the sample used would not be statistically representative of the relevant population, it is viable because the sample can be matched to objective criteria or proportions in a manner that is appropriate to the particular research exercise. Where a lot is known and measured about the various attributes of a population, non-probability sampling is automatically easier to carry out. It is harder to use it in developing countries, for example, where little data may exist concerning the constituent make-up of the entire population.

Quota sample

A quota sample (also known as a purposive sample) is a type of non-probability sample where the required numbers of sample units with particular characteristics are specified. For example, where a population has known demographic characteristics relating to age, gender and social class, a quota-sample-based survey would want to replicate the proportions of each demographic characteristic. Quota samples are still considered to be very reliable even though a statistical confidence level can not be attributed to the result as it is not based on probability.

Judgement sample

This is a type of non-probability sample where the selection of units is based on the judgement of the researcher, using criteria appropriate to the research aims and objectives. A survey of 'very fashionable people', for example, would require the interviewer to approach only those people that he/she judged as being very fashionable.

Convenience sample

A type of non-probability sample is a convenience sample, where the units have been selected because they are conveniently accessible to the researcher (which may not necessarily be the optimum sample for the research project). For example, if a fashionability survey relating to young people is required, then standing outside a fashion college would have a high chance of providing many young respondents. (However, it is likely that such a group might be overbiased towards extremely fashionable, rather than just fashionable, respondents.)

Choosing a sampling process

In planning the sample to be used, it is important to make a decision about the sample unit to be used – how it is to be constructed and who is to be surveyed. As a general rule, probability sampling is the best approach statistically, although it can be very costly and take a long time. Non-probability sampling is therefore more likely to be used in day-to-day marketing research. Every research project will require a different approach, depending upon the accuracy required and cost/time limitations. It is important for the researcher to try and avoid selection bias, particularly when undertaking non-probability sampling techniques. Experience is essential when planning sampling procedures and, of course, when writing and framing questions and questionnaires.

Low response rates

Poor response rates can undermine the validity of a survey, especially if it is based on a quota sample. This is because the quota sample is based on assumptions about the structure of a particular population. If certain categories of the population are left out or underrepresented in a survey owing to low response rates, then the survey can not claim to represent all views. Further, the views of non-respondents may have a significant bearing on the findings. A general reaction to a low response rate is to increase the sample size. However, other risks are linked to increasing the sample size, in particular the increase in non-sampling errors associated with data collection and analysis arising from the larger volumes of data that need to be handled. As society becomes increasingly more researched, questionnaire fatigue is a major problem facing the fashion-marketing researcher. It is therefore common practice to try and reduce low response rates by offering respondents rewards and prizes as an encouragement to participate.

Data collection methods

The means of collecting data is a critical element in market research as the methods employed can impact on the accuracy and credibility of the results. Data in this instance is a generic term that refers to all kinds of factual information, not simply numerical information. Data may be collected to suit qualitative and quantitative research aims. Qualitative data collection normally uses forms of interviewing that involve longer answers from respondents than is typical in quantitative surveys. This is because the rationale for qualitative research is generally exploratory, requiring the researcher to go below the surface and seek reasons and explanations for opinions and decisions.

Interviews and surveys

Interviews and surveys are both primary research data-collection methods. Interviews are normally used to gather qualitative information whereas surveys are typically used to collect quantitative data. Qualitative information can enable researchers to gain insights into decision-making processes whereas quantitative data are used to measure specific outcomes.

Interviews – focus group and depth

Interviews normally involve one researcher and one or more respondents. They are conducted using different methods, including face-to-face telephone and, on occasions, computer-mediated conferencing. The response rates vary by method, with some being lower than others. Personal interviewing is sometimes better, especially if the subject of the interview involves complex or technical terms. The two most common categories of interview type are focus group and depth interviews.

Focus group interviews

Group interviewing is a method of gathering qualitative information from small numbers of relevant consumers simultaneously. The group normally comprises between six and ten individuals and quickly gels to form its own identity. Focus groups are often audiovisually recorded so that time can be taken to undertake deeper analysis of the more complex elements or ideas discussed. Such 'post-analysis' reviewing will often reveal ideas or words, not previously thought very important or relevant to the topic being surveyed, thus enabling an avenue for further research or the uncovering of a potential marketing opportunity not previously understood.

The interviewer acts as a facilitator of the group, asking questions to generate discussion among group members. The focus group method is used to research issues that require respondents to provide deeper and more considered responses than is possible to record using a quantitative questionnaire. For example, a fashion brand would use this method to understand how a representative sample of its customers perceived its brand image. Interviews would enable a researcher to elicit the deeper thoughts, opinions and feelings of the target consumers (respondents) on how the brand is perceived. This sort of qualitative data can then be used to inform a more focused and structured quantitative survey of a wider sample of the same 'population' (target market).

The concept of focus group research is simple, which can mean that researchers underestimate the level of planning and skill required for a session to be effective and credible. Focus-group sessions need thorough planning and skilled moderation to ensure that the results are meaningful. For instance, the discussion should be directed and not led, all participants should have an equal chance to contribute (without one individual dominating the discussion) and all the research objectives must be covered. A well-facilitated focus group is free-flowing and spontaneous, although occasionally one individual can dominate a group by overpowering the rest and therefore invalidating the session. There are specialist research companies who are expert at devising, organising and facilitating focus group research. This is a specialised field requiring professional methodologies. Some key tips are shown in figure 2.2. Focus groups are ideal in helping to develop understanding in difficult areas of consumer research, and often act as a precursor and more specific guide to the development of a later questionnaire/survey.

Focus groups can be expensive, typically costing £2,000–£3,000 per session and requiring up to ten sessions.

Depth interviews

Depth interviewing is a qualitative method of data collection that enables the researcher to obtain detailed information from a respondent. The method is appropriate when a researcher needs and expects to collect information that is both deep and complex. This would include detailed information that may

Planning

1 Select sample(s) group(s) of 6–8 respondents
2 Develop semi-structured questionnaire (open questions and prompts for probing answers)
3 Plan and script the session to guide the discussion
4 Select visuals and other props for prompting, stimulating responses and clarification of subject content
5 Decide on recording methods (flip chart, audio/video and written notes) and whether or not the session is to be observed by a third party
6 Ensure that two researchers are used to conduct the session (one to question, and the other to record), assign roles

Implementation

1 Start the discussion and begin audio/visual recording
2 Monitor time
3 Involve all group members
4 Probe where further clarity is required
5 Prompt according to the research aims (e.g. use of visuals of an advertising campaign)
6 Check that all objectives have been covered
7 Close discussion

figure **2.2**   **effective focus-group interviewing**

require probing to elicit further explanation and the articulation of feelings, attitudes and beliefs. Such interviews are commonly undertaken on either a face-to-face or telephone basis. The interviewee normally possesses specialist knowledge that is important to the researcher, who may need to probe a respondent's answers to achieve the desired level of detail and explanation from the answers. For example *Vogue* magazine interviews leading designers such as Karl Lagerfeld to reveal insights into the thought processes and concepts behind collections. The depth interview is typically unstructured, although it should have clear aims and preprepared questions and themes.

Surveys

A survey is arguably the most common method of data collection used in generic market research. It is certainly the one that most people will have experienced at some time. A survey is a process of interviewing a large number of respondents using a predesigned questionnaire and is implemented in different ways, for example in the street, over the telephone, by post or over the Internet.

The accuracy of a survey depends on a number of factors including:

▸ the sample mix;
▸ the method of data collection;
▸ the process of data collection;
▸ the relevance and validity of the questions.

Surveys need to be carefully planned and developed, with most importantly the problems and issues to be surveyed needing to be defined in the first instance. Untrained researchers find it hard to write clearly focused questionnaires, often failing to phrase questions correctly or indeed in a logical order. Survey planning and writing requires the skill of planning the sample so that it accurately reflects the profile of the proposed target market, using the full range of question types needed to elicit the information being sought. In general, questions fall into either structured (closed) questions or unstructured (open-ended) questions.

Key types of closed question

Closed questions are the most easily analysed types of question for marketing research purposes and can help measure a range of fashion issues very accurately (often they can be used to measure consumers over time to ensure that marketing activity is having the desired effect, i.e. customer satisfaction is moving upwards).

- **Dichotomous** – questions with a yes or no answer.
- **Multiple-choice** – a list of alternatives, usually with a final 'other – please specify' box at the end.
- **Likert scale** – a statement to which the respondent has 5- or 7-option range of answers from, often used to measure attitudes and opinions:

STRONGLY DISAGREE – DISAGREE – NEITHER AGREE/DISAGREE – AGREE – STRONGLY AGREE

- **Semantic differential** – a bipolar scale, often using 7 levels, which can be used to measure a respondent's feelings about a research issue (a fashion retailer, for example, could be measured over a series of bipolar attributes):

CHEAP	1	2	3	4	5	6	7	EXPENSIVE
FRIENDLY	1	2	3	4	5	6	7	UNFRIENDLY
GOOD SERVICE	1	2	3	4	5	6	7	BAD SERVICE

- **Importance scale** – allows respondents to rank a feature or attribute in the following 5-scale rating:

EXTREMELY IMPORTANT – VERY IMPORTANT – SOMEWHAT IMPORTANT – NOT VERY IMPORTANT – NOT AT ALL IMPORTANT

- **Rating scale** – often on a 10 scale, it enables respondents to rate different aspects – similar to marking students' work. For instance 1 would be poor, 5/6 would be average and 10 would be exceptional. This is often used when measuring aspects of service in a fashion context.
- **Intention-to-buy scale** – a 5-point scale, used to determine the likelihood of the respondent buying a product – ideally suited to many aspects of fashion product research:

DEFINITELY BUY – PROBABLY BUY – NOT CERTAIN – PROBABLY NOT BUY – DEFINITELY NOT BUY

Key types of open question

Open questions are used to elicit more qualitative information, where consumers may have difficulty in comprehending an idea or articulating their feelings. By being unstructured they allow a degree of personal thought-flow to emerge, which can prove an invaluable source of information for fashion researchers. They can often be used at the start of surveys to allow the respondent to relax a little and to help get them talking:

- **Completely unstructured** – the questions are normally aimed at eliciting overall interest and understanding from the respondent. They can be answered with one or a thousand words but can be hard to analyse effectively. They often help delve more deeply into the respondent's subconscious.
- **Word association** – a word is mentioned and the respondents are asked to mention the first thing that comes into their mind. These questions are often used for helping to make decisions about fashion brand names.
- **Other types** – there is a raft of pseudo-psychological question types often cited in marketing texts, including story and picture completion as well as thematic apperception tests. These are very rarely if ever used in the fashion industry.

  - **Computer-aided personal interviewing (CAPI)**: CAPI is used where the responses to a personal interview or questionnaire are keyed directly into a computer, with the administration of the interview managed by a specifically designed computer programme. The programme checks for invalid responses and will not accept responses outside prescribed limits, hence subsequent editing and keying-in of data is avoided. Very often response rates to surveys can be improved by the use of prizes or offer coupons for the respondents. These can be done by an interviewer present with the respondent or directly via the Internet.
  - **Computer-aided telephone interviewing (CATI)**: the use of well-designed CATI, where the interviewer carefully guides the respondent through a well-designed series of questions and skip questions, greatly speeds up the data- and information-gathering process. It has the advantage of being easily analysed and is a very valid and robust form of marketing research, and in many cases it can be carried out without the need for a live interviewer, relying instead on very well-developed speech recognition systems. However, many respondents often prefer a live interviewer.

    The greatest benefit of CATI is the fact that it is fast and accurate, enabling changes to be made quickly to research areas being investigated, as patterns and information emerge from the early interview sample. CATI is currently used by WF and mentioned in the case study that follows this section.
  - **Continuous panels**: a continuous panel is a market research tool which is most commonly used in consumer research. This is because it enables

researchers to gather various data about relatively low-value but frequently purchased items in a systematic way. Panels are selected to represent a large population and usually number many thousands of respondents. For example the TGI continuous panel survey comprises 25,000 individuals and covers nearly all consumer products. WF use 15,000 respondents and focuses only on fashion clothing, accessories and footwear. Panel surveys are normally longitudinal and very detailed data are collected on a frequent basis. These are particularly useful in monitoring consumption market and consumer changes over time.

CASE STUDY

WF (WORLD PANEL FASHION; FORMERLY FASHIONTRAK)

WF is part of the TNS market research group, which operates a global market research business with a wide client base. The WF division specialises in delivering fast and accurate, quantitative market research about the size, structure and performance of fashion markets. However, it uniquely provides detailed insights into consumer buying behaviour based on data obtained from a continuous panel of 15,000 individuals. These respondents who are selected according to the criteria of age, social grade, heavy/light users and TV region, are between 12 and 74 years of age and from the following UK regions – London, Midlands, Tyne Tees, Yorkshire, Lancashire, South, Scotland, East, Wales/West and South West.

In addition to the age and geographic parameters detailed above, respondents are selected on the basis of further demographic, lifestyle and attitude data, which is gathered from a pack of information sent to potential panel members. TNS also operates an omnibus street survey to seek potential new recruits to join the WF continuous panel. This survey uses a quota-sampling approach to target individuals who fit these categories where there is a shortage of respondents.

Data collection

WF sends panel members cards listing details of the products they are to record and memory boards on to which purchase information is written. Respondents record all purchase information on the memory boards, which are divided into sections to help accurate and systematic recording by the respondent and information-gathering by the researcher. Respondents wipe the boards clean after every fortnightly telephone interview. The participants are asked to record details of all relevant purchases (menswear, womenswear, childrenswear, accessories and footwear) and whether the purchase is for themselves, a family member or as a gift for someone else. The information only relates to purchases made by the respondent and not by anyone else. Only new products are included and so no information is collected about second-hand items. WF researchers conduct a brief quantitative telephone interview with each member of their panel every two weeks to gather specific information about their purchases. The interviewers use CATI and CAWI technologies and gather information for each item that includes the following:

1 **Brand name** the name of the brand which made or retailed the product.
2 **Price paid** the actual price the respondent paid (for mail order this is the total price, not the instalment price) and whether it was full price or on sale/discounted.
3 **How many (identical) items** or multi-packs of the same product were bought.
4 **Where bought** the name of the catalogue, shop or location from where the item was purchased.
5 **Who bought for** whether bought for self, or the age and gender of the person for whom it was bought.
6 **Purpose** the main use or purpose for which the item was bought.
7 **Fibre (clothing only)** the fibre or material from which the item is made.
8 **Method of payment** how the respondent paid for the item (e.g. cash, credit card, debit card, store card, vouchers).

EXAMPLES OF TYPICAL WF DATA

**12 months ending January 2007
(women's clothing and accessories)**

Retail share by	% volume (units)	% value (£)
Clothing multiples	20.4	33.7
General stores	17.4	16.9
Supermarkets	18.2	6.5
Department stores	4.8	9.2

**12 months ending January 2007
Women's clothing and accessories key retailer shares
(£/% expenditure) by age**

Under 20		55–74	
Topshop	8.7%	M&S	21.1%
New Look	12.4%	Tesco	2.0%
River Island	7.7%	Debenhams	5.1%
Dorothy Perkins	2.0%	Matalan	2.5%
Next	2.7%	Bon Marché	3.9%

When compared with previous years, these data provide companies with valuable insights into market changes.

WGSN/WF – is one better than the other?

WGSN and WF are two leading providers of fashion research data to the fashion industry, but offer very different types of research information. Many fashion brands subscribe to both as the information has different strategic and tactical marketing uses. WGSN is an online provider of primarily qualitative information, much of which is visual. Its offer is unique, not simply because of its online delivery but also because of the scope, depth, currency and speed of information that it delivers. As the world becomes 'smaller' with faster media communications, greater international travel and more cultural blending, so consumers are more open to influences on taste and style. Fashion is a visual medium and, as such, those working with it need visual references. Much of WGSN's material is concerned with sketches and photographic images of colours, prints, and silhouettes, styling detail and fashion store windows. Although its service is used for research purposes, it is not a market research business. Its information is not about product sales and market-share data or even about understanding the opinions of a group of consumers about a brand. However, it is an indispensable source of research information for many different kinds of business that trade in the fashion and style industries.

WF does fit the more traditional image of a market research company, as it provides hard quantitative data about fashion markets and consumption. It is vital for a fashion company to know in which direction markets are moving and to have access to up-to-date information on customers' attitudes towards their brand.

Both WF and WGSN deliver cutting-edge research data to address the increasing demand for fast information. A major advantage that both companies offer to a fashion client is the currency of their information. WF's quantitative data are updated from its fortnightly continuous panel interviews and WGSN's site is updated daily with images, commentary and analysis from around the world. Some people view market research as limited because the information it provides only offers a snapshot of a situation at the time the research is undertaken. The modern world of fashion research delivers continuous information and analysis in text, numerical and visual formats to address the diverse and fast-changing needs of the fashion industry. Although both companies charge for their research services, the business and marketing information provided can deliver even larger bottom-line benefits.

Observations/accompanied shopping

Observational research is undertaken in fashion to learn about consumers' behaviour and responses to a stimulus. For example, a brand may wish to analyse and evaluate customers' reactions to a trial store format in preparation for a wider 'roll-out' of a new store design. Selected consumers can be taken around the trial store and asked to give their views on specific aspects such as ease of access, sensory impact, ambience, service facilities and other features that will impact on customers' shopping experiences and behaviour. Fashion retailers may also undertake accompanied shopping to assess customers' reactions to promotions, in-store visual marketing, product presentation and the frequency of particular routes taken by customers around the store. The latter can be useful information for planning the location of product areas (e.g.

high value or important to try on), logical product adjacencies, information points and advertising.

Fashion retailer brands regularly carry out 'competitive shopping', which is observation-based. Typically, members of product teams visit the stores of competitor brands in order to gather information about their new fashion lines, price points, promotions, in-store and window presentations and customer flows. Current information of this sort is critical to fast-fashion retailer brands in making tactical decisions regarding stock deliveries, store layouts, sales promotions, mark-downs and window presentations.

What about luxury?

The luxury goods industry has grown out of all recognition since the early 1990s. This dynamic industry and some of the reasons for its growth are discussed in chapter 8, but a key issue for market researchers to tackle is how to identify and question luxury-goods consumers. There are many problems with researching such consumers, the first of which is to establish who they are, since they are not typically found in high streets and shopping malls. Another is the problem of accessing individuals, many of whom, unlike ordinary fashion consumers, are elusive and have homes all over the world. Interest in researching luxury consumers has increased since the luxury-goods global market has grown to be worth anywhere between $100 billion and $140 billion depending on which investment bank or wealth management report you have to hand.

The Hasley Group

The Hasley Group provides a specialist tracking study, using a sample of luxury consumers who buy luxury goods and services across multiple segments such as travel, the automotive industry, electronics and food and drink. Its 'luxury decoded panel' provides information on consumers' values, brand perceptions, product ownership, lifestyle activities, media consumption and aspects of their buying behaviour (e.g. reasons for purchase/rejection). The panel data also provide a complete brand assessment of companies in each of the luxury goods and services sectors, allowing full comparison.

Limitations of market research and marketing research

When researching only the opinions of a small number of people who are supposed to represent a much larger population, there is of course the possibility of error. After all, researchers generally are not able to research the views of an entire 'population' owing to cost and time constraints. Whilst statisticians insist that a small sample can accurately reflect the views of a much larger group, it can only be done if the mix of the sample accurately reflects the mix of the larger population in terms of important discriminating variables. Such discriminators will differ according to the topic being researched, but might include demographics and geographical factors.

Through being aware of and understanding the limitations of marketing research it is possible to reduce errors at the design stage of the research process. Common sources of error include:

- errors in sample design: inappropriate mix of respondents, high levels of non-response;
- inappropriate data collection methods and techniques: poor questionnaire design and biased interviewing;
- erroneous and unclear initial research objectives;
- poor data analysis and wrong deductions drawn from the data or information provided.

Readers are always advised to ensure that before undertaking any form of fashion marketing research they are clear about what they need to find out and what is already known about the subject/issues to be researched. Much time, effort and money can be wasted undertaking valueless research that will never be of any use for future marketing decision-making. Marketing research is always an expensive process and marketing resources need to be used wisely.

Undertaking useful marketing research

Throughout fashion businesses generally, there is often a tendency for organisations to undertake their own marketing research, rather than employing qualified and capable practitioners. The idea that writing a quick survey questionnaire is either easy or likely to deliver good information for decision-making purposes is one of the greatest modern-day fashion-business fallacies. It is important for those intending to undertake market research to appreciate the fundamentals involved. Simply standing in the street with a questionnaire is unlikely to reveal much of worth to anyone, as the legitimacy of the location, the relevance of respondents and the depth of information may be in doubt.

Readers are advised to use trained market researchers when undertaking this highly important business activity. MRS maintains lists of members and experts to help with this process.

Recently, the UK has witnessed the rapid demise of some large fashion names. Examples of businesses that have ceased trading, had trading problems, been absorbed or had to be rescued include Allders, Army & Navy Stores, Etam, Pilot, Ciro Citterio, Kookai, Mark One, Dolcis, etc. – in fact a list covering the past ten years could fill a page. It is more than probable that many of these companies failed to subscribe to and accurately utilise available research, to assess their own position and standing in the market-place and, more importantly, to assess how their customers' perceptions to their product and service offer were changing over time. It is easy, when an organisation is doing well, to cut market research budgets, believing in your own and the organisation's skill and invincibility. All fashion organisations, whether large or small, need to carry out ongoing market research to ensure that their marketing and marketing-communications activities are having the planned effect. Arrogance is particularly dangerous in the fashion business.

Some final thoughts on fashion marketing research

There are many ways to use marketing research in the fashion context. Conventional approaches to market research can be supplemented by sometimes cheaper and more innovative research methods. It is imperative to link research outcomes with appropriate marketing strategies – misinterpreting marketing information or using it wrongly can be costly and dangerous. All good marketing research will deliver outcomes that can directly assist in the accurate management of the vital marketing mix.

Fashion businesses that 'fly by the seat of their pants', choosing to resist marketing research, will eventually crash if their pilots ignore the value of market and customer insights that are achieved through research. Always spend time on identifying the research issue and problem before leading straight into the actual formal research phase – even the most experienced marketing researchers need to keep reviewing their research objectives during a project as more information comes to light. There is no such thing as a perfect fashion marketing research solution, but only a fool would suggest that it is ever a waste of money.

fashion marketing segmentation, targeting and positioning (STP)

Understanding the needs, wants and demands of UK fashion consumers will be essential to future marketing planning. Although every customer is different, it is possible using segmentation, targeting and positioning techniques, to place them into understandable groups and to then ensure that we deliver the right fashion products to them.

Alison Thorne – Partner and formerly Director of Otto UK, BhS, George, Mothercare and B&Q

Introduction

The main aim of this chapter is to explain how the sequential marketing processes of STP are actually carried out in the context of modern fashion marketing. These processes and their terminology are key to marketing – this chapter describes how they can be used and applied in practice.

Today's fashion market is evolving in a highly fragmented and complex way, compared with previous generations. Global consumer choice is expanding exponentially in nearly every area. The fashion consumer is often overwhelmed and confused by the wide range of products and brands on offer. At the start of the Industrial Revolution, markets were simple because of the limited manufacturing capacity available. Consumers did not demand choice, they were simply glad to get hold of almost anything that was reasonably well made and offered at a price that they could afford. This uncritical consumer would be the modern fashion marketer's dream: easy, non-demanding and relatively gullible! However, history has conspired to turn the modern fashion consumer into a more knowledgeable, wealthy, educated and discriminating individual, who has developed a number of sophisticated needs and wants. Today's more selective fashion consumer is much harder to track down, to understand and to provide with a suitable fashion product.

As markets have become ever more complex, we see the continuing fragmentation of consumers within all areas into small groups which desire and demand very different products. The huge increase in ethnic subgroups has spawned new fashion looks or segments of the market, for example the smart gangster rapper look created internationally by US-inspired Afro culture. In the UK since the 1950s, a period that was really hailed as the start of the modern youth movement, there have been various waves of style dressing, all very different and distinct from the mainstream fashion and clothing market. Table 3.1 is a chronology of influential youth dressing styles by decade.

In each decade since the 1950s, influential youth dress cults have emerged, usually only worn by a minority of that generation. Although fashion historians wax eloquent about trends and cults, it is important for the reader to understand that throughout history most people have worn clothes rather than fashion. It is probable that the recent success of supermarket clothing brands, such as Florence & Fred at Tesco, George at ASDA and TU at Sainsburys, has mainly resulted from the fact that they are simply offering well-priced clothes of a reasonably acceptable fashion genre. Youth is undoubtedly more susceptible to fashion trends and changes, although today's baby boomers are a generation who have not totally given up on fashion at the age of 50+. Their aim is not necessarily to stay at the frontiers of fashion, but simply to remain reasonably fashionable. In the words of Nick Hollingworth, Chief Executive of Austin Reed, 'Women of fifty no longer act, look or shop like fifty-year-olds, they want to be like thirty-five-year olds.'

When previous generations turned 50, there was a natural assumption that they would give up on fashion. The relatively new concept of wishing to remain contemporary longer can be likened to Peter Pan – the boy who never grew up. 'Peter Pan marketing' is now likely to be one of the greatest challenges to the current generation of fashion marketers, who will need, as never before, to focus upon the expanding 50+ fashion market. Many large retailers have wrongly concentrated on trying to market their fashion products only to the young, failing to remember that the fastest-growing and richest age group over the next 15 years in many countries will be the over-50s! They do so at great risk to their long-term survival. It is estimated by the National Statistical

table **3.1**   **influential UK youth dressing styles by decade**

1950s	Teddy boys	Based upon elegant Georgian dressing with elaborate hairstyles
1960s	Mods	Smart and casual, clean-cut
	Rockers	Motorbike-based with leather and jeans
	Hippies	Indian-inspired ethnic dressing
1970s	Glam rock	Outrageous, exaggerated, feminine stage fashion
	Punks	Nihilistic, make-do and DIY fashion
	Heavy Metal	Rock-based leather, chains, motorcycle-inspired
1980s	New Romantics	Floaty, glamorous styling
	Yuppies	City-inspired dressing
	Grunge	Anything unkempt goes
1990s	Streetwear	Sportswear taken to the street
2000s	Chavs	Conspicuous consumption of obvious luxury brands

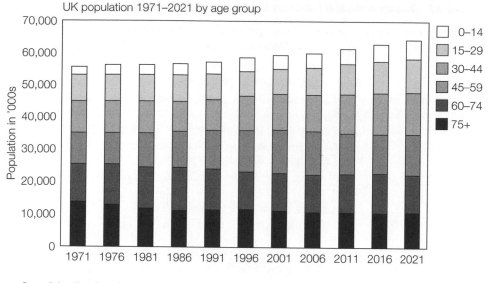

UK population 1971–2021 by age group

Legend: 0–14, 15–29, 30–44, 45–59, 60–74, 75+

figure **3.1**   **the changing age balance of the UK population**

source: Derived from National Statistics (ONS)

Office that by the year 2021 more than 50% of the UK market will consist of people who are over 45, compared to around 33⅓% in 1971. Figure 3.1 shows a population projection by age. A similar pattern is emerging in other developed global economies. With middle-aged people now looking and acting younger, the old adage of 'act your age and not your shoe size' is now likely to be revised and reversed.

The need to understand the changing population dynamics and market segmentation is a prerequisite of successful fashion marketing. The slavish assumption that 'only youth = fashion' has been and will continue to be the downfall of fashion companies. It is vital to understand, through good marketing research, which segments are worth pursuing. Positioning a fashion product or service for each segment is a sequential process. This chapter reviews and comments on the detail of successful STP marketing activity.

Fashion consumer segmentation

Changes in the social and demographic constitution, as well as fragmentation into smaller distinct groups of fashion consumers, are making it more important for fashion marketers to understand the make-up of different market segments. Understanding how a market is segmented makes it easier to plan marketing strategies, to target consumers and position products more accurately. The main ways of segmenting fashion consumers are shown in table 3.2.

table **3.2**   **the main methods of fashion marketing segmentation in the UK**

Demographic segmentation (main rationale for fashion marketing interest)

Age	Younger consumers tend to spend more on fashion more than older consumers
Gender	Women generally spend more than twice as much per annum on clothes than men
Family size	Larger families have differing spending priorities and patterns from smaller ones
Stage of the family	Young families without children generally have more to spend on fashion than those with them
Income	Higher income earners tend to spend more per capita on fashion than the average
Occupation	Usually directly relates to income level and therefore likely annual spend – some occupations demand a different style of dressing
Education	A good indicator of future potential earning power. Graduates have a higher lifetime earning potential
Religion	Fundamentalist religions tend to have stricter dress codes
Race	Certain races have traditional, or sometimes more flamboyant or conservative, dress codes
Nationality	Different nationalities have certain dress-code norms: e.g. US dressing is casual and sports/outdoor focused

Purchasing behaviour segmentation

User occasion	Weddings, evening wear, outdoor pursuits, sports, casual, formal, etc.
Benefits wanted	Image-enhancement, value, high quality, service excellence
Loyalty level	Regular purchasers as compared with fickle brand-hoppers Purchase frequency: daily, weekly, monthly, annually or other
Readiness to purchase	The stages through which consumers move from awareness to interest to desire and finally action

Geographic segmentation

Country	Defines likely income, size and number of consumers and style of dressing
Town v. country	Likely style of dressing and preferred method of retail distribution
Actual street	Individual postcodes can reveal a great deal about the resident profile and value of the house and are therefore a rough guide to likely social grouping
Drive time	Out-of-town retailers need to understand how long it will take for customers to drive from major conurbations to their outlets
Climate	Prevailing local weather and seasonal patterns define clothing weights and types of garment
Hemisphere	North or south denotes seasonal demand timings

Psycho-graphic segmentation

Social class	May denote spending power, education and job status
Lifestyles	Descriptive systems that categorise people into how they live their lives
Personality type	Inwardly or outwardly directed – may indicate likelihood of following fashions
Spending attitude	Some consumers are natural spenders, whilst others are savers – this is called their propensity to spend. Easy credit availability changes consumers' propensity to spend

Although the methods listed are currently the most important and relevant ones, it is a fact that socio-cultural shifts may cause marketers to re-evaluate the way in which they analyse and segment markets in the future. When societies were more homogeneous, in the past, the analysis of their constituent segments was much easier. With today's more varied and fluid social structures, marketers are constantly looking for new ways to understand and analyse their customers and their needs, wants and demands.

Demographic issues and their influence upon UK fashion consumer segmentation

Age and gender are two of the most basic ways in which to segment fashion markets. Women generally spend more money than men on clothes, with young people usually spending more than older ones. There are also cultural differences: women in the UK, for example, have typically spent more on luxury fashion than women in China. However, men are gradually spending relatively more on fashion than before, with older customers now staying fashionable for a longer period. The old order of market segmentation is no longer fixed, making the need for regular, clear and accurate segmentation analysis a critical 'must-have' tool for fashion marketers.

In a number of countries, women are the major purchasers of men's clothing and the decision-makers about what men wear. It is women who buy a large share of the men's shirt and tie market, although they now have less influence on major garment purchases such as suits. The increasing availability of menswear within supermarkets is a keydriver of this trend. Income levels are also an important aspect of fashion consumption. However, this must be balanced with an individual's propensity to either spend or save. The higher the total household income, the more likely a consumer is to have disposable income (the income left after essential bills are paid), which can then be spent on fashion. Income, therefore, along with age and gender, is a key area of interest for segmentation analysis.

Occupation and education also play an important part in the way in which people tend to dress. The work-based clothing requirement for an office worker is likely to be different from that of a manual worker – although this does not apply outside the work environment. For some, the wearing of older, worn-out branded clothes may still be an essential part of their dress code. Again, there are no hard and fast rules. Although the office worker is stereotypically dressed in smart tailoring, the reality is in fact that many offices now adopt a much more casual dress code. The US concept of 'dress-down Friday', during which casual clothes may be worn to work, is still spreading. Some US observers have noted that many organisations have had to introduce subsidiary dress codes and etiquettes to stop employees going a little too far. One US company even insisted that female workers wore 'foundation wear' on Fridays, to avoid any office titillation!

The way people dress still generally relates to their type of employment, as social-group pressure and peers influence taste. Formal education remains a major driver in terms of life and work opportunities, and is therefore important in terms of defining the likely type of work and ultimate income level of the customer. Higher levels of education may also make an individual more 'fashion-savvy'. Keeping up with the latest styles and trends, if done properly, can be quite demanding intellectually. The skills derived from higher education often impact upon the quality and depth of the individual's fashion decision-making processes. Although this is so far only an unproven theory of the authors, it could make an interesting topic for future academic research.

A result of globalisation, the world fashion market is firmly entrenched in an American–Western casual fashion ideal, there is still a huge number of the world's population who wear national costume. The wearing of 5-pocket Western jeans, sports clothing and casual dress is firmly based upon the ideals and imagery of a relaxed and wealthy American life-style. Sometimes religion and ethnicity can impose strict dress-code norms, especially upon followers of the more fundamental religions. In those religions that expect women to cover up their entire body and face, it is interesting to note that fashion can still play an important part, especially shoes. Wherever governments or religions have tried to impose dress codes upon the population, there are always some who find ways around the rules, without offending the basic precepts of the religion. The strict imposition of blue suits imposed by Chairman Mao in Communist China and black garments by the dictator Pol Pot in Cambodia bear witness to attempts to subjugate personal choice and ultimately fashion. Such rigid edicts are usually resigned to the scrapyard of history.

The UK is one of the most multicultural and dress-tolerant places in the world, especially London. It is true to say that London fashion gains as a result of the fact that it is a huge cultural melting pot. Many of the foreign-based students who have been taught by the authors speak enthusiastically about the freedom and inspiration they enjoy when they come to London. They say that, as few dress codes and protocols are expected of them, London is a very tolerant and relaxing fashion capital. Possibly the rich multicultural mix of London might be responsible for the eclectic nature of UK youth fashion trends. Each capital city enjoys specific tribal dress codes, as young people around the world all seem to seek the assurance of wearing what is acceptable to their peers.

Purchasing-behaviour issues and their impact upon fashion-consumer segmentation

The UK consumer is expected to dress up for certain key occasions such as weddings and funerals, although less so than in the past. The archetypal 'mother of the bride' outfit is still alive and well throughout almost all the multicultural diversity of Europe. The declining attention given to religion by the predominantly white indigenous population of Europe is compensated for by the growth of other more conservative religious groups. Many religions still have an expectation that their followers will respect the religion's customs and will attend religious ceremonies and holy places wearing correctly respectful dress. It is important for any fashion marketer of any religious, national or cultural identity to be aware of the fashion demands of the varied racial, religious and ethnic groups that make up the global fashion base.

Some of the garment benefits sought by fashion customers are simply for their physical needs – such as a basic pair of gloves and a scarf for warmth. Other customers will place high store on designer or luxury brands, whose wearing will sometimes imply an increased social standing. The conspicuous wearing of brands can also give the wearers a personal psychological lift and enable them to both stand out and fit in simultaneously.

The high prices paid by consumers for luxury and other brands depend heavily upon the psychology surrounding the buying of the brand. Objective and qualitative tests reveal that paying an extra £295 for a £300 pair of jeans compared with a £5 pair from the supermarket does not automatically improve the quality by a similar proportion.

The improvement of customer loyalty must now be a key fashion-marketing objective. The reality is that most young fashion consumers are inherently fickle in their tastes and purchasing habits. Certain consumer products, especially food, make-up, toiletries and technical goods, attract more loyalty since the benefits are not linked to constant change. Fashion, on the other hand, is primarily about change, and brands can be easily substituted.

Although there is undoubtedly some brand loyalty within certain segments of every fashion market, this loyalty is often superficial and tends to lose its hold in direct correlation with the loss of the perceived fashionability of the brand. Internationally, fashion consumers are notoriously fickle, with women being noticeably more fickle than men. Many large international retailers and fashion brands at times experience substantial losses of consumer loyalty. Successful brand names such as Levi's (over the past decade) and more recently Next (during 2006) lost their market dominance. They were once believed to be resistant to market trends, having enjoyed such a solid historic heritage and continuous growth in sales. Fashion marketers must note, however, that no fashion brand is ever unassailable by good competition – nothing is forever.

The variable nature of the fashion consumer's purchasing behaviour can often make it difficult for marketers to understand the triggers that actually make them part with their money. Some consumers, described as 'fashionaholics', even admit that they are compulsive fashion shoppers who often return their unworn clothes within days of purchase because of personal financial circumstances. In many cases they get their fashion kick by simply going shopping and undertaking the transaction. One of the authors, when on holiday in Key West, Florida, noted a simple sign in a smart fashion-shop window – 'Enlightenment through shopping'. Perhaps this sums up one of the many feelings experienced by fashion shoppers who are obviously living on a higher spiritual plane!

Geographical issues and their impact upon fashion-consumer segmentation

Despite the UK being, at its closest, only 36 km from mainland Europe, it is interesting to note that fashion trends, styles and colours do not automatically transfer easily between countries. Street fashion in London is often very different from that found in metropolitan France. Although common threads can be found, and many international brands work in both countries, the more mainstream fashions often diverge. Even between adjacent European countries, with no physical borders, there are often very different and long-lasting trends within the middle-market fashion offer. Germany's love affair with tailored and structured garments is still evident today, to a far greater extent than in many other European countries. Italians also like tailoring, but stylistically it is usually much softer and more unstructured than traditional British tailoring. French women have for many years purchased underwear which is more styled and feminine than that in Britain, although this is rapidly changing.

M&S has been, and still is, the largest retailer of women's underwear in the UK. New underwear ranges in 2006/7 positioned them well away from basic designs. It is interesting that many of the generic underwear retailers are looking for greater market share, with more exotic and explicit ranges. Ann Summers, for instance, has experienced considerable growth. As women have become wealthier and more discerning, and have travelled more widely, dull underwear styling is no longer acceptable.

Each season the international colour organisations, such as the British Textile Colour Group and the Intercolour Group of France, meet to deliberate on and recommend the colours and fabrics that are likely to be fashionable for the coming seasons. Again, across Europe colour acceptance at all levels of the fashion market will vary from country to country. In the warmer countries bordering the Mediterranean, the brighter colours worn over contrasting brown skin often look out of place on the paler Northern European complexion. Many ethnic sub-groups living in Europe are renowned for wearing stronger colours than the indigenous population. It is therefore almost impossible for even the largest European fashion businesses to be certain that a specific colour will be universally accepted across all countries equally. Throughout fashion retail history there have been many examples of international retailers who believed that they would be able to impose a pan-European style and colour policy. Countries, and even towns and regions within them, can deviate dramatically from the styles and colours accepted in the capital city. Despite cartoon stereotyping, women living in rural France do not all wear high heels, a chic hat and a Chanel suit while walking a poodle. Rural France is sometimes more unfashionable than rural Britain. Modern fashion marketers should not assume that a brand, business, style or individual colour will automatically receive total international acceptance. It is to this end that the trend forecasters, buyers and designers try and work towards delivering the ideally positioned product in the targeted market segment.

Geo-demographic modelling systems and their use in fashion segmentation

In many developed countries, postal addresses have been designated with computerised postcodes, or zip codes as they are also known. Postcodes can accurately position an address to within about fifty metres, making it possible to group them into similar types of residence. For example, it may well be that one group of postcodes relates solely to government-owned housing, whilst another postcode relates to a wealthy, privately owned area. In most countries, the type of house that you live in is a good indicator of the level of income or wealth you possess. Although this kind of socio-economic segmentation can never be 100% accurate, it is nevertheless a good approximate indicator of the types of goods, services and lifestyle desired by the occupants. This computer-held information can be used to develop complex geo-demographic modelling systems, which can assist fashion retailers to decide on the best locations for new stores or distribution networks. When overlaid with socio-economic patterns, the actual market level of the outlet can also be quite accurately planned. It is senseless to put up-market shops in down-market locations, and vice versa.

In the UK there are several proprietary data-based modelling systems such as Mosaic and ACORN. ACORN is a well-proven system. In the right hands it can help fashion marketers open their store in an optimum geographic location for their targeted socio-economic group. For example, up-market fashion retailers, given alternative trading locations, would normally try to site a new outlet close to a residential area with an up-market socio-economic profile, on the assumption that people living close to the outlet would have more spending power and would therefore be likely to make the outlet more profitable. Conversely, a discount retailer might use an area with a lower socio-economical profile in which to site its new outlet.

Fashion retailers have been slower in using geo-demographic profiling systems than have the major food supermarket chains, possibly because of the massive investment requirements of supermarkets compared with smaller-scale fashion retailing. There are many free internet-based socio-demographic profiling systems, which will profile any specific postcode: upmystreet.com will give anyone a good review and analysis of the local socio-economic and lifestyle background. The more sophisticated geo-demographic modelling systems, and the organisations developing them, are beyond the scope of this book. Readers are advised to be aware of their likely future impact on retail fashion geography, and the potential support they can give to the ranging and pricing decisions of fashion retailers.

Another key factor for modern out-of-town retailers is the drive time from towns and suburbs to retail outlets. In the UK it is estimated that approximately 8 million people live within a 45-minute drive time of the Lakeside Shopping Centre in Essex. The Lakeside Shopping Centre, located on the eastern section of the M25, is within easy reach of many car-borne shoppers, even those living on the west side of London (M25 traffic conditions permitting). If people living on the fringes of London were to try and drive, or go by train, to the West End, it is probable that they would have to spend more time, effort and money getting there than getting to Lakeside by car. Retail geographers, using sophisticated road-condition and drive-time modelling systems, can now also pick retail sites that are the best and most conveniently positioned for the majority of car-owning shoppers. Fashion retailers have been slow to use this emergent planning technology, preferring to use time-proven but unsophisticated 'guesstimation'. The huge investment required when opening a new retail outlet makes the use of intelligent modelling systems an important and essential part of the fashion marketer's armoury. Most fashion retailers employ external specialists for support with this work.

Climatic and hemispheric issues and their implications for fashion industry segmentation

The UK is, by international standards, a relatively small and densely populated island – the third most densely populated place in the world. Many foreigners remark upon our open obsession with the weather. As an island situated off mainland Europe, with only the Republic of Ireland to provide protection from the prevailing Atlantic winds, the UK's climate is described as maritime. It is typified by very changeable weather, although the temperature of the current generally makes the UK a little warmer in winter than its land-locked European neighbours.

Higher or lower temperatures than normal can have a profound effect upon fashion shopping patterns, with above-average sunshine often causing weekly sales increases of 30%+ over the norm, especially for sun-related items such as T-shirts. Unusually cold or wet weather can cause consumers to stay at home. In some towns and cities, shopping centres are enclosed and therefore climate-controlled, making shopping a pleasurable experience during extremes of weather.

The large fashion groups usually have a mix of both climatically uncontrolled outdoor and controlled indoor retail outlets, which normally experience substantially different sales patterns during extremes of weather – with shopping centres and their controlled climates being less weather-reliant that those in exposed town and city streets. It is for this reason that the larger fashion chains frequently experience greatly differing trading patterns on a weekly and daily basis across geographical locations.

Coping with the micro v. macro impact of the climate on fashion marketing

The variable nature of UK weather can have a huge impact upon consumer shopping habits, both positively and negatively, which can confuse even the best fashion marketers and planners. A sudden rainstorm, for example, will drive up store traffic and sales as pedestrians take shelter, whereas prolonged stormy wet weather will make people stay at home. To help fashion marketers understand the reality of prevailing weather, a number of specialist weather-forecasting organisations can provide detailed weather-analysis services for fashion marketers, for example, in the UK, the Met Office (see www.metoffice.gov.uk/retail/) and Planalytics (see www. planalytics.com).

Both organisations provide information that can assist fashion businesses to understand the historic, current and forecast weather impact upon sales patterns. By using sales data from the retailer and weather information from meteorological experts, their systems can fuse the historic, current and forecast weather patterns, together with the historic, current and forecast sales pattern by location. This fused data can assist fashion marketers in understanding how much the weather has affected sales in either direction. When undertaking fashion market planning, it is essential to use historic sales data, smoothed of any positive or negative weather-driven sales patterns, to avoid over- or under-estimating future consumer demand. Weather pattern recognition systems in fashion marketing are now becoming important tools in planning forward product demand. The topic of weather is always important to fashion businesses.

In the US, weather extremes of Alaska and Florida mean that snow and near-tropical sun happen simultaneously, and the issues and problems of weather extremes are even more problematic. In North America fashion retailers use weather information technology applied to fashion merchandise management to its fullest. It is a highly complex task to provide both hot- and cold-weather merchandise to one continent in the same season. Getting the wrong product in the wrong place in North America can be an expensive error to rectify. The UK's comparatively small area, combined with the relative ease and speed with which stock can be moved around, can often justify moving highly seasonal stock from one end of the country to the other. Adverse weather, especially as a result of disruption caused by global warming, is going to become increasingly relevant to global fashion marketers.

There are a few international fashion retailers and brands which operate equally or significantly in both the northern and southern hemispheres. In most instances, because the bulk of the world's developed population lives in the north, southern hemispheric fashion takes it lead from the styles and trends of the north. For any fashion business trading in both hemispheres, there is always the potential to move excess or poor-selling stock from one to the other, thus hopefully reducing overall mark-down costs of season-end stock (often referred to as terminal stock). Moving stock halfway around the world is an expensive logistical operation and is one usually only undertaken with lines and styles that are deemed both to be fashion-safe and to have strong sales potential. However, as and when northern hemisphere retailers and brands move more fully into the southern hemisphere, the inherently inverse weather and trading patterns will require careful marketing planning. Fashion businesses that have the ability to launch and understand their best-selling trends in the northern hemisphere, a season ahead of the launch in the southern hemisphere, would seem to have a huge business advantage – although in reality styles and trends generally need 'hemispheric re-interpretation' to get them ideally positioned for any particular market.

Socio-economic segmentation and its uses in fashion marketing

For many years one of the main ways of segmenting fashion consumers in the UK was by socio-economic group. Socio-economic groups are defined using a combination of factors, mainly occupation and education. These were originally conceived at a time when class was more prevalent and in an attempt to try and break UK society down into understandable segments, probably with the ultimate aim of helping plan future government taxation.

In most countries the convention was to use a mixture of social class and income to break societies down into meaningful segments. Socio-economic groupings still mainly used in the UK are those established by the National Readership Survey (NRS), and fall into the categories shown in table 3.3.

These groupings were for many years the major framework used by all marketers to help them understand their consumers to help them create effective and efficient ways of targeting marketing activities and communications at them. This system worked well in post-1945 Britain, when the very rigid class system ensured that class stereotypes correlated specifically with income, taste, knowledge and aspiration. The working class

table **3.3** **the current UK socio-economic groupings by the NRS**

A	Higher managerial, administrative or professional
B	Intermediate managerial, administrative or professional
C1	Supervisory, clerical, junior administrative or professional
C2	Skilled manual workers
D	Semi-skilled and unskilled manual workers
E	State pensioners, widows, lowest-grade workers

kept working and the rich stayed rich or got richer. Society was stable and generally class mobility was minimal. If you were born working-class, then generally you stayed working-class. However, this is no longer the case. As post-war society saw the introduction of societal cushions, such as the welfare state and the National Health Service, a substantially wealthy middle-class society emerged for the first time in British economic history. This pattern of social stability was mirrored throughout most economically developed countries.

The socio-economic groupings shown in table 3.3 fitted in well with the societal patterns of industrialised Britain, although as mass prosperity combined with better and more available state education, mobility between the working, middle and upper classes became more possible. Interestingly during the mid- to late-nineteenth century, in the Victorian era, social mobility was very high – Charles Dickens wrote about social mobility in both directions in many of his novels. In many ways the current dream of becoming a celebrity may well be likened to the lot of poor Victorians wishing to escape their lowly class. Social mobility is increasing in most developed societies, especially India and China, and is impacting upon fashion product demand.

For the modern fashion marketer, social mobility, equalisation of income and increased class movement have combined to create an increasing demand for luxury brands across a wide social spectrum. The wearing of luxury brands by lower socio-economic classes appears to be one of the first requirements in the climb out of poverty. Many previously prestigious international brands have suffered brand diminution as a result of their being purchased and worn by lower socio-economic groups, for example, Lonsdale in France and Burberry in the UK. The brands are often used as tribal markings, especially among youth groups such as football supporters – this can have negative implications for a brand. This problem is discussed more fully in chapters 1 and 8.

The classic socio-economic groupings have, until relatively recently, been used as the main way to undertake socio-economic segmentation. The problem now is that these classifications do not reflect current society and also do not make fashion sense. As industrial society has moved into the information age, and as class barriers and their associated dressing protocols vanish, this old system is effectively obsolete and often unworkable for fashion marketing.

The realisation of this problem by both government and general marketers has in part been the driving force behind the introduction of a new system of socio-economic classification called the NS–SEC. The British government in 2001 introduced this new system, which is shown in table 3.4. The NS-SEC aims to reflect the new industrial structures of UK employment

The authors were interested to note that teachers ranked higher in this new classification system, giving them a relatively high socio-economic status in modern Britain, which appears to conflict with pupils' respect for them. However, despite our cynicism, the new system is probably better than the original for the purposes of fashion marketing segmentation. At present it is not being widely

table **3.4**   **the new socio-economic classifications**

Analytic classes	Operational categories and sub-categories		
1.1	L1	Employers in large organisations	
-	L2	Higher managerial occupations	
1.2	L3	Higher professional occupations	
-	-	L3.1	'Traditional' employees
-	-	L3.2	'New' employees
-	-	L3.3	'Traditional' self-employed
-	-	L3.4	'New' self-employed
2	L4	Lower professional and higher technical occupations	
-	-	L4.1	'Traditional' employees
-	-	L4.2	'New' employees
-	-	L4.3	'Traditional' self-employed
-	-	L4.4	'New' self-employed
-	L5	Lower managerial occupations	
-	L6	Higher supervisory occupations	
3	L7	Intermediate occupations	
-	-	L7.1	Intermediate clerical and administrative
-	-	L7.2	Intermediate sales and service
-	-	L7.3	Intermediate technical and auxiliary
-	-	L7.4	Intermediate engineering
4	L8	Employers in small organisations	
-	-	L8.1	Employers in small organisations (non-professional)
-	-	L8.2	Employers in small organisations (agriculture)
-	L9	Own account workers	
-	-	L9.1	Own account workers (non-professional)
-	-	L9.2	Own account workers (agriculture)

used within fashion marketing. As dress styles can cut across age, wealth and social status, there are those who would argue that any socio-economically based system is totally irrelevant to the UK fashion industry.

Lifestyle segmentation and psychographics in fashion marketing and its current usage

Psychographics refers to the study and understanding of societal groupings based on lifestyle and personality types. It is important to recognise that people from different demographic groupings often have very different psychographic traits. The technique of measuring lifestyles is known as psychographics and mainly studies an individual's interests, opinions and attitudes to a wide variety of stimuli. The way in which individuals receive information about fashion, interpret it, buy it and ultimately wear it depends very much on their attitude and interest in the subject. There are many lifestyle systems used for measuring

table **3.4** **(continued)**

Analytic classes	Operational categories and sub-categories		
5	L10	Lower supervisory occupations	
-	L11	Lower technical occupations	
-	-	L11.1	Lower technical craft
-	-	L11.2	Lower technical process operative
6	L12	Semi-routine occupations	
-	-	L12.1	Semi-routine sales
-	-	L12.2	Semi-routine service
-	-	L12.3	Semi-routine technical
-	-	L12.4	Semi-routine operative
-	-	L12.5	Semi-routine agricultural
-	-	L12.6	Semi-routine clerical
-	-	L12.7	Semi-routine childcare
7	L13	Routine occupations	
-	-	L13.1	Routine sales and service
-	-	L13.2	Routine production
-	-	L13.3	Routine technical
-	-	L13.4	Routine operative
-	-	L13.5	Routine agricultural
8	L14	Never worked and long-term unemployed	
-	-	L14.1	Never worked
-	-	L14.2	Long-term unemployed
*	L15	Full-time students	
*	L16	Occupations not stated or inadequately described	
*	L17	Not classifiable for other reasons	

source: National Statistics

and analysing consumer groupings. The VALS lifestyle system was originally developed by the consumer futurist Arnold Mitchell in the 1970s and has, over the years, been developed and modified, as in the case of the VALS 2 version, developed by Taylor-Nelsen and shown in figure 3.2.

The VALs system

All the different lifestyle segmentation systems used within marketing try to place consumers into clearly defined descriptor segments. As a lifestyle consists of so many variables, marketers are faced with the problem that each consumer lives, acts and behaves very differently. It is very hard to place one individual into any single lifestyle category, since most people's lifestyles cross over into several kinds. As our lives and cultures become more complex, the marketer's dream of being able to place consumers into an individual category is becoming increasingly problematic.

Principle-oriented fashion consumers (more conservative dressers, unlikely to be swayed by the media and modern fashion trends)

Fulfilleds: more mature, fairly responsible and likely well-educated consumers. They are fairly home-centred and reasonably open to moderate levels of fashionability. They do not mind spending on clothes provided they are quality products that will wear well and last in terms of style and durability.

Believers: very conservative and quiet consumers, who do not have a lot of money to spend on highly fashionable or expensive clothes. Will buy from reasonable mid-market retailers especially.

Status-oriented fashion consumers (status-driven groups, who amend their fashion purchasing to align with their resources)

Actualisers: classic buyers of luxury fashion products, seeking exclusive and hard-to-obtain designer products. They are open to the latest and the best in terms of fashion product.

Achievers: similar to actualisers, but this group really like to show off their wealth to friends and family. Likely to be high spenders and wear very conspicuous and current-vogue branded merchandise for work and play.

Strivers: although short of both financial and psychological resources, these lower-socio-economic-status consumers would be likely to wear cheap, fast-fashion copies of celebrity-worn clothes and brands – probably not worrying about wearing fake or counterfeit brands. Despite their low income, they wish to be seen to be fashionable.

Strugglers: usually on a low income, they will shop in charity shops for branded bargains and will be content to shop at low-end discounters and supermarkets, where garment prices are low. Despite their lack of resources they tend to be loyal to brands.

Action-oriented fashion consumers (highly spending-driven, although some groups spend for show, while other spend to save the planet)

Experiencers: the heaviest spenders on clothes, who spend far above the average. They are probably young and have relatively high disposable incomes. Their clothes have a very short life-cycle. Being highly active and sociable, they need the right clothes for every occasion, e.g. sportswear and evening wear. They like to try new brands and designers and tend to adopt new fashion trends fairly early on.

Makers: these consumers are environmentally aware and will want to wear clothes that have been made responsibly and from sustainable sources. They are less worried about brands and fashion design than about being very ethical consumers.

figure **3.2** **the VALS 2 or Taylor-Nelsen lifestyle segmentation system**

At best, lifestyle segmentation can only ever be an approximation of how any one customer is likely to live his/her life, and behave at the point of sale. Nevertheless, it can work more effectively than the old socio-economic segmentation system. VALS is only one of many different types of lifestyle system or analysis methodology available. Many marketing agencies and even individual fashion companies create analytical parameters more closely suited to their own specific segment of their targeted market(s).

The critical importance of the pen portrait or customer profile

Fashion businesses often use lifestyle segmentation systems to help create pen portraits of their customers. A pen portrait is simply a written and illustrated description of their targeted customer(s), or specific customer segment. The creation of a clearly defined and illustrated pen portrait or customer profile can greatly assist in gaining a better understanding and mental picture of who will be wearing their product and for what occasion. The fashion industry and its marketers are notoriously prone to making sweeping generalisations about their customers, often relying greatly upon personal interpretation when deciding marketing strategy. A totally wrong fashion product can be offered to market if the business does not clearly understand who its customers are. However, readers should understand that a pen-portrait must be based on valid market research about consumers, as opposed to being made up.

Profiling customer information

Readers will probably come across both socio-economic and lifestyle segmentation being used within the fashion industry. As marketing information systems become more sophisticated at storing and analysing greater amounts of customer data, we may eventually move towards segmentation by individual, whereby every customer has a unique profiling that enables products and services to be personally targeted towards them. Financial services organisations are at present an example of a sector that is able easily to profile its customers via the huge amount of financial transaction data that they record as a matter of course. They can target product/service offers suitable to each individual client's financial situation. Fashion marketers, again using historic transaction data, could easily record customer size, style, colour and brand-preference data, with the potential of exactly targeting customers with very relevant merchandise as it arrives in the shops. Currently there is little evidence of the widespread intelligent use of such data, except by a few of the more progressive fashion marketers.

Consumers no longer want simply to follow the crowd, making mass-marketing communication and activity wasted. The individual and self are now more mission-critical, with the segmentation of self being the ultimate holy grail in fashion marketing.

Personality trait segmentation and its use in fashion marketing

Personality is a fundamental driver in the purchasing process of the fashion consumer. With more outrageous fashions, the wearer needs to be self-confident and aware of the impression (good or bad!) that a particular style statement is making to the beholder.

This whole area of personal individuality links very clearly with the concept of brand personality. Brands develop and generate strong personalities, which in turn project their images upon their wearers and users. A strong product brand personality can help support and possibly enhance an individual who may have a neutral personality. Clothes, and the style in which they are worn, often give off an external air that does not reflect the true personality of the wearer. One of the authors often experiences a very frosty response when wearing motor-cycling clothing. This attitude changes immediately when the helmet and leather jacket are removed and the wearer is recognised as being approachable. Psychologically, the wearing of certain clothing styles has for centuries given off signals and messages both good and bad. Wearing different clothing can fundamentally alter people's psychological state of mind, with some clothes creating a perception of formality, and others, casualness. Whether formal or casual, the delivery of confidence to the wearer is a key benefit bestowed on the consumer by a brand.

Personality profiling of both brands and individuals moves more into the area of psychological testing, usually beyond the budgets and understanding of fashion companies and fashion marketers. Understanding where to position the personality of a fashion brand, retailer or designer is one of the most important fashion marketing decisions taken by a business. Any fashion brand that conveys confusing or negative signals to its targeted group may well disenfranchise itself from them. There are good examples of brands with either a brand personality benefiting by being associated with a celebrity or influential individual. The argyle-pattern Pringle sweater has enjoyed this twice in its long and famous existence by being worn both by the Duke of Windsor in the 1930s and by David Beckham in the 2000s. Both men have been deemed style icons in their time, with the Pringle sweater benefiting from the association.

Spending pattern segmentation within the UK fashion industry

In the UK, female consumers spend more than double the amount of money on clothing as men. The problem with averages is that they fail to show the discrepancies in the spending habits of different groups. Young people are fundamentally higher spenders on fashion than are more mature customers. The level and frequency of spending and the places where that money is spent are unique to each individual. Sophisticated data-warehousing facilities and the information they contain enable brands to understand customer-spending patterns and therefore to plan what, how and when to market products.

Despite huge technological advances within retail IT, there are only a few fashion retailers that appear to be making any obvious intelligent use of the customer data that they hold. Interestingly, however, there are many small up-market fashion businesses which hold simple records about individual consumers' brand and style preferences. Small businesses are able to target and communicate with consumers individually, as a result of their small scale. Such businesses are in a minority, however, with larger fashion businesses generally using their detailed customer data to support broader marketing decision-making. Food supermarkets, where customer loyalty is generally greater, however keep and use a great deal of customer data. The more consistent purchasing patterns of food consumers make this task a great deal easier than for the clothing retailers.

There is evidence that in the future fashion businesses are likely to employ much more effort in segmenting and profiling the purchasing patterns of their high-spending customers. Special invitation-only preview evenings and the privileged use of a personal style and shopping adviser, as well as special home, office or hotel visits, can make financial sense when the customer concerned is an above-average or high spender. Focusing marketing and promotional activity only on high-spending customers is sometimes called 'cherry-pick marketing' – a self-explanatory term. The more we know about how fashion consumers spend, the more effectively and efficiently fashion marketing activity can be targeted at them. Currently, wasteful marketing activity, in terms of unfocused general mailshots, is typical of most large UK fashion retailers.

The ability to maintain the detailed brand, style, size and colour profile of an individual fashion customer remains the holy grail of fashion marketing, and is likely to become a major task of fashion marketers over the next few years.

Concluding comments on fashion market segmentation

Throughout this section most readers will have realised that the segmentation techniques and categories apply mainly to the retail consumer. However, it is important to note that similar techniques must also be applied to the fashion B2B context. The most successful fashion retailers undertake detailed supplier analysis relating to such fundamental business performance issues as quality, delivery reliability, price-competitiveness and creativity. It is now so important to get the fashion retail supply chain right that retailers need to be certain that their preferred supplier list contains only those who fully match their required segmentation criteria. Whether you are a fashion PR agency or a fashion magazine, or indeed any type of fashion business, you should apply marketing segmentation techniques when deciding to work with another business. The chances are that they will already have placed your business in a segment!

General methods for selecting which fashion market segment(s) to target

The increasing complexity of smaller, faster-fragmenting market segments is creating new problems for marketers. As segments become smaller and more complex, the decision about which to target can be difficult.

It is important first to try and evaluate the size and value of each segment before making any decision about which one(s) to target. Most important of all is to evaluate the overall sales and growth rates that can be expected. There are several widely available international marketing research reports that contain general data about market size, clothing categories, retailers and brand trends by gender and age group. This basic information is usually the first building block for helping to evaluate a segment size. With the exception of lifestyle segments, most of the other segment types are reasonably easy to assess, using basic marketing research survey techniques. It is helpful to analyse sector attractiveness in terms of the following key criteria:

1 **Segment size and growth in the future** – the actual value and the current v. forecast growth rate are probably two of the most important things to examine when deciding to market to a segment. Obviously there is a correlation between high sales and high profits (although high costs of sales can reduce profits). Small segments often present just as many, if not more, problems than larger ones. Large potential sales turnovers can have a magnetic attraction for marketers, who often see the benefit of economies of scale and potentially larger profits. It must nevertheless be realised that small segments are often very attractive to small specialist companies, which have the time and expertise to service them. Large market segments are not always the right choice to target if you are a small fashion business with limited resources.

2 **Segment outlook and attractiveness** – of all consumer goods sectors, the fashion industry is probably the most volatile. Fashion fads, styles, shops and brands can experience huge fluctuations of consumer demand within a matter of hours. Styles that have sold well for a few weeks often die suddenly without explanation and, conversely, styles or brands that were deemed minor to the total range suddenly become star sellers within days or even hours, simply as a result of a celebrity wearing them at an awards ceremony. Such wild changes in demand make the future outlook of segment attractiveness hard to forecast.

Despite these swings in micro demand, there are macro trend changes going on all the time in global fashion. For example, the move away from the male formal suit (despite evidence of a recent mini-revival in its fortunes) appears to be a continuing trend. Throughout fashion history, fashions have moved on, making certain styles redundant. Such a garment would be the gentleman's frock coat, an early predecessor of the formal suit. Now consigned to being worn exclusively by bishops and field marshals on formal occasions. It can otherwise only be found in fashion museums, textbooks or possibly theatrical productions. Conversely, the adoption of the sports trainer in the 1970s moved on to become a major macro fashion trend, with nearly a quarter of all footwear now bought in the UK being a trainer or close derivative.

A fashion marketer must ne careful not to mistake a small, short-term micro trend for a large, long-term macro trend. Doing this might be risky if business and marketing resources were to be deployed in the targeting process. Fashion is an inherently risky and unstable business, making medium- and long-term forecasting a difficult task.

In general, medium-term in fashion marketing means between six and eighteen months; long-term means no more than three years, and short-term is between three and six months. Many generic business textbooks suggest that long-term planning means anything between five and ten years. The volatility of fashions makes such a long planning period unworkable and illogical for the majority of fashion businesses. Segment attractiveness, though important, has to be measured with a degree of caution.

3 **Resource requirements, resource potential and business objective issues** – the UK fashion retail market, unlike that of many other European countries, is dominated by a few very large national retail chains, for example M&S, Next, Arcadia and Mosaic. Between them they control around 50% of the total fashion market. With such generally well-run businesses competing in the market, there has been an inexorable decline in independent retailers. It is quite difficult for undercapitalised smaller companies to have any great effect upon the main market leaders' dominance in the short term. Even large international fashion retailers which have entered the market in the last few years, such as Zara, Mango and Gap, still have small UK market shares. This is a tough, unyielding and hyper-competitive fashion retail environment.

When any decision is taken about targeting a market segment within UK fashion, the extremely competitive trading conditions (by most international standards), must be considered. Such a mature market requires a huge effort if the hold of the well-established home player is to be broken. In less well-established and less competitive markets, the necessary level of resource investment would probably be much less than it is for the UK. When considering entry into any segment, or market, the fashion marketer must always undertake primary research to discover not only the effort required to establish successfully in that sector but also whether or not the organisation has the will and resources to back up the decision. Resources are not simply about having money but include having good selling space, well-trained and motivated staff and most importantly, the right product. Of all the 4 Ps of the marketing mix (Product, Place, Price and Promotion), fashion marketing is especially unforgiving if the Product fails to meet consumer demand.

4   **Segment accessibility issues relating to fashion marketing**

When deciding to target any specific segment within fashion clothing, a key consideration must be the ease of getting product to the segment and communicating directly with it. As well as market segment fragmentation, many developed countries are experiencing media fragmentation. Audiences and readerships are generally becoming smaller and more specialist, meaning that fashion marketing may need to use a variety of marketing communications for longer periods to have the same impact as twenty years ago. Fragmenting media, together with falling TV and radio audiences and declining newspaper readership, is discussed in chapter 9. Media fragmentation makes it more difficult for fashion marketers to communicate with their target consumers.

It is also worth noting that attention spans appear to be declining, especially among younger consumers who are used to short, sharp interactions with the media, possibly as a result of the many distractions and fundamentally busier and potentially more interesting life alternatives.

Students, and young people in general, were and still are the mainstay customers of fashion retailers, simply as a result of their fashion interest and their general propensity to spend more per annum than older consumers. The successful iPod (the high capacity internet downloadable digital media player) and more recently the iPhone, together with the mass availability of home computers, may well have reduced traditional TV viewing and radio listening habits forever. In addition, with busier lifestyles and the many alternative amusements on offer, young people are also tending to read fewer newspapers and magazines. All these factors conspire to make it difficult to utilise conventional marketing communications techniques with this group. Although young people are hard to communicate with using conventional media, there are other segments of fashion consumers that pose similar problems.

The conundrum of the 50+ customer

With a rapidly increasing population of over-50s, a majority of fashion retailers appear to be failing to develop marketing strategies to market to and service this important market segment. Most marketing expenditure is being used to target the 15–24-year-old population, possibly on the basis of the segment's historic market share significance. Some of today's fashion chains can trace their heritage back to the mid-1960s through to the late 1970s, for example Miss Selfridge, Topshop, Wallis and Warehouse. Many earlier-established businesses also took the 1960s and 1970s as a time to reposition themselves to meet the youth demand of that period, for example Burton Menswear. A company such as Dorothy Perkins (for many years the only fashion shop in many small UK market towns) could provide an offer for three generations of women – grandmother, mother and daughter. However, over the past decade this highly recognised business has apparently put more emphasis on its younger customers. Many would argue that the department stores should be the ideal vehicle to serve older customers, but again many of these store groups have become obsessed with the cult of youth or have failed to create a truly tangible fashion offer to cover all age groups effectively.

However, the 50+ fashion customer is now finding it difficult to know quite where to shop. Why this situation has occurred remains a marketing mystery, given the huge financial resources available to these consumers. Many of the larger fashion retail chains inexplicably seem to be targeting the ever-younger and ever-diminishing youth market and to be ignoring older and potentially more loyal customers. Research by the advertising agency Young & Rubicam has revealed that by the age of 35 most people have a fixed brand portfolio, which has been learned and embedded in their lifestyles after many years' consistent use. It is reckoned that it requires four times the marketing expenditure to attract a customer to your brand if they are aged over 35 than if they are in their twenties. As people get older they like the comfort and certainty of tried and tested brands; they do not remain the experimentalists that they were when younger. There are many older customers walking round the retail brands of their youth who feel completely alienated by what appears to be an increasingly young and sometimes extreme fashion offer. Little research appears in the public domain about the frustrations of the 50+ shopper.

Gaining access to fashion segments is therefore not always as easy as it at first appears. Communicating with consumers is one issue, but then there is the question of just what marketing effort it will take to get them to trial or switch to your fashion product. This assumes, of course, that your business is offering the right product for that segment.

In conclusion, when considering the targeting of any fashion segment, it is important for the fashion marketer to answer five critical questions before embarking on the task:

1 Is it possible accurately to define and measure the segment proposed? Can the size and key characteristics of the segment be discovered using either secondary or primary research?
2 Is the segment proposed large enough to make the marketing effort worthwhile?
3 Is it possible to connect easily with the proposed segment in terms of marketing communication and also its geographical or physical location?
4 Do the marketing organisation and the fashion business involved have adequate human, financial and intellectual resources successfully to undertake the marketing to, and the entry into, the proposed segment?
5 With which distribution channels and/or outlets is the segment most comfortable?

The effective targeting of new market segments and the analysis and understanding of the scope, scale and dynamics of existing target segments is a complex and important step in successful fashion marketing. The complexity of most developed fashion markets and their continuous changes make effective targeting an increasingly difficult task.

Once the decision to target a segment, or number of segments, has been taken, the next priority is how to develop a marketing strategy for each segment. Most marketing academics, especially Kotler et al. 2001, suggest that there are basically three major approaches to target-market-coverage strategies, which are reviewed below in a fashion context.

Undifferentiated fashion marketing

This is where the business tries totally to disregard the variations of different segments and simply offers the same fashion product to every segment. With most fashion and clothing markets, of course, this would be almost impossible to achieve, as it would be extremely unlikely for one type, style or item of clothing to be worn by everyone. Possibly the only situations in which this might occur would be during a war or where a population is under the rule of a totalitarian state. During the Maoist rule in China and under the Khmer Rouge in Cambodia, citizens were under strict rule to wear prescribed clothing colours and styles. In more conservative times, during the 1940s/1950s and especially in post-war civilian Britain, there was indeed a high level of uniformity in male dress codes, for example the suit, shirt and tie. To some extent, this uniformity enabled the growth of many men's mass-tailoring chains, of which the only real remaining example is Burton Menswear. Most of the other established tailoring chains had died out by the mid-1970s. Today Burton Menswear has metamorphosed into a more fashionable, casual male-clothing chain, while its competitors have been relegated to retail history. It is unlikely that today's much more fragmented clothing market segments could ever accept undifferentiated marketing. The demise or stagnation of the larger variety chain stores was the inevitable result of trying to continue into the new millennium using undifferentiated marketing strategies, more suited to the Britain of yesteryear. The older variety multiples, including M&S and BhS, also once used undifferentiated marketing approaches – which has clearly taken a toll upon their once-mightier market shares. Today, we see clear range differentiation among these once undifferentiated giants. In M&S the use of in-house brands including Per Una, Autograph and Blue Harbour are examples of such differentiation.

Differentiated fashion marketing

Using this type of market-coverage segmentation, a business will target various segments, marketing fundamentally different offers to each. Fashion offers will ideally be positioned and targeted at specific market segments. The best example of this approach in the UK is the famous Arcadia Group, currently owned and controlled by the retailer Philip Green. The various fascias of Acadia are targeted at fundamentally different segments of the market, some of which are shown in table 3.5.

table **3.5** **the Arcadia fascias – current target segmentation**

Fascia	Segment	Age range
Topshop	Young females	16–25
Selfridges	Teenage females	14–19
Dorothy Perkins	Females	20–35
Evans	Larger females (sizes 12–24)	All ages
Wallis	Female	25–35
BhS	Males & females (all sizes)	5–70

source: adapted from Mintel.

The benefit of owning such a wide and well-differentiated portfolio of retail brands is that it allows a greater and more focused coverage of the total UK women's and men's markets. Although they could all theoretically be put under one roof, to form a complete clothing department store, it would be strategically more risky. Each fascia, by having its own individual store style, and stock content which can be targeted at specific segments, can be more finely tuned than the whole. Smaller, specialist retail brands also enable a business to be more fleet-footed in repositioning each brand as market demands change. Burton Menswear is an example of a brand that has survived nearly ninety years by constantly refocusing on the changing market demands of the segments it targets.

Retail brands are themselves subject to the usual rise and fall of the PLC. With marketing research and the careful development and implementation of a clear marketing strategy, the speed of fall can often be slowed or hopefully reversed. Fashion retail history is full of examples of fashion businesses that rise, fall, and then are successfully repositioned and driven on to new levels of success. No fashion business has a winning formula for all time, each one always requiring an element of market repositioning and adjustment to keep it ahead of the competition.

Concentrated or niche fashion marketing

In some instances smaller fashion retailers in particular focus upon marketing a narrow range of fashion products. Such businesses often prefer to take a large share of a small market segment, rather than a small share of a large market segment. Sometimes they have historically excelled in the development of one product. Good examples of concentrated fashion marketing in the UK include famous names such as Accessorize, Tie Rack and Boden.

In general, niche businesses are able to trade from smaller retail outlets than the norm, simply as a result of carrying one type of product. Although very focused, unlike more general clothing retailers, small niche specialists run the risk of their product becoming the victim of the PLC. Equally they are at risk of being eclipsed by better offers within other major fashion outlets. It is not beyond the realms of possibility that men's ties will go the same way as cravats – a once popular form of male neckwear that is now rarely seen or worn – and this could undoubtedly create pressure on niche tie retailers in the sector. Being too focused can also become problematic in terms of the overreliance upon one product in one segment, as was proven by the demise of Sock Shop in 2006.

Final comments on choosing a fashion market coverage strategy

Most fashion businesses choose a combination of marketing coverage strategies in order to avoid being locked into one segment with one product. The fickleness of fashion consumers and their changing fashion demands makes this choice important. This cannot be planned lightly or on a 'gut-feel' basis. It is at such decision points in fashion marketing that the benefits of good, consistent and well-analysed marketing research come into play. The relatively high cost of longitudinal marketing research becomes insignificant in the scheme of things when large fashion businesses start to lose sight of their core customer segments and fail to target them effectively. The authors believe that many problematic fashion businesses currently find themselves in difficult trading situations as a result of having singularly failed to use fashion marketing research techniques to their fullest.

Introduction to fashion positioning

Positioning products accurately within any industry is probably one of the hardest marketing tasks of all. The fashion consumer is fickle and unforgiving if the product or service on offer is not right. In other industries where there is little change from year to year, positioning and repositioning products is not as critical as it is in fashion. In fashion there is a need to change products and/or services almost on a daily/weekly basis. To position a fast-changing fashion product offer, and to keep it positioned in the consumer's mind as being just right, is difficult. Not even the best fashion designer or buying operation could guarantee to get their product offer right ten times out of ten. Fashion is always a compromise, with the very best buyers probably never getting it right more than seven times out of ten. There has been no fashion industry through history with a 100% style or line success rate – even the best buyers always have some element of failure within their ranges.

Fashion businesses are always seeking product attributes that give them substantial differential advantages over their competitors. Differential advantage can be delivered in any fashion product in a variety and combination of ways. Some examples of differentiation issues faced by UK fashion businesses are discussed below:

1   **Uniquenessof design** – design is a critical differentiator in fashion, which determines market position. Although the fashion-forward customer can cope with wearing the very latest fashions, the majority of consumers are fashion followers.

2   **Highly price-competitive** – pricing is one of the most difficult positioning approaches to take in fashion, as any business can cut prices by simply marking them down on the price ticket with a red pen. Fashion products or businesses that rely predominantly upon continuous price reductions can often create a substandard feeling about all of their fashion ranges. There are many consumers who feel uneasy about purchasing anything at a reduced price, for fear of buying something that is substandard or deemed by others to be totally unfashionable. There is no doubt that supermarkets have succeeded in gaining market share through a successful combination of product benefits that include fashionability and low price. In 2006, Asda's George brand sold men's jeans at £5 for two pairs.

3   **Exclusivity** – as increasing prosperity has put higher-priced and luxury brands within the reach of a wider customer base, many luxury brands risk losing their once-exclusive status. Limited-number editions or limited distribution or special superior label colours and names are now being used by some brands to try and re-establish their exclusivity. Economists realise

that if supply is reduced and demand is increased, then customers will pay higher prices. The luxury brands, and indeed some of the more mainstream international retailers such as H&M, have successfully created demand with a price premium, using capsule designer ranges by Stella McCartney and, more recently, Victor & Rolf. Scenes of customers fighting over products during launch days bear witness to this idea of supply limitation. The terms 'fashion ration', 'fashion torture' and 'once it's gone, it's gone' have been applied to this type of marketing supply manipulation. Zara uses a strategy of buying limited quantities per style to stimulate consumer excitement and demand.

4   **Unique product benefits** – occasionally some garments or fabrics offer specialist benefits or attributes. Examples of specialist breathable or thermal insulating fabrics such as Goretex and Sympatex have an element of uniqueness created as a result of a technical advantage. Sometimes design elements offer unique benefits, such as a reversible garment. Obvious design benefits can of course be easily copied. There are however more subtle garment design benefits which are harder to copy, for example the fast-changing ranges of Zara or a sports garment using a patented, highly technical performance fabric.

5   **Level of product quality** – throughout the global clothing and textile industries, product quality has generally improved over time, as consumers constantly expect more for the same price. The modern motor car provides a parallel, where new purchasers expect to have every possible accessory and a high level of reliability included in the basic price. Modern clothing must be able to withstand machine-washing and ironing, possibly many hundreds of times, without fading and looking limp. Many fabrics have built-in crease- or stain-resistance, mainly as a result of chemical treatments. A detailed examination of fabric and clothing of only twenty years ago often reveals minimal levels of fabric quality and garment construction. Quality is a difficult fashion attribute for the average consumer to understand. Only a person with a high technical ability and access to laboratory testing equipment could truly be certain of the quality of many mass fashion products.

Product positioning in practice

The position that a product assumes in the UK fashion market-place is defined by the key attributes that it displays, and how these are perceived in consumers' minds. Consumers generally compare the attributes of one product with those of a similar one before making a buying decision. It is the role of fashion marketing to try to position products and services in the most competitive way for each consumer segment. Extensive marketing research will usually have to be undertaken to understand current consumer perceptions, and hence positioning of a product, before making any changes to the marketing mix. Understanding, planning and continually monitoring a product's position over time is an essential on-going task for the fashion marketer. The authors' experience is that many fashion organisations, particularly when enjoying a spell of success, stop undertaking continuous research, dangerously believing that they have found some permanent positioning strategy which will guarantee them eternal prosperity. With so many external factors at work in any fashion situation, this is a very wreckless and arrogant management strategy.

As mentioned in chapter 2, there are a minority of managers who do not believe that marketing research plays any part in fashion. Although marketing research may not help with short-term decision-making in terms of what styles to buy for the following month, good marketing research will always provide a clear view of customer perceptions. Absolute objectivity is the sign of good marketing and marketing research. The need to plan positioning and not simply to leave it to chance ensures that the product is placed exactly where it should be relative to the competition. Figure 3.3 shows a positioning map that has been produced by Long Tally Sally, a specialist business targeting

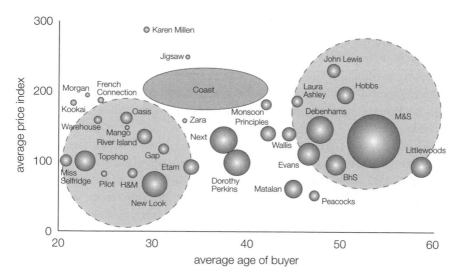

figure **3.3 Coast positioning map of competitors**

This perceptual map clearly indicates where Coast is in relation to its key competitors, as well as showing their relative turnovers. (*Note*: The size of each business is in proportion to its turnover.) In this example Coast is looking at both fashionability and relative pricing. Normally when developing new products, brands or ranges, or when undertaking an overall marketing review, the fashion marketer will research the positioning of all the main competitors in order to try and find a market position that is free and currently unoccupied. With established products, the task may well be to change the marketing mix in order to move the product into a more favourable position. Whatever the task, the use of the marketing mix is the key to moving positioning in any direction. Most businesses will monitor their own and their competitors' positioning over time to ensure that their marketing activities are moving the business in the right direction. It also helps to keep an eye on the performance of key competitors.

Products may have several different attributes that are deemed important in the target consumer's mind. To help marketing teams be certain of a fashion product's positioning, the perceptual map is a key analytical tool that is used extensively in UK fashion marketing.

The use of positioning or perceptual mapping in fashion marketing

Perceptual mapping is usually carried out using two aspects of product or service attributes at any one time, creating a cruciform diagram. Each axis is typically split into ten parts, to allow relatively accurate positioning. The most common attributes perceptually mapped by fashion marketers are the level of fashion, sometimes called 'fashionability', normally plotted against the general price level. Of course, a customer's perception of the fashionability of a business is often far different from the perception of the management. There are many examples of fashion retailers who have failed regularly to measure their customers' perceptions and have finally paid the price by going out of business.

Although most perceptual mapping is undertaken using two attributes, there are various more sophisticated methods involving a multi-attribute methodology. With this approach it is possible to map any number of attributes (in multiples of four) so that they can all be viewed together, as shown in figure 3.4. Because of its high complexity, it is normal to use this format only when preparing comparative perceptual maps between two businesses. Although more than two businesses can be compared, the diagram tends to become too complex to read and makes quick analysis slightly confusing.

All fashion, whether B2C or B2B, large or small, should undertake perceptual measurement on a regular basis, probably twice a year, to ensure that ranges do not negatively impact upon consumer perceptions. Particularly when using market repositioning tactics and strategies, companies will often show changing perceptions as a time series on one diagram. This can then clearly demonstrate how consumer perceptions are changing over time.

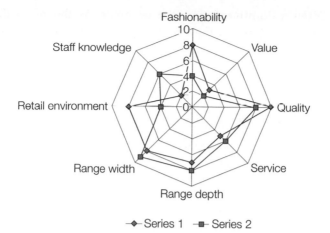

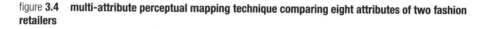

figure **3.4** **multi-attribute perceptual mapping technique comparing eight attributes of two fashion retailers**

How fashion repositioning is carried out in practice

Probably one of the least understood and most difficult aspects of modern fashion marketing is how to reposition a product. Repositioning in fashion is carried out for any one of a series of reasons:

1 **Increasing market competition** – this occurs when new competitors enter a market or established competitors enter an organisation's existing segment(s). Zara repositioned many fashion retailers as 'slow fashion' businesses.

2 **Product development pressure** – a new fabric or garment construction technique changes a product fundamentally. A new fabric or production method, for example, can improve product-handling characteristics and possibly lower the price at the same time.

3 **Major external macro-marketing and/or macro-economic force changes** – these can upset the fundamental equilibrium of the market. Major price reductions have occurred, for example, as a result of cheaper imports from China, deriving from basic changes to the Multi-Fibre Arrangement (MFA).

In a real trading scenario, the need to reposition a particular fashion business would be caused by several factors, rather than one alone. Failure to respond to change, and to reposition a business that is no longer aligned with customer demand, ultimately results in business demise. No business can stay locked in one position for eternity. Demand for repositioning is really driven by the inevitability of the PLC, which ensures that demand for a product is never consistent, since it is continually changing. Repositioning a business on the basis of gut feeling is used a great deal by some fashion businesses. Often a dominant manager or owner is the main driver of a repositioning process. Positioning which is poorly carried out often creates problems.

ALLDERS – A STORY OF REPOSITIONING THAT WENT WRONG

Allders, founded in 1886 by Josiah Allder, was a family department store that had traded soundly for many years. Throughout the 1960s and 1970s it was part of UDS (United Drapery Stores). During the early 1970s it was such a powerful name that UDS was at one point in a potential takeover battle for Debenhams, now the largest department store group in the UK. At one stage Allders traded over forty stores, but always had a strong household department and a much less influential clothing offer. In common with many other traditional department stores, it had an ageing clientele, mainly over the age of 35 and with the majority in the 50+ bracket.

During recent times, Debenhams, the UK's leading department store group, has flourished under the new ownership of the Burton Group. The takeover of Debenhams in the early 1980s was led by the famous Sir Ralph Halpern of Burton Group fame. Latterly Burtons was renamed the Arcadia Group under the careful stewardship of John Hoerner, the US department-store guru. Debenhams, unlike Allders, refocused itself upon becoming a department store based mainly upon own-brand and designer-brand clothing – whilst at the same time withdrawing from more traditional household goods.

During this period, Allders continued to trade as a traditional department store, with the associated high running and infrastructural costs leading to diminishing success. Some efforts were made by management to improve the fashion and clothing offer, but Allders' strength was traditionally more in household goods than in fashion.

Under recent management (many of whom had helped John Hoerner, the former Chief Executive, to transform Debenhams), Allders set about trying a similar positioning strategy, focusing on higher-margin clothing. A brand new store had even been opened in hypercompetitive Oxford Street in London, virtually opposite the famous Selfridges – another department store that had also chosen to reposition itself more towards fashion.

The repositioning that Allders attempted, in a matter of a few years, failed to attract the customers in enough numbers to sustain the business, causing it to go into administration in January 2005. Although other business factors may have exacerbated its poor financial position, the repositioning task undertaken by Allders was too great in the fiercely competitive fashion market-place of the new millennium. Hundreds of employees lost both their jobs and their pensions as result of this repositioning error.

This repositioning plan was simply too difficult for Allders – the task appears to have been too large to undertake in such a relatively short space of time. The rest is retail history, but shows clearly the danger of trying to reposition a large business too far, too quickly, without ensuring that your customer base is moving in line with the repositioning process. There have been many other similar examples of problematic repositionings throughout the history of the UK fashion industry.

Key methods of differentiating fashion businesses during repositioning

Differentiation is the key for any fashion business in distancing itself from its competitors. Not all fashion businesses can easily differentiate themselves, the general rule being that the larger you are, the harder it is for customers to follow any differentiation process that might be undertaken. Recently, M&S has successfully repositioned itself, by ensuring that the product meets consumer expectations and then effectively communicating this to them via well-targeted advertising. Often fashion businesses improve their product but, having previously alienated their core consumers, expect them to return automatically once the product is right. Consumers need constant communication, especially if the product or service proposition has been altered. Using good research, well-targeted repositioning techniques and good advertising communications, M&S continues to return to its old levels of trading success but, more importantly, to restore consumer confidence. The collapse of Allders bears witness to the danger of trying to reposition a large business too quickly.

Repositioning a fashion business using a differentiation approach can be achieved by using one of the following four methods:

1   **Product differentiation** – probably the most usual approach for fashion businesses undertaking differentiation. It will only work if your existing customer base understands what is going on and wants the new product offer. Hopefully, it will also expand the total appeal of the business to other targeted segments. Product differentiation is a way of life in most young high-fashion businesses, which undertake a mini repositioning process every time a new range enters the market. Product differentiation as a re-positioning strategy for larger and more staid fashion businesses can be far more problematic.

2   **Selling environment differentiation** – fashion businesses have long realised that an enticing retail environment can substantially enhance and encourage consumer purchasing. A trendy environment confers trendiness upon the fashion products it contains, simply by association. Most fashion retailers regularly refurbish their outlets, with brand owners and designers realising the marketing power of a modern showroom in a trendy area of town. 'New' is a powerful attribute in fashion marketing, with fashion retailers needing to refresh and renew their trading environments on at least a two-to-three-year cycle. Store modernisation has the effect of increasing sales by anywhere between 50% and 70% upon reopening. Store modernisation programmes are an important and

ongoing fashion marketing activity which require a high level of accurate forward planning.

3   **Service and personnel differentiation** – despite the fact that mass-market fashion retailing has become less service-oriented, some effort has been expended by companies such as Topshop, who provide home visiting and home shopping services. Many of the larger department stores such as Harvey Nichols and Selfridges will offer the assistance of a personal shopper, to help the individual with the whole retail experience. Some extend this through to personal styling advice; others, at the very top, tailor an individual VIP shopping and styling service for their best customers. In a world of increasingly bland service, especially in the UK where service has never been highly rated on any international scale, new levels of service provision may well be the next 'fashion' in fashion business differentiation. Currently working on the sales floor is not seen as an important role in fashion marketing. Good fashion marketers realise that it is here at the customer interface, the business is either won or lost.

4   **Value or price positioning differentiation** – the UK fashion market has, from an international perspective, always been seen as a high-price market. From cars to branded jeans (despite the level of the pound against the dollar or other leading currencies), foreign suppliers and brands have mercilessly milked the UK consumer with some of the highest prices in the world. However, as a result of the entry of fashion value retailers such as TK Maxx, Matalan, New Look and others, the average price of clothing in the UK market has fallen significantly over recent years. The average price of mass-market clothing has fallen by at least 20% over the past three years, with the likelihood of further falls as a result of increasing levels of cheap Chinese imports. As supermarkets now enter into fashion clothing as serious players, virtually all market segments are reviewing their price positioning. Value positioning needs very serious levels of strategic planning for it to be successful in the long run. Pricing will become of increasing strategic importance, rather than a mainly tactical activity, as supermarkets and other international low-cost retailers start to attack the apparently attractive global fashion markets. Mid-market regular-priced retailers should remain alert to this threat.

Communicating positioning and repositioning effectively to customers

One of the most important aspects for fashion businesses to understand when undertaking any type of repositioning is the long lag in consumer perceptions. Many consumers simply fail to understand changes in product, environment, pricing or service. Although many do see and understand change, a large percentage of fashion consumers seem oblivious to their external environment. Fashion marketers have to assume that it may take years, rather than months, for all their customers to tune in to a new strategy. Customers are simply not as smart as fashion marketers believe.

The length of time taken to move consumer perceptions depends upon many factors, but in general the level of marketing-mix activity is a key driver of perceptual change. People do notice advertisements, provided they have a clear and comprehensible message. Advertising, however, is only a support tool for positioning change in the fashion industry. The recent advertising campaigns of M&S, using famous models and celebrities such as Twiggy and fellow M&S models Erin O'Connor, Laura Bailey and Noémie Lenoir and, for the men's range, Brian Ferry, has managed to reconnect the business as being fashionable and relative to its older target market.

Concluding comments

The fashion industry widely uses the terms 'segmentation', 'targeting' and 'positioning', with many businesses regularly undertaking these most important of marketing processes. Unfortunately, even many large, well-known names have undertaken major repositioning programmes without first finding out exactly where they are positioned in their customers' minds relative to their competitors.

Often using a 'shoot from the hip' approach, fashion businesses have embarked upon fundamental strategic changes without spending a penny on good marketing research to assist them with their decision-making. A leading executive of a prominent and recently failed fashion business once told the authors, 'I do not believe in marketing, only in advertising'! The fashion market is probably one of the most competitive and unforgiving in the world. Readers of this book fail to believe in fashion marketing at their peril!

marketing mix: the fashion product

When well-designed, good-quality product is at the root of a marketing campaign it often adds a degree of authenticity and sincerity to the marketing strategy that can't be attained by any other means. Trust is essential to brand loyalty. The marketing communication should really be the icing on the cake – if a company places too much emphasis on marketing activities over product, it can ultimately be damaging to the brand. Putting huge marketing spend behind products that are below par to generate sales is ultimately a very short-term approach – where this is the case, good sales will inevitably undermine long-term brand loyalty and repeat purchases in the future.

Gary Aspden–Adidas

Introduction – the marketing mix

The aim of this chapter is to explain and analyse the term 'product' within the context of fashion and the marketing mix. Marketing theorists use the concept of the 4 Ps of the marketing mix to explain the interdependent relationship of Product, Price, Place and Promotion within successful business. The marketing mix was initially researched and explained by Neil Borden, a Harvard economist back in the 1950s. In essence the theory suggests that any business (fashion or otherwise) needs the right Product, at the right Price, in the right Place and using the right Promotion – hence the term the '4 Ps'. Each 'element' (of the mix) needs to match the needs, demands, resources and behaviour of target customers for the overall package of marketing effort to be successful. The basic theory has been subsequently revised to include another three Ps – People, Process and Physical evidence, which combine to form the services marketing mix. This more developed mix is discussed in chapter 7.

Whilst the definition of the marketing mix might not appear to be of world-shattering significance, its understanding and subsequent application has probably had one of the greatest impacts upon the growth of consumerism and directly contributed to the general economic well-being of society as a whole.

The fashion product

What is a product?

A product is the tangible offer that a business sells to make money. Conceptually, it is also a response to a customer need and/or a solution to an associated problem: for example, a consumer needs to fit in with the views of a peer group and the problem of how best to do this is solved by wearing brand X's trendy new products. One can argue that fashion creates continual problems, as each season consumers are faced with making decisions about what to wear.

Fashion is a perfect means of demonstrating membership of a social group, and clothing is a common vehicle for associating with particular reference or peer groups, since products and brands are conspicuous when worn. In many respects it is the job of (the wider) marketing (function) to identify customers' needs and solve associated problems with the provision of a product.

The fashion product is the most important part of a fashion marketing mix as it is:

- what consumers buy;
- the most common way for people to convey how fashionable they are;
- a brand statement of quality;
- the principal output of a fashion design process;
- the focus for the other marketing mix elements;
- the tangible representation of a brand.

The last point refers to a particular brand association that consumers have with a fashion company based on the differentiated nature of the products that it designs, makes and sells. The trend towards the customisation of fashion products underlines the importance of the product to the relationship between brand and consumer. At a recent conference on luxury goods, François-Henri Pinault stated that 'high luxury and the brand itself are defined by the product' (2006). This is very much the case where a luxury brand is selling products using the name of a heritage designer such as Chanel. Prada, Gucci, Christian Dior and Armani. For example, all have uniquely identifiable signatures to their clothing lines. However, such distinctiveness is less obvious in the mass fashion market as brands and retailer brands tend to follow fashion trends using similar trend information.

The importance of the fashion product is further illustrated when Tom Ford stated, while working as the creative director for both Gucci and Yves Saint Laurent luxury brands, 'I cannot emphasise enough the importance of product. It is the key. All the advertising in the world can't help sell a pant that makes your butt look wide, or a dress that makes you feel fat, or a shoe that makes your ankle look thick. For me the ultimate test for a product is sales' (Ford, 2001).

If a fashion product is fundamentally wrong (for a market and a season), then no level of price reduction, widened distribution or increased promotion will necessarily make it sell. This is called 'terminal stock', or simply stock that has failed to sell within a season. Often, even after mark-downs, it has to be 'jobbed off' (sold to market traders, etc.) to avoid storage costs and brand dilution (see chapter 7). Having high levels of old-season or terminal stock dramatically reduces profitability.

Demand for fashion products is perishable, since they are normally only relevant for a season. Increasingly fast fashion means that products have a very limited commercial lifespan. It is all the more important, then, for buyers to get the product right for a market.

What is fashion?

In many respects fashion, like marketing, is an overused term referencing everything from seasonal trends and celebrity style and to a global industry comprising many eclectic business activities. Fashion is frequently a theme used to sell a variety of products ranging from furniture to cars. Advertisements for many brands of car, furniture and mobile phone use fashion references such as seasonal colours to convey a sense of desirability and trendy product positioning.

The reason fashion can be applied so liberally is that it reflects a zeitgeist and is an expression of the times in which we live. The recognition and meaning of fashion is contextualised by the mass adoption of a particular design, style or trend which results in something being 'in fashion' or on trend within a specific season. It is directly linked to the conspicuous use of products and clothing, to convey meanings such as social status and success. Fashion is also synonymous with terms such as style, mode and dress and specific types of products within a range of clothing, which are sometimes referred to as fashion items. Brands frequently produce a collection of products that are more fashion-forward in terms of their design, to generate press coverage in the fashion media.

Two fundamental requirements for fashion to exist are constant change and mass adoption. Gabrielle Chanel once said that fashion does not exist unless it goes into the streets (Charles-Roux, 1981, p. 237), which implies that a design is not 'fashionable' unless it is adopted by a majority of people, hence the terms 'in fashion' and 'fashionable', both of which imply a large degree of consumer adoption and recognition.

In some people's minds, the terms 'fashion' and 'style' are often interchangeable. However, style can exist outside the parameters of a fashion season and indeed one's personal style may run against prevailing fashion trends. In today's media-driven culture, stylists are very influential in creating particular looks for adverts and editorials, which are then worn by media celebrities, who in turn influence consumer buying behaviour.

The particular style of fashion product that constitutes fashionability varies from customer to customer and changes consistently over time. Customers' own attitudes and perceptions are the main drivers of what constitutes a fashionable product for themselves, although whether or not the fashion selected actually suits them is often debatable.

Fast fashion

The term 'fast fashion' has emerged strongly over recent years in Europe and in particular the UK to reference a specific type of fashion business. It is characterised by a quick turnaround of fashion products, which reflects fast-changing fashion designs and styles. One of the principal retailer brands associated with fast fashion is Zara, which is able to change its stock approximately seventeen times in a year. Zara is able to achieve a very fast 'design-to-stores' supply chain largely owing to its vertically integrated business (in-house design, manufacturing and retailing).

Of all consumer and business products, fashion items present a particularly difficult marketing problem in terms of how the marketer can ensure that the product is right before it gets to market. The fast-moving nature of fashion makes pre-launch marketing research an irrelevance, as consumers generally do not know what fashion they will be wearing until they buy it.

New fashion products hit the market on a daily basis with fads, styles, colours or brand trends which can explode on to the market simply as the result of a celebrity photograph. No amount of carefully planned market research, whether primary or secondary, can predict fast-evolving fads. The serendipitous nature of fashion trends is the very thing that makes fashion an exciting business, but a difficult business to plan.

However, the authors recall from their past experiences in fashion that many big, established retail brands have historically been able to achieve 1–3 weeks' stock cover on garment types. Fast fashion, therefore, may not be as modern as popular commentators make it out to be.

Fashion product benefits

A basic concept of marketing is that people buy products for the benefits provided. In other words, a fashion garment is primarily of benefit to the consumer because of the intrinsic feeling of being 'in fashion'. Clearly other benefits exist that are associated with the physical product. For example, if the fashion product is an item of clothing, then other more functional benefits also exist linked to covering the body (modesty and protection): durability, the feel of the fabric, and so on. Such an amalgam of benefits is theoretically explained in the augmented product model illustrated in figure 4.1.

The model describes three conceptual levels of fashion product – the core products, the actual product and the augmented product. The core product is the basic benefit that the product or service delivers. In fashion terms this could mean the warmth that a coat provides. However, a basic coat is likely to have other attributes, for example, the colour, the fabric, waterproofing, special pockets, etc., that provide the user with a range of benefits. These physical attributes, combined with any brand image, describe the actual product and deliver another set of benefits to the consumer. It is unlikely that even the most unfashionable individual would purchase a coat without making some decision relating to their most preferred garment attributes.

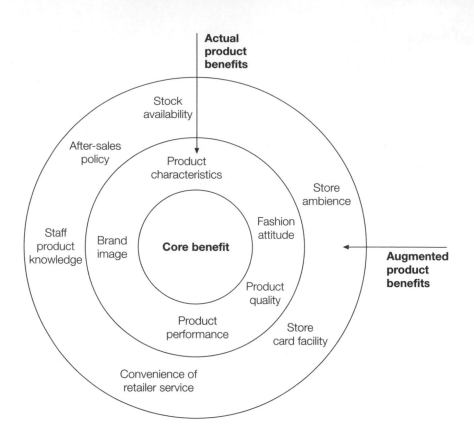

figure **4.1** **augmented product model for fashion retailers**

Source: adapted from Kotler et al., 2001

At the third 'augmented' level, benefits are primarily associated with service features. Thus a decision to buy a coat from one brand or another will be influenced by how many benefits the consumer can acquire for the price. In a competitive market consumers inevitably compare the package of benefits offered by one brand with another and come to a conclusion about which provides the best value (for money).

The continuum of fashion

Fashion is sold across a range of price and quality levels. At one end there is functional clothing that is unbranded and sold through market stalls. Choice extends right the way from this generic form of fashion clothing through supermarket and retailer own-branded fashion to luxury and couture brands at the very top end. This can be conceptualised as the continuum of fashion.

Luxury

Fashion products are becoming increasingly diverse, ranging from apparel, accessories and cosmetics through the other categories of conspicuously

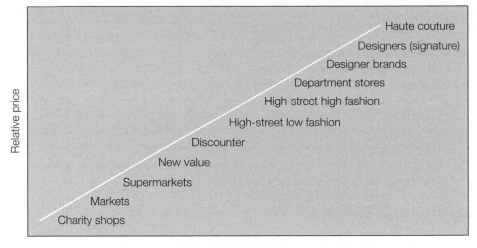

Relative price

Haute couture
Designers (signature)
Designer brands
Department stores
High street high fashion
High-street low fashion
Discounter
New value
Supermarkets
Markets
Charity shops

Levels of aspiration

figure **4.2 the continuum of clothing and fashion**

used products such as watches, jewellery and mobile phones. Interestingly, luxury 'fashion' brands are represented in each of these categories. Readers will be familiar with the names of luxury fashion brands, such as Armani, Prada, Christian Dior, Louis Vuitton and Gucci that sell apparel (clothing) and accessories. However, fewer will be familiar with some of the brands that specialise in cosmetics, watches, jewellery and other products such as phones (see table 4.1).

The luxury goods sector differs from the mass fashion market in obvious ways such as price, but also in some other less obvious but equally significant ways. Luxury brands typically have a heritage that goes back many decades and, for some clothing brands, to the turn of the twentieth century. The heritage is frequently associated with a particular product category for which the brand has developed a reputation for craftsmanship and quality. Prada, Gucci and Louis Vuitton, for example, all began life selling leather goods and not fashion clothing. The heritage, expertise and knowledge base of a brand typically determines its product specialism.

table **4.1 example of product categories and brands in the luxury sector**

Product Category	Luxury brand
Cosmetics	Benefit (LVMH)
Jewellery	Asprey and Garrard, Boucheron (Gucci), Cartier (Richemont),
Watches	Omega (Swatch), Tag Heuer (LVMH), Tissot (Swatch)
Perfume	Aqua di Parma, Guerlain, Jo Malone
Phones	Vertu, Prada

Note: The company names in brackets are the parent company of the brand mentioned.

In very general terms global sales of luxury goods can be categorised proportionally (by product category) as follows:

- Leather goods – 33%;
- Watches and jewellery – 30%;
- Apparel – 10%.

Other categories include cosmetics, perfumes, pens, wines and spirits.

It may come as a surprise to some readers that apparel is one of the smaller categories, given its disproportionately larger perceived association with luxury. This stems from the use of fashion shows and fashion weeks to communicate brand positioning and identities to consumers.

Product classifications

It is important for those involved with fashion marketing to understand that the complexity of fashion products has made it necessary for the trade to develop ways in which to categorise the multitude of garments, accessory types and genres. The next few pages aim to explain their taxonomy. Each fashion business tends to develop its own vocabulary and descriptors, which may vary slightly from those used in this chapter. The basic nomenclature of fashion revolves around the basic garment descriptors, for example, dress, suit trousers, shirt, etc. Over time, many widely used fashion garments have fallen out of fashion and they survive only as historic or generic fashion names, for example, the liberty bodice – a basic buttoning undergarment made from 1900 until 1950. Throughout history new fashion garments have developed into mainstream product, often gaining a new name as the product becomes more accepted. The plimsoll, for example, developed into the sports shoe, ultimately to become the trainer – the generic name for all casual, sports-related shoes. The trainer is now moving stylistically towards becoming a fashion-footwear basic. (*Note*: One style of Nike trainer in 2004 was highly embellished with Harris tweed – part of a genre of fashionable trainers now commonly referred to as cross trainers.) However, although garment descriptors are adequate as a basic descriptor, fashion falls into broader generic categories, often based upon price level and/or styling and fabric issues, for example budget jeans and jersey-wear.

Whilst the basic garment types (for example dresses, coats, blouses, etc.) are the key descriptors used throughout the trade, fashion product also falls into the larger generic categories described in table 4.2. These are typically grouped around market positioning. Today branded merchandise represents a major part of all fashion on offer. Issues surrounding branding and what constitutes a brand are discussed in chapter 9.

At the high/luxury/designer end (there is not a universally agreed term for this very eclectic sector) of fashion, it is not easy to create clearly defined and discrete segments. This is because some luxury brands are based on a designer's name and heritage. Some of these designers are alive (for example,

table **4.2**   **the major fashion product genres**

Major generic descriptor	Example
Unbranded clothing	Market stalls, boot fairs and discounters
Second-hand, recycled and vintage clothing	Charity and vintage shops
Discount fashion brands	Primark, Matalan and Bon Marché
Branded clothing	
• Designer	Biba, Paul Smith, Ellie Saab
• Luxury	Gucci, Chanel, Burberry, Armani
• Manufacturer's	Diesel, Levi's, Adidas
• Retailer	Top Shop, Zara
• Retailer's own	Moto, KM*, Per Una (M&S)
• Supermarket	George (ASDA), Florence & Fred (Tesco)
Counterfeit	Any well-known, high-value brand/designer label

* Kate Moss for Top Shop

Giorgio Armani) and others are not (e.g. Chanel, Christian Dior, Balenciaga). It is therefore arbitrary to classify Armani as a luxury brand and Ellie Saab as a designer brand. The former, however, is a globally known and distributed brand that sells everything from clothing and perfumes to home furnishings and even runs its own hotels. Ellie Saab is a great, but less well-known, couture designer with a narrower range of products.

Table 4.2 endeavours to locate all clothing into high-level descriptive genres, although it is not a definitive taxonomy, owing to the significant proportion of clothing that can fall into more than one descriptor. The UK clothing market, in common with that of several other European countries, may well continue to fragment and develop more sub-descriptors, as fashion markets and consumers continue to want increasingly varied individual dress styles.

Fashion product groupings

Whilst the main thrust of this chapter examines fashion clothing in its totality, it is important for us to consider the full scope and scale of what constitutes a fashion product. This is because brands need to plan and manage at a micro level of line detail to achieve optimum product sales. There are normally three key gender-/age-specific areas of trading activity – men's, women's and children's products, which themselves subdivide into major fashion product groupings (see table 4.3).

The main product groupings shown in table 4.3 can be further subdivided into men's, ladies' and children's fashions, although some groupings are obviously absent from children's products. It is easy, when discussing fashion, to forget the increasing number of new products that can now be described as fashion-related. For example, optical glasses, once seen merely as utilitarian aids to support poor eyesight, are now deemed to be an essential fashion accessory. Chanel was an early luxury-brand pioneer of well-designed optical frames, with Dolce & Gabbana now offering designer-labelled mobile phones. Undoubtedly

table **4.3** **fashion product groupings**

Product grouping	Key examples
Clothing	Every type of fabric item worn, for example, skirts, trousers, jackets and suits
Accessories	Bags, belts, gloves, hats and scarves, etc.
Jewellery	All levels from 'junk' to designer, including watches and pens
Cosmetics and fragrances	Everything applied to enhance physical bodily appearance + fragrances
Shoes	All types – sports, formal, casual, etc.
Optical products	Glasses and sunglasses
Technical products	iPods, MP3 players, mobile phones, etc.

more previously unconsidered product areas will in future have the potential to be branded using fashion designer names and logos.

Various types of fashion garment

It would be impossible within the scope of this book to list every type of garment and garment category currently available within the total global fashion market-place. In some countries, there are unique national costumes available which are rarely found or worn outside that country and which may be worn solely for special occasions, for example the Scottish kilt or the Indian sari. During the past twenty years, certain garment types of one kind or another have virtually vanished from high-street stores and personal wardrobes, for example waistcoats for men and corsets for women. Whilst virtually extinct garment types are often still available from specialised sellers, many slip out of common usage, only to be relegated to a reference in fashion dictionaries, encyclopaedias, fashion books or museum collections. Table 4.4 is a list of the major garment types found today in the average high-street retail outlet. Under each garment type, there are normally many categories and subcategories, some of which are peculiar or exclusive to certain specialist retail formats, for example hunting, shooting and fishing apparel. Table 4.4 shows the major garment types used for merchandise or stock-control dissection purposes and as in-store department descriptors.

From the table it is evident that the female and male wardrobes have become very androgynous, with most garment types being worn by both sexes. Throughout history men have often dressed more opulently and flamboyantly than women, although the increasing gender equalisation within modern society may be driving the current more androgynous dress code. The only major difference between the genders generally relates to the wearing of dresses and skirts by women, although the wearing of the Scottish kilt is becoming increasingly popular and David Beckham has also been seen wearing a sarong. As transvestism becomes a more openly accepted and discussed lifestyle, old assumptions may need to be challenged. Where the situation regarding acceptable male and female attire will be in twenty years' time is anyone's guess.

Although childrenswear has not been included in Table 4.4, most adult garments easily transpose into children's sizes, with the exception of certain unique specialist unisex garments, normally worn by babies and toddlers under the age of two. The pre-toddler age groups, for example, normally wear romper and sleep suits – the blue and pink garment colours being a common differentiator between boys and girls. Childrenswear garment types, with the exception of baby and toddler wear, generally closely mirror those of adults.

Fashion buying ratios

It is of interest to note that there is a fairly fixed ratio between the annual clothing expenditure of women, men and children. Currently European women spend at least twice as much annually as men on clothing and footwear. In some European countries they spend nearly three times as much. At the other end of the scale, childrenswear expenditure is the lowest, usually representing only half that of men. However, in some countries the level of children's clothing expenditure is higher than in others. The UK has historically spent relatively little on childrenswear, but with increasingly wealthy consumers and improved up-market brands and designs becoming available, expenditure on children's clothing has risen. As a rough approximation the fundamental clothing expenditure ratio is:

Womenswear	Menswear	Childrenswear
4 :	2 :	1

table **4.4**   **the major garment types**

Menswear	Womenswear
Shirts	Blouses
Ties	Tops
Knitwear	Skirts
Jackets	Jackets
Trousers	Trousers
Suits	Suits
Jeans	Jeans
Shorts	Shorts
T-shirts	T-Shirts
Nightwear	Nightwear
Accessories	Accessories
Swimwear	Swimwear
Underwear	Underwear
Rainwear	Rainwear
Coats	Coats
	Dresses

There are other similar fundamental ratios to be found when planning fashion merchandising or marketing activities. There is, for example, a fundamental sales ratio between women's top and bottom garments. Typically, women on average buy about 2.4 top garments to every 1 bottom garment. The logic here is that tops are normally more colourful and design-intensive, with many bottom garments being sold in more basic and neutral colours and in less fussy designs, for example the basic navy or black skirt or pair of trousers. Crucially for the consumer a different top, when combined with the same bottom garment, creates a different outfit.

Fundamental ratios also tend to vary by retailer and/or brand, with some having built up a historic customer-following for a certain aspect of their range. Despite market and product offer changes, some customers remain firmly loyal over the years as a result of historic reputation. Dorothy Perkins, for example, was originally an all-underwear retailer, but even today, with their full product offer, they still maintain a larger than normal market share of ladies' underwear.

The shift towards casual wear

There has been a fundamental shift over the past twenty years towards a casual rather than formal style of dress. There may be many reasons for this, from more liberal societal attitudes through to the use by brands of cheaper and simpler sources of production, limiting their manufacturing capabilities and leading to simpler, less structured garments. Many casual-wear products are simple to manufacture, lending themselves to low-cost mass production. The once rigorous split between work and leisure, requiring formal attire for work and casual clothes for leisure and home use, is no longer the norm. This has caused a fundamental change in the use of clothes, with a resultant explosion in the demand for casual clothing and a consequent reduction in the overall demand for formal clothes. The notion of 'dress-down Friday', which allows employees to come to work in less formal clothing, is relatively common in the UK and in the US. In a typical fashion 'about-turn' the US has reverted to the idea of 'dress-up Tuesday' – a day when staff are supposed to make a real effort to be smart. Office and work dress codes change over time and will continue to make a big impact upon overall clothing trends.

Garment construction and fashion trends

In general, the main attributes of casual clothing are softer fabrics, less structured construction, brighter colours and non-crease easy-care fabrics. Formal clothing is of a more structured construction, using formal and sometimes less comfortable fabrics and generally sold in more muted colours. As with any rule set, there are exceptions: we now see tailored jackets, for example, being extensively worn with jeans. How long this mixed fashion look is likely to last remains to be seen. Many fashion observers believe that the 'casualisation' of fashion may also be linked to the general deterioration in societal behaviour, for example the loss of good manners, no orderly bus queues and a general lowering of standards. Undoubtedly this area of debate is more suited to a sociology book rather than a fashion marketing book.

However, there is currently a definite revival in the demand for a more formal male dress codes, especially on the club scene. Many pubs and clubs do not allow baseball caps and trainers, with others going as far as banning jeans – insisting instead upon a smart casual dress code. Stories abound of Burberry baseball caps and Prada trainers now also being excluded by clubs wanting to keep out a 'certain type of person'. The demand for men's formal suits is very much 'in' at this point in fashion history, possibly as a response to many years of casual brands dominating the youth clothing scene. The mass availability and wearing of luxury brands by all social classes may be one driving force behind this current trend for a return to smart clothing. Fashion marketers must at all times be prepared for the casual v. formal swing within consumer demand. Knowing whether such a trend is a long-term or short-term change is difficult to predict.

CASE STUDY |

TRAINERS/SNEAKERS

Arguably the most iconic symbol of casual wear is the trainer/sneaker. The classic casual outfit for men, women and children is a pair of jeans, a T-shirt and a pair of trainers or sneakers. However, some consumers will now also wear trainers with formal wear when commuting to work and then change into formal shoes upon arrival.

BACKGROUND

Trainers, or sneakers as they are known in the US, have a heritage based on technological innovation and sport. In the late 1800s Goodyear (the rubber company) invented the vulcanisation process, which allows rubber and cloth to be moulded together – the basis of modern sports shoe design. An early term for this type of footwear was the plimsoll. The plimsoll emerged from Victorian holidaymakers wearing Dunlop's first sports shoes on the beach. Arguably one of the earliest forms of rubber-soled shoe was Keds, which were named sneakers by Henry Nelson McKinney as the rubber soles make no noise when the wearer walks.

EARLY ENDORSEMENTS

In 1917 Keds/sneakers become the first mass-marketed athletic shoe. At about the same time the Converse shoe company released the first performance basketball shoe called the Converse All Star, followed by the Chuck Taylor All Star ('Chucks'). This was possibly the earliest celebrity sports endorsement. Dunlop's design classic Green Flash was produced in 1933 and worn by Fred Perry when winning Wimbledon three times in succession from 1934. Adidas formed in the early 1930s and Puma in the 1940s, with both companies formed by different brothers. In the 1950s the jeans-and-sneaker look emerged from cinema (James Dean et al.) and revolutionised youth culture. This is reflected in Edison Youngblood's 'Tennis Shoes' (Hanover Records, 1959): 'Wear your sneakers wherever you go, even a smooch in the drive-in show.'

TRAINERS AND FASHION

The trainer/sneaker sits alongside denim jeans and cotton T-shirts as a staple item in many people's wardrobe. When trainers moved out of the specific sports arena and into popular culture as a fashion and lifestyle product, it provided the wearer with the ultimate shoe: something which is comfortable, cool and makes a statement about values. Sneakers, like jeans, may become a fashion evergreen and continue for over a hundred years – being worn and socially acceptable by all age groups. This is one of the interesting things about fashion – for most people fashion is about 'fitting in' and 'standing out' from the crowd simultaneously. A sneaker acts as a uniform which allows the wearer to fit in and then enables the wearer to stand out through the use of a particular brand or model. The average person is a fashion follower and would probably feel cool in any pair of branded sneakers, having seen the advertising and connected with the celebrities endorsing it. Each brand, Adidas, Nike, Puma or Reebok, has its own distinctive logo. Interestingly the trainer is often seen as a statement product whenever a luxury brand designs its own version. PPR, the parent of Gucci Group, also owns the Puma brand, for which one of its designers (Alexander McQueen) designs a special collection of trainers.

TRAINERS AND CULTURE

The sneaker transcends generations simply because each generation interprets it slightly differently – in its own image. Sneakers are a symbol of youth. Those who used to be young have grown up wearing sneakers and are likely to carry on wearing them – just as they will continue to listen to the pop music they grew up with. Fashion and music have always had close links, as do sneakers and music. Hip Hop, for example, helps reinforce the links between sneakers and tribes and between brands and tribes through groups such as Grand Master Flash and particularly the Run DMC/Adidas collaboration. Other examples include The Streets, who sang about their 'Reebok classics', and The Strokes are often photographed wearing their 'Chucks'. Bob Marley loved wearing Adidas – well before the notion of celebrity endorsement was a common marketing tool. He wore them because he liked them – more powerful than product placement. He was photographed wearing the blue Adidas TRX Comp in the 1980s.

STATUS – AN IMPORTANT PRODUCT ATTRIBUTE

Trainers are viewed by many as a vehicle for conveying status. This is often because of the imagery associated with particular brands and models, generated in part by marketing campaigns and in part by the sporting and cultural heritage of individual brands and shoes. Some consumers recognise limited-edition sneakers or original sneakers from years ago. Such enthusiasts know, for example, the chronology of a brand's portfolio of shoes, including the limited editions. In 2006 Puma introduced a limited edition Clyde shoe, named after the gangsters Bonnie and Clyde. The name alone assured copious amounts of publicity, although the model was limited to just over two hundred pairs. Everyone has the potential for wearing trainers/sneakers – it's a transgenerational product. Like all shoes the sneaker finishes off an overall 'look', makes the wearer feel good and potentially adds to his/her self-esteem through status recognition from peers. Much of the status of individual sneaker brands and products is associated with the shoes' links to fashion and popular culture.

SOME FAMOUS TRAINERS

Adidas Samba – probably Adidas's biggest-selling shoe and the longest-running model in production.

Adidas Stan Smith – designed in 1965 and went on to sell more than 30 million pairs – well-known all around the world.

Puma Clyde – there was controversy over this 2006 limited-edition Bonnie and Clyde product.

Nike Air Jordan (1985).

Nike Air Max 1 (1987) was the first trainer to show a visible air-comfort cushion.

Nike Cortez – one of the first shoes Nike made, a design classic given credibility when adopted by urban street gangs.

Managing product ranges

Garment types and their subcategories

Although garment types have clear generic names, which are usually self-explanatory in overall terms, within any one garment type, there are endless subcategories of garments. If we look specifically at men's shirts, for example, table 4.5 starts to explain the wide variety of categories and subcategories that are demanded by customers.

Table 4.5 shows that certain categories of shirt normally come in only one sleeve length. Polo shirts, for example,usually have short sleeves and evening shirts usually have long sleeves. Of course, whilst the subcategories of shirts may appear relatively simple, this garment has other complicating factors such as collar types. Men's shirt collars, in common with ladies' hemlines, are notoriously prone to fashion fads – collars may be pointed, rounded, button-down, etc. It is therefore necessary to further define shirts into even lower subcategories, in order that the buyers, merchandisers and designers are able to track what to design, buy and sell, and more importantly what quantities

table **4.5** **men's shirts – category and subcategory descriptors**

Formal shirts	Long-sleeve	Short-sleeve
Plain colours	X	X
Stripes	X	X
Patterns	X	X
Prints	X	X
Dress/evening	X	

Casual shirts		
Polo	X	
T-shirts	X	X
Plain	X	X
Stripes	X	X
Patterns	X	X
Prints	X	X

and ratios of size and colour to buy. Modern merchandise tagging now utilises optically read bar codes and sometimes radio-frequency tagging to help control stock buying and replenishment. Stock control systems, by using well-defined 'merchandise descriptor' fields, help buyers and merchandisers to group like-styled collars, sleeve lengths, colours, etc., in order that the business is able to get an overview of the current levels of customer demand for any particular feature, for example the total percentage of men's shirts being sold with button-down collars. Without such detailed information, it would be impossible to present balanced ranges to customers.

The importance of garment subcategories in marketing and merchandising management

The way in which marketers describe, analyse and control garment types, categories and subcategories depends very much upon the IT system employed, as well as the type of business involved and also the level of sophistication of the merchandise-planning management systems, processes and protocols. There are no prescribed ways to categorise and analyse fashion merchandise, but in general clear logic and experienced management are the main facilitators of good merchandise planning and practice. By using clear department, category and subcategory names to describe the huge number of garments available in large clothing stores, marketers are able to monitor and control stock levels effectively and efficiently, with a view to meeting demand accurately and therefore maximising sales. Clothing is an inherently complicated product offer and fashion marketers face one of the toughest stock control problems of any retail sector.

Some departments throw up greater complexity than others. Probably the most complex clothing department of all is ladies' underwear. Here we have not only a huge miscellany of garment categories and subcategories, but also the added complexity of bras needing to be available in both back and cup size. The range of colours, sizes and cup sizes needed for even the most basic style of bra is a mind-boggling stock control problem – often one style can involve several hundred options.

The fashion marketer relies heavily upon detailed merchandise sales and stock information supplied from the merchandise planners, to help in both tactical and strategic marketing decision-making. Knowing quickly and accurately what is selling, by size and colour, is a critical success factor in fashion marketing. Although fashion merchandise buying and planning is not carried out by a specific fashion marketer or marketing deptartment, it is the buying and merchandising department's ultimate responsibility to ensure that the right Product is in the right Place at the right time with the right Promotion (i.e. the right marketing mix).

The stocking decision process

The reader will by now be realising the huge and changeable number of product options that need to be controlled by fashion businesses. These often extend into many thousands of brands, styles, colours and sizes, each of which is known as an SKU (stock-keeping unit). Alert fashion marketers are aware, at any minute of any day, how many of an individual style by size and colour have been sold. Each style, category and size will need to be adequately represented on the shop floor if customer product demand is to be effectively satisfied – customers do not come back if a fashion SKU is not available – they will simply move on to a competitor.

The right number of style options?

The next major problem/product issue facing a brand is to determine the number of style options that should be displayed on the shop floor. If a wide variety of styles were to be stocked, but in only one size and one colour, the customer would be faced with a huge choice of style but not colour and little likelihood of their size being available. Such a wide choice of styles on display in a shop can also create a sense of customer confusion and a lack of range coherence. This type of store ranging would be described as wide and shallow. At the other end of the scale, we might consider a shop with only a few lines on sale but with a wide range of sizes and colours. Here customers might gain an immediate impression of seeing only a very limited range, with few style options to attract their attention. In this case the range would be described as narrow and deep.

These two descriptions are extremes, but for a good retailer the reality is somewhere in the middle. The width and depth of product offer varies immensely but, as a general rule, the more expensive a retailer's product offer, the more likely it is that they will carry a narrower range of products than, for example, a cheaper discount shop.

The planning of fashion product range and depth is rarely a pure marketing decision, typically being undertaken by the merchandising management team. Overcrowded and confused fashion product offers can often drive customers away, as they simply give up in the midst of the confusion. It is essential for any business to ensure that it has a clear and understandable product offer at the customer interface. Retailers with limited ranges are often deemed as having a narrow and uninteresting product offer. The best fashion marketers must aim at getting the correct range width and depth for the target market level being targeted.

The problem of variable store size and shape relative to product marketing and planning

As a result of local geography, history and trading accident, UK fashion retailers rarely have outlets of exactly the same shape, layout or size. This is especially the case in city and town centres, where retail areas have developed in an unplanned way as a result of many hundreds of years of shop-building history and geographical accident. Most established retail chains find that in some towns their trading area in a store is either too small or too large in relation to the size of the local market and general product demand. Many of the large groups undertake regular site reviews and often move into larger or smaller outlets to ensure that they are trading on the correct amount of floor space for selling. However, this is a very expensive proposition and is often not viable owing to the length of the lease, usually in the region of ten to twenty years. It can often take several years to locate and move into the right trading site.

The right-sized trading space – a key ingredient of fashion product marketing

For large-space out-of-town retailers, store size and department layout variation is less of an issue – therefore making the planning and laying out of ranges much easier. New out-of-town retail developments normally have enough space from the day they are built. The size of any particular shop or layout determines the number of garments and therefore styles that can be displayed. If too many styles are sent to a small shop, the product offer can often appear crushed and without depth of stock; if too few ranges are sent to a large outlet, the product offer can look thin and understocked. Getting the right balance of stock is the role of the merchandising and distribution teams.

The use of IT systems to plan space and visual layout

Some of the more forward-looking fashion retailers are now utilising computer-aided visual merchandising packages, which allow the individual fixtures and layout of every store to be data-warehoused, and employ trained visual merchandisers who are able to develop the most logical and aesthetically pleasing individual product layouts in each virtual store. Computer-assisted spatio-visual merchandising, such as Intactix by JDA, is at the forefront of this exciting new aspect of fashion marketing. Once the tailored, ideal and optimised layout has been developed, the plan and imagery are transmitted electronically to each store. Central control of spatio-visual merchandising is a normal marketing practice, but can detract from the local development of store visual-merchandising skills. However, the rationale is that central control ensures product display consistency across the chain – ultimately to ensure a coherent product range with the right depth and width for the space available.

Product-mix marketing decision-making in fashion businesses

Although fashion marketing is predominantly concerned with clothing, footwear and accessories, there is an increasing trend for fashion retailers to widen their product mix through the inclusion of new fashion-related items. Watches are increasingly being stocked as a fashion accessory, probably as a result of the development of fashionable watches by companies like Swatch (launched in the early 1980s). Next and Burton Menswear trade 'boy's toys' ranges, with even small departments stocking a wide variety of electronic and other gadgets. However, it is essential that new products add to the total business and deliver incremental sales, rather than simply replacing clothing sales. Often fashion businesses undertake fundamental and strategic product-mix changes in answer to pressure, competition or change in a specific sector of the market. Generally, product-mix alteration through time is as a result of natural changes in consumer demand. However, it is essential for businesses to monitor that demand and proactively rather than reactively to all demand-led changes. Many fashion businesses fail to respond effectively to changes in demand, simply carrying on offering what the customers patently do not want – catering only for historic demand is lethal.

In these highly competitive times, fashion businesses are forever seeking ways to differentiate themselves from the competition – the addition of new products and services is a tempting marketing option, but it can take time to establish, particularly if its launch does not have adequate marketing communications. Fashion shoppers are often creatures of habit and have been known to miss new products or brands completely, even after several visits to an outlet where product/service changes have been made. A large proportion of consumers have limited powers of observation and fail to notice even major changes to the marketing mix.

Sources of fashion product ideas

The demand for new product ideas and designs is insatiable for all levels of fashion product. At both the high and the low end of the market, consumers are constantly seeking something new. In the past, fashion was not as dynamic and changeable; customers were less discerning and knowledgeable than they are today. Fast, cheap and plentiful electronic communication is bombarding consumers of all ages with new ideas. Whether it is via satellite TV, iPod or the camera phone of a friend, fashion ideas and images are able to travel across continents virtually instantaneously. The cliché that the world is becoming a smaller place is very relevant in the context of fashion marketing; the explosive international growth of Nike, for example, has resulted in their 'swoosh' logo probably having a higher level of recognition than the Christian Cross or the Hebrew Star of David.

Fashion forecasting services

Specialist fashion forecasting companies such as WGSN are now able to provide immediate online fashion information across the globe. This UK internet-based fashion information and reportage business supplies text and image data and analysis, sourcing fashion information from around the world. Within minutes these images are available online to clients for a fee. The theory that fashion looks would gradually 'trickle down' into the high street has become more of 'raging torrent theory', with fashion consumers now being overwhelmed by an endless choice of completely up-to-date fashion products. Other fashion-forecasting businesses such as Promostyl, by contrast, provide printed trend-forecasting books and customised consultancy.

Are all fashion products simply a copy/derivation of something already in existence?

It would be wrong to assume that all fashion is simply created as a result of the immediate copying and altering of designer- or couturier-inspired products. There are of course new ideas and designs being generated all the time, at every level of fashion. As a result of faster idea information flows, even fashion retailers and producers at the lower end of the market are now having to put a much greater effort into the design of even the cheapest of garments. Good design and styling are no longer only required at the top end of the fashion market.

Most global retailers have added to and enhanced their own in-house design facilities. Before the creation of what is now known as the designer retailer, the average British multiple fashion retailer would rely almost entirely upon their garment and fashion product suppliers to act as the main source and inspiration of new designs and ideas. Manufacturers (having to keep their own brand label constantly renewed and refreshed) were often ideally placed to help retailers do the same job. However, as the market-place has become more demanding, and retailers need to create a more unique house style, it is the norm for own-brand retailers to run their own in-house design departments. Increasingly, freelance designers (who continually change, constantly bringing new ideas into the business) are useful to in-house retail design departments. The increasing inclusion and development of in-house brands/labels by fashion retailers has also been a key driver of better and larger in-house design facilities.

In-house design departments vary in size, status and authority. For some fashion businesses they are simply a department that synthesises and collects information from the fashion environment. At the other end of the scale they will act as a point of original inspiration and total design creation, starting almost with a clean sheet of paper. In reality, most mid-market fashion retailer brands and producers tend to use a mixture of original innovation and an element of what is known as 'knock-off' or modified copying. The fashion industry is continually plagued by the problem of illegal copying. Fashion designers in the EC enjoy some degree of design protection, through the system of design registration supported by ACID (Anti Copying In Design) (see www.acid. designsales.co.uk). This service enables small designers to register a design for a modest fee, in case of future copying disputes. However, design is a notoriously subjective discipline, open to widely differing interpretations. A good designer can always take the main innovative element of another designer's completely new idea, and then redesign it enough for it not to be legally deemed a copy.

The global policing of registered ideas across nearly two hundred different judiciaries would be an impossible task. Copying is culturally acceptable in many countries, where it is almost impossible to win a legal case against a home producer, especially when you are a foreigner and not seen to be supporting that country's economic cause. Whichever way design is approached, it is clear that over the past decade, all fashion businesses have had to add value to their

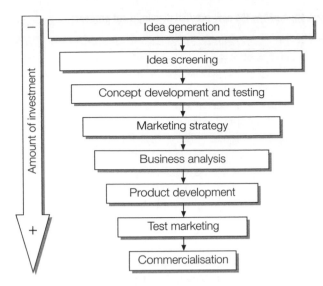

figure **4.3** **the classic marketing approach to the new-product development process (after Kotler et al., 2001)**

marketing proposition by the use of more and better design input. In some countries, clear legal guidelines are laid down as to what extent any design can be copied or incorporated into a new garment. The whole issue of copying is a highly emotive area at all levels of fashion.

Fashion product idea and concept testing

Innovation and new product development (NPD) are two of the most important drivers of business success. This is most pertinent to fashion marketing. In the marketing management process of most other consumer products, where there is almost certainly likely to be a more stable PLC, conventional marketing textbooks describe the very linear way in which new products are conceived and the stages through which they are tested and finally arrive in the market-place. Kotler et al. (2001) suggest that the process runs sequentially through eight definite stages, as shown in figure 4.3.

Such a long ponderous and prescriptive process would simply not work in the fast changing world of fashion products. The more likely route to market for the average fashion product would consist of only five or possibly six stages.

The proposed model of new product development shown in table 4.6 assumes that there are no totally new designs, with every new fashion idea and garment being built upon a previous style. Idea generation is likely to result from an old design that has been improved or modified to fit in with the modern fashion idiom. Occasionally a completely new fashion garment type, which has no historic precursor, will hit the scene, for example the bikini, which was designed in France in 1946 (although even this has been disputed). However, it is fair to say that there are very few entirely new garments designed

table **4.6** **a fashion approach to the new-product development process**

Kotler's NPD	Fashion NPD	Business functions likely to be involved
Idea generation	Idea gathering and synthesis	Marketing/buying
Idea screening	Idea generation & adaptation	Marketing/sales/buying
Concept development and testing	Sometimes focus groups may be used	Marketing
Marketing strategy	Internal product review	Buying
Business analysis	Merchandise planning and control	Merchandise planning
Product development	Ongoing and forward range development	Buying/merchandising
Test marketing	Very occasionally small trial lines may be tried with less fashionable products	Marketing
Commercialisation	Range fully launched into market	Retail operations

from scratch. The fashion industry, especially where mid-market fashion is concerned, is often loath to go towards the leading edge of style for fear of being too early. To try and reduce the risk of a full-scale failure, some larger retailers will trial new designs, brands or fashion ideas in a small number of trial shops or stores which are generally selected on the basis that they are representative of the whole chain. If the initial trial result is successful, larger quantities will be bought for an all store/shop distribution. In this way, any product failures are kept to a minimum and quickly liquidated using price reduction, or mark-down, as it is more commonly known. Unfortunately, as fashion appears to be changing faster, trial lines are used less frequently than they were.

More avant-garde young designers do take risks, and this is probably the major cause of business failure for many fashion design graduates. Fashion is a risky business that is immediately unforgiving if you design or buy the wrong product. The difficulty for all fashion marketers is to achieve the correct balance between being too innovative or being too safe and staid. The problem for many of the larger mid-market retailers such as C&A (no longer in the UK), M&S and BhS is that even middle-market customers have moved up a notch in terms of their own fashionability. Now only a minority of consumers regard clothes as a commodity purchase. The increased availability of supermarket fashion means that it is now possible for most people to have access to reasonable fashion products – even those on a tight budget.

The importance of new and fast product idea-generation for fashion

The continuous development and improvement of new products is therefore essential for all types of fashion business, as old formulas soon tire and quickly become dated. Brands and retailers are forever needing to reinvent themselves in order to keep abreast of their smarter competitors and to cater for increasingly sophisticated consumer tastes. Although most fashion businesses start to plan future seasons' ranges up to eighteen months ahead, the first plans are only made at a high or broad level, with the specific design and styling of lines left to the last possible minute before clothing production is due to start. Last-minute styling reduces the odds of the buyer making wrong decisions. In an ideal world, buyers would make styling decisions one week ahead of delivery, thus ensuring that their product was always correct for next week's customer. However, in the real world of fashion, even the very fastest of the fast-fashion retailers probably makes final styling decisions about four weeks ahead of delivery. The need for both in-house and external design teams to be providing a continuous flow of designs and ideas is critical. Increasing demand for more and better fashion designers would appear to a natural byproduct of fast fashion, at all levels of the market.

The fashion PLC(s)

In common with all types of product, fashion follows cycles and products follow the PLC. This fundamental of marketing theory explains that all products have a defined life cycle, which means that no product can go on selling forever.

The theory is that once a product has been accepted by consumers, it goes through various stages of introduction, growth, maturity and decline until it becomes obsolete. Clearly the time taken for a product to go through a complete cycle varies according to type. It is important for readers to appreciate that for some fashion products a life cycle may last many decades, such as in the case of denim jeans. However, a very specific fashion accessory may only last for a few weeks within a fashion season. In both cases, those managing the products will need to determine the point of optimum sales and profitability and the point of decline when mark-down and stock clearance may be necessary.

The fashion industry, being so prone to fast change, is probably the industry with the widest variety of PLCs. It is important for all fashion marketers to be aware of the huge variation in PLC types that are affecting the products and services that they offer.

The typical or classic PLC is shown in figure 4.4. The two curves show the relationship of sales and profit income over any typical fashion or non-fashion product. The classic PLC has essentially five different stages:

1 **The design development stage** – fashion designers undertake the design development stage ahead of the product launch. At this stage there are no sales and, of course, design development costs create negative profitability. In figure 4.4 readers will note that there are no absolute measurements on either the time or the money axis. The reason for this is that the classic PLC in fashion may extend from a few weeks (e.g. Topshop selling a fast-fashion fad item) to several decades (e.g. Burton Menswear selling a classic pinstriped suit).

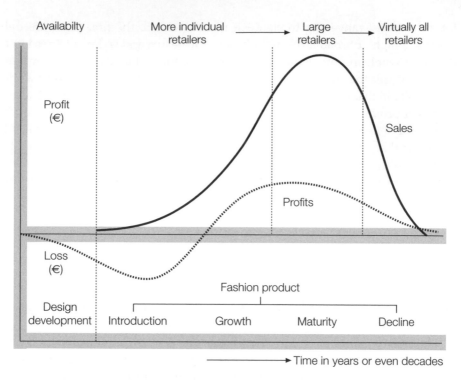

figure **4.4** **the classic fashion product life cycle stages (after Kotler et al., 2001)**

2 **The introduction or trial line stage** – here the product is launched in the market, sometimes as a small trial quantity but usually in a limited number of outlets, especially if it is avant-garde or leading-edge. Sales start from zero and the business has to wait for profitability to move positively once goods start to sell in reasonable quantities.

3 **The growth or mass acceptance stage** – during this stage the fashion/style/brand is now gaining much wider public acceptance. It will now become available in many mid-market shops. Probably the new fashion is now being accepted by a greater percentage of the total population. It is probably no longer deemed high fashion, but rather the norm. (Who would have thought back in the 1950s that blue jeans would be worn by three generations?) Sales and profits rise dramatically, and it is at this stage that large profits are made in fashion.

4 **The maturity of fashion saturation phase** – at this point in the PLC, the market is now probably saturated with the specific fashion product. What was once seen as fashionable is now so widely worn and seen that the original wearers no longer want the look. Every type of retail outlet, from designer stores through to market stalls, has flooded the market, with a resultant price war. Reduced prices ring alarm bells with even the least fashion-forward of consumers, who then totally withdraw from buying until prices are slashed and eventually the product 'withers on the

vine'. Here profits are hit dramatically as a result of the price-cutting that happens as retailers become keen to dump their remaining stocks – at almost any price.

5 **The decline or 'fashion get out' stage** – here are the final death throes of a fashion product. By now the more astute marketer will have got rid of the majority of this dead fashion look, hopefully having moved on to the next up-and-coming style or look. However, no matter how 'dead' a look is, there are always some fashion laggards who continue wearing a style/ look after other customers have moved on. Examples of this are the 'Teddy boy' and 'Mod' looks of the 1950s to 1970s, respectively. Even today there are still businesses catering for the small minority of consumers who chose to continue those lifestyles. Although sales and profit levels head quickly downwards, there are always some small niche businesses that can make a living out of a fundamentally dead product/look.

Although the PLC is an accepted underpinning of all marketing theory and practice, the major problem for the fashion marketer to grapple with is the fact that the actual position of a fashion product on the cycle at any point in time is hard to define accurately. Fashion sales patterns are notoriously variable as a result of simple external variables such as competitors' promotional activity and changeable UK weather patterns. This makes an accurate mathematical model of the PLC an impossibility. Astute fashion marketers aim to get out of a high-fashion look or fad as it approaches the peak of the maturity or saturation phase. Buying more stock at this phase, in an endeavour to grab those last few sales before the fast decline, is a dangerous tactic, as you are probably simply buying stock that may eventually have to be sold below cost. It is advisable not to be greedy in the fashion market; instead allow your competitor to buy too much stock. Getting out just ahead of peak sales is always the most profitable policy.

However, with experience and by continually monitoring product sales, the PLC can be effectively used as a marketing management tool in fashion. Successful fashion businesses have new products coming in all the time to replace the lines that are about to be discontinued. Managing the PLC effectively in fashion is the key driver of ultimate profitability.

Other types of PLC curve faced by the fashion industry

At the start of this section on the fashion PLC, the hugely variable lengths of fashion PLCs were discussed. In fast-fashion businesses such as Top Shop and Zara, fashion looks or fads can sometimes come in and vanish within a matter of three or four weeks. A short and sharp peak (see figure 4.5(a)) typifies this type of life cycle. At the other end of the spectrum there are some fashion products that have survived for over a century, and could be described as being of iconic status. Such an example would be Levi's jeans, whose origins can be traced back to the US Gold Rush of the 1850s (see also figure 4.5(b)). Here we see a current fashion product that has had a PLC of over 150 years – albeit that the current product has been modified somewhat to meet modern demands. Here we see two PLCs described with a variation of a hundred years at least.

Another PLC that is to be found, particularly in the fashion industry, is the flop, sometimes referred to as the 'dog' line, that simply bombs from day one (see figure 4.5(c)). This line usually requires an immediate mark-down, but sometimes it is so bad that it can still prove difficult to give away. All seasoned fashion store buyers will have a story to tell about their own 'dog' lines. Any buyer claiming never to have bought one is a liar – all fashion buyers make mistakes, but hopefully not too many.

Seasonal lines also have a very cyclical and defined PLC, with the peaks and troughs often being very closely related to the prevailing weather and seasonal trading patterns. Figure 4.5(d) shows a classic seasonal PLC curve. Seasonal items include swimwear, winter coats, gloves and scarves, etc. – all heavily driven by prevailing and recurring weather patterns. Sometimes, previous fashion styles or trends re-emerge many years later (usually with a slightly new twist). This is known as the revival life cycle and is shown in figure 4.5(e). A good example of this in 2006 would be the return in womenswear to a more tailored and formal look.

Long-term and short-term fashion PLCs are an endemic part of the fashion industry, and it is clearly important to differentiate between long-term and short-term changes in fashion product demand when using the PLC to assist in both the tactical and the strategic marketing planning. To complicate the situation, fashion often stages trend revivals, when a once-thought-dead look is resurrected in a slightly changed format – normally to be hailed as a 'brand-new' fashion movement! Readers should note that there is nothing really original in the fashion industry. Philip Green, the owner of the Arcadia Group, once remarked on BBC TV, 'there is nothing original in fashion – probably only Leonardo da Vinci could truly be described as original!' Although many fashionistas might dispute his rather radical view, there is an element of truth in his comment. Most new fashion product could be described as having been built upon what has gone before.

The implications of fashion product PLCs for marketing decision-making

In all fashion marketing there is always a need to decide what to do in terms of the best marketing strategy for a product at a particular point in the fashion PLC. At the beginning there is likely to be a need to spend a great deal of the marketing budget on promoting the product, in order for it to gain a wider consumer acceptance. When a product is selling well in the growth stage, however, it may be better to decide to spend nothing and to undertake no promotional activity. It is at this point that profit generation is normally at its highest level. Marketing activity in itself can, therefore, alter the shape of the PLC. In fact any marketing activity or inactivity will impact upon it in one way

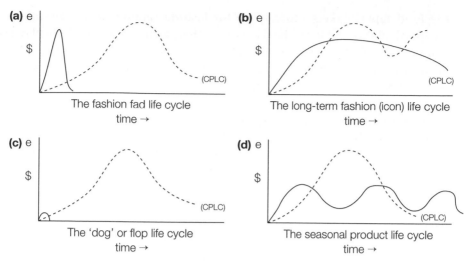

note: All overlaid with classic product life cycle for comparison (CPLC)

figure **4.5** **the shapes of the main types of fashion product life cycle**

or another. Marketing used both tactically and strategically can be both the cause and the result of the PLC. Fashion marketers must be alert to the quick changes in consumer demand that can often result in reduced profitability. As a result of the advances within retail IT, smarter, more intelligent merchandise-control systems can be readily programmed with statistically based 'detect and alert' systems which can alert management to slight shifts in demand – these shifts are otherwise often almost undetectable. To be ahead of the competition by being either first in or first out of a new fashion product is the ultimate objective of the game. Fashion businesses that do not get out of a fashion trend before the PLC maturity stage starts to head downwards will generally find themselves left with excesses of unfashionable stock. The secret is not to be greedy; it is better to 'sell short' or run out, even when there is still reasonable demand for a fashion product or trend. This trading maxim is used by all of the more successful fast-fashion businesses, who introduce new lines all the time to replace those in (or about to) decline. More profit is made by selling short than by trying to squeeze the last penny of turnover out of a line.

Other fashion issues affected by PLCs

Although fundamental textbook marketing implies that the theory is generally line-specific, in the fashion industry it is essential for the reader to understand that the PLC extends over more than just individual lines or products.

Brand PLCs

Fashion brands are also susceptible to the PLC effect. There have been many fashion brands that, whilst once strong, have vanished or have become greatly diminished in terms of their presence within retailer offers. As with the food supermarkets, store space for fashion retailers is at a premium. If any particular brand is on the way down, then generally its retail display area will be reduced, usually as a precursor to the range being discontinued. The fashion floors at Selfridges experience brand attrition as buyers drop older, poorer-performing brands and bring in faster-selling one. This is increasingly the normal course of events when dealing with branded products. Brand managers need to undertake affirmative marketing activity, in an endeavour either to stop brand decline or to hold and/or increase brand market share. Brands generally require continuous change and development if they are to survive and thrive.

Retailer PLCs

Fashion retailers are retail brands in their own right. Retailers and their merchandise are seen by consumers as a type of brand. Any fashion marketer reviewing the UK's fashion retail landscape over the past few decades will find examples of retailers who, once strong and well represented, are now either extinct or greatly diminished in size. At the other end of the scale, we see that Primark has rapidly grown to become one of the UK's largest fashion retailers. The once sleepy Primark retail brand has become a major force to be reckoned with by its competitors. Fashion retailing is an unforgiving business, with the ever-increasing level of international competition. There are likely to be many more business casualties in the future. Recently, we saw the grand old lady of basic fashion retailing M&S reeling under marketing attack from all and sundry, only to re-emerge again in late 2006 as a strong high-street brand, only to suffer again with the 2008 'Credit Crunch'. Until its revival in 2006, M&S's once-safe middle-of-the-road marketing proposition was no longer exciting enough for many 'fashion-young' older customers. Without consistent product and marketing activity development, the road to obscurity can be fast and painful, as nearly happened to M&S.

Style, colour and fabric PLCs

Although, throughout most PLC literature, writers generally refer to product in the singular and by by implication convey the idea that only individual fashion styles are subject to the vagaries of the PLC, whole groups of lines of one general style or genre can alter their PLC either up or down as result of fast-moving fashion trends. Similarly, colours and fabric can be subject to sudden fashion demand changes. Colour PLCs can often change over the course of a few weeks.

Some final thoughts on fashion PLCs

It is therefore evident that any fashion outlet, large or small, consists of a range of fashion products which are all somewhere along some type of long-term or short-term PLCs, as well as being potentially affected by an overall PLC trend – such as the continuing general change from formal to casual

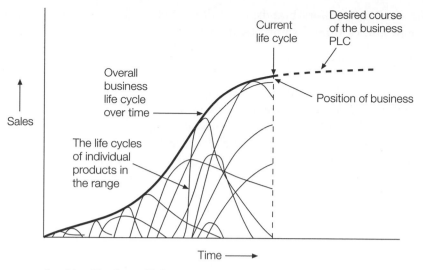

figure **4.6** **the combined product life cycles of a fashion retailer's range = average total business product life cycle**

clothing. It requires an astute understanding and interpretation of the PLC at all times, if a fashion retail business is to ensure that it has more lines rising to support and improve the overall PLC trend. Businesses that fail to keep winning upwardly moving combinations of styles, colours, fabrics, trends and brands are destined to go to the graveyard of failed fashion businesses. Figure 4.6 shows a hypothetical fashion business with many products at differing stages in their individual PLCs. As it shows, the combination of individual PLCs makes the PLC of the entire business more obvious. At any point in time it can be seen that some lines are on an upward trend, while others are on a definite downward trend. Having more going up than going down is essential for long-term business success.

Some strategies for ensuring a continuing positive PLC for a fashion business

For fashion designers and manufacturers, the need for winning designs to be developed all the time is an essential part of their successful marketing strategy if long-term survival is to be assured. For large fashion retailers who may have a lacklustre product offer, there are a series of alternative marketing tactics/strategies that will help ensure that their business quickly introduces fast-selling fashion product offer, without actually having to develop, manage and source their own brand ranges. The main ways are listed:

▸ milking existing successful designs in season or potentialisation;
▸ concessions;

- new manufacturers' brands;
- new non-clothing fashion brands/products.

With all four methods, the retailer is able (often quickly) to enhance the overall fashion offer, without going through the labour-intensive process of design development. The four methods are described in more detail below.

Milking existing successful designs in season or potentialisation – as a line, style or colour becomes clearly and apparently successful during the course of a season, it is often possible to introduce newer versions, in order to 'milk' potential sales. It can often extend the life of a particular fashion look across the main part of the trading season and, in so doing, it can generate extra sales and profit on a product or look that would otherwise have 'died off' earlier. This strategy needs to be approached with extreme caution; buying it too far into the season runs the risk of creating unprofitable terminal stock. The 'milking' process is shown in figure 4.7.

Concessions – these are normally run as wholly externally designed, bought and managed departments – normally by own-brand wholesalers or manufacturers. Retailers, whilst maintaining some style censorship of the ranges offered, do not undertake the original design work or indeed take the risk of actually owning the stock. Instead they simply take a fixed and agreed percentage of sales from the concession operators, who are effectively paying a commission to be able to display and sell their range in the retailers' outlets. Concessions are used extensively by large-space retailers, who would simply be duplicating their own ranges, were they to try and fill all their space with their own-bought stock. The percentage commission made by the host retailer is anywhere between 15% and 30% of gross sales net of VAT. Some concession owners will, within the terms of their formal agreement with the retailer, also

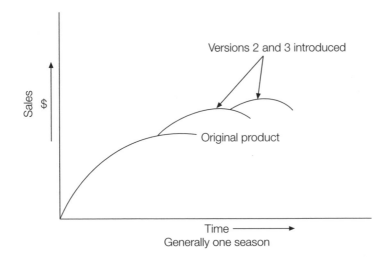

figure **4.7   product optimisation across the season**

provide sales staff and specialist branded fixturing from which to sell their stock. For the concession, this will ensure that their stock is well maintained, managed, displayed and, more importantly sold effectively. Unstaffed concessions rarely take as much money as do staffed ones.

The technique of concessioning has been extensively used and developed by department stores, which often have many floors and many difficult-to-trade retail spaces, although many smaller multiple fashion-clothing groups will utilise concessions for the provision of specialist product, outside of their normal product buying patterns, for example shoe brands in fashion multiples.

New manufacturers' brands – these are again used extensively by department stores, which may be replacing older, less successful brands throughout the season. Brand life cycle is also a continual problem for retailers. The Selfridges flagship store in London is reputed to stock 2500+ fashion brands at any one time, with over two hundred being discontinued each season. They continually need to replace the older, weaker brands with strong, new, exciting ones.

New non-clothing fashion brands/products – this is also a way to maintain customer interest, whilst at the same time enabling the retailer to enter into previously untried potential fashion-related product areas. This can be done by buying directly from or concessioning with brand owners. An example of this might be the external provision of technical products or gadgets, which are increasingly being seen as fashion items related to clothing.

The ultimate style, range, brand and colour product decisions taken each season by fashion companies, whether retailers or concessions, are critical if the business is to remain successful. It is for this reason that fashion buyers are so well rewarded or quickly fired for their success or failure!

The quality of fashion products – is quality tangible or intangible?

As society becomes wealthier, the quality of most mass-produced products has improved over time. The reasons for this are that technological advances in manufacturing and more exacting quality assurance techniques deliver better products at the end of the production line. Rising living standards have also raised consumer quality expectations, and fashion garments are no exception. If readers were able to examine closely the examples of mass-produced garments made in the 1950s and 1960s which are held in fashion museums, a closer scrutiny of the fabrics and sewing would, despite the nostalgic appeal of the garments, more often than not reveal a pretty poorly made item. Today's mass-produced fashion garments are generally better sewn and made of better and more durable fabrics.

The modern consumer expects garments to last, wash or dry-clean well, iron easily, resist creasing and staining and still look good to wear after they have been screwed up in a suitcase! To prove a point, readers need look no further than their local charity shops to see the good condition of second-hand garments.

The problem of fashion product quality is that, to an untrained eye, it is not easy to recognise and understand. Many customers believe that they can recognise quality, but this is questionable. For example, without using sophisticated 'rub-testing' laboratory equipment, it would be difficult for the average consumer to establish whether one particular suiting fabric would withstand heavy wear better than another. The durability and strength of a fabric is intrinsic, not extrinsic. The regularity of the stitching is more obvious, although again the layman is unlikely to be as observant as a trained factory quality manager. Very often a brand name can act as the subconscious guarantee of quality to the less-informed fashion customer. It is therefore very unlikely that quality can ever be easily marketed as a key extrinsic attribute of an augmented fashion product. It is sometimes assumed that the price paid for a garment is an indication of its quality, a high price indicating that a garment must be of high quality, and a low price indicating low quality. Later on, in chapter 5, the whole issue of whether paying a higher price for a garment automatically delivers a garment of proportionately higher quality is discussed. Whether the consumer really gets value in terms of quality and style when purchasing high-priced designer brands is a continuing debate among fashion academics.

The danger of marketing low-quality or substandard fashion products

The only certainty about quality is that there is no future in marketing fashion products which are substandard or of marginal quality. Many of the larger fashion retail groups in the UK have reduced their quality standards over time. Whilst it is possible to make small and almost imperceptible reductions in quality without affecting consumer demand, eventually the cumulative effects of continual quality reduction become evident even to the less quality-conscious consumer. Reducing fabric quality in pursuit of larger profit margins is a short-term profit-generation tactic – in the long run it will have a negative impact on the brand.

It is the authors' opinion, although this is hard to prove without continuous and objective quality testing, that, over time, a number of fashion retailer brands (or possibly their manufacturers) have undertaken a tactical process of downward quality migration. Quality migration is a barely perceptible lowering of fabric quality and garment-making standards, almost invisible to the untrained eye of the consumer. By reducing standards, retailers and indeed garment manufacturers are able to make more profit. However, eventually consumers do realise that the retailer is selling clothes which once lasted many years and now only last for a season. Such a tactic is often used on more basic fashion products such as men's underwear and socks, as well as ladies' underwear and hosiery. It is a dangerous marketing strategy in the long term.

Most fashion garments, unlike the majority of consumer products, are rarely highly packaged. There are of course exceptions such as basic underwear, socks, hosiery and formal shirts. As consumers usually like to try on garments, packaging would simply be impractical. However, once purchased, garments are sometimes wrapped and then placed into a bag or garment carrier, which enables homeward transportation. Outer bags and carriers normally display the retailer's name, logo or some other sales or promotional message – thus also acting as a promotional tool in their own right. Most bags are discarded once the product arrives home, although some bags from quality brands and retailers such as Harrods and Selfridges are retained and used again – possibly because of their snob value or cult status. There is therefore a lot to be said for developing quality bags with a longer life-expectancy, to maximise the potential for sustained brand or business promotion – this also fits in with the general thrust of fashion sustainability.

As well as outer packaging, it is essential to ensure that garments have sewn-in labels giving care instructions and information about fibre content, brand name, size and sometimes country of origin.

Care instructions – in today's hard-working, time-constrained society, the need for easy-care garments is a must. One of the key drivers behind the casual modern dress style has been the need to make garments easy-care – hence their less structured make and more minimalist design. The use of laundry-marking schemes (which often vary nationally) ensures that washing-machine users and makers, consumers and textile and garment manufacturers are all aware of the required washing temperatures and cycles involved in the laundering process. Some of the more common marking schemes and the symbols used are universally and internationally recognisable and are shown in figure 4.8. The main international body working on universal laundry marking schemes is the International Association for Textile Care Labelling (GINETEX: Groupement International d'Etiquetage pour l'Entretien des Textiles, www.ginetex.com). Textile care symbols developed by GINETEX are the subject of the International Standard ISO 3758. This standard is the result of an agreement between GINETEX, the owner of the trademarks, and the ISO. Information on the use of the textile care symbols in ISO 3758 can be found on the GINETEX website.

Fibre content – it is an EU requirement for garments to show fibre content/mix percentages. Fibre mixes down to a minimum of 5% are a mandatory requirement. The range of available fabrics and fibre mixes currently used by global fashion garment-makers could fill many volumes – needless to say, the major drivers of fabric selection in a garment are durability, ease of care, manufacturing compatibility, end use of garment, fashionability and overall suitability. As with garment manufacturing, the cost of world textiles has reduced in real terms as a result of the huge expansion of supply, the move of production to cheap labour areas and the technological improvements in textile machinery which, in

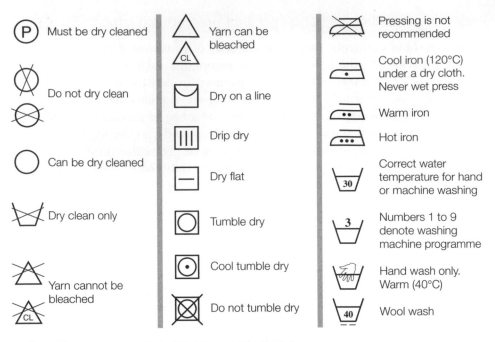

figure **4.8** **some commonly used laundry-marking symbols**

turn, have led to increased and more efficient output. The UK still retains many specialist areas of textile expertise, for example cashmere knitting and quality wool fabrics, although even these remaining areas appear to be fighting severe global competition, and their survival is by no means guaranteed.

Brand name – it is claimed that the earliest person to put a brand label in a garment was Charles Frederick Worth (1825–95), who founded one of the early couture houses in Paris. Brand names were once only to be found on garment labels, but the recent bling craze has underlined the importance of ostentatious brand logos that are conspicuous when a consumer uses the product. Branding a logo can sometimes work against a company. French Connection (FC) used their name in a quirky way with FCUK, but ended up creating a new identity which may have eclipsed the French Connection brand. Now the company is finding it difficult to maintain its brand proposition 'post-FCUK'. Overuse of a brand, logo or slogan can ultimately lead to brand overload with potential brand burnout. Fashion marketing is beginning to understand the dangers of brand overexposure.

Country of origin – in the EU there is no legal requirement to show the country of origin, although this is not the case in all parts of the world. The average UK consumer appears to be unconcerned about where products are manufactured, unlike in other countries where consumers are encouraged to support their own national manufacturing industry. Even as late as the 1980s, M&S was proud to advertise the fact that the majority of their garments were still manufactured in the UK. As a result of the inexorable decline of the UK textile and garment-manufacturing sectors, combined with the ambivalent approach to manufacturing by UK politicians, it would appear that there is now no logic in trying to support the home industry. Economic history will be the ultimate judge of the wisdom of our increasing reliance upon imported fashion products.

Garment-sizing – internationally there are three main clothing and footwear sizing systems (see table 4.7). These are based upon American, European and UK sizes, which relate to the use of inches in the UK/US and to centimetres in Europe. Most garments will contain at least one permanent sewn-in label to indicate the size. Glove sizes are generally the same in all countries. With more casual garments, which are looser-fitting, the use of S (small), M (medium), L (large) and XL (extra large) is normal. For very large sizes the term XXL is used, with 2XXL up to 8XXL used to designate garments which can fit people with a chest measurement of up to 60 inches.

Vanity sizing

Vanity sizing is a recent trend in the labelling of sizes (for jeans in particular) among some fashion brands in Europe and the UK. The term refers to size

table **4.7**   **international clothing and footwear sizes**

Men's suits and overcoats							
American	36	38	40	42	44	46	
British	36	38	40	42	44	46	
European	46	48	51	54	56	59	

Women's suits and dresses							
American	8	10	12	14	16	18	
British	10	12	14	16	18	20	
European	38	40	42	44	46	48	

Shirts							
American	14	14^1/$_2$	15	15^1/$_2$	16	16^1/$_2$	17
British	14	14^1/$_2$	15	15^1/$_2$	16	16^1/$_2$	17
European	36	37	38	39	41	42	43

Men's shoes							
American	7^1/$_2$	8	8^1/$_2$	9^1/$_2$	10^1/$_2$	11^1/$_2$	
British	7	7^1/$_2$	8	9	10	11	
European	40^1/$_2$	41	42	43	44^1/$_2$	46	

Women's shoes							
American	6	6^1/$_2$	7	7^1/$_2$	8	8^1/$_2$	
British	4^1/$_2$	5	5^1/$_2$	6	61/2	7	
European	37^1/$_2$	38	39	39^1/$_2$	40	40^1/$_2$	

note: Clothing and footwear sizes are all approximate. Glove sizes are the same in every country.

labelling that understates the actual size of a garment, presumably to make the consumer feel slimmer. This has been easier in womenswear, which uses a size system (8, 10, 12, etc.), as opposed to specific measurements to denote sizes, e.g. men's shirts. Accuracy and consistency in the sizing of womenswear garments has been the subject of much debate and consumer irritation for many years as sizes refer to different measurements across brands. A size 12 in one brand, for example, may well be the same measurement as a size 14 in another. However, vanity sizing now also occurs in menswear, particularly in jeans. Menswear sizing is traditionally more transparent than that for womenswear since the sizes reflect the actual measurements in inches (UK and US) or centimetres (Europe). In some cases a pair of jeans carrying a label marked 32 inches can measure as much as 36 inches, making the consumer believe that he/she is slimmer than is actually the case. There are moves afoot in the UK to use specific garment sizes based upon actual dimensions – to ensure universality between retailers. Many consumers would appreciate half- or in-between sizes being available.

International issues that should be considered by fashion marketers

The concept of the global brand and global fashion, with its underlying assumption that fashion can easily cross national and cultural barriers, is regularly promulgated by the UK's fashion media. The ability for fashion looks, retail formats and brands to cross international boundaries is often a major issue confronted by the international marketer. As fashion looks from all over the world are distributed almost simultaneously by fashion forecasting agencies such as WGSN, it is often wrongly assumed that all fashion is automatically accepted by every nation and culture. The reality is in fact far from this, as in many countries their cultural and religious codes would simply not allow certain styles to be worn in public. Tastes are often highly driven by lifestyle issues, such as opinions, attitudes and interests. For example, one country or culture may have a liking or preference for one colour – in Germany many tailored and outer garments are offered in loden green. In France, despite its image as the key country for sophisticated ladies' fashion, the average girl does not walk around the streets of a provincial town looking like a model in a Chanel catwalk show. The truth about universal fashion acceptability is that fashion often does not travel easily – even across European borders.

There have been many instances of international retailers failing to deliver the right product and/or service when starting to trade in a new country. There are some UK fashion retailers who, after starting to trade in a new country, have either totally withdrawn from that country or have fundamentally changed their fashion offer. Both New Look and M&S have withdrawn from their French operations (New Look now trade in France under a French brand name). Gap have had to review the way they source merchandise for the UK, with the retailer announcing the opening of its new European sourcing/buying operations which closed again in mid-2008. Often international fashion companies often fail to realise that the unique and sometimes quirky nature of UK fashion does not enable them to potentialise their UK businesses, without making regular range and product changes to meet the different tastes of the UK consumer.

There are almost no examples of an international fashion business that has been able to trade globally without making some changes and concessions to their products, service offers or other trading issues. Undertaking extensive early marketing research is a cheap investment, as well as ensuring that a fashion business really does understand the foreign customer and the likely trading conditions to be faced in a new country.

Fashion product issues relating to ethics and corporate social responsibility (CSR)

In the UK particularly, the media are increasingly interested in and concerned about ethical and green issues surrounding the international manufacture and sale of fashion products. Table 4.8 lists some of these key aspects.

Although the UK media campaigns vigorously against these practices from time to time, the reality is that many UK consumers do not really care very much about the provenance of the fashion they are buying. Consumers are described as 'armchair green' – slightly worried about an issue, but not really motivated to do anything about it. Most leading UK fashion houses such as Next and John Lewis have very clearly defined and publicly available policies relating to CSR. Others are less candid about their stance on the subject, whilst some designers, such as Katherine Hamnett, have pioneered the use of sustainable, organic and Fairtrade fabrics and yarns. The use of fur in couture still happens, with Julien

table **4.8** **the main issues affecting/driving CSR in UK fashion**

Low pay	Sometimes almost at subsistence levels – often around $1 a day
Long hours	Workers, especially women and children, have been known to work for up to 120 hours a week
Use of child labour	In some countries children are put to work from the age of 6 – certain countries legally allow work from the age of 12
No/minimal job security	In certain developing countries, workers often have no job security or other social benefits at slack times. Trade unions often are not recognised
Endangered species	Fur from rare or near-extinct animals banned in most developed countries
Pollutant issues	Dye and other textile-related chemicals often released into rivers – variable national environmental standards
Non-sustainability	Food crops are replaced by cash crops, e.g. cotton, often in a non-sustainable manner
Unhealthy conditions	Factories are often dirty, hot, dusty and unhygienic – bad environment for workers and final product
Non-organic products	Fibres such as cotton are often grown using dangerous and environmentally damaging insecticides such as DDT
Large carbon footprint	Cheap fashion products shipped by aircraft appear cheap to the consumer but are costly to the environment
Unfair trade	Manufacturers/retailers are often accused of paying a pittance for raw materials to growers in the developing world

Macdonald continuing to be a major advocate of its use. M&S is a leader in the retailing of the Fairtrade label, as well as being a major user of organically produced cotton.

Hopefully the ethical and socially responsible manufacturing, sourcing and acquisition of fashion will move up the fashion consumer's agenda, and fashion marketers must keep abreast of the current public mood, to ensure that their products and promotions are socially acceptable to the majority. However, for any fashion business to take a totally ethical and socially responsible stance may be to the detriment of bottom-line profitability.

Offering the right Product is the most important aspect of the fashion marketing mix – with the wrong Product on offer, no amount of Promotion will result in a profit. The fashion marketer is often remote from the actual product decision-making processes, these being mainly the remit of the designer, buyer and/or supply chain executive. In smaller owner-driver fashion businesses, the product decision-making process is clearly in the hands of one individual – whilst in the larger corporations there are normally several people/ departments involved.

Providing the right product in the fashion business is essential, owing to the nature of the product – like food, it has a very limited shelf life. Price reductions and promotions will not move a really unfashionable garment.

Concluding comments about fashion products

Fashion products differ from almost all other product categories in at least two main ways. First, products are design-led, which means that brands dictate the choice available to consumers each season (with the small but notable exception of those brands allowing some degree of product customisation by consumers).

Second, fashion has traditionally created an expectation of change twice a year and has two main seasons, spring/summer and autumn/winter (or fall/ winter in America). In countries with no or limited seasonal differentiation, e.g. the Tropics, fashion brands and retailers 'invent' new seasons in order to mirror major global fashion trends. Fashion brands do not therefore have the burden of trying to generate interest in new products as there exists an inbuilt demand pattern contextualised by the fashion seasons. Fashion does not need to sell 'new and improved' fashion designs and products as consumers are already sold on the idea of the need to update. Fashion seasons are themselves subject to change as fast-fashion brands provide new products every 2–3 weeks. In some respects fast fashion is educating consumers to expect change even more frequently. This can obviously work to a brand's advantage if the designers and buyers can successfully persuade consumers to buy their brand's products as opposed to those of a competitor.

Those responsible for creating fashion products also face different sets of problems according to their brand and market. In the luxury sector, for instance, many argue that the country of manufacture (also referred to as 'made in') is a key element of what consumers seek in a luxury product. This is especially the case for many Italian leather-goods brands, which have a heritage based on artisan quality, in terms of both manufacture and raw materials. However, the country of manufacture appears to be much less of a worry for consumers of mass-market fashion, much of which is sourced specifically from low-cost countries. A key aim of all those involved in producing fashion products must be to excite their customers. As a Moschino advert stated in 1999, 'Fashion without passion is just another business.'

marketing mix – pricing in fashion

Pricing is one of the most important decision processes that the fashion marketer undertakes. Customers are becoming increasingly price savvy all the time and therefore are unlikely to be fooled by false value claims and deliberate price confusion.

Martin Parker – Managing Director, Urban Outfitters (Europe)

Introduction and background to fashion pricing

The aim of this chapter is to explain the concept behind pricing and how fashion businesses use it as both a strategic tool and a tactical element within the marketing mix. The principal aims of fashion retail pricing are to optimise sales revenues, maximise profits, provide value to consumers and reflect the brand positioning of the fashion business. This chapter is mainly concerned with retail pricing, which is the price that a consumer pays for fashion products and services. The reason for this is that many pricing decisions made by brands are directly or indirectly concerned with the impact on consumers' purchasing.

What is a price?

In simple terms price refers to the amount of money that a customer (b2b, b2c or c2c) is willing to pay for a product or service. In this sense price is directly linked to value. The price paid by an end-user consumer for a product is known as the retail selling price (RSP). Throughout a season the RSP of a product can vary depending on whether it is 'full-price' or discounted in some way. Fashion products are normally full-price during the season and then gradually marked down or reduced if they do not sell.

The current fast-fashion trading environment encourages fashion retailers to clear stock as they go, to make way for new product ranges. Consequently, the pressure to achieve sales targets quickly means that stock can be sold or marked down during mid-season or, failing that, cleared as 'terminal stock' in the seasonal sales. Some online and catalogue retailers adjust their RSP according to demand. This results in a smoother and less dramatic use of mark-down when clearing slower-selling products. An exception to stock entering the retail business at anything other than full price is 'special purchase' stock, normally slow-selling brands or manufacturers' lines. This normally refers to products or lines that are bought by fashion retailers specifically for the annual sales. It is common for such stock to supplement the current season's ranges to boost the amount of stock trading in the sale period.

Readers should appreciate that the RSP achieved by a company is normally its only source of revenue. The profit achieved in the RSP has to fund its entire operational expenditure and its investment in future developments.

The concepts of price, cost and value

The word 'price' and 'cost' are sometimes interchangeable in business, as companies negotiate prices among themselves. For example a fashion retail buyer from a brand such as Top Shop will pay a cost price (CP) for fashion products that they have ordered from suppliers. The price will obviously be a selling price from the perspective of the supplier. The CP paid by Top Shop will have a mark-up (or profit) added to achieve its RSP. The notion of the RSP value as perceived by Top Shop's consumers will be influenced by the benefits that are built into the product by both the supplier (e.g. product quality and design) and Top Shop (e.g. the status of the brand).

In 2006 Stuart Rose, the CEO of M&S, explained his success in improving the fortunes of the company by quoting a formula: price x quality = value. Price is a clear and tangible criterion for consumers to evaluate. Quality is also tangible but many consumers are willing to trade quality for a lower price so long as the product achieves a minimum performance and standard of manufacture. Consumers have different priorities, experiences and reference points, and each perceives value very differently. Understanding why some consumers are prepared to spend several hundred pounds for top-end, branded jeans, whilst others make do with a pair for £3 from George, is an essential element of all fashion organisations' ongoing consumer research. Aldo Gucci, the son of the original Gucci brand founder Guccio Gucci, observed, 'Quality is remembered long after price is forgotten', and this is the ultimate truism of all good fashion-marketing management.

Pricing strategies for fashion marketing

A background to clothing price levels

Standard marketing theory suggests that there is a wide variety of pricing strategies and mechanisms that can be applied to general goods, although in reality the fashion trade tends to use only a relatively small number of them. The price the consumer ultimately pays for a fashion product is the result of a combination of several factors. The economists' view of pricing is that demand for any product will rise if the price is reduced – the laws of supply and demand.

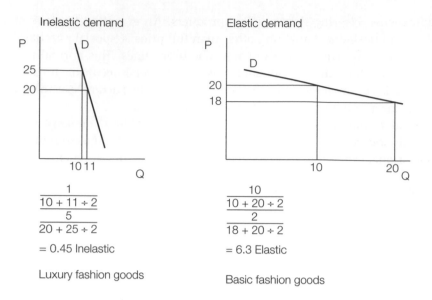

figure **5.1**   **traditional representation of inelastic and elastic demand for fashion goods**

The actual level of the change is described as the 'elasticity of demand' and is shown in figure 5.1.

Demand for fashion products is described as inelastic if the percentage change in the unit quantity sold is less than the percentage change in the price. In other words, a price increase does not deter consumers from purchasing, and vice versa. The arithmetic used to calculate elastic or inelastic demand is shown in figure 5.1. Demand for most luxury fashion goods appears to be fairly inelastic, with customers prepared to continue buying them, even at very high prices. However, the 'democratisation' of luxury (which has seen many brands increase their ranges of 'entry-level' products, especially accessories) has created an elastic demand at the cheaper end of the price spectrum. Many 'mass-market' consumers will increase their spending on luxury products as the prices fall (on the entry-level products) during the annual sales.

Elastic demand exists if the percentage change in the unit quantity sold is greater than the percentage change in the price. In this case, a price reduction can stimulate demand and generate more profit. The trick for retailers is achieving the right balance between price reduction and uplift in sales revenues. Equally retailers need to be aware of the effect that any price increase may have on customers, frightening them away or encouraging them to switch to a cheaper product.

Despite economic models, there are many fashion products that do not follow the normal graphical representation of price elasticity shown in figure 5.1. The lengths to which relatively poor consumers will go when buying luxury branded clothes – often sacrificing the basics of life such as food to ensure that they are seen wearing the latest brand/look – defy the basic and logical economic and behavioural assumption that food is more important than clothing.

The key determinants behind the setting of RSPs

The price at which any fashion garment is sold in a fashion store is determined by a sequence of factors:

1   The cost of making the garment (e.g. fabric, trimmings, labour and manufacturer's own profit margin).
2   The total costs and overheads of running the selling operation (e.g. staff costs, rents and other store running costs).
3   The accepted or normal level of profit that is naturally taken by all participants in the supply chain, for example the manufacturer, the wholesaler and the retailer. All need to make a profit and survive and thrive.
4   The value of the buyer's own home currency relative to the currency that the product is purchased with. (*Note*: Most European fashion retail buyers purchase in US dollars, whilst needing to sell fashion products in their outlets priced in euros.) When a home currency is 'strong' in foreign exchange markets, the fashion buyer can buy at keen prices and deliver value to the home fashion consumer.

In some countries, at certain product levels and within certain categories and clothing brands, manufacturers do not sell directly to retailers – instead they sell into the supply chain using an intermediary such as an agent or wholesaler. Wherever there is a 'middleman' you can always assume that, at that point in the supply chain, costs will be increased to cover that company's or person's operating costs.

Table 5.1 shows a simple fashion supply-chain flow indicating approximate profit margins throughout the various parts of the supply chain.

The percentages shown are only approximations, and will vary depending upon the trading circumstances of the company. As is shown, retailers add the largest percentage profit in the supply chain, as they have the highest trading overheads in terms of stores, staff and stock costs.

The traditional linear supply-chain model is now under pressure as retailers aim to work directly with manufacturers to cut out the middleman in an endeavour to reduce the cost of their products. The price of a fashion product at various points in the clothing supply chain varies dramatically, depending upon the manufacturing country, the trading level of the market segment being targeted, the quality and nature of the fabric used and the sewing complexity

table **5.1**   **categories of business activity and approximate profit margins**

Category of business activity	Approx Profit
Raw material producers = natural + synthetic fibres (animal/plant/mineral)	5% to 20%
Fabric + trimming manufacturers = woven and/or knitted products + other	5% to 20%
Product or garment manufacturers = various product types	10% to 25%
Agents and/or wholesalers	10% to 15%
Retailers	50% to 80%

required to make the garment. In chapter 7, different distribution-channel models are explored. In theory, reducing costs means that the saving may ultimately be passed on to the fashion consumer. However, in reality fashion retailers are usually focused upon making a profit for themselves rather than making goods cheaper for their customers, meaning that not all savings are automatically passed on. The recent deflation in clothing prices is mainly a direct result of increased international competition.

Some manufacturers (although not generally in the fashion business) would rather not have to deal with retailers – preferring to deal directly with the consumer and so making more profit for their own business. Direct selling from factories/brands to fashion consumers can be achieved by operating factory shops – often located on or near to the factory site or in a trading location well away from the town centre so that it is not in direct competition with the high street. Some manufacturers have successfully used the Internet and mail order to create the ultimate direct-to-consumer supply chain. There is a steady growth in fashion internet sales, especially of branded products, but mail order and catalogue sales have generally been in decline for many years.

Mail order, once a source of credit for poorer consumers, has come under pressure as a result of the wider availability of credit and store cards and the vastly improved product offer from the high street and clothing discount sector. Catalogues also use local agents to take orders and deliver their products, but this aspect of the business has declined rapidly, adding to the problems of the older specialist catalogue businesses. There are, however, signs of interest in a few of the more specialist mail order catalogues, for example Boden and TBD. The large expansion in fashion selling via the Internet is discussed in chapter 9.

What constitutes the cost of a garment?

The main constituent parts of the total garment cost required to be paid for by the time it reaches the consumer are shown below:

- sample making;
- management and marketing;
- design development;
- fabric;
- lining;
- trimmings;
- making-up costs;
- testing and technology;
- factory overheads;
- storage;
- transportation and distribution;
- general business overheads;
- business profit requirements.

The huge variations in fabric usage, garment/style complexity and work content are the major complicating factors. (*Note*: There are huge differences between the fabric and garment-making costs of a basic T-shirt and a luxurious evening dress.)

At all stages in the fashion supply chain, each person or organisation is trying to make a profit – this is simply the business norm. Companies often describe the final or net profit made at the end of the trading year as the 'bottom line'. In UK retailing, the bottom-line profit for retailers after all costs have been paid averages around 5–15% of gross sales. This means that if a garment is sold for around £100, the retailer generally ends up with a profit of between £5 and £15. Selling fashion is not really as profitable as it at first appears. Fashion retailing is one of the most risky forms of retailing, with the huge variations in fashion and style demand, variable weather patterns, uncertain economics and perverse consumer buying behaviour all helping to create a very uncertain sales and profit outcome.

Profit/retail price expectations

The relatively low RSP and profit margin generated by supermarkets when selling clothes is probably based upon the historically low margins achieved when they sell food products. It is as a result of this, and also of their relatively large-space/low cost/rental retail sites, that supermarkets are able to offer such comparatively low-priced clothing.

At the designer end of the market, the high RSPs and profit margins are needed to support the high promotional costs and also to pay for the high cost/rental of prestigious retail locations. It is important to note that high-end designer clothing often requires high levels of mark-down activity at the end of a season, to move out slow/non-selling lines – especially a problem of avant-garde design. (*Note*: Designers and high-end brands generally have more of an end-of-season stock problem as a percentage of the initial range than do more basic/lower price-fashion retailers.)

Retailers at any level of the fashion market will always be left at the end of a season with some element of slow-selling merchandise. It is normal to build this assumption into the RSP so the price reductions do not unduly affect the retailer's overall profitability at the end of the season/trading year. This means that in some respects the consumer (in the initial price paid for a garment) is actually supporting an 'insurance policy' that enables the retailer/designer to get out of their slow-selling lines/ranges when they use the price mark-down process to clear stock.

When looking at the costs complexity in table 5.2, it is difficult for the average fashion consumer to understand that when they buy designer clothing, the actual CP of the garment is probably only a fraction of the RSP price that they pay in the shop. Generally the better the design/quality of the garment, the higher the RSP and, more interestingly, the higher the percentage and scale of the initial profit margin made by that type of business. Table 5.2 is a very approximate guide to the uplifts on the initial CP applied by the major types of fashion retailer/product.

Table 5.2 can only ever be an approximation – as there is no one CP uplift or mark-up formula that can be applied to every fashion retailer. Each business has a different buying margin requirement, which is mainly driven by their overall trading profit requirement, which in turn is largely affected by each company's costs, overheads and general business efficiency.

table **5.2**   **approximate CP uplifts**

Retailer	Uplift factor
Haute couture	RSP = CP x 8 to 10 times
Luxury	RSP = CP x 5 to 7 times
Designer	RSP = CP x 5 to 6 times
Department stores	RSP = CP x 4.5 times
High-street chains	RSP = CP x 3.5 to 4.2 times
Discounters	RSP = CP x 2.5 to 3 times
Supermarkets	RSP = CP x 1.5 to 2 times

Key factors affecting fashion pricing

In any fashion business, the way individual garment prices are set varies widely, depending upon a set of internal and external factors. Prices are never set in isolation and the fast-changing, competitive trading environment is adding to the problem, especially as most markets are facing cheap imports. Fashion businesses will normally set prices using a combination of the following key internal, controllable and external, uncontrollable factors.

Key internal controllable factors

Current marketing objectives – all good fashion companies have clearly defined marketing objectives. Mostly these will be quantifiable and easily identifiable targets such as market-share maximisation, profit maximisation, product design and/or quality leadership, etc. If a business has clearly planned and accurately defined its marketing objectives, this makes setting prices a much easier task. In some instances, company survival may be the single driving force behind pricing decisions – an objective that certainly focuses the business. In this case, selling as much and as fast as possible at a low margin might be the survival tactic. Profit maximisation aims at delivering the best possible price for the goods whilst at the same time maximising revenue, cash flow and profit. Sometimes, planning one marketing objective may detract from another, e.g. a high profit and price maximisation strategy may be detrimental to achieving large-volume sales and ultimately a higher market share. Most marketing objectives tend to play one off against another. Gaining market share through lower initial unit prices is often achieved at the loss of percentage profitability. Fashion companies sometimes try to maintain a high-quality image by maintaining high prices, sometimes with little justification when the product's price, quality and value are examined objectively against those of competition. Low pricing on the other hand can sometimes wrongly project an image of low quality – often unjustified when we look at the quality and value currently being offered by UK supermarkets such as Tesco and ASDA. Probably the most important objective of fashion marketing is to maintain consistency, in order to avoid customer confusion.

Variable types of general marketing strategy – in all marketing situations, pricing is simply one aspect of the marketing mix that can be used to position a business. Promotion can range from the use of advertising in *Vogue* at the high end to a variety of price-driven offers at the other end. The full range of promotional tools is found in chapter 6. The suitability of either would of course depend upon the planned ultimate positioning of the product in a chosen market segment.

Fashion can also be sold in a wide variety of outlets (or places), ranging from Selfridges to a market stall or boot fair. Quite obviously, the type of product sold in either would probably reflect the customer's product and price expectations. Although it may be possible to find higher-end brands for sale in both types of outlet, consumers would not normally expect to find them on a market stall. Even if available, the question of doubtful authenticity might prevent the more wary consumer from buying top-end goods from a low-end retailer – consumers can be suspicious.

When considering pricing decisions, these are nearly always heavily influenced by the decisions already taken concerning the other elements of the marketing mix, i.e. the product style and quality, the type and suitability of the place/retail environment in which it is to be sold and the most appropriate form of promotion for the type of product and outlet. All pricing decisions are therefore governed to a large extent by the planned market positioning of the product and the chosen marketing-mix strategy.

Actual product manufacturing costs – the base cost of actually manufacturing a fashion product is normally the main factor driving the level upon which the RSP is likely to be set. Retailers of course have the high overheads of wages, rents, business rates, utility costs, mark-down provision for slow stock, maintenance and cleaning, etc., which can require RSPs to be set at anywhere between 2 and 10 times the CP of the garment. In general the more upmarket and highly positioned a fashion product, the greater the CP uplift required to meet the retail overheads, marketing costs, etc., and, most importantly to achieve a profit. The lower overhead costs of supermarkets, combined with their large buying power and low clothing-margin expectations, enable them to price very keenly in comparison to regular-priced clothing multiples. The keener CPs currently available from India and China are also helping to drive down clothing prices. The whole pricing dynamics of the UK retail clothing market may change over the next few years as a result of the current clothing developments within supermarkets. (*Note*: the launch of the new TU range by Sainsburys at the end of 2004 reputedly required a £100 million investment and was another indicator of the importance being attached to clothing by the supermarket sector.)

Market circumstances – the background trading conditions of the UK fashion market are quite different to those in other parts of the world. Our fashion retail outlets are conglomerated into several large groups of brands such as Arcadia with Top Shop, Burtons, Dorothy Perkins and many others, and Rubicon with Principles and Warehouse. The Mosaic Group (the relatively new Icelandic-backed retail investment group) is rapidly buying up smaller niche brands such as Oasis, Whistles and Karen Millen and in 2006 bought House of Fraser – another example of the way in which UK fashion retailers are being conglomerated. In other parts of Europe the independents still have a significant market share, unlike independent clothing outlets in the UK, which have been struggling to survive. We are now also seeing the rise of interactive TV shopping as a result of rapid technological advancements and the development and proliferation of digitally enabled cable, satellite and terrestrial TV stations. As a relatively small country, we have more nationally based TV services and radio stations. In many larger developed countries (such as the USA) there are often very few fully nationwide commercial TV and radio stations.

Although in the UK we do not legally allow monopolistic retailing, such acquisitive chains as Arcadia might one day reach the limit of their legal expansion level, which is continually monitored by the Office of Fair Trading. Whether consumers' interests are served by such large retail conglomerates is open to question. Although monopolies will not be allowed, the possibility of an oligopolistic market may not be of benefit to consumers. For example, if Arcadia were to acquire M&S, nearly 30% of the UK fashion market would one day be under the control of one organisation and its private owner. The UK market is, nevertheless, still one of the most internally competitive markets, although before the serious entry of the supermarkets there seemed little incentive for the established and new-entrant clothing chains to become either internally or internationally more price-competitive.

Consumer perceptions of price and value – fashion consumer perceptions of what constitutes the right price and what represents good value are the key to successful fashion pricing. Whether fashion consumers can actually differentiate between quality levels being offered by different fashion labels and brands is doubtful, owing to the complex nature of fabric manufacture and garment construction. A good-looking, more expensive garment may wear badly, surviving only a few washes, whereas the cheap and cheerful T-shirt bought from a market stall may wash well time after time. Although it is obvious, even to the untrained eye, when a garment is fundamentally poorly made, small imperfections in manufacturing, combined with a low-quality cloth, are not so easily noticed. The consumer, faced with the complexity of the garment-buying process, usually assumes that branded products will be of a more-than-adequate quality. In reality, the problem is that there is not always a direct correlation between high price and high quality. The true value delivered to a consumer is one aspect of garment value, but the consumer may also perceive other less tangible values in high-end, high-priced clothing brands. The psychological value to the consumer, in terms of the improved self-esteem bestowed simply by being seen wearing the brand, cannot easily be measured in financial terms. A few years ago, a youth wearing the latest trainers became trapped by the incoming tide. He decided to climb a steep cliff – upon which he ultimately became trapped, risking his life – rather than simply getting his precious new trainers muddy by walking back over a flooded beach. The ultimate cost of his air-sea rescue ran into many thousands of times the cost of his trainers. This is a real example of the psychological value placed upon fashion items by some consumers. Many top designer and luxury brands depend upon the psychological value systems in consumers' minds, rather than upon any real price/value criteria – here the psychological value of the purchase to the consumer turns rational economic theory on its head.

The relationship between price and demand from the consumers' perspective – according to the basic laws of supply and demand, fashion goods sold at lower prices generally sell in higher volumes than those sold at higher prices. More prestigious fashion brands generally gear supply levels to the lower demand required at higher prices, and vice versa. Expensive brands, however, which are sold at very low prices arouse suspicion in the consumer's mind, often creating a low rather than a high demand – consumers often feel cheated if a prestige brand is offered at well below the 'normal' high price. Consumers often go against the rational laws of economic theory. Again, this phenomenon demonstrates the psychological power of the brand. The continual discounting of a fashion brand will ultimately cause the consumer to question the 'normal' price. Many fashion brands try to avoid too much discounting activity to avoid this happening. It can, in some instances, be better physically to destroy excess fashion product and write off the cost value, rather than sell large quantities at discounted prices, which may destroy the future value integrity of the product. In an attempt to increase demand levels, certain designer brands introduce diffusion labels. These are generally a cheaper version of the original, which although priced more competitively, retain the original design essence and ethos of the higher-priced brand. A diffusion range can enable a brand to enter a slightly lower segment of the market without destroying the brand's overall integrity. The increased volumes sold of the diffusion brand can obviously be beneficial to the overall business success of the main brand. At the other end of the spectrum, many brands create a luxury high-end diffusion label aimed at the super-rich. Some top-end brands undertake a degree of product rationing, which enables them to drive up demand for a scarce product for which they are then able to charge a very much higher price than normal. 'Fashion rationing', as it is known, is achieved by creating limited editions which, if well publicised, can also create huge levels of fashion-media interest. Fashion rationing has also been described as 'fashion torture' by some of the popular media. This approach has been mainly used by the luxury and designer brands, but is now being employed by mid-market clothing multiples, which make a point of deliberately not repeating (buying more of) best-selling lines, as in the case of Stella McCartney's range for H&M. If consumers know that once a line is sold out it is unlikely that they will see it again, then this has the effect of increasing immediate demand. Fashion consumers quickly learn how individual fashion retailers operate and change their own purchasing patterns accordingly. Fashion marketers are beginning to realise that by limiting supply short-term, demand is often increased.

Price and its impact upon profitability – although increasing unit sales volume by lowering the price can increase the overall amount of revenue, it does not automatically mean that profit levels will also increase in proportion to sales. There is no direct relationship between the level of price reduction and the level of unit sales increase needed to make the same, or hopefully more, profit than that made at the original price level. The level to which unit sales increase as a result of a price reduction is known as the price sensitivity of a product. Small price reductions of 5% have far less of an impact on unit sales than does a 50% reduction – obviously the deeper the price cut, the greater the increase of unit sales. It requires good marketing judgement, rather than any mathematical formula, to decide upon the right level of price cut when selling off a fashion line. Most fashion marketers refer back to history for clues as to the likely volume sensitivity of a certain level of price reduction. The state of the overall fashion market is often a driver of discounting levels, and fashion marketers need experience to decide whether discounting is appropriate, needed or financially sensible. Mark-down strategies and tactics are mostly controlled by the buying and merchandising function – although fashion marketers are often pivotal in the strategic planning of these decisions. Price reductions without adequate communication and promotion can often simply turn into a profit and stock value reduction exercise, without fundamentally improving the trading position of the organisation. The industry is now seeing the development of pricing optimisation software that helps and guides fashion merchandisers and marketers to make better and more rational approaches to phased price reductions. Using complex mathematical modelling, these systems ensure that profit is optimised by using logical pricing throughout the fashion trading season. SAP, the German retail software suppliers, are currently leading this emerging area of retail marketing systems development (see www. sap.com).

Competitors' pricing policies – the average fashion retail business, during the course of a trading year, stocks many hundreds of lines, spanning a wide range of prices. A business such as Topshop at Oxford Circus in London would carry thousands of lines, ultimately creating many tens of thousands of size and colour options. Throughout the fashion seasons, fashion retailers undertake regular price reductions to help them move slower-selling merchandise – normally during special promotional periods, although some retailers discount on a continuous basis. For their competitors carrying similar slow-selling merchandise, if they fail to follow suit and to reduce their slow-selling merchandise at the same time, their rate of sales will become even slower, usually leaving them with unwanted residues at the end of the season – known as 'terminal stock'. During each season, fashion businesses need to track carefully the pricing policy of their competitors in order to maintain a competitive or at least logical price stance relative to their market segment. Regular and highly detailed competitive price analysis is an essential part of the ongoing longitudinal marketing research process for any successful fashion business. Short-term tactical pricing is a day-to-day part of fashion marketing, but sometimes pricing takes on a more strategic importance. Local pricing policies are common among food supermarkets, with some of the larger grocery chains stocking the same merchandise across the country at differing prices. (*Note*: Readers will often note higher prices being charged in Sainsbury's local stores, compared to those in their larger supermarkets.) There are also limited geographical price variations – normally undertaken on a store-by-store basis, to compete with intense local competition. Although most price changes in the fashion business are of a relatively tactical nature, at other times price changes may have a more strategic significance. For example during times of economic recession, it is normal for prices to drift downwards over time. During times of inflation or when the purchasing power of the pound is suffering as a result of an adverse exchange rate in relation to the dollar, fashion businesses may have to move prices upwards strategically in order to preserve their overall profitability. As supermarkets are now setting their pricing policy well below that of mainstream clothing retailers, it is likely that as the established fashion retailers lose market share to the supermarkets, they will be forced strategically to realign their prices downwards to maintain a reasonable competitive stance. No fashion business can isolate itself from external pricing factors driven more often than not by the competition or by economic factors. The 2008 'Credit Crunch' will clearly have a major impact on all global fashion policy

The numerous external factors listed are changing constantly, meaning that pricing tactics and strategies also need to be reviewed and changed. There have been several examples in fashion history of businesses failing to remain profitable by being either too cheap or too expensive. There is no formulaic approach to pricing, with experience of the market being one of the most powerful ingredients of good pricing decision-making. The next part of the chapter examines practical approaches to setting fashion prices.

Some specific fashion pricing strategies

Normal cost-plus pricing

Most fashion businesses, whether manufacturers or retailers, try to control their overall profitability by simply putting a percentage uplift or margin on the CP of the product, to arrive at the price at which they must sell their product. However, taking this very simplistic approach has the danger of ignoring competitors' pricing. (*Note*: the importance of overall price competitiveness is dealt with under 'going-rate pricing' or competitive pricing strategies.) This approach takes into account the cost of the garment and manufacturing, pays the company's overheads and then leaves a reasonable profit, to enable the business to both survive and thrive. All fashion businesses have differing infrastructural costs, which need to be added to the cost of the garments to arrive at the total cost of selling the product, sometimes also referred to as the cost of sales. Once a business is aware of these total costs, an executive decision is taken to decide what percentage profit needs to be added to each garment (sometimes known as the gross selling margin) in order for the business to be able to make its overall required percentage trading margin – normally described as its net trading margin. The profit level needed by a fashion business to trade successfully varies dramatically depending upon whether it is a high-priced and expensive department store needing high percentage profits or, for example, a low-price, low-overhead out-of-town discount or shed operator.

This rather simplistic explanation is of course underpinned by a complex planning process, which, whilst involving the fashion marketer, is mostly driven by financial requirements and targets. Some fashion businesses may have high infrastructural costs and overheads (e.g. a luxury brand with a prestige flagship store in an expensive location, such as Ralph Lauren with a large shop in Bond Street), whilst other discounters or 'large-shed' fashion retailers (e.g. Matalan) trade from large, cheap stores on the edge of town. No-frills retailing enables discounters to deliver value to the customer simply because they have low overheads. Each business historically builds up knowledge of its costs and there is a continual battle to keep them under control and preferably down on the previous year. Fashion retailers generally need to start their pricing planning from a cost-plus perspective, in order to ensure that they will make an overall profit at the end of the trading season/ year. Merchandisers and merchandise planners are the front-line personnel who make day-to-day line-pricing decisions, basing their assumptions on the overall target profit of the business. It is in this area of pricing activity where the operational activities of merchandising and marketing become jointly involved. Merchandising is a critical part of the marketing planning process.

Going-rate pricing or competitive pricing strategies

Although businesses need to ensure that they are selling their product with an adequate margin to keep the business trading successfully, in reality just adding a margin on to cost fails to look at the price created in terms of its competitive stance. All fashion businesses also need to understand what price level a product can command, taking into account competitors' pricing strategies. Clothing prices in the UK have historically been high by international comparison. The basic pricing strategy of many fashion businesses has often been only to try and charge as much as everyone else. With supermarkets and discounters taking market share from established businesses (at an ever-increasing rate), it will be interesting to note how mainstream fashion business reacts to these low prices. Going-rate pricing only works if the going-rate price reflects a truly competitive situation in the market. It appears that many fashion retailers, especially the variety retail stores, still believe that they can command a price premium, even if their competitors are pricing at lower levels. Eventually consumers realise that they are receiving poor value and migrate to the lower-level competition. Consumers always have the final say as to whether or not a price level represents value to them – based upon whether or not they reach for their wallets. Many marketing textbooks also describe 'price skimming' where extremely high prices can be charged for high-fashion or high-demand 'must-have' products. This is also a type of going-rate pricing – except that the going rate happens to be very high. Normally, price skimming is a temporary aberration; it is usual for the RSP of a product to drop once a fashion/trend/fad starts to mature and die away. Many fashion products can command high prices at the start but, as a result of the increasing speed and shortness of duration of the fashion PLC, prices can often fall fast as the smarter retailers react quickly and decisively to sudden drops in demand. Not having too much residue stock of a slowing fashion product/trend and reducing prices efficiently and effectively at the right time is the role of the experienced fashion merchandise planner. It is his/her job to reduce risk and to potentialise as many full-price sales and to leave the business with as little terminal stock as possible. Undoubtedly, going-rate pricing is the main way for fashion marketers to create a logical and sustainable competitive pricing strategy

Geographical pricing strategies

Sometimes the retail price levels of a given product within a country may vary from those charged in another similar country. Very few internationally recognisable fashion brands are sold at exactly the same price in every country. For example, cars have always been more highly priced in the UK – with many European and Japanese car manufacturers delighted at the UK consumer's willingness to pay higher prices than almost anywhere else in the world. In the fashionable luxury-brands arena, many companies do not have a unified, global pricing strategy for their product ranges, instead charging different, but locally sustainable, prices in each national market. However, with any branded product there is, of course, the potential for consumers to undertake internet comparison and then use mail order to obtain the product at the lowest international price. Some brands take steps to prevent consumers doing this, in order to maintain as high an RSP as possible – often they refuse to undertake international shipment. Such restrictive practices are deemed illegal in some international jurisdictions, but fashion brands continue to operate differential geographical fashion pricing none the less.

Most readers will be aware of how much cheaper international fashion brands are in the US than they are in the UK. Low fashion prices in the US are partially the result of the huge buying power of the US fashion business (enabling economies of scale and therefore cheaper production costs per unit) and partially the result of the historically low price expectations of US consumers. This of course is the opposite of the situation in the UK, where consumers have become used to paying high prices. International manufacturers of unbranded fashion products are well aware of the average RSP that can be obtained for a brand/garment in any particular country. As a result, they often use that target RSP to work backwards towards the CP that buyers in that country would be likely to be prepared to pay, rather than charging them the true cost of making that garment, plus a normal profit margin. So differential international pricing works at both a B2C level and also at a B2B level within fashion. As global sourcing becomes easier as a result of improved communications, especially the Internet, and supply chains because increasingly transparent, it seems likely that the ability of manufacturers, brands and retailers to support differing international price structures will be difficult to sustain in the longer term. Although international price variations are normal, variations within a national market are more unusual, although occasionally an individual fashion store/shop manager may have the authority to take his/her own mark-down initiatives, particularly if trade is temporarily problematic or if there are a few lines that are not selling. When this happens, it is generally only carried out on a small scale. Unlike food retailers, fashion retailers generally prefer to maintain a national product-pricing policy. Finally, from a theoretical economic perspective, perfect competition requires perfect knowledge on the part of both the buyer and the seller. Whether the fashion trade, with all its international fragmentation, will ever arrive at the point of perfect knowledge and therefore perfect competition remains doubtful. It is a large, fragmented and very imperfect market.

Temporary and permanent discount pricing

At all levels of the fashion industry, there are problem lines that simply fail to sell and this becomes obvious almost as soon as they are displayed on the shop floor. This can also be a problem at the B2B stage, where a line fails to sell to the retail buyers. Poor or slow-selling stock is the equivalent of dead money. If poor stock builds up in a retail outlet, stock overcrowding and poor range presentation is the inevitable outcome for the customer. This creates a vicious circle of failure, with customers more likely to walk away without purchasing and going on to a better-stocked and more exciting competitor. For this reason, all fashion businesses have to develop their own clearance or mark-down strategies, to ensure that slow-selling merchandise does not clog up valuable floor space. Most businesses will reach for one of the most powerful marketing tools – promotional pricing or mark-down – to try and encourage customers to buy problematic or slow-selling lines. At the top end of the fashion market, there is always a need to maintain an upmarket ethos, with such retailers and brands trying to limit not only the amount of merchandise put into a price-promotional event but also the duration of the promotion. Limited-period price reductions used in this way are known as tactical price promotion. All fashion businesses dream of selling all their merchandise at full price, as reducing any price erodes the overall profit of the business at the end of season. The cost of marking down slow-selling or problematic fashion merchandise is one of the greatest problems and the largest 'costs' facing any fashion business.

Many lower-end discount fashion businesses use continual price reductions as a strategic marketing tool. In terms of discounting, there are fundamentally two types of discounting – either permanent or temporary POS mark-down. Permanent mark-down is generally used as a final clearance tool to move problematic lines. The level of mark-down or price alteration varies in line with the severity of the problem, i.e. how long a poor line is taking to sell. For lines which are selling very poorly, most retailers know that customers' favourite level of mark-down is 50% – or half price. A mark-down of only 10% does not have the same impact. If a retailer wants to clear lines, then anything less than 25% to 50% off may not be sufficient to make the stock sell effectively. However, if a retailer has a small excess of stock of a particular line, then it is normal to offer a small reduction of perhaps 10%. Such a reduction will temporarily stimulate consumer demand and hopefully return the stock to a normal level in a relatively short time. During difficult retail trading periods, it is not unusual to see a 70% reduction off slow-selling stock.

Often a small temporary price reduction, such as the M&S 20%-off discount day, has the twofold benefit of both encouraging sales and increasing overall customer footfall. These temporary price reductions are sometimes referred to as POS reductions, and are different from the normal end-of-season permanent price reductions, whose main purpose is the final clearance of poor sellers. Whatever the type of price reduction used, both ultimately affect the bottom-line profit achieved at the end of a season. Making any price reduction is an extremely important marketing decision, although it is the merchandise managers and merchandise planners who normally make such critical profit-impacting decisions.

Customers undoubtedly enjoy and respond to the right level of price reduction on the right garment. Some discount offers are made confusing. An offer of 70% off a price, for example, whilst easy for many readers to calculate, can often confuse the less numerate of the population. Mental arithmetic standards are dropping internationally as education systems increasingly allow children to use calculators rather than doing calculations in their heads. Fashion marketers should take heed of this and never try to convey over-complex price offers to an increasingly innumerate population. Also '% off' rather than '£ off' discounts can intellectually challenge customers who may have low levels of numeracy. A reduction of £10, for example, is easier for consumers to understand and is widely used by retailers. Every fashion business has to face the problem of moving slow stock at one time or another – discounts and cash off are the main ways of getting rid of problematic fashion stock or generally increasing unit sales.

Slow-selling fashion stock is not like fine wine, which often gets better over time; it has to be dealt with fast, on the basis that there is a need to make room for the next new line. Hopefully the new line will always be a faster seller. Implementing mark-down as soon as a problem appears, rather than delaying it and hoping a line will sell later, is generally the most financially astute approach. Customers always know bad stock – they leave it on the rails and counters, having snapped up the good stock as quickly as possible. The cost of clearing and reducing stock is one of the highest of all business costs – and must be considered as a real cost, rather than simply a trading activity. (*Note*: Annual mark-down costs almost always exceed total marketing costs.)

Business problems related to price reductions

Although it seems logical to assume that all fashion businesses need to reduce prices, if a business becomes too reliant on this marketing tool, then it may be storing up problems for the future. For example, if a business regularly reduces a certain brand or line, consumers will no longer believe that the higher price is justified. As a result, they will put off purchasing at the top price and wait until an item is reduced, possibly during the next 'Blue Cross Day' sale (a one-day sale often used by department stores). Continual on/off discounting debases the customers' belief in the original price and then customer demand is simply stalled until the next period of price reduction. Price reduction in any fashion business has been likened to drug addiction – to achieve the same effect next time you need to take more of the drug than you used originally. Eventually a fashion business can become completely addicted and unable to survive without continuous mark-down. Customers are becoming an increasingly canny breed and quickly learn about the sale-reduction patterns of a retailer – waiting like vampires to suck blood at the appointed hour. One of the most important things for any fashion marketer to realise is the huge increase required in the number of units sold to make the same amount of profit as the percentage price cut gets deeper. When making any price alteration decisions, the fashion marketer should consider whether he/she is confident of maintaining overall profitability. It is not always immediately evident, even to trained fashion marketers, how many more units need to be sold to maintain overall profitability at different price reduction levels. There is no direct correlation between the cash reduction taken on a line and the increased unit volume sales required to take the same amount of cash. (*Note*: At 50% reduction, it will often be necessary to sell four to five times as many units as normal to generate the same amount of profit as at full price.)

The best way to phase price reductions

No fashion retailer likes having to mark down stock, as in some ways it is an admission of failure. It is essential when reducing the price of slow-selling products, to reduce them to a price that will clear them quickly. Fashion businesses are sometimes tempted to introduce a small initial reduction of, say, 10%, hoping that this might be enough to tempt customers. If a product has been a very slow seller, then probably a cut of at least $33^{1}/_{3}$% would be more logical. Very often, having realised their mistake, retailers will go back and make a further reduction. The problem of doing this is that during sale periods, probably 80% of the sale customers come through the store in the first week of a sale. Marking down a second time can often miss the main customer flow, leaving little opportunity to sell out of the problem line before the end of the sale. Getting the right level of reduction first time round is essential.

Price points and price architecture

All fashion businesses observe some form of logical price-point policy as well as a logical price architecture. Price points often tend to end in 99p, or £9 – with a view to creating a psychologically lower price in the mind of the buyer: £199 sounds cheaper than £200, and £4.99 sounds cheaper than £5. Although the pound- or penny-off price point is deemed to be a psychological draw, its origins go back to the old days of retailing, when if you opened up the cash till a bell rang – hence the expression 'hearing the tills ring'. By making a transaction an odd amount, the cashier was obliged to open the till in order to put the money in and then to give back change to the customer. The eagle-eyed floor manager would of course hear the till ring and then could look to ensure that the money was going into the till and that the change (hopefully the right change) was returned. With the advent of credit cards, the idea of tills and change are relegated to history.

Any fashion business needs to employ price points that are not only understandable but also logically stepped. For example, if a menswear business only sold branded shirts at £19.99 and at £99.99, they would quite clearly miss the mid-market in the UK for branded shirts around the £30 mark. Customers could feel that the lower-priced shirt might not be very good quality and not understand the fabric and make quality of the £99 shirt.

Generally, all fashion ranges have what is known as a lead-in or entry-level price, and prices should then move up in a logical sequence of steps to a final top price. In any range of prices, or price architecture, as it is commonly known, at each price level the lines or products sold represent good value for money.

If, for example, a range of men's branded shirts sold at £19.99, £24.99, £29.99, £39.99 and £49.99, the differences in fabric quality, design and style should be obvious enough to justify the different price points. Some retailers confuse customers by having too many price points. When customers are confused by a complex pricing policy, the tendency is for them not to purchase but simply walk away.

Fashion marketers, especially in fashion retail companies, often have a minimal involvement price decisions relating to individual garments. However, they do need to have an overview of price points and price architecture to ensure that the range of prices is logical. An objective reality check on a regular basis is good advice for any fashion business.

A UK perspective on retail pricing

This chapter has been written against a backdrop of declining clothing and footwear retail prices throughout much of the developed world over the past decade. For example, a UK garment costing £100 in 1996 would have cost only £60 in 2004 (see table 5.3). The UK consumer has for many years had to pay considerably higher prices than much of the rest of world for a wide range of imported consumer products.

Any reader who has shopped for branded clothing in the US over the past ten years will have noticed that RSPs can be anything between 33.3% to 50% cheaper in the US than in the UK. Also, many foreign and British cars sell at very high premiums in the UK when compared to Europe. It is still usually cheaper to import a UK-manufactured motor vehicle from a continental dealer than it is to purchase it in the UK. Table 5.4 shows the results of some research into international price comparisons undertaken in the UK by the authors during 2005.

This shows the huge price differentials being achieved on some of the world's most famous brands and well-known iconic fashion items. Often RSP

table **5.3**   **a comparison of price changes 1996–2004**

Year	General prices (% change)	Clothing and footwear prices (% Change)
1996	100.0	100.0
1997	101.8	97.5
1998	103.4	93.8
1999	104.8	88.8
2000	105.6	82.3
2001	106.9	76.2
2002	108.3	70.7
2003	109.8	68.0
2004	111.2 +11.2%	64.7 −35.3%

note: Price variations are expressed as a percentage of the price charged in 1996.

source: CSO

table **5.4** **internatonal price comparisons**

	UK	US	Canada	Germany	Australia	Caymans
Local sales tax included (approx.)	17.5%	8%	7%	n/a	22%	low
Levi's Men's 501	**£65**	£27.29	£35.35	**£52.94**	£44.12	£34.61
CK boxers	**£18**	£9.49	£11.78	£17.82	**£23.50**	£10.98
Coco Chanel 50 ml	**£39**	**£47.47**	£35.82	£34.43	£34.32	£36.26
Adidas Superstar II	**£50**	£35.60	£42.36	**£56.10**	£26.39	£41.20
Burberry Trench M	**£895**	£371.88	N/A	**£798.6**	N/A	N/A
Timberland Basics	**£120**	£86.04	£103.57	**£105.53**	£54.83	£70.87
Clinique (Dram. Diff) 50 ml	£14	£6.53	£14.61	**£14.52**	**£15.54**	£5.40
Ralph Lauren SS Polo	**£45**	£38.57	N/A	**£46.20**	£41.99	£41.20
Hermès Birkin bag	£4000	**£6824**	N/A	£2970	**£4508**	£N/A

note: bold = highest price; bold and underlined = second highest price.

differentials are the result of differing levels of sales tax levied by governments. Where known, the local sales tax has been indicated. This can have a dramatic impact upon final retail prices. Many developing and poorer countries impose large taxes or levies on imported luxury goods, deeming them a waste of valuable foreign currency.

Examples of brands trying to defend differential international pricing policies

Levi's took legal action against Tesco during the mid-1990s to try and block their importation of cheaper Levi jeans, originally planned only for consumption in the US. Tesco had started to sell these 'grey imports' at prices that undercut Levi's-accredited European distributors. Levi's had for decades been able to command higher prices in the UK than in the US, and therefore wanted to stop Tesco undercutting them. The European courts upheld the action by Levi's, on the basis that the brand might be damaged in the European market. Levi's is, therefore, still able to command higher prices in the UK than in the US. Another example of higher pricing in the UK can be found when comparing the prices charged by Zara in Europe and in the UK. Before the advent of the euro, Zara used to show the key European currencies on its price tags. The UK price was generally higher than elsewhere in Europe. UK consumers still seem content to pay top prices, although there is now some evidence of price resistance. At present, there is no easy way to assess how much tourists and holidaymakers are spending on shoes and clothing when travelling abroad, although anecdotally this would appear to be on the increase and there is evidence that fashion consumers are making greater efforts to shop internationally, in order to get better value.

Some possible explanations of the causes of international clothing and footwear price variations

The cause of the variations in international consumer goods pricing cannot be explained using any simple economic rationale – it may simply be a result of the 'softness' of the market – or, put simply, the UK consumer's willingness to accept high prices. A number of reasons have been put forward to explain the continuing price differences of many basic clothing brands between the UK and countries like Spain, Australia and the US:

- The UK market does not buy sufficient quantities to enjoy the economies of scale of a market the size of, for example, the US.
- The margin or profit put on the CP by the retailer is larger in the UK than in other markets.
- The government's sales tax or VAT (value added tax) in the UK is at a relatively high level compared to other countries
- Retail rental costs in the UK are some of the highest in the world.
- Retail wage costs in the UK are higher than in other parts of Europe.
- The levels of direct and indirect taxation levied upon UK retailers are very high.
- UK retailers are inefficient in terms of their buying and supply chain management.
- The exchange rate of the pound against the euro and the dollar is so poor that UK retailer's CPs are higher in the first instance.

Only some of the above can be cited as being the cause of the UK's high-priced economy, sometimes dubbed 'Rip-off Britain' by the popular press. Probably the major reason is that the UK consumer is simply seen as a 'soft' target by foreign businesses, which see the huge historic wealth of the UK economy. This wealth was mainly created as a result of its long, but now historic, economic supremacy in manufacturing and dominance of world trade. Unfortunately for foreign fashion enterprises, the UK consumer is now becoming increasingly price-savvy as a result of the following:

- greater price transparency and ease of comparison as a result of wider internet availability and its international usage for online purchasing;
- greater levels of personal foreign travel, resulting in the better consumer awareness and knowledge of international pricing policies of UK consumers.

Increasing consumer understanding of fashion prices and value and the fast emergence of new manufacturing nations (whose labour forces are working for a fraction of the wages of the Western economies) are now reducing the price of retail clothing price. The UK consumer, unlike consumers from many other countries, has never been prepared to haggle over prices, believing erroneously that they must pay the price asked without question. Again, as a result of increased foreign travel and cultural exposure, British reserve is at last beginning to break down, with consumers trying to negotiate clothing prices in some retail situations. Still not the norm, haggling is definitely on the increase.

Consumer spending and debt

At the end of September 2006, the UK became Europe's most personally indebted country, with an average of £3000 of unsecured personal debt owed per head of population. With a total of £200 billion of unsecured debt and another £1 trillion owed on house mortgages, UK consumers seem happy to continue borrowing. Unlike in many European countries, home ownership in the UK is the norm; in countries such as Germany renting is deemed to be more economically prudent. There is no right or wrong – but clearly the capital locked into an owned house may well have been the key driver underpinning high levels of consumer spending in the UK. As house prices dropped during 2008, retail spending also appeared to suffer. Certain international economists are doubtful that renting is in the best interests of an economy – high rental economies may be fundamentally weaker than those based on saving and owner-occupation. Britain is a country where students have to pay for higher education and credit has become second nature to Generation-Y. There may well be some reduction in fashion demand from this generation as the impact of student debt starts to be felt.

The major causes of recent international clothing and textile price deflation

The major causes of recent international clothing and textile price deflation is shown below:

- **The export of European industries to cheaper manufacturing countries** – European clothing and textile manufacturing has been in a relatively long-term decline, mainly as a result of capital and technology being attracted to low-cost manufacturing nations, who are eager to use their own cheap labour to attract foreign currency, leading to improved incomes and living standards. It is likely that China will eventually become the world's greatest exporter of clothing. As clothing manufacture becomes increasingly uncompetitive in Europe and the USA, it is probable that many more developing nations will turn their hand to clothing manufacture. Making clothing does not require huge technological investment or understanding, as it still relies heavily upon dexterous hands of cheap workers and the basic technology of the sewing machine.
- **Improved international logistics** – with improving transport infrastructures, less-developed countries are now able to ship materials and finished goods with increasing efficiency, at high speed and at very competitive prices. Modern container ships can carry in excess of 8,000 containers.
- **Technological improvements** – sewing machines, weaving looms, knitting machines and other machinery used for garment and fabric manufacture are now many times faster and more reliable than even a decade ago, which in turn has led to improved manufacturing speed, quality and efficiency and generally to lower CPs. Output per worker has risen throughout most parts of the global textile and garment-manufacturing sectors – although where labour is cheap, output

efficiency per worker is not as critical as it is in developed, high-labour-cost areas such as Europe and the US.

Factors driving price trends of mass-market clothing

The current outlook for clothing prices within the UK is for them to continue downwards, with consumers likely to be the main beneficiaries. For the resellers, it is slightly more problematic, as they will need to increase selling volumes and become more cost-efficient if they are to maintain their current levels of profitability. The increasing market share being taken by supermarkets will put huge pressure upon the likely profitability of the main middle-market clothing multiples over the next few years. The clothing multiples have historically enjoyed high-street dominance, with only the variety and department stores to contend with as serious competitors. The relatively low retail-cost base of supermarkets, their low margin requirements and the high traffic flows of a wide socio-demographic range of customers have positioned them ideally to compete against their inherently high-cost competitors. The battle for the mass-market clothing share may only be in the early stages.

The only caveat to the continuing availability of cheap imported clothing in the UK might be if China were to revalue its currency, thus making imported goods more expensive. The US government is becoming increasingly concerned about its massive balance of trade deficit with China, and has mooted a potential 27.5% import tax on all imported Chinese goods unless the Chinese government allows their currency to float freely on world foreign exchange markets. Cheap goods generally become more expensive in the longer term – this appears to be an underlying pattern for marketers in most product areas.

The changing spending patterns of UK fashion consumers

Over the past fifty years, as consumers have become wealthier and in real terms clothing prices have gone down, the purchasing of clothing is no longer such an important part of consumer purchasing patterns. In 1950 clothing purchases took up nearly 30% of consumers' disposable income, as compared with a mere 12% today. As already explained, prices have reduced as a result of clothing manufacturing having moved to low-cost countries and the improved technology that has delivered economies of scale. For the first time in economic history, UK consumers in 2005 spent over 50% of their disposable income on non-essential products and services. Holidays, leisure pursuits and eating out rank far higher in the psyche of the UK consumer than does shopping for clothes. The reduction of clothing as a percentage of UK consumer's total disposable income over time is shown in figure 5.2. As consumers have become wealthier in real terms and as clothing and footwear prices have spiralled downwards, fashion represents an increasingly small part of overall consumer spending.

The UK fashion consumer is now faced with a bewildering choice of discount and off-price clothing retailers, most of which sell very adequate

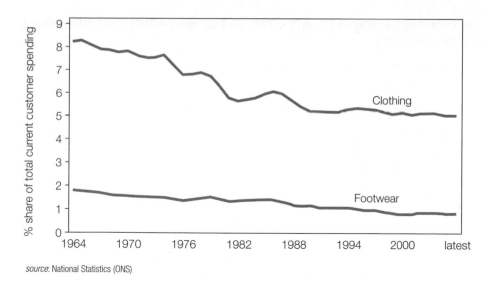

source: National Statistics (ONS)

figure **5.2**   **clothing and footwear shares of total consumer spending 1964–2006**

and reasonably made clothes at very competitive prices. The 1980s and 1990s saw the emergence of chains like New Look which became the masters of fast, cheap fashion. The 'pile it high and sell it cheap' maxim, originally used by Jack Cohen of Tesco fame, is now being applied to selling fashion, in a market-place that was for so long dominated by higher-priced operators. M&S and the department stores, which were targeting an older and wealthier segment of customers, were for decades able to command high prices – until the invasion of these lower-priced retailers. Other discounters such as Mark One and Primark also moved in on the scene when it became clear that the consumer was now in the mood to purchase cheap, disposable fashion. Consumers were now no longer buying clothing as an investment, but instead were aiming to wear fashion for a short period and then quickly move on to the next new style.

The huge growth of charity shops in the UK – there were approximately 7000 in 2008, may partly be driven by the disposability of these new cheap garments which, after a short period of wear, often find their way into the charity-shop supply chain. The intense price competition now being faced by middle-market 'high-priced' retailers such as M&S continues to increase as the food supermarkets join the fray. Although Sainsbury's was an early pioneer of clothing in its supermarkets, poor initial experience with Jeff & Co, designed by Jeff Banks, led to its replacement by the TU range in 2005, which is now trading strongly – again, this range offers excellent value when compared with many regular mid-market clothing offers.

The continuing supply of cheap clothing and its likely effect upon international fashion marketing

The basic tenet of supply and demand economics indicates that as prices fall, consumers will buy more of a product. As clothing prices have fallen and as fashion consumers have become wealthier, this has dramatically increased the demand for cheap disposable fashion. Despite the real and developing interest in expensive luxury fashion brands, the majority of UK consumers still wear mainstream, middle-market clothing. However, many consumers are willing and able successfully to mix cheap and expensive fashion brands – the 'Prada and Primark' phenomenon, as discussed in chapter 1. A basic requirement for all successful fashion marketing is an awareness of the entire spectrum of fashion and retail brands and an understanding of how they might relate to each other.

For many years the UK, in common with most other developed countries, protected its indigenous clothing and textile industries from being swamped by a flood of cheap imports. This was achieved using a quota scheme, negotiated under the aegis of the General Agreement on Tariffs and Trade (GATT). Under the section known as the MFA, developed countries limited the number of garments or quantity of textiles that were annually being imported from cheaper countries. The quota system was aimed at ensuring that developing countries would be able to undertake an orderly withdrawal from textile and clothing manufacture without causing massive short-term unemployment. In theory, an orderly withdrawal from manufacturing would give the workers time to retrain and the industry the opportunity to diversify and reinvest in more lucrative (and possibly more technologically advanced) businesses.

In 2005 this international textile and garment quota system was dramatically reduced and, as a result, increasing levels of cheap clothing and textiles are finding their way into developed markets. It is envisaged that within a decade China may well be supplying over 80% of the developed world's garments and textiles. With a labour force earning about 10% of the pay rate of workers in developed countries, there is simply no contest. Despite demands for increased wages by clothing and textile workers within countries like China and India, international fashion CPs seem likely to go down, rather than up, over the next few years. However, trading at the high end of the fashion industry normally requires a different range of marketing tactics and strategies from that at the low end. The following section looks at the various strategic-pricing options within the fashion context.

The importance of remaining price competitive

As the competition in UK fashion retailing increases exponentially, the need to keep abreast of the pricing tactics and strategies of competitors becomes more and more essential. Price-setting is both a tactical and a strategic essential of fashion marketing. To help to keep abreast of the prices being charged by the competition, many retailers employ marketing research companies or mystery shopping companies, who keep an eye on competitors on a daily/weekly ongoing basis. Both authors, during the course of their fashion business careers, would admit to having missed a competitor's sudden mark-down activity. Research companies can often provide ongoing field research programmes, aimed specifically at alerting their clients to changes in competitors' prices. Some organisations make a virtue out of their continually keen pricing policy: the company slogan of the John Lewis Partnership is 'Never knowingly undersold'. In the days before the growth of the national discount chains, this was a very powerful marketing proposition for consumers. Even today, if you purchase from John Lewis and subsequently find an item being stocked by another retailer at a lower price, John Lewis will (with proof and within a timeframe) refund you the difference.

Pricing is probably the easiest sales promotion tool to use. Any fashion business could effectively reduce all its prices within a matter of hours, using only a telephone. However, whilst price cuts are very sales-generative, they can impact badly upon long-term profitability, as well as creating customer confusion. For the first time in living memory M&S embarked upon special discount days in 2004, offering up to 20% off. They were reported as being very sales-generative, but may well encourage customers to change their spending patterns, as the canny hold back from purchasing in anticipation of the next discount day.

The continual use of regular discounting can have a long-term detrimental effect upon customers' full-price purchasing patterns. Once customers come to expect regular discounting to occur, especially on well-known brands with clearly stated suggested RSPs, the discounted price soon becomes the consumer's psychological norm. It then becomes increasingly difficult to get customers ever to pay the normal or suggested RSP. With ever-increasing retail overheads, discounting can often become a smart cash generator in the short term and a profit destroyer in the middle-to-longer term. The red pen used on price tickets is one of the most dangerous implements available to fashion retailers.

The main ways of improving and maintaining profit margins

There are basically four main ways in which a fashion business can generate higher overall profit margins. These four options are explained below:

1 **Raising retail prices** – prices can often be increased on fast-selling fashion lines or on identified key value lines, where the demand is seen to be higher than normal. There is nothing illegal about raising RSPs, although it can create some customer dissatisfaction if purchasing had been planned when goods were being offered at the lower price. The implication is that it is essential to check competitors' pricing before undertaking any price hikes.

Small price increases are often not spotted by today's sometimes confused customers. In practice, if an existing or currently selling line has its price marked up, there is then the administrative problem of having to get retail outlets and distribution centres to relabel any old stock with the new higher price. This can be time-consuming and labour-intensive. Also, the marketer must consider the potential unit sales volume decrease that can ensue as a result of a price increase. In some instances the overall profit is decreased, despite the increased unit profit, as a result of the decline in unit sales. The decision-making with regard to price increases needs careful consideration, and is normally the remit of the buying and merchandising department, rather than a purely marketing decision.

2   **Lowering CPs and extended settlement terms** – it has become an increasingly popular practice in recent years, during difficult trading periods, for the larger, more powerful retailers to exert pressure back down the supply chain to their suppliers and demand discounted prices below the formerly agreed price on all outstanding orders and deliveries. Another tactic is also to extend the payment period, making suppliers wait longer to be paid for their merchandise after delivery. In March 2006, M&S sent a letter to all its suppliers saying that it would unilaterally deduct 10%, together with a further 0.5% for 'marketing expenses', from its invoices. The Arcadia Group (which includes Burtons, Topshop and Miss Selfridge) did not make itself popular among its suppliers, when it extended its suppliers' payment terms from 30 to 60 days from 1 August 2006. At the same time Arcadia also imposed an additional 1% discount on all product from landed UK suppliers. The discount for Evans, Dorothy Perkins, Miss Selfridge, Outfit, Topshop and Wallis increased to 14.25%, while Burton and Topman discounts have risen to 11.25%. In the world of fast fashion, extending the payment period often means that the retailer will have received sales on the garment before the supplier is paid.

These companies quite clearly have made a profit gain by these actions, but on the downside they will almost certainly have alienated the suppliers whose profits they have dented. The buying power of the large organisations makes it almost impossible for suppliers to complain, although anecdotally some of the smaller suppliers have found the business relationship both unprofitable and untenable. Suppliers who make public comment and complain about what might be described as sharp practice will almost certainly put themselves in the firing line, risking their future business. Although most suppliers feel obliged to fall into line with such edicts, in the medium and longer term, they will undoubtedly seek their own ways of cutting production costs, which may be to the ultimate detriment of product quality. They may also actively seek out other more profitable business relationships, planning eventually to reduce their business relationship with the more aggressive fashion retailers. The balance of power in the short term is generally in the favour of the large fashion retail groups but, in the longer term, manufacturers and suppliers need to look after their own profitability and business relationships in the rapidly developing global market-place. Although there are many suppliers available across the globe, good, reliable suppliers are in short supply – upsetting and damaging a long-term relationship with a historically proven good supplier is not really a smart business move in the longer term.

A more logical way to reduce CPs with suppliers is to increase buying quantities with the aim of gaining economies of scale. However, this will depend upon the level of certainty that a retail buyer has about the line's future sales potential – the sixty-four-thousand-dollar question. Other methods involve selecting a fabric that can be used over a wide variety of lines, ranges and garment types. Again, bulk fabric buying will result in lower garment CPs as a result of economies of scale. In chapter 4, the problem of reducing quality over time – known as 'quality or product migration' – is discussed at length. Marginal reductions in garment or fabric quality over time eventually culminate in the creation of an inferior garment that customers no longer wish to buy, but it is a tempting approach on basic products such as underwear, basic knitwear and hosiery.

3 **Increasing the volume of sales at full price** – this is the most logical way of generating higher margins and profits. Classic techniques include the application of sales promotion techniques, including direct response advertising, public relations, direct marketing, gift or premium offers, personal selling, shows, visual merchandising and/or guerrilla marketing. Some promotional techniques tend to have a more immediate effect, especially incentivised personal selling and good visual merchandising. These techniques are two of the most popular applied in mainstream fashion retailing. Good sales staff who can implement innovative personal selling are increasingly hard to find in fashion. The casualisation of selling staff, with shift patterns now aligned to sales demand patterns, is tending to create more variability in the quality, motivation and professionalism of store sales teams. Working directly at the customer interface makes the role of the fashion sales person probably one of the most critical in the whole fashion marketing process. Unfortunately, this fact is poorly appreciated by some fashion marketers, who fail to see the personal selling process as a vital part of the whole integrated fashion communication process. The need for better-trained, high-quality, dedicated and motivated fashion-selling staff is one of the major issues for the modern fashion marketer. In the US and Europe, sales people are seen as professionals, but in the UK the shop floor is not seen as a prestigious and vital role in fashion marketing. Until this happens, UK fashion shops will continue to be criticised for delivering lacklustre customer service. All marketers need to focus on delivering service, but fashion marketers seem at present to lack the motivation to address this mission-critical issue. As global and internal competition becomes more intense, the marketing spotlight will undoubtedly focus on this currently unaddressed problem.

4   **Reducing the level of poor selling lines and ultimately the level of mark-down** – the problem faced by all fashion buyers is the continual need to select best-selling lines – sometimes known as having a 'high strike rate'. Modern merchandise information, planning and control systems can automatically monitor buyers' success rates, with some organisations actively monitoring, ranking and usually also rewarding those buyers with an above-average sales and profit performance. Buyers with high success rates are richly rewarded and are in short supply and great demand. All buyers can buy poor-selling ranges and lines at some time or another during their career, but of course the key question is how many and for how long. Some buyers work on a product that may be on trend that season and have few poor-selling lines, whilst other working on more problematic product areas might have a high line-failure rate. Senior management is aware of such temporary trading trends and will normally plan higher levels of mark-down in the more difficult departments than in those that are trading well.

Quite clearly, a good buyer with high sales and low levels of mark-down can have a profound impact upon the profitability of the company's overall trading performance. Buyers sometimes struggle when buying for a new company or a new department. Having an 'eye' for best-selling merchandise can be likened to being an artist. There are many parallels between a buyer creating best-selling ranges and an artist who paints good pictures. Poor buyers generally do not last long in modern fashion retailing – the impact of high levels of mark-down merchandise can be devastating to overall bottom-line profitability.

In essence, the impact of increasing and decreasing costs on the overall margin can be seen graphically in figure 5.3. Using the classic marketing cruciform matrix, the margin impact clearly emerges. In most fashion-pricing scenarios, the CPs and RSPs are rarely static, requiring the continual

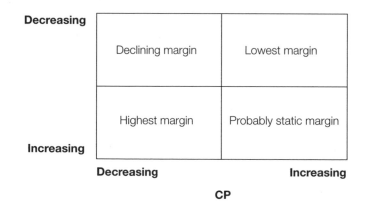

figure **5.3   the margin impact resulting from cost and selling price movements**

need for margin vigilance if the businesses overall profit target is to be achieved.

Are low prices a sustainable strategy or simply a useful tactic for fashion?

Although consumers benefit from reduced prices, it becomes a problem for the retailer, who, as a result of a price reduction, needs to sell more units at the lower price to take the same overall amount of profit. For the foreseeable future, especially as China and India supply even more clothing to the Western world, the downward movement of consumer prices is likely to continue. Readers should not confuse this general decline with the deliberate tactical and strategic price cuts that are normally undertaken by fashion businesses. In essence it can only mean that price competition will continue to get tougher as we move towards the end of the first decade of the new millennium. Undoubtedly, many fashion businesses will drop by the wayside as they fail to compete. In common with most of the European manufacturing base, manufacturing competition in cheap labour countries is set to intensify.

Recently the authors were offered over a quarter of a million white, men's, combed-cotton T-shirts, at the amazingly low price of 37p each, landed in the UK. No UK clothing manufacturer could or would ever meet such a price. If these T-shirts were to enter the UK clothing supply chain, they would make it hard for any normal full-price retailer to compete. Low prices, whilst good for consumers and certain retailers in the short term, are not really a strategic long-term alternative for the UK fashion industry. It remains to be seen if the cheap garment will work in the long term for the UK fashion industry.

The new phenomenon of confusion marketing

There is no one factor causing fashion to become cheaper; it is a combination of several factors. In this hypercompetitive marketing environment, pricing can be very confusing to customers, especially when they discover that a well-known international brand is sold at a fundamentally cheaper price in another country. Brand owners often place the blame on 'adverse exchange rates' or 'special local market conditions'. This can be a smokescreen for simple business greed on the part of large businesses, who believe that their consumers are easily confused. A good non-fashion example is mobile telephone tariffs, which are above the global average and totally incomparable as a result of the thousands of varying 'deals' on offer. Deliberately confusing the customer's understanding of prices is now referred to as confusion marketing. The hard-to-understand discounts and gift deals relating to the opening of notoriously expensive store credit cards are an example of confusion marketing being used in the UK fashion industry. However, it is true to say that the fashion industry uses confusion marketing to a much lesser extent than many other consumer sectors. Finally, beware!

As the old saying goes, 'You can fool some of the people all of the time and all of the people some of the time but you can't fool all of the people all of the time'. Fashion consumers are becoming increasingly savvy and any bad word-of-mouth publicity, as a result of confusion pricing, will soon damage even the largest fashion business.

Concluding comments

Although marketing theory generally assumes that purely rational approaches are used in making pricing decisions, the huge number of variable factors involved generally require that several pricing methodologies need to be rolled together to come up with a sensible solution. Some books talk of price-skimming (where businesses charge high prices for new and innovative products) and penetration pricing (where businesses want to buy market share at almost any cost). Both of these approaches are really no more than an intellectual abstraction, with fashion product pricing being a far more pragmatic and down-to-earth task.

Fashion consumers react in many different ways to higher or lower prices, and the level of price sensitivity may vary. The best fashion retailers are always watching, measuring and monitoring specific and more general price movements. Pricing is the most easily alterable element of the fashion marketing mix, as well as being one of the most dangerous if not used intelligently. The UK pricing of fashion goods in retail outlets is subject to various price-marking orders, all of which legally regulate how prices should be shown in the trading environment. Price-marking methods vary widely internationally.

The famous 28-day rule states that the top price of product must have been established by having stock available and selling at that price for 28 days prior to the date of reduction. Some retailers use this rather loose aspect of the law to create bogus top prices (prices that are really unsupportable) to try and fool the consumer into believing that they are buying something at a vastly reduced price.

In reality, many consumers are fooled by these 'created top prices', although, as mentioned previously, customers are becoming much more price-savvy. In other European countries, especially France, the rules concerning the price reductions are much more regulated, with clear protocols that all price reductions must be shown on the price ticket. This ensures that the consumer is clearly able to understand the value on offer and the history of the price alterations undergone by the item in question. In the UK, pricing is policed and monitored by local trading standards officers, normally attached to the local council. As a result of manpower reductions, many of these departments are not able fully to monitor all pricing issues in all consumer markets. Unfortunately, crazy top prices in fashion are still being quoted and going unchallenged as a result of inadequate trading standards enforcement. The UK fashion retail scene has been likened to the Wild West in terms of its ability to mount sales promotions based upon marginally legal pricing claims.

Correct fashion pricing assumes, therefore, that initially the right product has been designed and manufactured. Selecting the right product is the most important strategic decision. In the future, as competition becomes more intense, fashion pricing and its management will become increasingly fast-moving and complex. Fashion marketers cannot afford to get prices wrong!

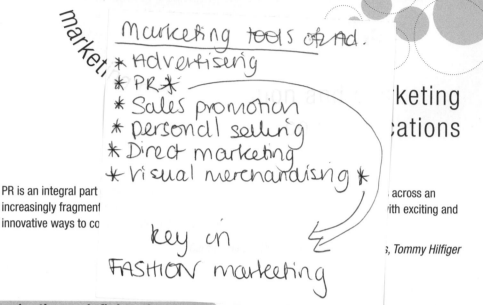

keting

:ations

PR is an integral part ... across an
increasingly fragment... ...ith exciting and
innovative ways to co...

..., Tommy Hilfiger

Introduction – defining the scope

The main aim of this chapter is to explain and analyse how modern promotional techniques are used in fashion marketing to deliver wider fashion business and marketing objectives. The chapter examines both new and traditional promotional tools in the context of their application to the fashion industry.

From a marketing perspective, fashion promotion includes the traditional marketing tools of advertising, PR, sales promotion, personal selling, direct marketing and visual merchandising. The fashion sector utilises the promotional tools in a slightly different way from other sectors, placing much more emphasis on PR and visual merchandising. To some degree this is due to the reciprocal relationship between fashion brands and the press and the prevalence of retailing in fashion. In simple terms, journalists need real fashion brands to write about and stores provide excellent vehicles for communicating with customers.

Furthermore, the process of trend development leading to a season generates points of media interest, such as fashion shows, that provide brands with opportunities to obtain pre-season editorial coverage of ranges and products.

A key part of that process is the use of shows to demonstrate and exhibit fashion in its various forms, ranging from fibre through to couture dresses. Some of the earliest shows are in fact yarn trade fairs and these are principally located in France and Italy. Throughout an eighteen-month period prior to a retail season beginning, there is a wide range of different types of trade fairs and fashion shows that help promote the products of fashion manufacturers, designer and brands.

The evolution of promotion

Since the early days of marketing theory the promotional methods used by marketers have changed in line with developing technologies. This has frequently led to innovations in communications techniques. The Internet arguably provides the greatest number of current innovations in promotion, as it extends the opportunities for mass communication. Some of these are referenced later in this chapter and again in more detail in chapter 9.

Marketing communications refers to the communications elements of promotion, including advertising (face-to-face and Internet), PR, personal selling, visual merchandising, word of mouth, corporate identity and direct marketing. Promotion includes not only communications but also sales promotions, with the word 'promotion' being commonly used as a synonym for consumer or sales-staff incentivisation. The distinction between promotion and marketing communications is minor and the whole spectrum of promotional and communications activity is frequently described as 'marketing' by the fashion industry. The marketing department, as an operational function of fashion branding, is concerned with promoting the brand and its products.

The major problem facing any brand wishing to communicate a message to consumers is how to penetrate the clutter of other information which is directed at them on a daily basis. The fragmentation of the media, from very targeted glossy magazines through to subscription television, means that more consumers are paying less attention to broad-based advertising messages. The public is not connecting with the media in the way that it did even ten years ago. For example, the growth of internet websites and specialist radio stations, as well as the developments in mobile communications, have provided consumers with wider choice about how and what they view and listen to. In parallel with an increase in media fragmentation, brands also face the problem of more sophisticated competitor communication. Over time, consumers are becoming increasingly sceptical about the marketing communications of many global brands. Consumers are becoming more educated in every sense, with many looking more deeply into the product and service claims of various sectors. The fashion industry has recently had several high-visibility stories about ethical issues, including the wearing of fur, child labour and low wages, exposed for media debate. Despite these problems, all fashion brands need to communicate with their consumers in order to stay relevant.

In response to such increasing public concern the Ethical Trading Initiative (ETI) has been created. It was formed in 1998 as an alliance of companies, non-governmental organisations (NGOs) and trade union organisations. Its main aim is to promote and improve the implementation of corporate codes of practice which cover supply chain working conditions. Their stated ultimate goal is to ensure that the working conditions of workers producing for the UK market meet or exceed international labour standards (see www.ethicaltrade. org). This initiative is not fashion-exclusive, but spans all types of goods and services.

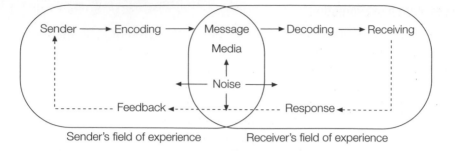

figure **6.1**   **the communication process (Kotler et al., 2001)**

Why effective marketing communications are essential

Whenever marketing promotion is used, it is always done for the purpose of communicating with another business or a customer for a particular reason. If promotional activity fails to connect with a targeted business or consumer, effort, time and, more importantly, money will have been wasted. It is therefore important for fashion marketers to understand the key stages of effective marketing communications. A model derived mainly from Kotler et al. (2001) clearly illustrates the whole two-way communication process. Figure 6.1 shows the key stages and processes of this traditional communication model.

This model identifies key stages in the organised marketing communications between a brand and its consumers. It applies equally to advertising and PR in circumstances where brands target segments with specific messages. The message content will depend upon the communications objectives: for example, to raise awareness of a new product or to reposition consumer perceptions of a brand image. In either case PR may be a valuable tool in persuading consumers.

The stages of the fashion communication process

Sender – the fashion business or brand creating the communication. Normally this will be the responsibility of the marketing or PR manager who will select and plan the marketing communications to ensure that they align with the target customer and the brand identity.

Encoding – the word 'code' is used to reference subtleties in the selection of communication ideas and the use of words, phrasing, images, symbolism, sounds and other elements which create a meaning and which are expected to appeal to the target market or segment. Sexy, young, highly fashionable, suave and casual would be examples of the subtleties required in a fashion communication context.

Message – this is the main point of the communication. It may well be illustrated by a visual narrative and reinforced by a slogan or strapline. The creativity of the communication and the marketing communications objective(s) being addressed will decide on what the message is. Luxury brands will use a fundamentally different message from that of a discount fashion retailer.

Media – this is the appropriate communication channel(s) through which the message is being sent. Some media are more ideally suited to fashion than others, for example, moving images of film and video generally have more relevance to fashion than radio broadcast messages.

Noise – this refers to the vast range of other communications and media trying to get messages across to the fashion consumer. In a fashion context this noise is immense, with many competitors jockeying to be heard and seen.

Decoding – this is the meaning that is interpreted from the message by customers in the target market or segment. This process is often the hardest part of the communication process to research and understand, as one person's perception of a fashion marketing communication can be fundamentally different to those of another person.

Receiver – this is the customer to whom the message is communicated. Sometimes the customer is not the consumer, for example, the purchasing of men's clothing is often undertaken by women. It is essential to understand which individual is undertaking the purchasing of a fashion product.

However, this theoretical communication model does not exactly explain what message is decoded by the receiver and how exactly the message is received and reacted to. For example, the hugely symbolic act of owning certain luxury brands may vary widely according to social class and culture. Feelings of prestige, worth and integrity are felt by some as a result of the ownership of a luxury product, whereas others would interpret such ownership as a crassly stupid waste of money – 'each to their own', as the old saying goes. For example, it is suggested that one person in four in Japan owns at least one item of Louis Vuitton merchandise. In cultures that put a high value on status, the conspicuous ownership of luxury brands is apparently believed to be a reflection of high social standing. In other cultures and religions, for example Buddhism, more humble and lowly lifestyles are admired and revered.

The main tools of the fashion communication mix

An important, but sometimes forgotten, consideration for any fashion marketer is that all marketing communications tools cost money and each has a very different role. Used effectively and efficiently, they can deliver a wide range of positive outcomes. Used wrongly, they are simply a waste and an expense. How each tool is used varies according to the type of fashion business, with each usually having different business and marketing objectives at different times of the year and trading season. As competition at all levels of the fashion market intensifies, most retailers have had to rethink the ways in which they promote their products, brands and businesses to consumers, to try and attract them away from the competition. The ten main types of promotional tools currently being used for marketing fashion in the UK and their roles are shown below:

1 **Advertising** – any paid form of non-personal presentation and promotion of ideas, goods, services or organisations aimed specifically at communicating with fashion customers. This includes internet advertising activities such as podcasts. The fashion show podcasts by style.com will soon be much more widely distributed and this will become an increasingly important form of very targetable fashion advertising.

2 **Direct marketing** – the processes and techniques used to communicate personally and meaningfully with individual fashion consumers. It includes internet-enabled facilities, telephone calls, personal contacts and/or written communications. Store cards are a key part of the armoury.

3 **Personal selling** – the personal presentation of goods and/or services by a company's selling operation aimed at building sales and relationships with customers.

4 **Sales promotion** – a short-term, incentivised selling activity to encourage the customer to buy goods or services.

5 **PR and publicity** – the processes used by an organisation to build mutual, positive, long-lasting and meaningful relationships with all the fashion-related publics that it comes into contact with during the normal course of business.

6 **Word of mouth** – the positive (although potentially negative), direct or indirect communications about a product/service/organisation between target buyers, friends, neighbours, family members or other associates. Such personal communications are very powerful but are also unfortunately the most uncontrollable.

7 **Visual merchandising** – the process of presenting and displaying merchandise in any trading environment in the best way, to attract the customer's attention and to encourage awareness, trial and ultimately transaction. Point of Sale (POS) is a term used to explain activities/items used to display/assist selling at the physical point of purchase.

8 **Packaging** – the outer wrapping used to present and deliver the product to the consumer. Its functions are also to protect and promote the product – also sometimes also to assist consumer usage.

9 **Corporate identity** – the physical manifestations of an organisation that are immediately recognised by the public and the trade, for example, logos, colours, fascias, uniforms, vehicle liveries, brochures, forms, buildings, company business cards, stationery, brochures, etc. A standardised and memorable corporate identity can reinforce all other aspects of marketing communications activity.

10 **Exhibitions** – generally these are aimed at trade buyers only – although the Clothes Show Live, held annually in Birmingham, now also targets consumers (see www.clotheshowlive.com). Shows exhibiting fibres, yarns, fabrics, prints and ready-made garments are held around the world on a regular cycle.

Using integrated marketing communications effectively

Each of these major promotional tools can be used by the fashion organisation to support and underpin its chosen marketing tactics and strategies. Most of the tools that are discussed can be used either individually or in combination with one another. The combined use of marketing promotional tools is usually termed integrated marketing communications (IMC). It is essential, when using them jointly, to ensure that they convey a cohesive message to their chosen target market or customer.

With any marketing promotion, the main aim is to communicate with the buyer or consumer in order to create a positive response. The types of response that occur can range from simply being aware of a brand, product or service, using that brand, product or service or even becoming an advocate of it. It is essential to have a clear set of marketing and marketing communications objectives when planning any form of fashion marketing promotion. Throughout the authors' careers, in many different areas of the UK fashion industry, it has very often been the case that promotional tools have been selected (often at great cost) using little logic or forethought. All marketing promotion is generally a cost to the organisation, so its random and unplanned use can be a wasteful expenditure.

The cliché that 'No publicity is bad publicity' cannot be relied upon, as the fashion-branding strategy of Burberry and the potential problems caused by the many media reports about chavs wearing Burberry as their brand of choice showed. The adoption of such a prestigious brand by such a potentially unsuitable segment of the market might have irretrievably damaged that brand's upmarket standing. Similarly, the persistent negative publicity that dogged M&S over its continuing poor trading performance (prior to the successful intervention of its CEO Stuart Rose) is another example of negative publicity potentially causing brand damage. At the lowest point when its ranges and business strategies were under attack by just about everyone, many of its more uncertain and easily swayed customers were undoubtedly of the belief that all the M&S fashion ranges were suspect. However, even at its lowest point, M&S was generating hundreds of millions of pounds'-worth of profit – with many products still being of excellent design and quality. The need to try and manage negative public perceptions of an organisation or its brands is probably more difficult and potentially more important than managing positive ones.

The key promotional tools of marketing

Advertising

Advertising has traditionally been the principal method of communicating a brand image. Its ability to create a powerful image and message in different formats across all media has enabled brands to gain customers' attention. The way in which fashion businesses apply different advertising techniques using different media is not a formulaic process; it is guided more by the current state of the market and by competitive activity.

Printed media

There are both specialist and non-specialist printed publications that are used to carry B2B and B2C advertising. Some advertising is specifically aimed at image- and brand-building, whilst other advertising has a more practical purpose, for example, promoting sales during the main biannual sale periods. The printed media used mainly to promote fashion in the UK are described below.

The daily and weekend national, regional and local papers – these have generally been classed as either tabloids or broadsheets. Until recently the tabloids took a more popular editorial approach, with a bias towards readers in the lower socio-economic classes; whilst the broadsheets were deemed more the preserve of the higher socio-economic classes and were written in a more serious vein. As a result, the types of fashion product and business that were advertised in each type of paper were determined by the readership. In general the more upmarket businesses advertising brands or biannual sales stayed with the broadsheets, whilst the tabloids were used more to promote the middle-to-lower-positioned fashion businesses.

Although some papers are published with full-colour pictures, a majority still only publish in black and white, making them unsuitable for communicating the exciting colours and textures of modern fashion. Some national daily and weekend papers do, however, have excellent colour supplements, which work well for fashion advertising on all levels. Newspapers are also a fairly transient medium, with many being disposed of at the end of the daily commute. With people's increasingly busy and complex lifestyles, national newspaper readership is on a decline. The availability of 24/7 online news services may be also undermining their raison d'être. Newspaper advertising, does, however, remain an important part of the communication mix of many fashion companies. The fast turnaround of newspapers enables fashion marketers to quickly mount tactical advertising campaigns in response to, for example, a competitor's pricing activities. Their associated colour supplements have a much longer production cycle and tend to be more useful for strategic, long-term advertising. It is therefore essential for a fashion business always to have adequate and suitable photographic material at hand, in readiness for publicity and/or advertising purposes. This can save valuable lead time if tactical advertising is needed at short notice.

It is important for marketers to remember the importance of regional papers. The UK newspapers *Metro* and the *Evening Standard*, for example, have a potential readership of at least 8 million in the London area. This is higher than the populations of Wales and Scotland combined. Despite some of the limitations described, newspapers are still a powerful and influential advertising medium for mainstream fashion retailers. The increasing availability of free newspapers such *London Lite* and *The London Paper* appear to be having a detrimental effect upon the circulation of the conventional regional papers. Although these papers do have fashion pages, the fact that they are free, and therefore more readily disposed of, may result in the shorter interest span of their readers. This could make the delivery of marketing communications messages more problematic. Whether free newspapers will be economically sustainable remains to be seen.

Weekly, bi-weekly and monthly magazines – The UK has a uniquely wide magazine offer, with over two thousand titles regularly published, catering for nearly every conceivable taste. There are dozens of fashion-specific magazines, with others containing elements of fashion. Certain fashion magazines such as *Vogue* have international editions with prestigious editors, whilst others focus less on the luxury and designer end of the market and more on women and high-street fashion in general. Regular advertising with a magazine can also help an advertiser's inclusion in editorial fashion comment. There is an uneasy alliance between fashion magazine editors, advertising departments and advertisers. Biased reporting is a fact of life in both magazines and newspapers –business survival often has a higher priority than editorial integrity!

Fashion magazine advertising is predominantly aimed at the final consumer, although in many countries there are also trade magazines, aimed specifically at professionals working in the fashion industry. B2B fashion advertising in the UK, whilst small compared to B2C advertising, is nevertheless sometimes an important part of the fashion promotion mix. In the UK, one of the most influential fashion trade magazines is *Drapers*, which has been in existence for well over a hundred years and was formerly known as *Drapers Record* – very few UK fashion marketers fail to read it on a regular basis. In the US, there is the prestigious *Women's Wear Daily* or WWD (see www.wwd.com), a newspaper-format publication that gives a global review of world fashion, as well as a wide US fashion business focus.

Levels of UK fashion advertising expenditure

The levels of advertising expenditure of the UK's leading fashion retailers vary dramatically as a percentage of sales. Each year the *Retail Pocket Book* (A. C. Nielsen) reviews historic advertising expenditure by the major clothing retailers and brands: there appears to be little correlation between the size of the business and the level of brand visibility. In 2003 Mango spent £401,000 against Burberry's £356,000. Considering Burberry's luxury-brand status and Mango's relatively low penetration of the UK market (less than 1% in 2003), this seems to make little sense. There is simply no rationale behind the level of advertising expenditure and the current or likely level of market penetration. For many years M&S had a policy of no advertising, believing that the strength of their product offer, brand and reputation would be enough to sustain their business. This policy worked well for a long time when their product offer was based upon basic classic garments requiring little fashion content and when general UK fashion competition was less intense. Now M&S regularly takes industry awards for the superb quality of its creative advertising. In 2003 the largest unisex advertiser was H&M, which spent just under £2 million, with their main rival Top Shop/Topman nowhere to be seen in the top five UK fashion advertisers. Many large fashion retailers appear to be revisiting their whole strategic approach to advertising in view of the hypercompetitive nature of the UK fashion market.

Finally, unlike black-and-white newspaper printing processes, the production processes of colour magazines have longer lead times of several weeks and sometimes months. The great advantage of magazines is that they have a longer life than that of newspapers. The more upmarket and exclusive fashion magazines are passed on to friends or kept as prestige coffee-table items. The total readership of a magazine can therefore be much higher than that of a newspaper, even though the initial circulation (number of copies bought) might be initially lower. Fashion magazines, unlike newspapers, are more tightly targeted at specific age groups, thus enabling a much more precise focus on a specified market segment. Although magazines generally have longer copy deadlines than newspapers, the use of detailed colour photography enables them to show fashion to best effect.

The impact of celebrities on fashion

The cult of celebrity is increasingly an important part of everyday British life. Celebrity magazines such as *Heat, Closer, Now, Hello* and *OK* feature the lives and circumstances of a wide range of famous people and celebrities. The huge growth in circulation of these magazines is having an increasing influence upon all aspects of UK fashion.

Celebrity influence is wide, with TV presenters, sports personalities, media stars and a host of other B- and C-list names taking the roles once played by royalty and politicians. This sudden upsurge of interest in celebrities has been put down to the increasing potential for social mobility within British society. The old order of the UK class system is now under pressure as a result of widening opportunities. The increasing social importance and visibility of celebrities has resulted in their dress style and fashion sense being keenly watched and analysed by an increasingly interested public. Celebrities, or celebrity look-alikes, are now replacing anonymous models in fashion adverts. The benefit of celebrity association is being extensively used by many leading fashion brands, for example David Beckham for Police sunglasses, and Bryan Ferry and Twiggy for M&S.

The importance of awards ceremonies and reality TV as a fashion influence

The increasing number of awards ceremonies and other celebrity-related events are an important influence on fashion journalists, who scrutinise every detail in order to analyse and understand the likely directions of future fashion. Table 6.1 shows the current calendar of significant international awards ceremonies.

The vast amount of fashion comment about what is worn at these occasions can have a profound directional effect upon mainstream fashion. It is believed by many that awards ceremonies are now gaining in importance, probably attracting as much press interest as the important couture shows.

Highly visible public figures have often been deemed to be the epitome of good taste. The late Duke and Duchess of Windsor were the style icons of the 1930s and 1940s, and every decade heralds its own new icons. As royalty has become a fashion irrelevance to many Britons, celebrities, with their assumed style confidence, have rapidly replaced them as the ultimate fashion role models.

Reality TV shows have enjoyed increasing popularity over the past few years, and have created a perception that anyone can become a star. The wearing of luxury brands by reality TV participants has not always helped to enhance the brand, as in the case of Burberry being worn by a Big Brother contestant. Although media exposure can enhance fashion brand awareness, overexposure or the wrong kind of exposure can have a very detrimental effect. It is important to try to avoid the wrong kind of product exposure, although good product placement is a tried and tested marketing tool. Product placement, i.e. the planned wearing of a fashion item by a celebrity in a high visibility public situation, can be achieved either by direct payment or sometimes by the giving of a free sample. Product placement as a result of a long-term sponsorship agreement is an accepted practice, as in the case of the Engand rugby team and their sponsorship by Hackett men's clothing.

table **6.1** **Internationally significant awards ceremonies**

Month	Awards ceremony
February	Brit Awards
	BAFTA (Film Awards)
	Grammys
March	Academy Awards (Oscars)
April	BAFTA (Television Awards)
	MTV Fashionably Loud Europe
October	Mobo Awards
November	British Fashion Awards
	MTV Fashion Awards
December	Golden Globes

Cinema

Cinema has enjoyed a renaissance over the past twenty years, as the new multiscreen cinemas now offer a luxurious and inviting environment for cinemagoers. Cinema attendance was at its peak in 1947 in post-war Britain, and then suffered three decades of decline as TV and video became available to every home. However, the modern multiplex cinemas are far removed from the run-down cinemas of the 1950s, 1960s and 1970s. Showing a wide variety of fast-changing films, the modern cinema is a medium ideally suited to advertising fashion products on both a local and a national basis. This is a result of the relatively young profile of modern cinemagoers. It has been used effectively in the promotion of several US brands such as Nike and Levi's. Its overpowering sound and all-embracing visual impact makes it very captivating for audiences. Despite the growth in the ownership of DVD and home cinema systems, cinema still remains a powerful promotional medium for younger fashion consumers.

Cinema audiences currently tend to have an average viewing age of late teens to mid-twenties, making it ideally suited for communicating with this important market segment. The relatively high production costs of top-quality cinema adverts tend to make it a more suitable medium for large fashion organisations. It is another medium that is used for paid fashion product placement. Clothing used in films often can become a cult 'must-have' item, thereafter spawning a demand for what was originally simply a styling prop. An example of this is the fedora hat worn by Harrison Ford as Indiana Jones. Again, what celebrities are seen wearing in films can be a very powerful generator of fashion demand.

Broadcast and other electronic media

The digital technology used in radios and TVs, telephones, video and computers is leading to a co-ordinated form of media delivery and reception. Soon all our personal communications will come into one electronic information centre, rather than several. Already the videophone, video camera, TV and radio are available as one instrument. As we now fully enter the digital age, it is envisaged that virtually all media will broadcast using digital rather than analogue signalling. The advantage of digital signalling is its ability to carry greater amounts of information within a much narrower electromagnetic bandwidth. This has the benefit of providing faster information delivery, as well as enabling more signals to be sent at the same time, hence, for example, the high number of digital radio and TV stations. Enhanced video technology will undoubtedly improve the quality of electronically communicated fashion imagery, thus making remote fashion purchasing by consumers more likely.

Television

The British Broadcasting Corporation (BBC), along with several large commercial companies, dominated UK television viewing for the first fifty years of its existence from the mid-1930s. Using the large commercial TV stations for fashion advertising (even with their high viewer levels) is a fairly expensive proposition. As we enter the digital age, the number of TV and radio channels is increasing exponentially, causing audiences to fragment into smaller segments, leading inevitably to lower advertising costs. In general, radio and TV stations with large audiences command higher advertising revenues than smaller ones. (*Note*: see British Rates and Data (BRAD) for a station-by-station listing of TV advertising slots and their costs.) Television advertising is mainly used by large international brands for image-building and by large national retailers to communicate details of special promotions and offers. Small, locally based TV stations are now being granted transmitting licences. Small-scale local TV stations may well prove a very cost-effective form of communication for localised fashion businesses. Interactive terrestrial, cable and satellite television is being used to sell fashion, providing various methods of customer-ordering interactivity. Pioneering shopping channels such as QVC are taking an increasingly large share of the fashion market. More recent developments using digital cable television enable customers to transact directly via their television remote controls. With the improvement in the clarity of television images, together with the likely development of full 3D imaging, fashion advertising and promotion via television may be on the threshold of a new era.

Internet

The Internet in its own right is developing out of all recognition, with broadband delivering high-speed downloads, thus enabling fashion advertising and information, as well online purchasing, to reach a global audience. Although only a relatively small proportion of fashion clothing is currently sold via the Internet – under 10% of the total market – it is also importantly a key source for seeking information about stock availability and for making price comparisons. In this way it is playing an increasingly important role at the information-search stage of the consumer's buying process. The outlook for fashion taking a much larger percentage of sales via internet purchasers is excellent. However, there is still an intrinsic need for the fashion consumer to see, feel and try on fashion products they plan to purchase, making it unlikely that internet trading in fashion will ever gain a majority market share. In the US, fashion companies such as Cotton Traders run affiliate schemes which enable site owners of smaller personal sites to derive income as a result of carrying the advertising banners of the larger traders. The idea is that such banners generate 'click-throughs' to a specific trader's site. A small fee is payable to the smaller site owner, often a percentage of the sales generated as a result of the click-through. The whole idea of affiliated websites works well in the US, where many individuals have their own websites, but at present is not that significant in the UK.

Radio

Using radio advertising for fashion is a difficult proposition, simply because of the very visual nature of fashion products. Radio stations are proliferating as a result of digitalisation, again leading to generally lower listening figures – the latest internet radios receive 7000+ international stations delivered with perfect audio quality. When used by fashion marketers, radio is mainly for creating consumer awareness, for example during sale and promotional periods or for the opening of a new outlet. As digital technology advances, radio may have increasing potential as a fashion-advertising medium. The possibility of a radio set which provides regularly updated, still pictures on a small screen is already being suggested. As digital technologies – cameras, telephones, computers, radios and TVs – merge, our current box-like thinking will have to change accordingly. Radio listening, whilst fragmenting as a result of station proliferation, is in fact on a general upward trend. RAJAR (Radio Joint Audience Research) issued the following information in August 2007:

- radio listening rises to 45.6 million listeners per week;
- increase in radio listening via mobile phone;
- listening to podcasts via mp3 player up 40%.

This is mainly as a result of increased car ownership, car usage and traffic congestion, as well as an increasing number of young people listening to radio via their mobile phone. It has recently been estimated that the average British motorist is likely to spend up to three years of his/her life behind the wheel of a car. It is therefore probable that radio listening will grow accordingly.

Mobile phones

Fashion retailers are already experimenting with the sending of short message service (SMS) texts to targeted mobile-phone users, usually when the customer is in the vicinity of a shop or a shopping centre such as the Lakeside Shopping Centre in Essex. This service is used to notify customers about special deals, events or happenings. This new and ingenious location-finding technology enables companies to know the exact whereabouts of their customers, and it is also being used by the police to track down criminals. There is a huge potential for the more intelligent use of mobile phones, particularly the new generation of videophones.

Word of mouth (sometimes called 'viral marketing')

Until recently, marketers believed generally that word of mouth was outside their control and was a cost-free form of marketing communications. However, within the UK fashion industry this perception is rapidly changing. Word of mouth is now being spread by the use of 'seeding techniques'. Guerrilla marketing includes illegal activities including the unusual use of flyposting on street furniture, on the inside of toilet doors in clubs and other unusual but highly visible places. Although there is a charge for guerrilla flyposting, this more unusual form of communication tends to remain in the targeted consumer's mind longer than conventional advertising. By choosing specific venues and using a targeted message or tone, the communication is more likely to be seen by and to appeal to the targeted consumer, and to have a high impact and recall level. Guerrilla marketing communications techniques are still in their infancy – new ideas and methods develop daily. Getting 'more bang for your bucks' is the requirement of all modern fashion marketers. This area is covered in more detail in chapter 9.

Outdoor and ambient advertising

As society has become wealthier, personal travel has increased. This has encouraged the growth and development of outdoor advertising. The use of poster sites and electronic telecasters has enabled fashion advertisers to connect with people as they walk, drive or commute. Posters carried specifically on the back of specialist lorries (called mobiles) are often used on a localised basis to launch new fashion shops and/or products, and are often seen driving continuously around the main shopping areas. It is well known that the best way to advertise to young males is via posters, as this segment of the population spends a great deal of time in groups on the street. Commuters waiting in traffic jams may have nothing else to do but to sit and read posters, hence the placement of posters at bottleneck road junctions and intersections. The same occurs with rail and air travellers, who often spend time waiting for delayed connections.

Advertising livery is also being used by trains, lorries, buses and taxis, and is highly visible as the vehicles move from place to place. As society becomes increasingly mobile, the opportunities for new and innovative types of transport advertising grow accordingly. The Arcadia Group is one example of a fashion business that uses liveried vehicles to deliver to its 541 widely located Dorothy Perkins outlets, many receiving two or three deliveries a week. The huge advertising opportunities provided by these vehicle movements is immense.

Ambient advertising is a genre of outdoor advertising where adverts are placed in unusual or unexpected places. Fashion examples include the use of adverts on the back of London Tube ticket machines, as well as on the steps leading out of railways, Tube stations and bus depots. These often small and cleverly placed advertisements have the power to catch the viewer's eye, simply as result of their unique and often odd positioning. Their ability to attract attention is their main raison d'être, in a world where advertising overload makes it hard for adverts to stand out. Ambient advertising is often used as the major support tool in guerrilla marketing campaigns. Recently British Telecom launched a new type of public telephone booth that has one flat side to be used specifically for advertising.

The media selection planning process

All fashion advertising has the major purpose of raising awareness about a brand, product, retailer or related service. With so many different types of advertising media available, it is essential to consider carefully the advantages and limitations of each when planning an advertising campaign. Fashion is generally a very visually exciting concept and it is advantageous, therefore, to be able to show colour and style in great detail. However, for certain fashion communication tasks, some media are more suitable than others – radio, for example, would be ideally suited to announce the start of a fashion sale, but could not easily be used to describe styles, colours or trends.

In general there are four main issues to consider when selecting the most appropriate advertising media to use in any fashion marketing campaign:

1 **Reach, frequency and media impact** – relates to the percentage of people in the target market that you want to expose to an advert over a set period of time. Frequency is the number of times an average person in the target segment is likely to see an advertisement, and media impact is the qualitative value of the message exposure through the selected medium. Some media

have more impact for fashion than others, particularly where they can show colour, texture and movement. Reach multiplied by frequency is a formula used to create the performance indicator 'gross ratings points'.

2 **Type of media** – certain target groups are more exposed and can react to different media in different ways. Young people, for example, are notoriously hard to advertise to, owing to their declining levels of TV viewing, although their cinema attendance and internet usage have increased. The nature of the fashion product/service is often a major driver in this element of the decision process.

3 **Best media vehicle** – when advertising fashion products on television, it is best to place the advertising slot during or around fashion-relevant programmes, for example during popular music shows. The recent TV series *Sex in the City* was a very influential programme for generating new fashion looks, and would be highly suitable for the placement of fashion-related adverts. If a new fashion brand were being launched in the UK, it would be important to promote trade-buyer awareness, in which case advertising in a major trade magazine such as *Drapers* (see www.drapersonline.com) would be logical. The fortunes of the media change continuously and it is important for the fashion marketer to refer to BRAD, which is the best guide to media costs and their likely impact upon selected target groups.

4 **Media timing** – many fashion products are seasonal by nature, therefore making advertising planning and timing critical. Also, it is often necessary to launch a product into the market and to start advertising ahead of its general availability. This can help to build buyer awareness and create a sense of consumer anticipation. Advertising to support special in-store promotions generally needs to tie in closely with the visual merchandising calendar. Co-ordinating window and in-store displays with an advertising campaign helps to reinforce the advertising message and ultimately increase the impact upon the consumer. The need to co-ordinate advertising with all marketing activities to ensure maximum impact is a key responsibility of the fashion marketer.

Advertising campaigns can be either continuous or burst, in terms of the way in which adverts are scheduled. Sometimes media buyers and planners use a combination of both. A new fashion brand or product launch often requires a high number of early adverts to ensure that consumers are made aware of its presence – this is known as burst advertising. If a fashion brand, product or retailer is well-established, it is sometimes necessary to run a continuous or drip campaign, to keep the brand or product 'top of mind'. Many of the best-known international consumer products such as Coca-Cola continue to advertise to ensure that they remain top of mind. Global fashion enterprises are no different – companies like Nike and Gap advertise continually all over the world. Media planning and buying is normally carried out by specialist types of advertising agencies, or within the media-buying section of large, full-service agencies. It is technical and highly competitive, and its sole purpose is to get the best value out of the advertising monies available. Fashion businesses rarely become directly involved in the media-buying process.

The fashion advertising media and their relative usefulness for conveying fashion messages are described below:

- **Black-and-white publications** – ideally suited to black-and-white photographs, line drawings and text to convey basic factual information about styles, sales promotional information, new store openings and other general information. This mainly involves newspapers which have a short shelf life and which are normally read quickly and thrown away. As such, their advertising impact is very transient. Production costs are relatively low.
- **Coloured publications** – good for detailed coloured images, for brands and for showing high levels of fashion detail. These are mainly glossy magazines, which have a long shelf life and the potential for being passed on to others within the targeted segment. The wide variety of highly targeted colour magazines available in the UK makes the medium ideally suited to targeting selected market segments.
- **Cinema** – excellent for the transmission of strong audiovisual images to younger target audiences, although its messages are fast and transient. It is ideally suited for geographically targeted advertising campaigns, although it can also be used on a national basis. Production costs are relatively high.
- **Television** – good for detailed coloured images with movement and useful for brand and atmosphere advertising, although it is still a relatively expensive medium, delivering transient, short-lived messages. In the fashion context, larger retailers often use it for communicating sales promotional information. Interactive home-shopping TV stations can be used to sell and market fashion clothing. Interactive marketing companies such as QVC have enjoyed considerable success in selling a wide variety of fashion brands and products. Although customers are unable to feel or try on the merchandise, there is little difference between selling merchandise off-page (mail order) as against off-screen (interactive TV). Improving TV definition, especially 3D TV, may well make home fashion purchasing even more attractive.
- **Radio** – mainly used for passing on more basic information and for raising awareness about, for example, store openings and sales promotions. They have the ability to target either locally or nationally – ideal for getting to people on the move with personal and car radios. They have relatively low production costs, but are creatively limiting for fashion.
- **Internet** – used a great deal for comparison, education and some on-line shopping. The problem of consumers being unable to try on the product still appears to be a major barrier to major growth in the fashion context. It has proven an effective way to buy intimate apparel, such as ladies'

underwear and outsize clothing without embarrassment. Over the past few years Ann Summers has enjoyed huge growth in their internet trading.

- **Direct mail and catalogues** – printed and electronic catalogues create awareness and historically provided a credit facility before the widespread availability of credit cards. Their effectiveness relies heavily upon the quality of the database design and its maintenance, as well as upon the quality and design used to show and display the merchandise. Originally targeted at poorer socio-economic groups, or at geographically remote communities, fashion catalogues were once a key marketing communication tool for consumers disseminating the latest fashion look. Today's multitude of nationally based retail chains are having a detrimental effect upon mass-market catalogues. However, in more specialist and niche garment areas such as larger sizes, for example Bravissimo lingerie, they are enjoying steady growth. Some larger retailers produce edited seasonal catalogues that are distributed on either a mass or a targeted basis. Their aim is to act as both a promotional and a transactional medium. Paper-based catalogues generally have long lead times, making them unsuitable for high-fashion items targeted at younger people. It is a medium more suited to the marketing of more classic styles aimed at the older customer, for example Cotton Traders.

- **Outdoor and ambient advertising** – increasingly useful for connecting and advertising to youth markets, especially young males. High-quality images make it a versatile medium for fashion. When planning a poster campaign, the key factors to consider are the physical size of the site and the quality of the location. Location quality is driven mainly by the level of vehicular and pedestrian flow, as well as the site visibility and the area's socio-economic profile and/or relevance.There are many specialist poster site owners, who provide both local and national poster sites. Poster advertising and transport advertising are both growing as traveller and passenger numbers increase. Nearly every type of transportation system offers a range of advertising approaches, from completely liveried trains to carriage and platform posters. Ambient advertising is being used in new and innovative ways, especially in connection with guerrilla marketing, and is therefore highly compatible with young fashion. Reasonably long lead times are needed to set up outdoor poster-transport or ambient advertising.

Concluding comments on the selection of fashion advertising media

In many non-fashion product areas, the distinction between the use of media solely for advertising and its use for direct selling is blurred. Sales promotion and direct selling are often seen as separate marketing tools. However, they will often use the same media, but with different final business and marketing objectives in mind. As both fashion retailers and fashion consumers fragment, fashion marketing will need to use specialist and better-focused marketing communication techniques both to advertise and to sell to their customers.

With the fragmentation of the media, audiences have become smaller. Advertising campaigns and strategies need, therefore, to become more focused at the micro level. Analysing, planning, implementing and controlling increasingly complex advertising campaigns requires a very detailed management approach to ensure that a campaign is delivering an effective and efficient outcome.

If advertising is to work effectively, it must have a strong message and identity. It is important never to spend on advertising without continually researching its effectiveness. Passion alone is not enough to ensure that advertising is supporting the achievement of planned marketing communications objectives.

Evaluating fashion advertising

During their careers in the fashion industry, both authors have been aware of fashion businesses that have embarked upon advertising campaigns without really setting any clear business objectives. Fashion companies have been known to spend their advertising budgets simply on a 'feel-good' basis. Fashion executives, with little consideration given to a tactical or strategic rationale, often undertake advertising for reasons of personal self-aggrandisement. No advertising should ever be considered until there are clearly planned marketing and marketing communications objectives.

Marketing objectives commonly include sales plans, market share, distribution, market penetration, etc., all of which are objective, quantifiable and measurable. However, marketing communications objectives tend to refer to how the communication will affect or impact upon the minds of the target audience, for example levels of consumer awareness, attitude changes, product/brand/service interest and the likelihood of trial or purchase.

The use of advertising should not be considered without first measuring the levels of consumer awareness, perception or understanding of a fashion product. Understanding consumer perceptions and awareness at the start of any campaign is essential. It is important that marketing research should measure and evaluate where a fashion business is, in order to establish the starting-point on the route to achieving marketing communications objectives. The evaluation of advertising and marketing communications before, during and after an advertising campaign ensures that the planned marketing tactics and/or strategies are the correct ones to achieve the overall objectives. If they are not being achieved, then clearly tactics and/or strategy may need to be reviewed and modified accordingly. It is very unlikely that any marketing or advertising strategy will work perfectly first time. When planning a marketing communications campaign, there will almost certainly be a need for changes and alterations to be made. There is no such thing as the perfect marketing or marketing communications plan.

Testing fashion advertising

When undertaking any fashion advertising campaign, it is necessary to ensure that the communication will work effectively, and that ultimately the advertising is helping to improve sales and bottom-line profitability. The major tests that need to be carried out before, during and after an advertising campaign are listed below

- **Direct rating test** – A panel is asked to rate one advert against other similar ads for similar products.
- **Portfolio test** – A group of targeted consumers are shown a relatively large portfolio of similar adverts and are then subjected to a recall test. Their level of recall is a good indicator as to the likely future impact of an advert.
- **Laboratory test** – Where a group of individuals are tested for physiological reactions to reading or looking at adverts. Heart rate, blood pressure, perspiration levels and pupil dilation are good indicators of whether an advert is having an impact upon the receiver. Unfortunately measuring these reactions is no certain indicator of the potential level of impact or recall that an ad might have.

- **Post-testing fashion advertisements** – post-testing may be carried out in either of the following ways:

  - **Recall test** – asking people who have been generally exposed to publications and TV to try and recall what adverts have stuck in their minds. These tests are sometimes given using specific advertisements as a prompt to aid the respondent's recall – this is called assisted recall. This can be a good measure of the level of impact that a particular advertisement may have had upon a consumer. However, the actual creative content of an advert can sometimes overpower the respondent's recall of the product and/or service being advertised. Many famous award-winning advertisements through time have been guilty of this, for example the Benetton advertisements featuring shocking events/ situations of world significance actually obscured the message that the organisation was trying to convey, i.e. that it sold good, well-made and fashionably coloured casual clothing. Humour has been proved to be a good messaging tactic to grab consumer attention and to assist advertisement recall. There have been few examples of fashion businesses using humour in their advertisements.
  - **Recognition test** – target consumers who read a certain publication or watch a certain channel are simply asked to recall which advertisers and advertisements they can recall. This can be useful to compare one advertiser with another, within one specific publication or programme. The results of this type of post-testing enable advertisers to see just how much impact an advertisement has had. Usually this type of test will be

carried out mid-campaign, allowing the advertiser to change creative direction, should their advertisement not be achieving the planned marketing communications objectives. Changing the creative platform midstream can often prove expensive, but it is necessary in the long run to achieve marketing success.

In any fashion marketing scenario, where advertising is likely to play an essential part of the marketing communications strategy, it is important for fashion marketers always to set aside part of their planned advertising budget for research into just how effective their campaign is/has been. Without this sort of measurement, there is simply no effective indicator, except for hopefully improved sales in the longer term, by which to judge advertising activity.

Setting advertising expenditure budgets in the fashion industry

Once a fashion business has clearly defined marketing communications and advertising objectives, it is important to plan the level of advertising expenditure that will be needed to meet those objectives. Most advertising expenditure is, in the longer term, aimed at increasing consumer demand for the product and/ or service in question. In reality, many fashion organisations (both large and small) set their advertising budget simply based upon what they can afford, trade norms or what their competitors spend. However, it is a good idea to consider all of the following factors before undertaking the advertising-budget planning process and settling upon a budget.

- **Current or expected level of market share** – businesses with a higher market/brand share generally require/use a higher percentage of expenditure than those with a lower share. When trying to build market share from a low base, high percentage levels of advertising expenditure in relation to sales are usually essential. Once a brand starts to gain awareness, word of mouth is probably the most powerful way of spreading brand awareness. With so many new brands emerging on to the UK fashion scene, the costs involved in creating and establishing new fashion brands are increasing.
- **Current level of differentiation of a fashion product or service** – if you have a unique product that is highly recognisable, understandable and therefore sought after, it is likely that you will require a much lower level of overall advertising expenditure. In the fashion industry, consumers and trade buyers are always on the look-out for new and exciting brands. High design and product detail are often the key ingredients in their decision-to-purchase process.
- **Current stage of a product in the fashion PLC** – during the early stages of the PLC it is normal to apply high advertising expenditure, in order to gain consumer awareness. However, once the product has matured, the need for advertising diminishes because the product's reputation is already implanted in the consumer's mind. Sometimes, at this stage

in the PLC, small improvements, modifications or an extension to the range are used to extend and possibly to revive an ailing brand. In these cases, advertising expenditure will again be increased to levels that fulfil the market and marketing communications objectives of the fashion organisation.

- **Current level of competition and market confusion** – in today's increasingly crowded fashion environment, there is a huge amount of clutter and confusion. To undertake any type of fashion marketing communication is becoming more and more expensive. It is therefore increasingly important to have fashion products and services with unique selling propositions that enable them to stand out from the crowd. Having a bland fashion range is now a recipe for disaster. The new mantra is that 'the brand has eclipsed the bland'. There are many bland fashion retailers still continuing to try and sell the same old-fashioned product, often at increasingly uncompetitive prices. These organisations have marketing myopia and will not survive in the long term. Using publications such as the *Retail Pocket Book* by A. C. Nielsen, it is possible retrospectively to calculate competitors' levels of advertising expenditure as a percentage of retail turnover to assist with the advertising budgeting process.
- **Level of fashion advertising frequency needed** – in some markets and with certain products, there is an increased requirement to keep repeating an advertising message if a fashion product/service is to stay at the forefront of the consumer's mind. This often happens during annual sale periods, when fashion retailers vie for each other's bargain-conscious customers. Other well-known brands and retailers (usually of higher-priced products) undertake shorter bursts of more prestigious advertising, often to announce the new season's range.

At the end of the day, it is very difficult for any fashion business to be prescriptive in terms of the level of advertising expenditure it needs to apply at any specific point during the trading year. The fashion trade is notoriously volatile and so is susceptible to unplanned external influences beyond the control of even the best-planned fashion marketer. Although planning in a more long-term and strategic way would appear to fit in better with larger fashion organisations, the reality of the fashion business is that many organisations try to plan strategically but, in reality, react tactically because of the levels of market volatility.

Managing fashion advertising in the UK

Most fashion organisations employ one of three major methods to manage their advertising:

1. **In-house** – where a business uses its own advertising/marketing department to manage the full creative process and then to arrange, schedule and book the required media.

2 **Out-house** – where both creative advertising specialists and media-buying specialists are hired on a contractual basis to achieve the most professional result.

3 **Combination** – where there is a joint use of in- and out-house expertise, often justified by cost-saving rationalisation or external specialist skills, for example creative work undertaken in-house and media-buying done out-house.

In-house advertising requires a high level of specialist expertise and may divert the organisation away from its core raison d'être – fashion. Large retailers usually have enough human and financial resources to undertake this. However where high levels of creative thinking (especially with prestigious brands) are required, large companies often prefer to use external advertising agencies. Not only are they likely to be more creative, but they are also likely to be far more objective about a brand or product. It is essential for any fashion business to understand consumer perceptions and perspectives with regard to its own fashion offer. Being employed/involved internally by/with a fashion business can often blinker the individual, who can sometimes be mesmerised by current corporate thinking and viewpoints. Thinking rationally and objectively about a brand and its positioning in the consumer's mind is often more easily achieved by using an external agency.

Larger fashion organisations sometimes undertake a boutique selection of advertising services – doing their own creative thinking and then hiring specialist advertising-buying agencies to secure the best and most logical advertising slots and rates, or vice versa. There is no best approach; the decision may well be driven by the 'marketing maturity' of the senior management. Readers of this book are advised to acquaint themselves with BRAD, the UK's key publication listing the costs of placing an advertisement in virtually every conceivable medium, from hiring the side of an airship to covering a London taxi with your advertisement. The cost of advertising in/on every publication and TV and radio station is also clearly listed. Advertising rates for prime-time TV and prime editions of newspapers are clearly explained. The rates quoted cover only the placing of the advert; they do not include any necessary production costs. Taking fashion models to an exotic film location is no cheap affair, especially if the weather is poor and shooting takes much longer than anticipated. Buying advertising slots in any medium is a skilled process: media buyers aim to secure for their clients the best chance of exposing the advertisement to the highest number of targeted consumers at the lowest cost. Media-buying is an extremely specialised area of marketing activity.

Using advertising effectively in any UK fashion business is a costly process. A simple, one-page colour advertisement placed in a key edition of the prestigious UK *Vogue* magazine might easily cost £30,000, with the actual photographic shoot likely to cost around £12,000! The total cost of say £42,000, would, based on the average 8% net profit retained by the UK fashion retailer, need to generate extra sales of in excess of £500,000 to cover the cost. As readers will appreciate, it is almost impossible to ascribe extra sales to specific advertisements – advertising is often done with the objective of simply raising awareness or of making consumers more likely to purchase a fashion product at a later date.

Direct marketing

Direct marketing can be defined as any form of direct communication with a customer, aimed at creating a direct response that leads to a long-term relationship. Direct mail, one of the most widely used tools of direct marketing, is sometimes wrongly described as junk mail. There has been a strong growth in this medium, as a result of the overall decline of both large-scale TV viewing and printed media readership. Gathering addresses and contact details of specified target customers and groups enables businesses to target more accurately their consumers or business customers. As direct mail is so focused, there is less wastage than when using the major advertising media. Organisations can either create their own customer database over time, or buy in professionally built lists of relevant consumers or businesses.

Only a minority of fashion retailers effectively capture and use customer purchasing data, which are normally gathered from store credit, charge and loyalty cards. Fashion businesses that transact via the Internet are easily able to capture customer data. Data are often stored for many years to build a clear picture of individual customers' purchasing patterns, which can be used to target them more effectively in the future. Better individual targeting means less wasted marketing effort and expenditure. Direct marketing can be a fast and very accurate medium, often used to communicate relatively quickly with a highly targeted group. Untargeted, general mail drops can be used effectively on a local basis to promote and advertise local fashion retail businesses, but the less targeted the drop, the lower the response rate.

Direct marketing can also be used effectively for contacting targeted businesses and consumers via e-mail or by telephone. In the UK, consumers are able to filter out any unsolicited direct mail or telephone marketing by registering with either the Mailing or Telephone Preference Schemes. These screening systems allow selected addresses and/or telephone numbers to be deleted from all contact lists and databases (see mpsonline.org.uk and tpsonline. org.uk). This is a free facility that has recognition across the direct marketing industry and it is very effective.

The increasing use of the Internet has created huge levels of unsolicited e-mails, referred to as spam, advertising a wide variety of products. These are often poorly targeted and unlikely to have much impact. Well-targeted e-mails to quality customer lists could be used very effectively in fashion marketing, although currently most direct marketing used by the fashion industry is paper-based. La Redoute (a catalogue-based business) is one of a handful of international fashion businesses making effective use of internet-enabled direct marketing. The best customer lists are created using internal data-gathering procedures, although it is possible to use list-broking agencies that create and sell lists of likely prospective customers. The care with which such commercially available lists are built needs to be meticulous if they are to work effectively and yield high response rates.

The success of direct marketing depends upon the design, maintenance and logical use of databases. As computing power increases and becomes increasingly intelligent, fashion retailers will be able to more fully understand their customers' purchasing habits and patterns through time. This, in turn, has the potential to enable them more effectively and accurately to target personalised marketing communications to specific customers. Mass enclosures of irrelevant information to store-card holders is unfortunately the current norm for the direct marketing activity of most fashion retailers. Direct marketing is a powerful communication tool, but requires careful, targeted and intelligent use.

Personal selling

When talking about marketing activity, it is common for people to assume that marketing is synonymous with advertising. In fact, advertising in simply one of the tools available to marketers to achieve their planned marketing strategy. However, when we compare the UK fashion industry with other sectors, the overall level of advertising expenditure, compared to that of other marketing activities, is really quite low. In the layperson's mind, because advertising is 'obvious' it assumes a mantle of importance far beyond the reality. Personal selling, particularly in fashion retailing, is in fact probably the most significant marketing activity in terms of overall financial and human-resources expenditure.

Personal selling is the front-line activity of fashion. It is here that the consumer meets the human face of a fashion organisation embodied in the person selling to and assisting the customer. We all have stories (particularly in the context of UK fashion retailing) where we have been served by a disinterested person with little or no knowledge of the product. This is typical of many areas of UK industry where front-line service seems to be in terminal decline. Unlike in the US and most of Europe, people involved in any form of selling activity are undervalued. Selling is seen, even by the new middle class, as something to look down upon. Americans involved in selling – or indeed French waiters – are proud of their work and the role they fulfil. The British distaste for anything to do with service may lie in our own social history, where many were condemned to a life of domestic service for very low wages. That particular debate is beyond the scope of this book.

How to encourage skilled, motivated, intelligent and enthusiastic graduates to join the UK fashion industry in a selling capacity remains an almost insoluble problem. Until fashion retailing is recognised as a critical and important part of the economy, the situation is likely to remain unchanged. Some fashion colleges are now adding fashion marketing to what was a totally design-biased curriculum. An understanding of retail management and the retail process is almost essential for anyone entering any part of the fashion industry in any marketing capacity. Enthusiasm and a clear understanding of fashion retail management will help those at all levels of the fashion industry to bring their product successfully to market. Relying upon innovative design alone is not enough to ensure success within the UK fashion industry. The high business-failure rate among our best fashion graduate designers may well indicate a need to educate designers about the importance of marketing and selling their products and not simply teaching them design skills.

Sales promotion

Sales promotion is a tool that provides incentives for customers to buy. It is the one tool available to marketers that will ensure a sale. The incentives can be loosely categorised as those that add value through giving something away with a product and those that offer a discount on a purchase.

Sales promotion is usually used as a very tactical tool in fashion, with the specific objective of encouraging the consumer to buy now. It is used more as a tool for B2C than for B2B marketing. Unlike advertising, which aims at developing longer-term consumer relationships, sales promotion aims at getting the consumer to buy now, rather than in the future. Advertising is not used as extensively in the fashion industry as is sales promotion; with the huge emphasis on fashion retailing, rather than fashion manufacturing, a majority of UK fashion marketing expenditure is spent on all aspects of sales promotion. It is hard to analyse exactly what percentage of the total marketing expenditure is spent on each of the principal fashion marketing tools, but sales promotion may well be in excess of 70% of all national fashion marketing expenditure.

Sales promotion in the fashion context can be used to achieve several different types of sales-stimulation objectives. In main these objectives can be categorised as follows:

1   to stimulate consumer trial;
2   to improve the purchase or repurchase rate;
3   to cement long-term customer relationships.

All of these still basically aim at stimulating sales, although each for a slightly different purpose. Conventional marketing thought tends to see sales promotion as a very short-term marketing tool, which, if used wrongly or for too long, can actually damage a brand and ultimately consumer loyalty; advertising, conversely, works by building and defending brand loyalty. It is often the case that the more prestigious fashion brands tend to rely more heavily upon advertising, whilst the less prestigious and often cheaper fashion brands and retailers rely almost solely upon sales promotion. The reality is that even top fashion brands and retailers use sales promotion as a tactical way of clearing problematic lines during the biannual sale periods, despite trying, during the rest of the year, to use advertising for the purpose of brand-building. Even top stores such as Harrods have twice-yearly sale periods, despite trying not to discount fashion product outside these periods.

The use of sales promotion tools by the UK fashion industry

There are various ways in which sales promotion can be used by fashion businesses, in both the B2C and the B2B context. Over recent years, fashion sales promotion methodology has developed many new and innovative approaches – it is an area of considerable potential for creative fashion marketers of the future. In general, sales promotion techniques are either price- or premium-driven.

B2C fashion sales promotion techniques are as follows:

The price-driven techniques are:

1 **Selling-price reductions** – probably the main sales promotion tool used by fashion retailers across the globe – when prices are reduced, customers tend to buy more. Price reductions can easily be used either for clearing problematic fashion styles, colours, bands or ranges or for stimulating increased demand for a line. In the second instance, the aim of reducing the price is simply to reduce stockholdings back to the level required to meet the forward customer demand. Price reductions are normally achieved by using an absolute discount level (e.g. £5 off) or a percentage reduction. Normally the main discount percentages used in fashion retailing are 10%, 25%, $33^{1}/_{3}$%, 50%, or 70% off. Most customers, even if arithmetically challenged, can understand an absolute discount and the usual percentage discount levels. Unusual percentages may be difficult for some consumers to understand, e.g. $34^{1}/_{2}$% off. The level of discount given generally relates to the level of the problem – a very poor-selling line would need to be discounted heavily if there were to be any chance of clearing it. When a fashion business is simply trying to stimulate demand on mildly overstocked lines, then a 10% discount may well be enough to do the trick.

2 **BOGOFs (buy one get one free) or 'two-fors' (two for the price of one)** – both are methods of incentivising a consumer to buy more than they had intended. Typically this type of promotion is used either to clear really problematic lines or to be incredibly sales-generative. Giving the fashion consumer two for the price of one is exactly the same as offering two at half price. The discount and off-price retailers are the masters of BOGOF. If used with the support of good window and in-store graphics, this is one of the most potent sales promotion tools for moving large quantities of stock or achieving high sales. A derivative of BOGOF is the multiple-pack discount (sometimes used on underwear and hosiery), such as three for the price of two – this of course equals a saving of $33^{1}/_{3}$% to the consumer. All of these variants encourage high-volume unit purchasing. BOGOFs may also be used to encourage consumers to trial variations on a product. For example, some cosmetics companies use a BOGOF and banded-pack approach to

strap a new scent version of a soap product to an existing one for sale at the single unit price. Consumers are effectively getting two soap products for the price of one, but the second is a new version.

3   **Loyalty cards** – a recent innovation over the past ten years, loyalty cards were first used in this country by the food supermarkets. The idea was to encourage consumers to save points, in order to achieve a future saving on either the retailer's own products or on other sought-after gifts, such as travel, holidays or electronics. There are many other types of products against which points can be redeemed – the choice is now almost boundless. Simple cards that discount every nth purchase have been used by many young fashion retailers (e.g. buy four items over £10 and get the fifth item under £20 free). Where cards are electronically able to capture full details of the fashion consumer's purchasing pattern, as well as their address and contact details, the intelligent use of the data stored on the card could enable the retailer to make direct contact with specific consumers and to target them with specially personalised sales promotion offers. So far, the authors can cite very few highly intelligent uses of customer data by fashion retailers across the entire fashion spectrum. Better use of consumer data in the future will be a major direction for fashion marketing over the next decade.

The premium driven techniques are:

1   **Trial samples** – used extensively in the cosmetic and fragrance markets. Here the consumer may simply be offered a free sample, on the basis that most consumers will be more likely to buy a product if they have actually tried it. Trial is not used in most garment areas of the fashion industry, simply because of the relatively high prices of individual garments.

2   **Free gifts** – often used to increase consumer demand. Normally a higher-priced fashion item will be sold with a giveaway free gift, for example a free pair of sunglasses with every item of swimwear sold. If, for example, a swimsuit cost £39 and a pair of sunglasses, retailing at £10, were given away, the actual discount would appear to the consumer to be the equivalent of just under 20% for the two (cost of both being £39 rather than £49). In reality, the sunglasses may only have cost the retailer a little over £2 and could well be a slow-selling, problematic style. Therefore the sales promotion deal represents only a minimal real cost for the retailer and may well have accelerated swimwear sales, as well as having helped clear a problematic line. This is an innovative way of achieving several sales promotion objectives at the same time. Very often the 'free gift' is of very little real value, but is perceived by the consumer as being worth much more than it really is. Fashion magazines will often attach a free gift, for example a make-up bag, to the front cover – this type of offer is referred to as a 'cover mount'.

3   **Extra for free** – sometimes, especially with underwear and hosiery, a multiple pack will be bound together, offering an extra item free. This is a great psychological spur to get the consumer to react positively at the POS.

4   **Competitions** – any form of competition, most of which require an element of skill on the part of a player. An example would be to buy swimwear at retailer A, answer some simple questions about the range and then enter a prize draw for a first-class cruise – the player will need to state why retailer A's range is so good, thus turning this into game of skill rather than simply luck. This gets around aspects of the UK's rather complex gaming laws.

B2B sales promotion techniques

Most fashion manufacturers and brand owners generally have the ultimate focus of marketing their products to either fashion wholesalers or fashion retailers. The types of sales promotion tool available for fashion B2B marketing are fewer and quite different from those employed in B2C. The main tools available for this task are described below:

Straight price discounts – in this case the larger the order, the larger the discount offered by the manufacturer or brand owner. These increasing discounts are allowable as a result of the simple economic theory relating to the economies of scale. The more units of a product that are made, the greater the decrease in the unit cost of production. However, the overuse of discounting may undermine brand values in the longer term, i.e. people will wait for discount periods and never buy at full price.

Personal or team incentives – with the agreement of the client (usually a retailer), the manufacturer or brand offers incentives to individuals, teams or branches on the basis of selling the most or of meeting a pre-agreed sales objective. The term often used to describe this type of incentive is called a 'spiff'. In isolation, and if not well controlled, such events can distract selling teams from their general selling objectives, to the overall detriment of the retail business. They need careful planning, monitoring and control on the part of the retailer if they are not to create internal dissension and discontent. The incentives given to selling staff can range from cash prizes to the simple psychological reward of being voted best salesperson, with the public award of a trophy or certificate. Money is not always the best form of reward, with time off now being seen as one of the best prizes in today's time-starved world.

Fashion retailers do not always welcome the direct incentivisation of their selling staff via a third party, sometimes preferring to get general promotional support – such as for advertising or in-store display – rather than sales promotion support. To ensure that a specific fashion brand is displayed in some special way that makes it stand out from the others, brand owners will sometimes provide special fixtures and fittings free to a retailer. This sort of sales promotion support may go as far as to create a uniquely fitted department, designed specifically to draw the consumers' attention to the brand enhancing it and making it stand out from the crowd.

There are some who would argue that brand-funded display schemes are not solely sales-promotional in intent, but also a strategic way of ensuring that the brand is stocked and fronted by the retailer. In this instance it is helping several key marketing and marketing communications objectives at the same time. These schemes are expensive to arrange, manage and control and may have a payback period which extends over several years.

Public relations (PR)

PR is arguably the most important communications tool available to fashion marketers. It shares some characteristics with advertising in that it uses the same media to achieve similar objectives. For example, both are highly effective methods of raising awareness and generating shifts in the attitudes of consumers towards products and brands. However, they are used differently. Whereas advertisers will pay to place an advert in a specific publication, PR will aim to secure an editorial on the product or brand, which normally includes an image. Advertising and PR are frequently designed to work in an integrated way. Controversial advertising such as the Reebok sneakers 'I am what I am' campaign, featuring the rapper 50 Cent, and French Connection's FCUK campaign were designed to generate acres of press coverage following the release of the adverts.

What is PR?

PR is officially defined by the UK Institute of Public Relations (IPR) as follows: 'Public relations . . . is the planned and sustained effort to establish and maintain goodwill and mutual understanding between an organisation and its publics' (www.cipr.co.uk). In the context of fashion PR a public is virtually any external body, organisation or group that has a direct or indirect interest in what a fashion organisation is doing. In addition to consumers, the main publics of fashion PR are:

1 the fashion media – fashion editors and journalists;
2 the financial media – financial editors and journalists;
3 the general public – especially customers and local communities;
4 the staff – important always to keep them informed;
5 the industry – brands, manufacturers, retailers and support services;
6 government –local and national;
7 pressure groups – e.g. those focused on ethical issues of exploitation (cheap labour, the sexualisation of children, modelling – the size zero debate) and specific-issue groups such as PETA (People for the Ethical Treatment of Animals), sustainable fashion, etc.;
8 trade unions – mainly in manufacturing and retail sectors.

The IPR and other organisations provide lengthy definitions of PR, which outline the full extent of its scope. However, a concise definition which reflects its role in the fashion industry is 'a marketing activity that generates publicity'.

Readers should be aware that although PR can influence and shape people's view and perceptions, it can only do so through the publicity generated by its activities. As such it is the outputs of PR activities that are of most interest to marketers since they are relatively low-cost per output (and in some cases completely free) when compared with advertising and other forms of mass-market-awareness communications tools.

Is PR part of marketing?

Some fashion commentators are uncomfortable with the notion of PR being conceptualised as a function of marketing. Whilst the authors do not hold a particularly strong view on this, most fashion brands and retailers regard PR as a function that delivers specific communications objectives in parallel with advertising, direct marketing and sales promotion, to achieve overall marketing objectives such as increased market share and sales.

In fashion, PR has a unique and disproportionately significant role in communicating both product and brand messages in a season. This is partly because enormous opportunities exist to supply the fashion-hungry print media with seasonal stories and product samples to show their target readers.

As a result of the recent explosive growth of consumerism that has now become such an important and powerful driver of developed economies, fashion, clothing and textiles (in all their facets) have become a significant part of people's daily diet of news and views. What celebrities choose wear to awards ceremonies often appears to have greater social significance than major world events. The growth of reality TV and the general dumbing-down of programme content has put the spotlight more on what people wear than what they say and do! Similarly, a review of the editorial and reporting content of business publications and reviews reveals an inordinate level of interest in the business performance of luxury brands and high-street retailers. In the past, the general public was not often directly involved with the important aspects of the UK economy of the time, such as coal-mining and shipbuilding. As the old industries have lost their economic significance to the growth of consumerism, more people are involved directly with the economy, simply as a result of being shoppers.

Traditionally, UK fashion companies have not spent as much on advertising as FMCG brands. To some extent this is because branding in fashion companies is a relatively recent strategy of fashion marketing activity when compared with the FMCG sector. Further, it is the fashion retailers and some mass-market designers who really benefit from advertising, as opposed to the fashion suppliers, who tend to be unbranded manufacturers or agents.

The success of communications tools such as PR and visual merchandising in communicating to consumers has, to a large extent, reduced the need for fashion retailers to advertise. If the main and commonly accepted functions of advertising are to raise awareness of a brand or product and to influence customers' attitudes positively, then both can be achieved more cheaply by other means. The almost unique infrastructure of UK high streets has provided stores with a captive public for its brand-promoting window displays and store fascias.

Cost–benefits of PR

PR can deliver a relatively low cost per output of publicity compared with advertising since the principal cost is a fixed one connected to the employment of an in-house PR function or a retained agency. Good PR staff who generate significant publicity are, therefore, more cost-effective. The cost of PR will vary hugely according to the business model of the fashion company. For example, a fashion brand will normally be different from a retailer brand in terms of its communications budget since it does not have a large store network through which to communicate with consumers.

Since the outputs of PR activity, such as editorials in the press, are produced by journalists, the content and brand representation is often seen as impartial compared with brand advertising. This benefits brands since specialist fashion journalists and media are considered authoritative. Many fashion organisations employ press-cutting agencies, which monitor all the printed and broadcast media (for a fee) and usually produce a weekly/monthly press-cuttings book. Some people argue that Google News provides a media-monitoring service by allowing queries on the number of times a keyword has been mentioned in thousands of publications, based on the publications' websites. However, specialised services will very often provide a much more reliable service based on trusted publications and human reading.

In 2005, companies such as Global News Intelligence began using Java-based artificial intelligence. This can automate the process of coding and analyse media content, even for tone and sentiment. This type of technology is known as meta-analysis and will have huge potential for monitoring the media to measure the PR output.

The PR process

Although there are many ways in which PR activity may generate publicity for fashion businesses, there is generally a common set of shared activities that all fashion PR uses. In this sense we can talk of a process. This is further supported by the fashion calendar that sets dates for important PR events such as press days at regular and commonly adopted points throughout the year. This is explained a little later.

Frequently the aim of a PR campaign is to generate publicity on the back of other opportunities arising from newsworthy stories. Stories may have a range of sources, including:

> • company results (e.g. LVMH (Moët Hennessy Louis Vuitton) half-yearly profits);

- guerilla marketing stunts (e.g. '118 runners' standing out in the crowd);
- celebrities signed up to design a range for a brand (e.g. Kate Moss);
- the commissioning by a brand of a piece of trivial market research on a seasonal issue to capture news headlines.

In each case there is a chance that the PR activity will generate publicity across a range of media including (in the UK) non-commercial media such as the BBC. In that sense PR can reach media that other marketing tools cannot (to paraphrase an old slogan from a lager commercial).

How does PR work?

At the most basic level, PR has a reciprocal relationship with the fashion media. Journalists need fashion stories, editorials, features and products to include in their magazines or other media to satisfy readers' fashion interests. Similarly, fashion PRs need media coverage to communicate with their brands' consumers. It is a symbiotic relationship – each likely to gain from the other's existence.

A fashion PR will then set about developing and nurturing relationships with fashion journalists to ease the process of securing the coverage they need in the media they want. To do this they use a variety of tools.

PR tools

Press packs – these are folders that contain information intended for the press and are usually sent out ahead of the season, often given out to the press and the media at special pre-season press fashion shows or press days.

Look books – these are working photographic style books that clearly show key looks and styles, each garment being clearly numbered and referenced to enable the media to call samples to their offices for photo or styling shoots.

prshots.com – this is a specialist website that allows the media to download fashion images – to quote their website, 'PRshots is a free-to-use library of PR and editorial images from numerous partner companies including Debenhams, Laura Ashley, Arcadia, The Body Shop, Diageo and many others – the more we get the better for everyone. Our aim is to provide journalists and picture editors with a one-stop shop for images and company/product information'. Fashion journalists in the digital age working remotely and away from their offices can see the latest looks online.

News releases – one-off releases about specific events which are sent out to fashion journalists – often with ready-made photos or website links.

Sample collection – The press offices of the large fashion brands and retailers keep a sample selection of the key looks, readily available for photo shoots well ahead of the season. Keeping control of samples is a difficult job, with samples often being in demand by the media at the same time. Keeping the press well supplied with samples is critical if a fashion company wants good media exposure.

PR events – fashion shows

Press days

Three times a year there is a week set aside by fashion retailer brands and agreed in the annual fashion calendar for press days to promote their ranges to the fashion press. Brands invite journalists to see new collections at their PR office (or agency) or at some external location according to the budget and market positioning of the brand. Press packs, look books and gifts are given to journalists and the main point of a press day is to enthuse journalists about the forthcoming products.

Days are held in:

● April – for autumn;
● July – for Christmas;
● November – for the spring (the following year).

This allows for the different lead times of the media.

Fashion shows

A fashion show is a marketing event that is designed to convey fashion designs and marketing messages to its audience, which comprises mainly the press and buyers. Events marketing has its place in the promotional or communications mix, but it is normally eclipsed by the more commonly used tools of advertising, PR and sales promotion. These are the three big integrated tools for most mass-market businesses. Fashion, however, is slightly different. PR is arguably the most important and effective communications tool for mass-market fashion owing to the relationship between fashion brands (including retailer brands) and the press and to the perceived impartiality of the media. The subject of fashion provides newspapers and magazines with a glamorous topic that readers can find interesting and relate to. Celebrity and fashion features mixed with editorials can not only increase circulation but also aid in the market positioning of a publication. In all kinds of fashion-related consumer publications, branded products are included to illustrate a story or feature. The products are typically sourced from brands' own marketing or PR functions or retained PR agencies. The press need real products and brands to reflect the changing reality of fashion for their readers.

Advertising is much more common at the premium and luxury end of the fashion market since luxury fashion houses are very concerned with creating, communicating and evolving an exclusive brand image. The ratio of advertising spend to sales revenues is typically higher for luxury brands than for mass-market retailer brands.

Fashion shows are very important marketing events that help both new designers and established fashion brands to communicate the next set of ideas, brand positioning and product ranges to audiences of the press and buyers. Fashion shows may be used in a variety of ways. At the mass-market level it is common for retailers and small brands to use fashion shows in-house to showcase the new season's ranges to retail management and staff. At a more exclusive level, fashion designers and brands will use the biannual RTW fashion weeks to host runway shows that are targeted at the international press and buyers. Such shows have two main goals, which are to gain PR editorials from the invited press/media and to sell the collections to attending buyers. The latter may be from international department stores or boutiques. The shows enable designers and brands to obtain 'free' coverage of the shows, as fashion journalists review the event and frequently focus on particular aspects, including the products, models and creative direction conveyed in a show. The press coverage normally focuses on a story relating to the designer, brand or fashion themes paraded down runways, as opposed to specifics about products and prices. This is because the shows tend to be about five months ahead of the season they relate to (i.e. Sept/Oct RTW shows are for the following spring/summer season that retails between February and June).

Fashion weeks

These are the principal venues for design houses and luxury brands to show their ranges for a forthcoming season. Spring/summer shows for RTW designer 'brands' are held in September and October of the previous year. Autumn/winter or fall (US) shows are held in February of the same year as the season to which they relate (autumn). Although there are many RTW fashion weeks hosted around the world, the four principal shows are held in the cities of New York, London, Milan and Paris – in that order.

As all the major international fashion cities now host lavish biannual ready-to-wear shows, there is an increasing pressure on the organisers to justify the costs of these shows to both designers and brands. To a large extent each city hosts the RTW shows of its national designers and brands. For example, Milan hosts Italian heritage luxury brands including Prada, Gucci and Armani, Paris hosts Chanel, Louis Vuitton, Christian Dior, and so on. New York is packed out with the larger signature brands (America's brands tend to be more modern, with less heritage than those in Europe), including Calvin Klein and Ralph Lauren. A common element shared by the majority of the luxury fashion brands which participate in these fashion weeks is that they have an extremely large advertising budget. This budget is spread across different media, although most of it is spent on the print media, especially the glossy fashion magazines such as *Vogue* and *Elle*. Such a scenario is in sharp contrast with the RTW shows in London held twice a year during London Fashion Week (LFW), most of which have little or no advertising budget to spend in the main fashion glossies. Consequently, considerably fewer members of the international fashion press and buyers attend LFW compared with the other international fashion weeks.

LFW

Each season many in the British fashion industry begin a reflective process of navel-gazing in an attempt to explain London's apparent lack of status compared with the other three major fashion weeks. A debate about London's importance as a fashion city has been rumbling on for a number of years. The main complaints are that Britain exports fashion design talent to work for European luxury brands and that too many British designers choose to show their collections at the fashion weeks of the 'competing' cities New York, Milan and Paris. Various explanations have been put forward to explain the absence of British fashion designers, the influential foreign press and buyers from LFW. Some are to do with a perceived lack of professionalism, as well as the opportunity to attend other international shows, where more luxury brands and well-known designers show their ranges. The fashion on display at LFW also has an image of being quirky, which is directly related to its strength as a host to much of the innovative creativity of modern fashion. However, some buyers prefer to spend their budget on visiting the cities with the 'safer bet' global fashion brands, since that is what their customers are likely to want.

LFW hosts only a handful of global fashion names that have sufficient advertising spend to make them interesting to the powerful fashion press. Paul Smith is probably the brand which spends the most on print advertising. This is believed to be an important reason why the international, and particularly American, press and buyers do not attend LFW. In simple terms, the argument is that a publication will provide editorial and other coverage for those brands or designer houses that advertise with it. This view is supported by Vanessa Friedman, fashion editor of the *Financial Times* who wrote, 'It's the most basic of equations. A fashion house invests in a publication, the publication invests in the fashion house. There are only two fashion brands with any advertising muscle at all at that show in London – Paul Smith and Nicole Farhi' (Friedman 2006). Many other famous British fashion designers and brands have shown elsewhere – Matthew Williamson in New York, Vivienne Westwood in Paris, and Burberry in Milan.

Models

The recent debates concerning 'size zero' models reflect a dilemma facing the fashion industry. On the one hand, fashion is about the mass adoption of branded products by a wide variety of consumers of all shapes and sizes. On the other hand, fashion is aspirational and about making individuals feel attractive based on contemporary ideas of beauty and ideal body shapes. As such, most fashion advertising contains imagery that promotes a lifestyle which is different from that experienced by the average consumer. Indeed 'dream-keting' is now a term used by some to reference those models in fashion advertising features whose appearance is striking and out of the ordinary.

Size zero in perspective

Recently the global fashion industry has been criticised for perpetuating the view that slim or skinny women are beautiful through its use of such models in runway shows and advertising. Lily Cole, Erin O'Connor and Kate Moss have all come in for criticism for being too thin and, as such, providing the wrong sort of image for young girls and women to aspire to. However, the 'size zero' tag has also been used to reference celebrities such as Victoria Beckham and Nicole Ritchie. It provides a potential dilemma for hosts of fashion shows who will not use size zero models on runway shows, when such celebrities attend a fashion show and generate press attention.

The main criticism of size zero body shapes is that they are considered to be unhealthy. The belief is that women who have such a body size will probably have achieved it, at best, by extreme and unhealthy dieting or, at worst, as the result of an eating disorder. Body shapes have traditionally come into and out of fashion. The heroin chic of the early 1990s that made Kate Moss famous was replaced with the healthier look of models such as Elle Macpherson. Sophie Dahl provided women with a brief period where it was fashionable to be large but has subsequently lost weight. Health experts are now quoting a minimum body mass index (BMI) of 18 as being the benchmark for a model, with some suggesting that fashion agencies and brands should not employ models whose BMI falls below this. It is interesting to note, though, that while the trend for women's role models, celebrities and some models is to be thinner, the average woman is becoming larger. In fact obesity in men, women and children in the US and the UK is considered to be so serious that the government is involved in tackling it through a health budget. UK readers need to be aware that size zero refers to a US size and is in fact size 4 in the UK. This further reinforces the problems associated with variable intenational sizing. See table 4.7.

Most fashion consumers do not really engage with a fashion purchase at a very deep level. Style (including fashionability), price and quality are still the main criteria for the selection and purchase of a fashion garment. Ethical issues can impact on buying decisions for some consumers, especially when an issue is highlighted in the media. Brands are expected to reflect exotic and aspirational lifestyles that are not typical of most consumers' lives.

Celebrities and PR

There is an increasing association between celebrities and fashion as traditional role models, such as politicians and royalty, fail to stimulate consumers' imaginations. The use of famous celebrities to promote key luxury brands is shown below. Celebrity status is increasingly short-lived. None the less, the key brands seem to believe it to be a strong marketing plus for their businesses. Table 6.2 shows some current celebrity/brand associations.

Many designers and brands will deliberately offer free product or loan of product to key celebrities,

table **6.2**   **current celebrity/brand associations.**

Celebrities	Fashion / Luxury brands
Victoria Beckham	Gucci (Tom Ford)
	Donatella Versace
	Dolce & Gabbana
Nicole Kidman	Jean-Paul Gaultier
	Yves Saint Laurent
Kylie Minogue	Julien Macdonald
	Donatella Versace
	Chanel
Jennifer Lopez (J-Lo)	Valentino
	YSL

as they are pretty well assured that their designs, brands and looks will get massive media coverage. PR companies will work hard to get celebrities to wear their clients' merchandise. This is probably the purest form of product placement. The media events that currently figure highly on the celebrity fashion calendar are shown below.

- LFW;
- British Fashion Awards;
- Golden Globes;
- BAFTAs;
- Academy Awards (Oscars);
- Brit Awards;
- Tony Awards;
- Mobos;
- Grammys.

PR and the fashion calendar

The principal role of PR is to communicate to target audiences by taking advantage of opportunities provided by the media. All fashion companies have a variety of audiences, including current and potential consumers, business partners, regulatory bodies and other 'stakeholders'. There is a strong rationale for PR in fashion since a variety of different media feature fashion in their content. The increased interest in celebrities and celebrity lifestyles has further expanded the opportunities for the production and consumption of fashion features. New celebrity magazines such as *Now* and *Closer* not only show what individual stars wear and how they are styled, but also provide broader brand education to their readers.

The relationship between journalists and those responsible for the PR of fashion brands is a reciprocal one in which both media and brands benefit. In simple terms, journalists need to carry exciting features about the fashion brands and products desired by their readers, and brands need the low-cost and often authoritative exposure provided by the media.

The process of PR works within a well-established fashion calendar – the agreed set of dates when the fashion seasons begin and end. The fashion business still has the traditional seasons of spring/summer and autumn/ winter. A season is defined as the period of time in which particular products are sold. The aim of all fashion brands and retailers is to sell as much of their stock at full price as possible and to minimise mark-downs. A season covers the period of time that stock is sold at full price and then put in a clearance sale. The notion of a season is an important one to grasp since many of the commercial organisations working towards a season have their own deadlines and events. For example, a textile show such as PV, the global RTW shows and the main glossy magazines such as *Vogue* and *Elle* all have different lead times relating to the same season. However, the season that they are all contributing to in different ways has a start and an end date tied to the retail sales of products to consumers.

PR agencies and their selection

There are many specialist fashion PR agencies, which manage the publicity and related marketing activities for a portfolio of client brands. They can offer a wide variety of services from simply generating publicity and managing special events, through to helping in the development of the overall marketing strategy.

When a brand employs an agency it is effectively buying the agency's contact book of journalists. There are clear benefits to a brand using this approach. However, there is a strong argument that an agency will not be able to deliver the same kind of 'brand management' that a brand could achieve through controlling its own PR. Agencies will typically have several clients and individual account managers, who are unlikely to represent competing brands in a product area. The scope and scale of PR agencies and their services is immense. The best way to find out about PR companies and their competencies is start by looking at the *Hollis PR Annual* – which lists the key PR companies and their main clients. They have an online subscription facility at www.hollis-pr.com, providing a wealth of information covering both the UK and Europe.

Another key source of fashion information is a subscription service known as Fashion Monitor. It is the UK's leading provider of news, events and contacts information to the style and beauty industries. Available by annual subscription, the full service comprises:

▶ Fashion Monitor online, updated daily;
▶ a monthly news and events report;
▶ a quarterly contacts directory.

The in-house brands approach to PR

Many retailers, designers and fashion brands prefer to run their own in-house PR operation, usually citing lower cost and more direct control over the content as the main rationale. However, in essence much of their work is similar to that of the specialist external PR agency.

Regular liaison with the fashion media is critically important, usually involving meetings with editors, assistants and stylists. The media need to have the ranges, looks and brands clearly explained to them, to ensure that the brand is represented correctly in the media. *Tatler* might be looking for a 'gold story' for one of their autumn publications.

Most in-house departments keep a highly accurate database of the key fashion journalists in order that they can be invited to the brand's press day, or be sent the latest look books or press releases. There is a constant flow of samples backwards and forwards between the PR operation that takes up a considerable amount of management time and effort. However, having samples readily and quickly available is mission-critical for all successful PR departments.

Measuring PR

The measurement of marketing communications is diverse. The use of sales as an indicator may often be misleading since other factors are involved in a purchase. PR is quite different from advertising in the way it works and its budgets are spent. As such, it requires different measures of performance.

Common ways of measuring the effectiveness of fashion PR are:

● the volume of column inches/centimetres in all media;
● the equivalent advertising cost of each of these;
● the number of enquiries (if a direct response is facilitated).
● the number of website hits.

Opportunities for fashion brands to gain publicity in the print media will depend on when a particular magazine or newspaper is covering a season.

How PR works in UK fashion businesses

In general, fashion organisations have two approaches to managing their PR effort: (1) undertaking all PR activity in-house using trained PR specialists or teams, or (2) using an external PR organisation or individual. There is no best approach to undertaking PR, although larger fashion businesses with large turnovers and market shares often prefer to employ their own specialist departments, in order that they can take direct control over the total PR effort. Companies with smaller turnovers, lower market shares and small management teams often prefer to employ external PR organisations and consultants, in order to avoid diverting management time from its key objectives. Using external PR organisations can also bring a more objective approach to all aspects of the PR effort. Not being directly employed by a fashion organisation often enables external PR staff to 'think outside the box'.

The costs of running an in-house PR team can often be very high, particularly if the team is diverted away from key communication issues with the organisation's principal external publics towards other, peripheral issues such as arranging free samples for the MD's wife's charity work! External PR organisations, on the other hand, have the advantage of not being bogged down in corporate organisational thinking. External PR organisations are generally paid a monthly retainer to ensure that an appointed member of the PR team is dedicated to working for the client organisation for a specific number of days a month. The basic monthly/annual PR fee would exclude all other incidental costs such as travel, design and the production of corporate literature that are incurred by prior agreement with the client and are generally billed monthly in arrears. Good fashion PR is not simply about writing and sending out the occasional news release – listed below are some of the main activities of any fashion PR or press office, whether operating internally or externally. These activities obviously vary according to the type of fashion organisation, as well as the time of year. There is no exact formulaic way in which PR can be applied across all the diverse aspects of the fashion industry.

The main areas of likely involvement of PR within the fashion industry are:

1   the management, production and circulation of press releases;
2   the management of fashion samples for external media, especially for photo shoots;
3   the management, production and circulation of all sensitive internal marketing communications to staff;
4   the planning and management of trade shows, fashion shows and business conferences;
5   crisis management control;
6   general liaison with all external publics over a wide range of issues;
7   event and sponsorship management, where applicable;
8   product placement, especially in visual media such as TV and cinema.

There are, of course, numerous other areas and issues that an efficient fashion PR function might take on board in the normal course of events. The very varied nature of UK fashion businesses makes it hard to be too prescriptive.

Undoubtedly, the continual and consistent communication between the client and the various fashion and financial media is probably the most important part of fashion PR. Often, because of the rather specialist nature of financial PR activity, larger fashion organisations will use specialist companies to undertake this work. However, again there are many examples of large fashion companies where all types of PR activity are carried out within one central team.

Choosing and using external PR organisations

An effective and efficient relationship between a fashion organisation and its external PR provider is extremely important if a consistent and accurate message is to be communicated to the many internal and external publics involved. In many respects, this relationship has been likened to a marriage – there is always a need for understanding and give-and-take. Operating within the UK fashion industry are many different types of fashion PR organisation. These range from individuals working from home to huge multinational organisations. Some PR companies specialise in fashion, whereas others undertake PR activity across a wide range of consumer products.

Some of the smaller boutique PR operations, employing a very small number of staff, operate very successfully across several different areas of the UK fashion industry. As specialists, the principals of these organisations rely heavily upon their own networking abilities. These have often been built up over many years – some of these organisations' most important assets are probably their address books and contact lists. The best fashion PR operatives in the UK are likely to be those with the widest circle of fashion media contacts. Being able to pick up the phone and talk to the key fashion editors and journalists is a critical success factor.

Although personal contact with the media is best, a great deal of the communication process is undertaken using the ubiquitous press release. This is normally used extensively to herald and explain the launch of new ranges, brands and stores. Undoubtedly, it is much easier to create an interesting press release when dealing with a new or quirky brand, designer or retail format than when trying to maintain the fashion media's interest in something that may have been around for many years. Writing and enthusing about a basic cotton/polyester top for a middle-of-the-road high-street fashion chain is in fact much harder than writing about the launch of a new, young, designer brand in an upmarket luxury store. Good fashion PR press-release writers have to find some interesting 'hook' that will make their press release of interest to the fashion journalist or editor receiving it. It has been estimated that there is a fashion press release being sent every minute of every working day.

In reality, fashion journalists will tell you that only a few of the many hundreds of press releases received each week actually catch their attention. The relationship between fashion PR and fashion journalism is a symbiotic one, often described as a love-hate relationship. Each requires the other if their objectives are to be fulfilled. A good, exciting press release makes the fashion journalist's job easier, and an astute journalist will often be able to look at a press release from an interesting or unusual angle. The fashion industry needs something new to be exposed to the general public – fashion PR is the main conduit.

Good fashion PR communication requires the ability to communicate using a wide variety of differing methods. These include:

1 **written communications** – press releases, corporate literature, general written communications;
2 **verbal communications** – directly to individuals and organisations, face-to-face or by telephone, and may involve public speaking if addressing large meetings and conferences;
3 **audiovisual communications** – via television, the Internet or video conferencing using a wide variety of different visual sources.

Excellent communication is the key ingredient of all PR. This is especially the case for fashion PR, where the business is very driven by individuals and personalities. The ability to develop and select good visual images is again particularly important, as most fashion press releases depend upon a balanced mix of both written and visual communication.

As a result of the continuous fragmentation of the UK fashion market, as well as the huge growth and diversification of the fashion media, PR has become an increasingly powerful and useful marketing tool. The fashion PR industry continues to develop new and more effective ways of communicating and promoting fashion, and is still one of the most important tools available to fashion marketing.

It is often wrongly assumed that the reason why PR is both tactically and strategically more important to the UK fashion industry than advertising is because advertising is more expensive. PR has always been a more important tool than advertising, as the output of PR can deliver a much more personal, dynamic and believable message to the consumer via good fashion journalism. Good PR does of course incur costs – there is no such thing as totally free marketing.

As both the press and the public seem to be developing an increasingly large and insatiable appetite for fashion stories of every ilk, fashion PR continues to grow and develop. The growth in product placement, where a garment or other fashion product is worn on TV or in a film (usually by a star) is a relatively recent development within PR. The recent US TV series *Sex in the City* bears witness to the power that TV personalities have in confirming for a consumer that a product is 'right'. Such placement deals are often rather private and complex, and sometimes the accidental wearing of a style and/or brand can have an immense impact upon consumer perceptions, as is the case of David Beckham's public wearing of a classic Pringle Argyll sweater. This is an example of an accidental placement, which can provide a cost-free PR coup.

Finding the right PR resource

However, when involved in selecting an external fashion PR organisation it is useful to check the following aspects of that individual's or organisation's business portfolio:

1 Do they have a proven track record of success within the sector? Check this with current and former clients.
2 Do they have the ability to handle all types of media and are they well connected with key shakers and movers? Check this via word of mouth.
3 Do they have enough expertise in all the sectors of PR activity planned or will they need to outsource some of the work? Check the CVs of the PR team.
4 Are they creative in terms of tactical and strategic thinking? Ask to see examples of earlier campaigns, as well as marketing outcomes.
5 Will you be receiving the continual support of the key executives, or will a more junior team be left to run the account – meeting the principal players of a well-known PR organisation once and never seeing them again is a common occurrence!

There is, of course, no certain way to guarantee PR success, but the track record of an organisation is a useful barometer with which to make certain objective and value judgements as to its suitability. In today's increasingly consumer-centric society, and with the penchant for litigious activity, good fashion PR can often avert crises before they escalate. Bad publicity about an organisation tends to spread like wildfire, often with disastrous consequences for the organisation's trading position and its public image. There have been many examples of sensitive issues impinging negatively upon areas of the UK fashion industry.

Most of the recent interest stories in the media have centred on issues relating to the exploitation of people and resources. Size zero (US) models and celebrities inevitably attract attention around the time of the biannual fashion weeks. Special interest groups such as PETA have raised the issues of fur and the exploitation of animals for fashion in the media, using a variety of publicity stunts. In so doing, they aim to keep the topic of animal exploitation in the forefront of consumers' minds.

Each year the list of public concerns relating to the fashion industry lengthens, with many being trawled up again and again by those fashion journalists with limited horizons. People's perceptions about such issues are often at variance with the reality, requiring very skilful handling of the press by the PR representative. Poor PR in such situations can have a long-term detrimental effect upon future trading performance.

Word of mouth (or word of mouse)

In this increasingly interconnected and global fashion market-place, a lack of trust and belief in some of the large-scale global fashion companies is emerging. The publication of *No Logo* by Naomi Klein (2000) is seen as the watershed of a new movement that started to query and challenge the validity and motivation of the larger global brands. Throughout the more developed countries there is, in parallel to this, a growing doubt about the motivations of international organisations and national governments. It would appear, throughout the world, that the concept of followership, so beloved of governments and large trading organisations, is rapidly on the wane. The individual now wants to take control of his/her own future. Most of us claim to like change, although, upon deeper investigation, change appears to be all right providing that it happens to others! Undoubtedly certain young fashion consumers are becoming sceptical about the increasing power of some of the larger global brands, especially those with environmental and worker issues. The Internet is a powerful and fast driver of word of mouth/mouse marketing, which can quickly fuel both good and bad news fashion stories within hours, if not minutes. It takes very quick and skilful PR to manage negative stories that suddenly emerge on the Internet. A brand's integrity can now be destroyed very quickly as a result of the availability of the Internet.

The power of word of mouth in marketing communication

For any consumer, living in any culture, there are always individuals, groups, accepted practices, norms and a host of other factors that influence them in terms of how they react in any given market situation. These are generally referred to as cultural influences. Everyone is under the influence of the culture that he/she has been brought up in.

Culture, as defined by Armstrong and Kotler (2004), is 'a set of basic values, perceptions, wants and behaviours learned by a member of society from family and other important institutions'. No consumer can be completely unbiased in the decision-making processes, with friends and family seen as a particularly strong and reliable source of consumer information. Seeing friends wearing certain fashion brands, liking how they look in them and also hearing them extol the virtues of brands or products are influences which are normally more significant to an individual than any amount of advertising. As fashion consumers are bombarded with marketing communications, it becomes increasingly difficult for them to analyse and synthesise them, to assist in the purchasing process. The normal human response, when overloaded with consumer information, is to take a simplistic approach which gives a quick, comfortable solution – advice, information and knowledge learned from friends and family is the obvious answer. The phenomenon of viral marketing in its various forms, including flash mobs, is discussed in chapter 9.

These relatively recent groupings also point towards a decreasing belief and acceptance of global brands by Gen-Y. This generation is now less likely to accept conventional marketing communications such as advertising, preferring to rely more upon word of mouth and recommendation. This is the first text-reliant generation, heavily dependent upon one-to-one text messages to help their everyday decisions.

As a result of the emergence of Gen-Y, the UK has seen the development of new genres of fashion marketing tactics, such as guerrilla marketing and viral marketing. Both these tactics are used to ignite positive word-of-mouth communication between members of the Gen-Y age group and employ unusual marketing communications tactics.

Guerrilla marketing can be defined as the use of unconventional modes of marketing communication, usually tightly targeted at younger consumer groups, using media, timing and locations not normally used for conventional marketing communications. For example, small illegally placed posters, announcing the opening of a new retail outlet, are pasted to street furniture such as lamp-posts and waste bins, possibly with directional arrows to lead the consumer to the actual location of the store. Other examples are small, enigmatic logos of a new fashion brand, with posters advertising the brand's new website. Sometimes guerrilla marketing verges on the illegal – especially when flyposting is involved. The huge financial rewards potentially created by the guerrilla marketing tactic employed far outweigh the fines imposed for flyposting. Other ideas for guerrilla marketing include the leaving of strategically placed cards in clubs and restaurants, and at concerts/gigs or other public places likely to be frequented by the consumer group to be targeted. The marketing communications objective may be simply to raise awareness, or possibly to call the targeted consumer to action. However, once the message or communication has been seeded using guerrilla marketing tactics, the level and calibre of word-of-mouth communication that it creates is difficult to measure.

This sort of innovative communication/promotion technique is becoming increasingly popular as it is on a much more personal and human scale than, say, a large national advertising campaign. This small and very personal type of marketing communication can assume prominence and credibility and often has the advantage of being more unusual and therefore more memorable in the consumer's mind.

Although positive word-of-mouth communication can therefore be seeded using guerrilla marketing techniques, there is a major problem with negative word-of-mouth communication that arises, sometimes for no reason. Negative publicity that is fuelled by word of mouth can be very damaging to any fashion organisation. Sometimes such negative publicity is unfounded and untruthful. In these cases it is essential that untruths or fallacies be countered using corrective and positive publicity. Such incidents can even cause long-term financial damage to an organisation. Many of the recent problems encountered by M&S appear to have been fuelled by negative word-of-mouth communication between individuals. Once any fashion organisation appears to be in either financial or organisational difficulty, doubt is created in consumers' minds about the suitability of the organisation's fashion offer. Negative publicity spreads almost faster than positive publicity, especially in the fashion business where the product is inextricably linked to people's everyday lives.

In chapter 2 the importance of using marketing research on a regular basis is discussed at length. If consumers are becoming dissatisfied over time with any fashion offer, it is essential to pick this up early in order that the product can be realigned to consumer demand. Using effective and continuous marketing research can often stop negative word of mouth before it starts.

Visual merchandising

Visual merchandising is the process of presenting and displaying merchandise throughout any trading environment. It aims to present it in the best way possible to catch the consumer's attention and hopefully to encourage awareness and ultimately a transaction.

Generally it is a promotional tool likely to be used in retail trading or trade exhibition/showroom environments. The main purpose is to ensure that merchandise is displayed to its best and most eye-catching effect. Without good creative-display methodologies, even expensive clothing can have its value detracted as a result of poor presentation. There are several key golden rules of visual merchandising:

- **simplicity** – avoids sensory overload for the consumer – muddled and crowded displays tend to confuse and potentially drive away time-strapped consumers;
- **clear labelling of information** – to provide clear explanations for the customer;
- **logical positioning** – to ensure that it is seen by the customer, for example POS and in windows;

- **clear garment and colour co-ordination** – to help the customer understand how to wear or use the product most effectively;
- **logical adjacency** – it is important for displays to relate geographically to the correct department or area of the store;
- **innovation** – it is important to display the merchandise in an exciting, innovative and/or unique way to grab customer attention.

In today's modern fashion retail environment, exciting visual stimulation plays an important part in getting consumers into an outlet and then more importantly to purchase. The quality and calibre of visual display techniques has risen dramatically over the past decade. The excitement of Selfridges' windows always attracts huge PR attention, giving the visual merchandising a support role in PR. Other retailers, such as John Lewis, take a less flamboyant approach to visual display, using clean, crisp and uncomplicated visual merchandising to ensure that the product gets its message across to the consumer. Again, each retailer adopts his or her own approach to visual merchandising. Many fashion retailers, who simply look upon it as a cost rather than a major marketing tool aimed at attracting customers, sadly ignore not only visual merchandising but also its ability to encourage customers to try on and hopefully to purchase a garment.

Packaging

Although a large percentage of fashion merchandise is available for consumers to touch and feel, with very little packaging involved, certain fashion products are heavily packed for transportation, presentation and usage purposes, for example perfumery and toiletries. The average garment will have identifying swing tags and internal sewn-in labels and will normally be presented for sale on a hanger. It is important, however, not to trivialise the importance of the 'assistance' packaging – a good clothes hanger will stay with a customer possibly for many years after the garment has been disposed of. As such, it lives on as a potential advertisement, seen every time that the wardrobe door is opened. Garment labels are often left on the outside of garments as a form of cultural badge by many young consumers, who wish to make a highly conspicuous statement about their own purchasing habits. Recently a vogue for leaving price tags on garments even after purchase has emerged. It is probable that in some market segments this rather odd consumer marketing behaviour can be developed and exploited by retailers and brands serving that element of the market.

More basic fashion products such as hosiery and underwear, especially for men, do have external packaging to help assist in display, product protection and physical selection by the customer. At various levels of the fashion industry, the packaging varies in quality and design – but always aims to ensure coherence with the overall brand identity.

Corporate Identity

The physical manifestations of an organisation that are immediately recognised by the public and trade, for example logos, colours, fascias, uniforms, vehicle liveries, brochures, forms, buildings, company business cards, stationery and brochures, form an important part of the overall fashion marketing communications mix. All must be in harmony and must reflect the brand/retail personality. Most fashion businesses undertake a change/review of corporate branding, to ensure that the image is always relevant and of the moment.

The cost of changing a corporate identity can be massive, even for the smallest of businesses. Therefore the old adage 'If it ain't broken don't fix it' is especially relevant. Most organisations with a very notable corporate identity will undertake small, gradual changes, normally only making subtle alterations to the corporate identity such as a gradual change of colour tone or typeface. Anecdotally, M&S has changed its corporate identity about ten times since it first started trading.

Corporate identity includes all the physical manifestations of an organisation that are immediately recognised by the public and trade. A standardised and memorable corporate identity can reinforce all other aspects of marketing communications activity. Total conformity and consistency are the key indicators of a well-controlled fashion corporate identity. Most fashion businesses publish detailed guidelines of all their corporate identity, e.g. colours and typefaces, for use by external agencies.

Exhibitions

International exhibitions covering textiles, brands, fibres, yarns and ready-made garments of all types are held throughout the year. Many are held twice yearly, some annually. It is believed that there are about three hundred days a year when a keen (but foolish) fashionista could be in attendance at a fashion show somewhere on the planet! As the quality of internet imagery improves and as international fashion businesses become increasingly cost-conscious and possibly more environmentally aware, many fashion-related trade shows are suffering from declining attendances. The improving quality of digital images may lead to more fashion buyers visiting virtual rather than physical trade shows. A list of global fashion, textile or garment shows would take up many pages. Most shows are not open to the public, being by invitation to the trade. Some focus on small independent retailers and brands, whilst others are for the mass market.

Key sites giving information about trade shows are:

- www.apparelsearch.com/trade_show
- www.apparelnews.net/Events/index

Buyers simply do not have time to visit all the shows, but thanks to the high quality of trade-show reporting by WGSN, they are able to trawl the Internet and to get an almost immediate view of the key looks. The virtual trade show may be the norm of the future if international travel becomes more problematic.

Concluding comments on fashion promotion techniques

Fashion marketers have a wide armoury of fashion promotion techniques and tools available to them. The right tools must be selected and used at the right time to the right level if promotion is to work effectively in either a tactical or strategic way for the fashion organisation involved. Some promotional tools, for example price reductions, work more effectively at the lower end of the market, whereas advertisements in the quality fashion magazines work more effectively for upmarket brands and designers.

There is no formulaic approach to the application of promotional methodology within UK fashion. Experience and logic are the fashion marketer's best guide as to what to do. The importance attached to each of the promotional tools varies dramatically depending upon the type of fashion business and the marketing task. Whichever promotional tool(s) is/are selected, it is essential to realise that all marketing promotion incurs costs. Failure to select the right promotional tools, or to monitor their impact over time, is a certain way to waste the marketing communications budget.

marketing mix: place – channels of distribution and service

The location, aesthetics and shopping experience of any successful selling environment must inspire, involve and excite consumers.

David Riddiford – CEO, Arnotts of Dublin (formerly Buying and Merchandising Director of Selfridges, also President – Merchandising, Lane-Crawford Hong Kong)

Introduction and terminology

The aim of this chapter is to explain the Place element of the marketing mix within the context of fashion. In common with promotion, the term 'place' has a wide frame of reference in marketing theory and practice. Place is short for place of distribution and refers explicitly to the POS, where the fashion business sells directly to the customer, and implicitly to the process of physical distribution management. The latter is also referred to as supply chain management since products are supplied to customers in different ways according to the place of purchase (POS). For example, the process of supplying products to consumers is very different for a fashion brand that uses both stores and e-commerce. Stores require stock to be held on site and consumers take products away with them following purchase. An e-commerce operation typically requires the brand to arrange the delivery of products to consumers. In this simple example there are different logistical implications in the delivery of products to consumers. Furthermore, the word 'channel' is normally added to the word 'distribution' and refers to the holistic process of supplying products to various POSs.

A key point therefore in planning a marketing mix is the consideration of both the customer experience in buying a product or service, which is normally through some sort of store, website, catalogue or other place, and the issues associated with the efficient and effective delivery of a product from brand/manufacturer to consumer. Readers should also appreciate that 'Place' is used instead of 'distribution' to construct a convenient set of Ps that are collectively referred to as the marketing mix.

It is essential for the fashion marketer to be aware of the type and level of retailer or brand involved, together with the structure of the supply chain of that retailer or brand. Understanding speed to market and intrinsic product value is vital background information for any fashion marketer. Without this background knowledge much marketing activity can be wasted or wrongly applied. This chapter will help explain the complexities of the fashion market.

The fashion context

Fashion provides a very significant context for decisions on the type of distribution channel a brand will need to use to best serve customers and optimise sales and profits. At the high end of fashion (typically referred to as luxury) consumers expect a tremendous shopping experience that includes superb individual service within an immaculately presented and innovative selling environment. This often requires brands to invest in flagship stores that are differentiated, in terms of design and in-store experience, from normal branded retail outlets. Flagship stores at the very high end are typically designed by world-famous architects such as Peter Marino (Chanel store in Tokyo) and Rem Koolhaas (Prada store in New York). This type of store is discussed later in the chapter.

The different distribution channels

Fashion is a dynamic industry in which brands trade using complex global distribution networks. The globalisation of business opportunities arising in part from greater cultural homogeneity, the easing of international trade restrictions, faster and more reliable communications, increased wealth and saturated domestic markets have all encouraged companies to trade beyond their original national boundaries. Consequently, it is normal for fashion brands to use a combination of different distribution channel options that include retailing, franchising, wholesaling and licensing. All are served by sophisticated supply chain structures.

It is important to understand that brand can refer to both a type of business model and also, more commonly, to an image and identity. In the fashion industry a brand typically refers to a business that is able to command a premium for its products, due to the differentiated product benefits that are often connected with status. This may also apply to a retailer. However, the business model adopted by a retailer is one in which it sells directly to consumers through its own retail outlets. This point will be analysed and discussed later in the chapter. A (non-retailer) brand is different inasmuch as it distributes to consumers through a mixture of channel options that include retailing directly to consumers and also selling to other third-party customers (e.g. boutiques and department stores), who then sell on to consumers.

When operating in global markets, a fashion brand may use a combination of its own stores in certain countries, department store concessions in others, and

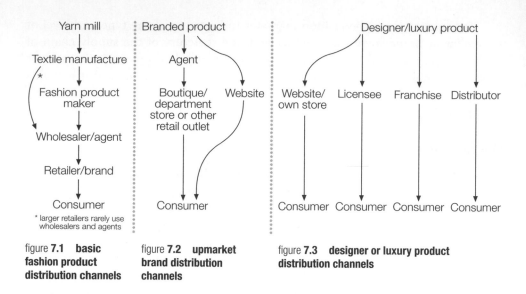

figure **7.1** **basic fashion product distribution channels**

figure **7.2** **upmarket brand distribution channels**

figure **7.3** **designer or luxury product distribution channels**

wholesaling and direct selling through a transactional website in others. The possible combinations are endless and utilised to fit in with local and national trading conditions and situations. Some typical distribution channel options used in international fashion trade are explained below.

Examples of fashion distribution channels

Figures 7.1, 7.2 and 7.3 illustrate a selection of distribution channels which feature different generic distribution options through which products can pass from creator to consumer. These are by no means the only options and it would be too complex to illustrate all the possible variations that operate within the global fashion industry.

Figure 7.1 indicates a distribution channel that is typical of mass-market fashion sold through multiple retailer brands. The particular business relationships between the various stages would depend on whether the retailer brand was operating on a CMT basis (buying its own fabric and sending it to a manufacturer to be made into garments) or simply buying products which have already been designed and manufactured (known as factored garments). Figure 7.2 shows the route that a fashion brand may use to distribute its products to consumers where it does not own any stores. This would also apply to a brand that owns a limited number of flagship stores (for brand presence), but distributes mainly through department stores, boutiques or other specialist shops, including sportswear outlets. Figure 7.3 shows the equivalent relationships between a luxury brand and its consumers.

Back room – front room

All marketers agree that the 'back-room' supply chain, which is responsible for the distribution of products to consumers, has a direct impact on the success of the 'front-room' place of distribution. However, it is more common for the subject of marketing to address the front-room (or front-of-house) issues, which include the selection of channel type and the appropriate strategies and tactics associated with each.

Distribution options

There are a number of channel options that marketers can select in making decisions about the best place of distribution to serve customers. These include wholesaling, franchising, licensing and retailing, which are all supported by an array of other fashion intermediaries such as garment-processing services and overseas buying and marketing offices. In retailing there are further choices to be made by fashion brands about the best place. These include own stores (also referred to as stand-alone sites or solus outlets), concessions within other stores, catalogues and transactional websites. This chapter goes on to discuss the options and to explain how each of these marketing channels operates.

There is a greater emphasis on fashion retailing, in view of its significant scope and scale within the context of the total fashion industry. This section deals with and explains some of the more hidden parts of the fashion distribution supply chain through which products pass before arriving at the fashion retailer and ultimately the customer. Although most global fashion clothing goes directly from the factory to the retailer's distribution centre before being split up and sent out to individual outlets, it is worth considering some of the less visible parts of the supply chain. An understanding of their working is essential for the fashion marketer.

Fashion wholesaling

The term 'fashion wholesaler' is used to define any organisation or business that buys in bulk and then sells directly to smaller fashion businesses at a profit. In general, fashion wholesalers do not deal directly with the public, as they usually operate from warehouses or distribution centres away from the main shopping areas.

Although the majority of wholesalers tend to sell a miscellany of lesser-known brands to the middle and lower market, the more prestigious fashion brands often have in-house wholesale departments. Brands have wholesale departments to sell ranges internationally and to boutiques or department stores that are in retail locations where it may be difficult to open a store of their own. This could be due to the cost or to the lack of suitable and available locations.

Both the host retailer and the incoming brands need to be sure that the respective market positions of the businesses are right and that neither suffers damage to the long-term reputation and perception of its brand. Although a relationship might make sense at a strategic level (in terms of brand positioning), some brands discover problems at an operational level where the staff of the host retailer fails to present the brands' products in the right way.

Wholesaling is a global phenomenon, with most capital cities having a 'fashion district' where wholesale businesses tend to conglomerate. In Paris there is the Sentier clothing and textile wholesaling area which has a strong Jewish influence, and in New York the main clothing manufacturing and wholesaling area in Manhattan can be found around Seventh Avenue and Broadway between 34th Street and 40th Street. In London, fashion wholesaling is mainly located in the West End in and around Great Portland Street, Great Titchfield Street, Market Place and the surrounding side streets. This area is one of the main fashion wholesale showroom areas of the UK, although another strong wholesaling area can be found in the Commercial Road area of London's East End. Internationally, wholesaling areas usually developed close to the historic manufacturing areas of the main cities, but as those manufacturing areas continue to decline, wholesaling lives on.

In the UK, manufacturers (either foreign or UK-based) often have a London showroom from which they sell their own brand directly to smaller independent retailers on a wholesale basis, as well as directly to certain larger retail groups on a more heavily discounted basis. As with any traded commodity, the large buying power of the UK's major fashion retailers ensures that their buyers can command very keen CPs, usually meaning that large retail groups rarely use wholesalers, preferring to purchase directly from the manufacturer or brand owner.

The distinction between wholesale and retail can often be blurred; the wholesaler sometimes allows regular admittance of the general public to buy directly from the showroom. Wholesale or discount cash & carry warehouses enable manufacturers to deal more directly with the public – this time cutting the retailer out of the supply chain. Whatever level of the fashion business is involved, it is fair to say that the shortening of the supply chain and the maximisation of profit at all stages of it are the main business objectives for all involved. In general – as a result of the increasing number of larger retail groups – wholesaling is not expanding in the UK.

Fashion franchising

Some retail outlets are not owned by the retailer whose name appears above the door, but by an individual or smaller company that takes on what is known as a franchise operation from the parent retail brand, as in the case of Benetton and Body Shop. A franchise is normally defined as a contractual arrangement made between a fashion brand manufacturer/retailer/wholesaler and another independent retail business, which buys the right to own and operate a shop in a closely specified format. Franchising is now becoming increasingly popular across a wide range of fashion businesses. In essence, it is a form of business expansion that enables retailers or manufacturers (usually referred to as franchisers) to expand quickly, without risking huge capital and management costs. Instead they use the capital and business energy of independent entrepreneurs, who invest in a proven retail/business format. Franchising is one of the fastest-growing business start-up methods being used in general US retail development.

How does franchising work?

The model requires individual investors looking for a retail format to approach a successful franchise operation and then buy a shop in a mutually agreed location, fit it out in the agreed corporate format and then, most importantly, buy all their stock from the franchiser. The investors or franchisees have the advantage of buying into an already proven retail format, thus removing the risks involved in starting a new, unproven retail business from scratch. They are automatically buying into an existing brand equity that, hopefully, will deliver higher profits than if they had gone it alone. The retailer or manufacturer will normally vet prospective franchisees to ensure that they are sound in every sense, i.e. that they have adequate capital and business experience. The franchisee has to sign a formal legal agreement which states that they will sell only the one brand and that they agree to adhere to all the rules, procedures and protocols of the lead business. Generally the contracts are for several years, with a long notice period by either party. The brand is then guaranteed that the franchisee will buy product from them and will retail it in the trading format agreed. The benefit for the lead company is that it is using the franchisee's money, effort and time to open a retail outlet, rather than risking and relying on its own capital investment. Franchisees, having made that investment, are often more driven and loyal than normally employed retail management.

The Body Shop, McDonald's, Benetton and Kookai are all examples of businesses that have successfully employed franchising as a method of business expansion. Mothercare and M&S are examples of clothing businesses that have used franchising as their preferred method of international expansion. Franchising is often the best way for a fashion retailer to undertake foreign expansion, as direct investment into foreign retail markets has proved to be a risky business for international fashion retailers. It is of interest to note that many luxury brands, especially Burberry, have more recently preferred to withdraw from franchising, in order to take stronger direct control over the way in which their brand is being retailed and marketed in other countries. By directly controlling all international marketing activities, brands are able to ensure consistency of marketing communications and ultimately the brand identity and its values. There are risks and capital issues involved with the direct international control of a brand. The trend in the luxury markets has been for brands to move away from franchising towards directly operated stores, where they have more control.

In conclusion, franchisers make their profit from the merchandise they sell to the franchisees, whilst the franchisees make their profit on the merchandise that they sell at retail. For both parties it is a relatively secure long-term income stream, as well as being one of the major drivers of global fashion retail expansion.

Fashion licensing is when a brand, manufacturer, retailer or wholesaler allows another party (usually in another country) to trade its products for a set fee or royalty.

Advantages of licensing

The advantage for the parent company is that it is a low-risk entry strategy into a foreign market, where customer tastes and preferences may be very different to those of the home country. The main advantages of using a licensee, rather than directly operating a business in a foreign country, are as follows:

1 the licensee generally has a better understanding of the market and its specific national demands;
2 the licensee has better grasp of any cultural and language issues relating to the promotion and management of a foreign brand;
3 the business risk is taken more by the licensee than the mother brand;
4 the licensee must guard and control the brand's image and integrity – impossible for a geographically remote brand.

How does licensing work?

Licensing deals require a watertight contractual deal between the partners, normally written under the national legal system that will give the licenser the best chance of legal control of the licence situation. The licenser normally demands on average around 5–10% of annual sales from the licensee, with a guaranteed 75% income on the annual turnover forecast. This protects the licenser against any poor management by the licensee in any one financial year. The licensing agreement will often be signed for a period of between five and ten years. The licensing contract will specify every aspect of the way in which the brand will be marketed, often going down to minute levels of operational detail. Brands that allow lax licensing, without adequate control of the trading method and environment, can be destroyed in a short space of time.

The complexity and extent of licensing deals varies greatly. Companies such as the Disney Corporation allow clothing manufacturers to use Disney characters on certain categories of product, although Disney is reputedly very protective of the quality of garment being printed and the quality, content and context of the print being used. There are some examples of organisations where the licence holder (licensee) has developed the business internationally very substantially differently compared to the parent organisation. One example is Austin Reed, which licences a garment and product range in the US which is very different from the range being marketed in the UK. In the textile-manufacturing sector, there are many manufacturing processes that have been internationally licensed, as well as trade marks, designs, patents, secret processes and individuals. In fact almost anything that adds value to a product or service can be licensed. Internationally there is a huge demand for licensing deals within the fashion sector.

The management and control of international licensing is a specialist area, with most leading international fashion brands needing a licensing department with specialist staff. Signing up with the wrong international partner for a long period of time has been compared to being married to the wrong person. Getting out of the marriage can be an expensive and messy business.

A number of fashion brands use franchising and licensing to avoid the cost of owning foreign stores and to achieve a broader and often faster market coverage. As both methods require brands to engage with partners who control the POS interface with consumers, many designer and luxury brands have moved away from these methods. This is because such brands need to manage the shopping experience of their consumers, believing it to have a fundamental and significant impact upon their total brand. This is especially important at the luxury end of the market where consumers' expectations are much higher, and where brands differentiate on esoteric qualities, which need consistent reinforcement through messages of innovation and sensory delight at the POS.

Other fashion intermediaries supporting fashion distribution channels

Throughout the fashion industry supply chain, there are many different types of intermediary that can be involved in bringing merchandise into and through the supply chain. Shown below are some of the main players. An intermediary can be defined as any individual or organisation involved anywhere in the fashion supply chain.

The manufacturer's agent

Foreign manufacturers mainly used to use agents to represent them in foreign markets. These individuals would act as a conduit between factory and retailer, often also acting as an import office and sometimes providing design input. Most modern, efficient fashion retailers now have their own import and design experts, making a manufacturer's agent largely redundant. Whether all cost savings made as a result of the exclusion of agents are fully passed on to consumers is a debatable point – often such savings were simply seen as a way of improving overall retail profitability. All the main international fashion retailing groups have moved away from dealing with manufacturer's agents or import agents. Import agents often carried several different unrelated fashion garment types and brands, which did not directly compete with each other, supplying smaller and independent fashion retailers with several ranges. Again, these are also disappearing as a result of the continued general decline of independent fashion retailers. Agents generally mean increased costs and confusion, with retailers preferring to deal directly with manufacturing sources.

Garment-processing companies

With huge levels of imported clothing entering developed markets, often the supply chain members have to employ garment processors whose raison d'être is to ensure that garments are unpacked and steamed or ironed to remove creases so that they are in a fit state to be displayed. Merchandise often arrives badly creased or wrongly labelled. To remedy such problems after merchandise has entered the formal supply chain would normally be very cost- and time-ineffective – probably slowing it down and losing profit. For this reason it is more logical to divert the problem product to a separate processing unit, have the merchandise made ready and then deliver it in to the distribution centre (DC) or retail outlet. Sometimes garment processing is known as pre-retailing. Reprocessing businesses are normally independent from the main players in the supply chain, and often offer warehousing, distribution and technical services as well as processing. It is interesting to note that with the increasing pressure on costs and the public's increasing desire for cheap clothing, many low-end and discount retailers are not concerned about the creased and crumpled look of unpacked garments, as their customers appear happy to receive cheaper goods in this state. This may be a dangerous avenue for them to go down. Garment processors are therefore coming under pressure as in-store product presentation levels decline and as manufacturers and retailers work more efficiently to get the product into good order before the shipping stage.

Jobbers

At all levels of the fashion business, from time to time stock in the supply chain far exceeds demand. It may that these lines are faulty, but more often than not, it is because they have not sold during the season as a result of poor design or, more probably, late delivery. Jobbers take advantage of such situations, buying up stock at highly discounted prices to sell it on again, usually at the lower end of the market, for example to discount retailers and market traders. Brands, particularly upmarket brands, do not want their usually higher market prices to be undermined by high levels of their own 'jobbed' merchandise. To this end, when selling to professional jobbers, they will often do so on the proviso that such merchandise is sold off in foreign markets, where it will not compete and undermine the current full-price offer. The world apparel market is currently oversupplied with fashion product, hence making jobbing an important and integral part of the supply chain.

There are an increasing number of other support functions in the fashion supply chain, including shipping and consolidation agents, as well as dedicated distribution and warehousing operations that work as outsourced third parties to the major players. In general they enable the supply chain to operate more efficiently and are more cost-effective. Speed of operation is assumed at all levels of the international fashion supply chain.

Fashion retailers' own foreign-based buying offices

Although many international manufacturers do have administrative centres based in other foreign markets, large-scale fashion retailers would often rather deal through their own foreign buying operations, which are usually set up in the main foreign garment manufacturing areas, such as Hong Kong for the Far East and China. These buying offices act as the preferred conduit between the retailer and their several manufacturers in the region. Foreign buying offices have the following key advantages for international retailers:

1 technical and commercial expertise on the spot to make decisions;
2 clear visibility as the main contact point for the retailer in that country/ region;
3 a good working environment and communication centre for buyers and technical operatives visiting the country/region;
4 clearly standardised work practices and methods for manufacturers to follow; creating an ethos of professionalism and of long-term business commitment.

One of the main issues relating to the use of a retailer's own dedicated buying office is the cost. It is usually very expensive to staff and manage a fully owned foreign-based buying operation. However, there are usually savings to be made in terms of the cost of travel and the time of the home-based buying management, as problems can be dealt with at source. Making quick decisions relating to styling and fabric substitution can also speed up product delivery into the supply chain and increase profits. Sometimes, retailers will use independently run sourcing and technical services, rather than setting up their own dedicated offices. There are several specialist operations available on a global basis to assist retailers with all their likely foreign sourcing requirements. In general, only the largest international fashion retail operations can justify the expense of owning and operating a dedicated foreign-based buying operation. As a halfway house, there are third-party operators who run foreign-based buying office representation for a number of smaller retail clients. These clients have a buying presence in a foreign manufacturing market, but at a much reduced cost. Whatever type of foreign-based buying office is used, it is very helpful to have a representative immediately available to deal with foreign manufacturers' brands because they are often able to give quick commercial decisions.

Concluding comments on fashion supply chain intermediaries

With so many different types of intermediaries involved in the supply chain, and with market forces constantly putting profit pressure on fashion retailers and marketers, supply chains are tending to shorten, and new lower-risk methods of market entry are always being sought. The customer is always the final arbiter as to whether or not the product, trading format and speed to market are adequate to meet his/her demands.

Fashion retailing

Fashion retailing is the largest and most customer-obvious element of the fashion supply chain – this section aims to analyse the different formats and the current dynamics of fashion retailing in a UK and international context. Most of the terms used are internationally recognisable.

A perspective on UK fashion retailing

Napoleon once described the British as 'a nation of shopkeepers', which was only partially true (there were apparently more shops in France at that time!). The term 'shopkeeper' reflects a historically second-rate perception of retailing as a career. In the UK the English term 'rag trade' also conveys the idea that textiles, clothes and the retailing of fashion are somewhat second-rate industries when compared with finance and professions such as the law, architecture and medicine. In stark contrast, Italy and France have historically had a strong, deep-rooted organisational support and cultural respect for their fashion industries. The French organisations La Chambre Syndicale and Comité Colbert are very influential in and supportive of French fashion. Information on both may be found on their websites (www.modeaparis.com and www.comitecolbert.com). Some information on the UK's British Fashion Council may be found within the LFW site (www.londonfashionweek.com).

In the UK there have been tumultuous changes in the structure of fashion retailing over the past 50 years. These include the disappearance of many local department stores, which have become assimilated into the large conglomerates like Debenhams and House of Fraser. However, as a result of the huge decline in the number of small, independent shops, combined with the explosive growth in large-space out-of-town retailing, the face of UK fashion retailing is changing fast. It is estimated that over two hundred thousand small, independent general retailers have closed in the UK since the end of World War Two. Many small specialist chains such as Dorothy Perkins, once only a women's underwear business, have developed into large multiple fashion chains. Throughout all retail sectors, the change continues at an alarming rate as supermarkets have successfully entered the clothing market and, in a matter of years, have achieved a significant market share of all UK clothing sales. It is estimated that by 2010 supermarket clothing sales might represent 10% by value and around 15% by unit volume of the total market. The supermarkets' recent and relatively fast expansion into clothing is likely to have a profound impact upon the future marketing activities of all fashion retailers. Here again we see how the significance of the Place element can impact upon the overall marketing decision-making processes.

The unique structure of UK fashion retailing

The structure of UK fashion retailing is different from that in other European countries. The UK fashion clothing market is strongly dominated by fashion retailers that have become brands in their own right. They are very different from fashion retailers in other countries since they only sell through their own retail outlets (single or multi-channel). Further, the UK fashion retail sector is typified by the small number of large, multi-site retail chains and a diminishing number of independents – approximately 30% of the clothing bought in the UK is from M&S, Arcadia Group and Next. Anyone visiting France and Italy cannot have helped noticing the many small, independent fashion shops, often selling a wide and eclectic mix of fashion brands. Criticism is often made about the level of homogeneity of high streets in the UK as a result of the proliferation of fashion retailer brands.

The shopping experience

Through the 1990s many fashion brands recognised a trend towards shopping as a form of entertainment for consumers. Sociologists and academic researchers have analysed a cultural shift towards shopping as a form of self-expression and a 'moment of freedom', as Vittorio Radice expressed it (2002). Under his management, Selfridges repositioned itself from a bland department store into Europe's leading 'house of brands', with a mission to create and operate places filled with brands and experiences that inspire and excite both employees and customers. In Radice's eyes the Place element was more important than the Product element. Department stores have always been at the forefront of what is now referred to as 'experiential retailing or branding' as the larger spaces and creative teams have traditionally presented very theatrical window and in-store displays.

Table 7.1 shows an approximate chronological development of the main types of retailing in the UK – many of the major changes have a similar chronology throughout Europe.

table **7.1   some key milestones in UK retailing**

1900	The introduction of public access to stores such as Selfridges – the real birth of the modern department store
1910	Woolworths opens in the UK – the US general/chain-store concept arrives
1920	Small multiple stores grow and flourish post-WW1 – Burton Menswear
1930	Major development and growth of the variety chains BhS and M&S
1940	Charity shops arrive. Oxfam opens its first shop in 1947
1950	WW2 clothes rationing ends and the first supermarket opens in Croydon
1960	The Swinging Sixties and Carnaby Street start a young fashion revolution in the shops
1970	The start of the design-led retail multiples, e.g. Warehouse, Wallis, Richards
1980	More aspirational fashion chains develop – Next and Principles. International fashion retailers enter UK, e.g. Gap
1990	Internet retailing starts in the UK
2000	Multi-channel retailers
2010	The multi-channel technology available to fashion retailers may threaten the traditional high-street format?

The fashion retail trading environment is in a constant state of flux, with certain retail formats and market segments increasing and others losing their historic dominance. The fashion marketer must be ever watchful for the shifts in market structure and size – many retailers have had fundamentally to reposition elements of their marketing mix, in response to market shifts. It is likely that the growth of fashion retailing by supermarkets and online retailers will create pressure on middle-market, slow-reacting high-cost operators.

Throughout fashion history, names have come and gone. A few of the names in the British fashion scene have either vanished or dramatically reduced the scale of their operation over the past few years, for example Richard Shops, Ciro Citterio, C&A, Allders, Dunns Menswear, Horne Bros and Etam. A full list of fashion retailers who have closed over the past twenty years would have in excess of a hundred names. Fashion marketers should appreciate that just as products have life cycles, fashion brands, fashion retailers and retail formats are also prone to the PLC.

The location of new retail developments

Most of the major retail development within the UK over the past ten years has been in areas away from the traditional city centres and older high streets. New purpose-built, indoor regional and local shopping developments are now being challenged at the planning stage, on the grounds of the detrimental impact they might have on the environment and the community of established local high streets. Large-scale retail shopping parks situated away from the historic shopping centres are also challenged because they are luring car-driving consumers away from the older shopping areas.

How retail locations are planned

When planning a new outlet and its location, large retailers are very interested in how long it will take consumers to drive to it. Often they will use sophisticated geographical modelling software that plots 15-minute drive-time isocrones. These look like weather maps, but clearly show that in London you could take 15 minutes to drive one mile, whilst if you are in the country you could easily drive 15+ miles if using a motorway. There is always a limit as to how far/long people are prepared to drive to do their shopping. Shoppers are not generally prepared to drive as far each week for the weekly food shop, although they might be prepared to undertake a long drive to a smart regional shopping centre to find a new wedding outfit. Large retail groups also use these geo-demographic modelling systems to check the locational logic and viability of their existing shop chains.

When Arcadia was under the management of CEO John Hoerner, it undertook a full review of the location of all their fascias in 'Operation Town Print'. During this exercise, it was discovered that Arcadia often had the wrong size of outlet trading the wrong type of fashion product, in the wrong town.

Burton Menswear shops were realigned to become Topman outlets, and vice versa. The overall effect was to make Arcadia's fascias work more efficiently and for the size of outlet to match more closely the market demand of each location. Many retailers find that over time the location of their outlet may go 'off pitch' as town centres start to develop away from their historical (once well-located) site. Towns often expand and contract, making the original outlet either too large or too small. Having the right location is essential for the Place element of the marketing mix. The old maxim states that there are only three important things in retailing: 'Location, location and location'! This is undoubtedly the greatest truism of UK bricks-and-mortar retailing.

The impact of new retail shopping centres

As in the US, these newer and more inviting retail environments act as a gravitational force, changing customers' shopping habits, sometimes forever. The large-scale modern shopping centre can be detrimental to the long-term survival of the smaller, older, local shopping centre, and there has been much lively debate about this in both the local and the national press. New large-scale regional and local shopping centres can lead to the overall deterioration of a local trading street, the first sign usually being the closing down of the smaller-upmarket shops, leaving the cheaper discount stores and more effectively managed national chains as the majority traders in an area. Ultimately, if this gravitational pull is too strong, even the larger national chains may pull out – leaving many empty retail outlets. Although an established part of our national retail heritage, charity shops often take up the empty retail units, mainly as a result of the lower rent now prevailing. Large-scale shopping centres tend to favour the larger national retail chains, again leading to a further diminution of the small independent retailers. Whether new retail shopping centres benefit the consumer in the longer term remains a matter of debate, with some parties arguing that fewer, larger retailers do not represent what economists would see as a competitive market-place. It is argued that if there are too few retailers in the market-place, there is a tendency for oligopolies to emerge, which ultimately tend to charge higher prices. On the other hand, large retailers are able to enjoy the economies of manufacturing scale which can lead to lower prices for customers. It is a circular and unanswerable debate.

From table 7.2 some general trends emerge, in terms of where customers are now choosing to purchase fashion products. It is important for readers to note that it is estimated that women purchase over 50% of male clothing on behalf of men, as well as purchasing or at least influencing around 80% of all childrenswear. However, female consumers are not as important in male clothing buying as they once were. Nowadays, younger men are taking greater control of the purchasing role as they become more confident about all things fashion-related.

The important emerging trend in the fashion retail business can be summarised as follows:

- clothing multiples still have a major market share in all areas;
- clothing independents are generally declining but are more important to menswear;
- supermarkets are making major advances in market share on all clothing fronts, including childrenswear, and are strongly price-/value-driven;
- multi-channel retailing is now very important in fashion retailing;
- general retailers including M&S are fairly static in terms of market share;
- department stores are still important – although there is no real evidence of growth;
- mail order is continuing to decline on nearly all fronts – some specialist catalogues and internet sites are doing well;
- discounters and cash & carry are gaining an increasingly important share;
- sportswear shops are declining for clothing;
- market stalls are generally declining due to the growth of discounters.

Table 7.2 shows a consolidation of the large UK fashion retailers, with supermarkets and discounters all grabbing market share. The department stores seem to be holding their own, but mail order and other miscellaneous types of fashion retailing are still on the decline. The greatest threat appears to be from supermarkets, which are adding clothing to their existing food offers as well as increasing clothing space in store. Many of the original supermarket clothing ranges were dull and unfashionable, but now we see more design being put into products that are being retailed at very keen prices. ASDA retails its George brand in both the UK and the US, Tesco retails Florence & Fred and Cherokee (a licensed US brand) and Sainsbury's has introduced its new TU fashion range. As more women shoppers become time poor as a result of their pressured working and social lives, buying clothes at the supermarket is seen as a great time and money saver. There is now no stigma attached to buying supermarket clothing, which is often seen as very stylish and incredible value for money. A recent and important media story was about Tesco offering jeans

table **7.2** **UK clothing and accessories expenditure – annual % retail shares**

Outlet	Men's	Women's	Children's
Clothing multiples	26.0	33.7	24.4
Clothing independents	11.1	8.1	7.0
General stores	14.0	16.9	11.8
Department stores	9.7	9.2	4.7
Mail order	4.4	7.2	3.9
Discounters and cash & carry	10.7	12.0	14.2
Sports shops	12.4	2.6	13.9
Supermarkets	6.2	6.5	16.3
Market stalls	–	0.8	0.8
Others (including internet)	5.5	3.0	3.0
Total	100	100	100

source: adapted from WF 2007

at £3; ASDA have more recently offered two pairs for £5. These fantastic value offers are creating major competition for the high-operating-cost mainstream fashion retailers. Even if these jeans were sold as loss leaders, the offers provided high levels of promotional publicity for both Tesco and ASDA.

Trends impacting on fashion retailing

In common with all areas of marketing activity, each sector has unique descriptors and jargon. A few of the more recent additions are explained below.

Fast fashion

Fast fashion places a different type of pressure on brands. Retailer brands are most commonly associated with fast fashion and have created an expectation of speedily changing fashions in the minds of their customers. Some argue that the influence is wider than that of specific segments of customers and that fast fashion affects the expectations of all types of fashion consumer and many associated fashion businesses, including the fashion media. However, the implication for the distribution of fashion products to consumers is profound, since stock turns and deliveries occur much faster. Zara, for instance, turns over its stock approximately seventeen times a year and the central London flagship store for Topshop, at Oxford Circus, can have six deliveries of stock per day. Fast fashion is here to stay and the speed of stock change at all levels of the market appears to be increasing.

Multi-channel retailing

Multi-channel fashion retailers are beginning to separate stock into the basic commodity items, which can be sold via their website, and the fashion items, which benefit from being seen by consumers in a stimulating store environment. The ways in which marketing planning and marketing communications can be used for each channel are fundamentally different and require different strategic and tactical methodologies – sometimes alone and sometimes in combination. It is unlikely that traditional fashion retailers simply using shops as a channel to market will survive in the longer term – the use of multi-channel retailing is an inevitable part of marketing development. It is now almost essential for all levels of fashion retailing to offer an online ordering facility.

Flagship stores

The term 'flagship' is derived from the fact that the admiral of the fleet's own ship was described as the flagship – the best and most important ship in the fleet. Similarly, international fashion brands (especially in the luxury goods sector) are being used as a key marketing promotion tool. They are generally in obvious prestige locations in capital cities, and aim to be a showcase for the brand, for example Nike Town in Oxford Circus, London. The quality of the displays, the newness of the stock and the expertise of the staff all provide a powerful marketing message – this is the brand to own. Some flagships are not profitable as a retail trading entity, but the publicity they generate and their image-making potential more than compensate. Luxury brands sometimes look upon them more as a marketing promotion tool than as a viable trading outlet.

The main fashion retail formats

Internationally, retail formats and definitions change marginally in different markets. Some of the key format descriptors are explained below. Each requires a slightly different marketing approach, although there is a high degree of cross-over and commonality in the marketing decision-making for successfully managing each.

Department store

These are large-space retailers, usually with several floors selling a wide variety of goods including clothes, furniture and general household goods in dedicated areas or departments. Originally a French invention – Le Bon Marché opened in 1834 in Paris – they are found in most developed countries and normally offer a wide range of upmarket goods and high levels of service.

Multiple retailer brands (including sub-brands)

Generally fashion-product-dedicated and mostly single-gender, these trade mostly on one floor and provide a clearly targeted fashion offer. They will sell all types of garments, footwear and accessories, with many now offering both manufacturers' brands and their own sub-brands, rather than trading solely on the business's overall brand name.

General or variety stores

The general or variety store was an American invention, and can be defined as a large-space retailer, generally focusing on clothing, food and some household items. Unlike department stores, they do not offer a full range of merchandise, most stores rarely trading on more than two floors. Prices are mid-market and service levels are generally low. The UK's general/variety store sector (which includes M&S and BhS) has struggled to retain its once-loved position in the UK public's affection. Some stores are finding it difficult to retain their market share, although the recent resurgence of M&S in 2006/7 appears to be going against this tide. These giant stores, with their large, cavernous retail spaces and more basic trading environments, no longer hold up against the smart and modern retail interiors being utilised by the fast-fashion clothing specialists. These general stores are also having to face a multi-fronted price attack by the discounters and supermarkets.

Value and off-price retailers

Clothing is increasingly being sold at cheap or discounted prices. There are three main types of cheap clothing outlet. First there are value retailers who sell at permanently low prices, offering minimal service and basic fabrics but increasingly fashionable garments. Secondly there are the permanent discounters who use continuous original v. new lower pricing as their major sales promotion strategy. Finally there are the off-price retailers, who sell mainly manufacturers brands at discount – using the suggested or recommended price as the top price then heavily discounting it. The various formats of value/off-price retailers are generally increasing their market shares. International TJ Maxx (US) and TK Maxx (UK) are good examples of this fashion retail genre. In the US over 40% of all branded clothing is reputedly sold off-price.

Supermarkets

Internationally, supermarkets are increasingly giving over space previously allocated to food and general household products to value-led fashion clothing. This phenomenon has accelerated in Europe over the past five years, particularly in the UK. The rationale for this switch is that clothing offers a higher profit margin than food. Supermarkets, as a result of trading in cheap-rental, large-space sites and offering minimal levels of customer service, are able to sell clothes cheaper than the high-street fashion chains. There is a large captive market of weekly food shoppers visiting supermarkets who find it convenient to be able to shop for clothes. Internationally it is likely that the consumer's willingness to purchase clothes in food supermarkets will increase – personal time pressure is an increasing international marketing issue.

Sports shops

Over the past twenty years, as fashion clothing has assumed a more casual style, the wearing of sports clothing for everyday dress has become an accepted fashion phenomenon across the globe. The brand-bearing, colourful, comfortable, easy-to-wear and easy-care attributes of sports clothing make it an ideal choice of dress in our ever more leisured society. Combined with the increasing celebrity status of sportsmen and sportswomen, there are powerful and logical reasons for the young, and increasingly the middle-aged and the old, to dress in a sporting style for everyday life. As a result, sport chains specialising in clothing and footwear are an important part of the modern fashion retail scene. In earlier times, the lower social classes, again wanting to dress like royalty and the rich (the celebrities of the age), aped the wearing of countrywear in town. The wearing of sport-related clothing has spawned several very large chains in the UK – JD Sports, JB Sports and Sports World. In general it is men who tend to wear sportswear as street fashion rather than women. With an ageing population throughout the developed world, it will be interesting to see if sports shops will still be so dominant in another thirty years. The US market has been the international driver of the sportswear revolution, with the global dominance of US sports brands such as Nike.

Independents

In earlier times, most clothing shops were owned and run by individuals and/or their families. The early part of the twentieth century saw the development of the multiple retail group, often based upon a local family business – the more entrepreneurial family clothing businesses would open another branch in the next town. Many of today's well-known UK retailers have their origins in a family business – Burton, Sainsbury, M&S, John Lewis, House of Fraser – as is the case in most developed countries. However, it is sad to note that across Europe the independent fashion store sector is declining in the face of large-scale retail competitors. The larger chains benefit from bulk buying and economies of scale, enabling them to offer better value than smaller businesses. Despite the high level of individual service available in independents, consumers seem happy to sacrifice service for value. In some more specialist clothing sectors, for example bridal wear, the independents are still taking an extremely large share of their segment – brides need the highest level of personal service and this is not normally widely available in the large multiple groups.

Mail order

Mail order's early origins and growth were mainly as a result of the relatively limited availability of credit, as well as a generally poorly developed retail offer. Before the days of easy credit and the wide availability of fashion outlets and products, many consumers would buy from a local agent's catalogue, or sometimes from small, local home businesses known as credit draperies. The grandmother of one of the authors was a credit draper, selling clothes to factory girls and then meeting them at the factory gate on pay day to get that week's payment before they had a chance to spend their wages. Today catalogues are in decline, although there is still interest in some of the more upmarket specialist catalogues such as La Redoute (laredoute.co.uk/com) and Bravissimo (bravissimo.com). Across the spectrum of fashion retailers and brands there is a strong growth in internet retailing. Nearly every bricks-and-mortar retailer has a website, which is colloquially known as clicks-and-mortar retailing. One of the fastest growing internet businesses is ASOS (As Seen On Screen) (www.ASOS.com), a site specialising in selling what the celebrities are wearing. In a similar vein, it is important to mention the increasing level of fashion shopping being undertaken via TV shopping channels such as QVC. As technologies, computers and TVs merge and high-definition television (HDTV) becomes more widely available, it is likely that more customers will be tempted to shop online, rather than risk traffic jams, crowds and out-of-stock lines in increasingly busy and confused traditional shopping areas.

Concessions (sometimes known as shops-in-shops)

These are normally branded departments operating within larger stores, on what is known as a concession basis. The area within the department store is presented and merchandised in accordance with the brand's external outlets, just as if it were operating outside of the host department store. The stock is owned by the brand and not the host retailer, with the sales staff typically employed by the concession brand.

How concessions work

When a concession negotiates with a fashion retailer, it will agree upon a fixed trading space in a relevant number of outlets. Sometimes a concession (known as a concessionee) may be asked to trade in several outlets, depending upon the confidence that the retailer has in it. The retailer (or concessionaire) will allow the concessionee to trade in the space, often allowing it to use its own graphics, fixtures and methods of display and sometimes its own selling staff. The actual terms of a concession agreement are thrashed out in advance, with the retailer receiving a set percentage of the weekly sales turnover – this can be anywhere between 15–30% or even more, depending upon the type of deal. Sometimes, the concession will be expected to provide own fixtures and staff, which normally engenders a lower percentage commission rate. Normally the contract will initially be for a few months, although if the concession is providing substantial counters and other specialist fixtures, the contract may extend into years. The benefit for the concession is that it can retail its product in a proven retail outlet, with minimal risk. The advantage for the retailer is that it can try out a new (possibly unknown) brand, without having to take on the risk of actually buying the stock – it can be a win-win situation for both parties.

The likely improved/extra sales performance from the proposed concession is of course a key driver behind its introduction. Some observers believe that a need to introduce concessions is an admission by the host store that its own bought ranges are not as good as those of the concessions.

Department stores' use of concessions

Department stores and other large-space retailers often have too much trading space, and offer concessions a logical way to fill that space. Fashion retailers may also use concessions in product areas where their own buying teams lack specialist trading knowledge, such as fashion watches or gifts. Many successful department stores such as Harrods and Selfridges have used concessions to complement their total brand offer. To a large extent, concessions represent the original co-branding partnership between brands. The host store benefits from the sales revenue, the concession's brand positioning and new customer traffic, whilst the concession benefits from a ready-made market with relatively low overheads. Fashion brands may find that concessions provide the only access to a particular shopping location where there are no retail outlets available. However, concessions can face restrictions in the way they trade. For example, concessions are not guaranteed access to department-store window space and there may also be a conflict if the concession brand operates its own store card and the host store does not allow it to be used.

The average consumer entering a fashion outlet can not possibly know whether he/she is shopping from a franchise or a concession, or whether the merchandise is actually bought by the retailer. Bought-in merchandise is usually referred to as 'own bought'. Managing the marketing effort of concessions can often be quite problematic for the retailer's marketing team, especially when trying to synchronise a store's promotional activities – biannual sales, mega-days or other sales promotion events.

Why retailers introduce concessions

The owners or manufacturers of fashion brands can often find it difficult (especially if they are new or unproven) to sell their merchandise to established retailers. Retailers prefer to sell their own brand or other well-known established brands, as they are assured of the suitability of the product and of its likelihood to generate profit. When new brands of riskier fashion looks/products come on to the market, bringing in a concession to take the initial trading risk often makes good business sense for the retailer. The main reasons why retailers introduce concessions are listed below:

1 The host retailer's own bought ranges are simply not enough to fill the trading area available.
2 The concession has merchandise of such a specialist nature that the host's own buying team has no expertise in purchasing it.
3 The concession is so cutting edge that buying and stocking own bought stock would be deemed too risky by the host retailer.
4 It is a facility for testing a new or unproven brand or product.

The concession is an ideal low-risk trading format for the fashion marketer to consider if uncertain about the trading viability of a new range/brand or product and internationally offers all types of fashion retailer a relatively risk-free way of quickly introducing new brands into their business.

E-commerce and the Internet in the fashion context

Following the global collapse in 'dotcom' stocks and businesses such as Boo. com in 2000, confidence in online shopping has taken a long time to return. Many e-tailers failed, having invested too much money in website design and marketing communications and too little in 'fulfilment'. Fulfilment refers to the delivery of products to consumers following orders being received on a website. Some fashion businesses such as Boo.com were successful in establishing brand recognition but failed to deliver the basic service expected of any retailing business by consumers.

In the early days of internet shopping it was felt that fashion would not be easily marketed online – this has proved to be fundamentally wrong. The *New York Times* reported on 14 May 2007 that online clothes purchasing in the US overtook online computer purchasing in 2006, when apparel sales reached US$18.3 billion as compared with US$17.2 billion for computers. The surging popularity of clothing on the web defies the prediction that fashion (which is hard enough to buy in stores, with the aid of sales clerks and fitting rooms) would be difficult, if not impossible, to translate on to the Internet. With the development of virtual shops in Second Life and virtual reality shops of flagship standard also available online, the number of fashion products bought online will increase both internationally and exponentially

Although still an evolving channel, e-commerce is now a significant retailing activity for many businesses which trade in products such as books, CDs, DVDs, small electrical goods and computer-related products. Internet retailing is more developed and sophisticated in the US as the take-up of broadband, website ownership and general experience of online shopping is much greater across the population. Successful American online clothing retailer landsend. com operates a website that is quick to download and easy to navigate, and encourages relationships with its customers through its affiliate marketing programme. It is important for readers to appreciate that online consumers are different from consumers who visit 'bricks-and-mortar' retailers.

Online consumers do not have a high street or a shopping mall to browse around; they use a website which they access via its web address or universal resource locator (URL), or which they find using a search engine. The latter requires the website to have specified the relevant meta tags to enable a search engine to include it within the results of a search enquiry. Online consumers spend less time accessing the brand's site than shoppers do entering a store. If the website is difficult to download or online shoppers can not find what they want relatively quickly, they will leave and be unlikely to return.

Internet usage in the UK is increasing and transactional sites such as Amazon and eBay are now mass-market businesses. Some niche e-tailers are now firmly established, including Net-A-Porter which won the award for best shop at the British Fashion Awards in 2004. Gap has recently opened up Piperlime which sells shoes, Amazon has launched Endless, a shoe and handbag site, and other such as Zappos.com are gaining popularity as a result of next-day delivery and easy return policies.

The critical success factors of fashion e-tailing

Just as with normal bricks-and-mortar fashion retailing, the store atmospherics of fashion clothing websites are very important. Kotler (1974) defined atmospherics as 'the conscious design of the store environment to positively affect the consumer'. Website design for fashion e-tailing needs to address the following main areas if it is to assist in stimulating and ultimately selling to the consumer:

1 **Product presentation** – ideally product is best sold from models, rather than seen folded or on a hanger. The three-dimensional representation of the garment being worn by a model is logically the most effective vehicle for the communication of an electronic image.

2 **Background music** – music has always been a good way of providing non-verbal communication and mood enhancement, with its clever use in the Levi's commercials on television being the best fashion example of the 1990s. Music on fashion websites can have the same effect. Adding

music to fashion websites can draw consumers' attention away from time delays, allowing them to surf the net in a more positive mood and leading hopefully to better product service evaluations later on (Cameron et al., 2003).

There is nothing more frustrating than surfing a fashion-based internet site which has poor-quality pictures, lack of clear colour/sizing information or a complex ordering procedure – especially if the site is slow, complicated and not user-intuitive. Fashion shoppers online can be very impatient and soon give up if the site fails to work effectively – this gives competitors an immediate opportunity to take advantage of the last sale.

The improving retail environment

Globally, retail environments and service levels in fashion retailing have improved dramatically, especially over the past two decades. During the post-war period between 1940 and 1970, European retail formats were in general quite basic. As society has become wealthier and as affordable fashion has become accessible to virtually all social classes, the design of retail environments has improved and this is now expected by consumers at all levels of the international market-place. The grand department stores of Paris, New York and London that were created at the end of the nineteenth/ early part of the twentieth century were, at that time, solely for the rich, with many stores barring the less well-off and poorly dressed. It was Gordon Selfridge who opened the first upmarket department store (in London in 1909) to advertise itself as being 'open to all' – in a way he was responsible for the start of the democratisation of fashion. In those early days, when labour was cheap, a high level of personal service was a normal and expected part of the shopping experience. As American self-service methods were introduced throughout Europe, service levels in fashion shops started to decline, in many instances becoming not self-service but rather a limited service, with customers doing much of the selecting and trying on of garments. As staff costs rose over time, the reduction of staff service levels became an exciting prospect for profit-hungry fashion retailers.

In common with many other product and service areas, international retailing (especially in developed, high-wage economies) is delivering less and less personal service, relying more on customers to undertake their own selection. Only at the point of purchase is the consumer assisted by a member of the 'selling' staff who simply transacts the sale. In more upmarket and luxurious retail environments where large profit margins are still attainable, good service is normally still available. Trained personal selling staff are expensive and in general they have been greatly reduced in most middle-market retail outlets. The reduction in selling staff on the shop floor has put the onus upon retailers to ensure that customers can easily find not only their way around the outlet but also, more importantly, the exact size and colour in the style they have selected. The need for clear and logically set-out fashion retail environments has increased as a result, with shop designers incorporating fixtures, signs and layouts that help the customer find the right product quickly and effectively. Fashion marketers are having to become more involved in understanding how customers interact with the fashion retail environment, and to devise and manage the aesthetics and the other more pragmatic issues related to good store design and layout.

Visual merchandising

It is the creative marketing skills of a good visual merchandiser that can turn a dead space into a vibrant and interesting area. Creative visual merchandising is clearly an important part of the total marketing promotional effort. So often, poor displays and store layout can actually detract from a product. A crisp, clean, modern and well-thought-out fashion retail environment can lift even quite mediocre ranges, as consumers' buying behaviour can be strongly and positively influenced by the quality and style of the trading environment. Good retail environments add value in the subconscious mind of the consumer. No one likes to purchase clothes in a dirty, cluttered and/or confused environment. If customers are caused stress at the POS, they often walk away. As time is such a valued and limited commodity, time-strapped consumers, particularly men, have a habit of walking away without purchasing. The need to make fashion merchandise easy to find has never been greater.

Scope

Visual merchandising covers all aspects of marketing communications activities relating to the in-store display of product and graphics, as well as the overall store sales-floor and window displays and general layout. It is a key responsibility of fashion marketing to ensure that the customer finds merchandise quickly and efficiently and also that the visual experience is as pleasant as possible.

Store windows and fascias

Over recent years, the term 'window and shop display' has been superseded by the term 'visual merchandising', which is now universally applied to any creative activity aimed at displaying fashion merchandise and/or services in the best and most attractive way to attract customer attention and/or desire. Fashions in visual merchandising change, as do fashion trends themselves. There are many historic and archive photographs of early fashion-window displays, which generally indicate a crowded and confused approach to window display where the retailer has tried to show every product. This approach is still used widely by retailers in less-developed countries which, being unable to afford any other form of marketing communications activity, rely solely on their windows to attract, inform and, hopefully, sell to their customers. Store windows provide excellent promotional opportunities for the host retailer. Innovative window displays involving the unusual, such as live models or interactive displays (through the glass), can all generate excitement and valuable PR.

De-cluttering – less is more

The modern fashion retailer now generally takes the 'less is more' approach to visual merchandising, with window displays that are less cluttered and allow those products which are displayed to be seen more clearly. The habit of closing the back of the windows has also changed: with backless windows the customer is able to look more clearly into the entire shop. The need to enhance the product and therefore the marketing proposition is paramount in such hypercompetitive trading conditions.

The large department stores have a long heritage of developing themed windows, and Selfridges of London has recently has turned its whole store over to international themes such as Bollywood, Tokyo and Rio Carnival. Although these exciting store themes have brought theatre back into retailing, historically stores such as Selfridges in London have often created innovative windows and in-store displays. For example, when Selfridges first opened in 1909, they put Louis Blériot's famous Channel-crossing aeroplane on display. In 1925 they also staged the first public demonstration of the new invention of television – to the amazement of their customers. The huge crowds watching soon blocked Oxford Street and, according to the father of one of the authors, who was present at the time, it required police horses to break up the crowd. Several modern retailers, especially the UK's first retail executive to earn £1 million a year, Sir Ralph Halpern, have always believed that retailing is akin to theatre, in terms of the need to make it exciting and spectacular. The product can often be greatly enhanced by unusual and exciting promotional activities.

Store atmospherics

The store atmosphere is an ever-more-important part of the Place element of the marketing mix. The quality and design of a store, both externally and internally, can fundamentally change the attitude of the customer and make him/her predisposed to purchase an item from the store. Internationally, famous architects and designers are being commissioned to design stores that have more in common with religion than commerce – sometimes known as temples of consumption. At all levels of fashion retailing, store atmospherics are having to improve in line with consumer expectations.

The golden rules of in-store visual merchandising

As the average international customer becomes wealthier and more fashion-design-aware, the modern fashion shop environment has improved dramatically in terms of the overall quality of the store design, its cleanliness and the ease of customer navigation. Most fashion marketing managers will look to visual merchandising as one of the key promotional tools in the fashion marketing armoury. It is simply no good having fantastic merchandise if you fail to show in its best light to the customer, explain where it is located in the shop and ultimately make it easy for the customer to try it on and buy it. Creativity in visual merchandising is now an essential differentiator of the fashion-retailing environment.

Good visual merchandising will create visual displays at key positions throughout the store. The main positions are usually located close to key traffic-flow areas such as escalators and major walkways and gangways, as well as till points and other areas where customers are likely to congregate. In most fashion retail environments, there are structural items, for example support pillars, that provide a backdrop or focal point around which to place special merchandise displays. Pillars may be anything from a place to hang stock to a plain background against which to display some key line or trend.

Some of the key rules of good fashion visual merchandising are listed in chapter 6 and below:

1 Ensure that only your best-selling new or key lines are shown in your windows – the windows are the key first point of contact with potential customers. New-line visibility is essential but window displays are also a major stimulus for best-selling lines.
2 Always ensure that your best-selling departments, themes or styles are close to the front entrance – this encourages customers to cross the threshold.
3 Always ensure that customers can easily reach merchandise and that rails and shelves are accessible – as customers will never work hard to pick up stock. Arrange potentially linked items close to each other in logical colour blocks.
4 Ensure that departments are placed logically adjacent to one another – men's shirts and ties, for example, are normally purchased at the same time.
5 Ensure that colours run logically – the rainbow approach to colour adjacency is often easy to achieve and, more importantly, easy on the eye; running the colours from red through orange, yellow, green, blue and indigo to violet works in most instances.
6 Ensure that merchandise featured in-store is just above eye level and in a clear sightline so that the customer's attention is grabbed.
7 Make all walkways uncluttered and wide enough for two people to walk past each other – customers do not like walking through a maze.
8 All fashion merchandise should be clearly labelled with the right price and size – it is important for customers to be able to find their size and see the price within seconds of handling the line.
9 Historically men's clothing and accessories have been located in the basement. This is because womenswear has been the dominant business. Customer traffic drops off significantly anywhere other than on the ground floor.

The shop and store layout should position related departments adjacent to one another. With fewer selling staff available on the shop floor, we have to turn the customer into his/her own salesperson by making their experience at the customer interface as easy as possible.

The need for clear and simple shopping environments

The way in which customers' physiology changes as a result of 'going shopping' has been accurately measured and it was found that their pulse rate lowers and they enter a trance-like state. Although these studies try to develop hypotheses and theories about the way in which people shop, the truth of the matter is that our psychological and physiological state varies dramatically, therefore making empirical measurement all but worthless. However, it is only logical that if the retail environment is well displayed and laid out, then the average customer is going to be brought more easily through the decision-making process to the purchase stage.

Less is more

Fashion retail environments that are overcrowded with merchandise, untidy, poorly signed and illogically laid out make it hard for even the most dedicated customer to find a suitable fashion product. It is interesting to note that some of the most upmarket and expensive fashion shops often display their merchandise very thinly. Usually they use a minimalist approach to stock levels, with window displays and in-store visual merchandising also kept to a minimum. This minimalist approach to retailing is aimed at creating an air of exclusivity and preciousness around the product. Conversely, the lower-targeted discount fashion outlets tend to have crowded stock fixtures and an untidier appearance, aimed at creating the the idea that there is a bargain to be found if the customer looks hard enough! Most middle-market retailers will use a combination of both approaches and more upmarket retailers tend to lower their standards during the annual sales and other promotional events. There is no hard and fast rule about approaches to stock and layout and visual merchandising; it is more a matter of the preferred and prevailing visual merchandising aesthetics of the time.

Customer flows into and around retail fashion outlets

One of the most important statistics that fashion retailers fail to measure is the number of customers who enter their shop and then leave without making a purchase. The percentage of customers who enter a store and then make a purchase is called the conversion rate. The way in which this can be measured is explained later on in this chapter. The next most important thing to ascertain would be the reason why they left the shop without purchasing. Common reasons for the non-purchase of products by consumers include the following:

▸ It was an unplanned visit to the outlet: browsing to fill time or sheltering from the weather (hot or cold).
▸ The visit to the outlet was not for purchasing purposes – possibly to use another facility or service, e.g. café, mirror, toilet, cash dispenser or other service.
▸ The product ranges, styles or brands did not appeal.

- The required style was not available in a specific size, fit or colour.
- The customer was unable to locate a product within the outlet.
- The shop was too crowded with people or stock.
- There were long queues at the till points.
- The changing rooms were not clean or were too crowded.
- There were no available selling staff to assist with the purchase.
- There were no mirrors available.
- There were credit card or other payment problems.

There are undoubtedly other more minor reasons for non-purchase, but in general fashion retail researchers seem to ignore this most important of considerations. The importance of planning the shopping experience for consumers is discussed towards the end of this chapter under the heading of blueprinting.

Measuring customer flow

Measuring the reasons for non-purchase – some more forward-thinking fashion retailers invest in what are known as exit surveys, in which customers not obviously carrying a bag from the retailer (generally a sign that they have come away discontent) are questioned as part of a marketing survey when they leave the shop. Although an expensive form of research, the information gleaned can be very illuminating. The best fashion retailers undertake such research on an ongoing basis – this is called a longitudinal survey – to ensure that they are making continual range and service improvements. It can also prevent small problems developing into larger ones. There are many large fashion retailers currently experiencing declining consumer loyalty who have stubbornly refused to pay for such research. In the scheme of things, the cost of such research is minimal when compared to the long-term survival of the business.

Measuring customer conversion rates (CCRs) – this is a simpler, relatively automated process, requiring only basic technology to gather the data. There are proprietary customer-conversion measuring systems such as ShopperTrak (see shoppertrak.com) being used by some fashion retailers. These systems use basic electronic customer sensors at the entry and exit points of the outlet continuously throughout the day to measure the number of customers entering and leaving a store. The data from these sensors are then merged with data obtained from the till transactions, and a clear measurement of how many customers are entering in any hour compared with the number who actually transact at the till gives what is known as the CCR – the equation is shown below:

$$\frac{\text{number of customers purchasing within a selected timeframe}}{\text{number of customers entering the outlet within the same timeframe}} \times \frac{100}{1}$$

= % CCR

Again, good fashion retailers will measure and compare this key ratio over time as it is a good indicator of whether or not the fashion retailer's ranges are being well received by the public. However, it is important to realise that there are many extraneous economic factors that can also impact conversion levels over time, such as the general macro-economic situation.

Measuring the CCR on a longitudinal basis is a good barometer of the general health of any fashion business, but it can also be a very practical tool in helping to create efficient shop-floor staff schedules. In most towns, the start of the day is quiet, with the trade building to a crescendo at lunchtime – usually between noon and 2 p.m. Other key trading periods can occur during late-night openings, sale periods and the run-up to Christmas. By knowing how many transactions are likely to occur during these peak periods, retail store management can ensure that the sales floor has adequate staffing levels to meet the increased demand. The problem of not having enough till capacity can be easily seen in food supermarkets, when not all the tills are manned and there are long queues behind the few that are. This is not rocket science, but it is fundamentally important for any fashion marketer to track and measure. Customers are the life-blood of marketing – simply taking what money we can at the till is not good enough in such a competitive industry. The authors remain amazed at the relative lack of interest shown by many large fashion retailers in such basic and easy market research. Fashion retailers ignore dissatisfied customers, or non-customers, at their peril.

Making it easy for customers to move around a store can add to the customer's overall feeling of well-being. Easy-to-find lifts and escalators, well-marked departments and good signage are a must for successful fashion marketing. It is important to undertake a layout and signage audit from time to time. Just as local authorities put up too many confusing road signs, so can a fashion retail business provide too much signage in the retail environment, which will confuse the customer, detract from the overall store ambience and represent a massive waste of time and money.

The need continuously to modernise fashion retail outlets

As customers have become more affluent, their homes and the retail outlets where they shop have simultaneously undergone both physical and decorative improvement. The house makeover is now ingrained in the British psyche, and fashion retail units are no different. When customers buy fashion garments, it appears to be a psychological boost to the process for the shop environment to be as fashionable as the products it is displaying and selling. Store modernity can be a huge driver in putting fashion customers into a purchasing mood.

On average, the modern fashion retailer expects to have to modernise and improve each outlet's retail environment on a three-to-five-year rolling cycle. Normal customer wear and tear, especially in high-traffic-flow outlets, soon takes it toll on fixtures, flooring and fittings. Small fashion outlets in a busy crowded shopping area will undergo tremendous levels of customer use and will probably have a shorter-than-average refurbishment cycle.

Fashion retailers targeting the fast-fashion end of the market normally plan for post-shop-modernisation/refurbishment sales levels to lift by over 50% immediately after the modernisation and then, after a few months, to be about 30% higher than before modernisation. The economic sense of keeping a fashion chain modern, clean and in good repair is obvious to even the least financially astute.

Good store visual merchandising critically assumes that the overall retail ambience will be clean and in a good state of repair. Customers soon stop entering tired and worn-out retail environments. In common with most aspects of modern marketing, customers are more attracted to the new, the clean and the exciting. New restaurants always seem to have a good launch period, because human curiosity is a powerful driver for first-time visitors. Whenever a fashion outlet is modernised or refurbished, there is invariably a huge lift in customer visits and purchasing as a result of the modernisation.

The main areas where visual merchandising has the greatest impact in any fashion retail outlet are (1) the window displays, (2) the POS and (3) the general layout of the merchandise.

Customer service in fashion retailing

The service levels of many middle- and lower-market fashion retailers have reduced to a point where they can only really be described as self-service. Self-service simply means that customers can only expect to get basic directions to a fashion product area within the store; once there, they are unlikely to get expert help in terms of fit, look or performance. Once found, the garment is then normally taken by the customer to a till point, where they are required to queue and then pay for their purchase. In previous times, when sales staff labour costs were lower, even retail outlets at the lower end of the market would have had sales staff who were much better trained to assist at the point of purchase. Most international fashion retailers are finding that their profitability is under pressure, and making a reduction in selling staff support is their first course of action. Only in countries where labour costs are still relatively low do we still see high levels of fashion sales staff, as is the case in India.

Personal selling in retailing

Fashion marketers must be aware of and understand the importance of the personal selling element of the promotional mix. Without well-trained, enthusiastic and motivated staff at the customer interface, other well-planned business and marketing activities can effectively be ruined at the final point of interaction. The need to differentiate between the perceived and real levels of service customer should be an essential part of the ongoing marketing research processes.

Fashion consumers who buy more expensive brands expect to receive a better level of customer service than those buying from, say, discount stores and supermarkets. Higher-priced and more complex attire may often require the reassurance and assistance of the trained salesperson. Good sales staff can help customers over the final decision hurdle and create a long-lasting customer relationship with either the brand or the retail outlet. The more unscrupulous staff, however, have been known to sell totally unsuitable items to consumers – this can be a short-term boost to sales, but a long-term destroyer of customer loyalty.

With the increasingly rapid changes in fashion trends and styles, it is now becoming difficult for fashion retailers to ensure that their customers are fully aware of the new merchandise on offer. To this effect, UK fashion retailers are now increasingly creating visual displays around shops with the aim of explaining to customers how to wear and coordinate their wardrobes. Although many customers believe that they are the epitome of good style, most would benefit from a second opinion when purchasing clothes – how can that eternal question 'Does my bum look big in this?' be answered, without the help of a second pair of eyes?

The use of websites by most larger fashion retail groups allows customers to browse through a retailer's range before leaving home, as well as to check out what styles, colours and sizes they are likely to find in the shop. Here we see the Internet being used as a sales and marketing enabler, and the customer has an increasing part to play in the process. As customers have less time to shop, the use of the Internet as a means of pre-shopping education may have a significant effect on long-term consumer buying behaviour. The Internet has many more uses for consumers than simply as an enabler for on-line shopping.

Retailers are principally service providers and so one would expect service to be an important focus of their overall customer offer. The level of service provision among fashion retailers and department stores in particular has moved on from the basics of fitting rooms, convenience of payment and accessibility of stock to more sensory attributes collectively grouped under experiential retailing. Many fashion retailers also offer some degree of customised shopping assistance in the form of personal shoppers or style advisers. It is interesting to note that personal service has always existed at the premium end of the fashion and luxury goods markets and is commonly customised to the needs of individual regular customers.

Service within the fashion industry

Service is an important element of distribution within fashion as it impacts on the Place element of the marketing mix, also referred to as the customer interface (POS), and throughout supply chains. Without an efficient supply chain to service the stores there can be no meaningful customer service from a fashion retailer. The extensive literature relating to services marketing has considerable relevance to the fashion industry, which is predominantly service-oriented. This becomes obvious when one considers the benefits sought by fashion customers and the level of pure service provision delivered across various categories of the fashion business.

Fashion businesses are typically associated with tangible products because for many people it is clothing, footwear and accessories that represent fashion. The majority of people interact with fashion as consumers and therefore understand it to be about the brands and products they buy and the designers they read about. Consequently, it is easy to assume that fashion businesses produce and sell tangible goods. However, on closer analysis the majority of fashion businesses are very dependent on service attributes in their delivery of benefits to customers. Some fashion businesses provide a mixture of tangible products and intangible service benefits, whereas others provide purely services. It is evident from tables 7.3 and 7.4 that there are many categories of fashion business that are either partially or totally service-centred.

It is important to stress that it is the benefits of their service-based business activities that are intangible, as opposed to the tools used in the delivery of the service. For example, trend prediction companies sell visual information in tangible formats that include trend books and webpages. However, the benefits to clients are not the tangible images but the accuracy of the predictions, design interpretations and insights into future consumer demand that are expressed through them. Similarly a PR agency may use fashion product samples to secure publicity in the media but the benefits to clients are the brand messages and the increased levels of awareness and the attitude changes that result from them. In fact, a large number of fashion businesses are pure service operations offering no tangible product to customers.

Table 7.4 features categories of fashion business that are predominantly associated with tangible products but which are chosen by customers on the basis of their provision of both products and services. Even if the end product of a fashion business is tangible, the chances are that the selection of that business by a customer is based on intangibles.

table **7.3   fashion businesses that deliver a service rather than a tangible product**

Business	Main customer benefit (B2B)
PR agencies	Publicity and other marketing services
Model agencies	A particular 'look' for a campaign
Trend-prediction companies	Fashion and style trend insights
Transport and logistics	Reliable movement of stock
Fashion agents	Brand access to retailers
Fashion recruitment	Supply of qualified employees

Business	Main consumer benefit (B2C)
Personal shoppers	Customised assistance with shopping
Hairstylists	Personal appearance

Business	Main consumer benefit (C2C)
Auction site (eBay)	Finding and trading hard-to-get items

table **7.4** **fashion businesses that deliver a mixed product/service provision**

Category	Customer benefit (B2B)
Fashion manufacturers	Products made to specification and delivered on time
Fashion sourcing agents	Location of appropriate manufacturers

Category	Customer benefit (B2C)
Fashion brands and retailers	Fashion products and differentiated service features relating to the shopping experience

It is not only retailers and brands that are judged on their service; garment (and other product) manufacturers are frequently selected on the basis of their service provision as much as on their ability to manufacture quality products. Garment manufacturers, whose customers are typically buyers from multiple retailer brands, are given orders and evaluated on the basis of a series of service-related issues. Service attributes that influence a retail buyer's decision to place an order with a manufacturer include on-time delivery, levels of returns, production and delivery in the correct quantities and flexible phasing of deliveries. The latter refers to a request from a buyer for the supplier or manufacturer either to bring forward or to hold back the delivery of stock according to the retailer's stock position. Similarly, a retailer may offer business to one supplier over another because of the design services available or because of its ability to source production effectively.

Even the benefits of a fashion magazine are mostly intangible, with the physical magazine acting as a conduit for information. Consumers buy fashion magazines for many reasons, including the way it makes them feel, a sense of belonging to a community of like-minded people, the information acquired and the sense of relaxation and enjoyment associated with flicking through it in a rare moment of personal time. The tangible characteristics are secondary to the principal reasons for buying and enjoying it. This is why many magazines translate easily to other physical formats, such as websites.

How services differ from products

Product and service characteristics

Zeithaml (2000) refers to a product service continuum, which expresses the relationship between tangible products and intangible services according to the particular qualities that they possess. Products are high in 'search' qualities, meaning that consumers can touch, feel, smell, try on (in the case of fashion) and thus evaluate a product prior to purchase. At the opposite end of the continuum are services that are intangible and so cannot be evaluated in the same way. Some services are so hard to evaluate, even after having paid for and experienced them, that the customer has to believe in the quality of what has been received. These are referred to as 'credence' qualities. A good example of this would be management consultancy and trend-prediction services, the benefits of which may not become apparent to a client until some time after the service is complete and the bill has been paid.

In between are businesses that provide a mixture of product and service. These include fashion retailers, garment manufacturers and fashion-related consumer services such as hairdressing. These businesses are high in 'experience' qualities, meaning that customers can only evaluate them after purchase and during their consumption (use) of the service. For example, a customer books an appointment with a hairdresser and sits through the process of having his/ her hair done before finally being able to judge the quality of the hairdressing service. Although he/she is not able to make an evaluation until the end there is evidence throughout the process of the quality. This would include the professionalism of the hairdressing staff (People), the appearance of the salon (Physical evidence) and the service features (Process), such as advice on hair care and other non-core service features. It is important for service providers to appreciate the potential for dissonance to occur and to manage customers' perceptions throughout a service process by providing evidence of good quality where it can.

The main differences when marketing services

Services require a different marketing approach from products for many reasons, including the fact that they are intangible, are difficult to standardise and are produced and experienced by customers simultaneously. Fashion products are tangible and so can be evaluated in terms of style, quality, fit and other criteria prior to purchase. In other words consumers can make a judgement about the benefits they are buying before paying for the goods. However, they also contain an intangible benefit centred on the status associated with the (fashion) brand's image.

It is not so easy to make a judgement when buying an intangible service that cannot be picked up, tried on or sensed in any other way; customers cannot see the finished service they want to buy as it is not produced until after they have ordered and sometimes paid for it. The service is in fact produced and experienced (by the customer) simultaneously. As a service is only experienced whilst being delivered, the customer can only fully judge its quality after it is complete. This makes the selection and purchase (commitment to pay) of a service inherently more risky for customers than when buying tangible products.

The 7 Ps – the expanded marketing mix

These points have major implications for the marketing of any fashion business that either has service as a significant part of its unique selling proposition (USP) or is a pure service. The additional three elements that supplement the traditional 4 Ps of the marketing mix are People, Process and Physical evidence.

People

People are crucial to the delivery of a service and convey important messages to consumers about the quality of what they are experiencing. In many instances the person delivering the service may be the main tangible component in the service that is experienced by the customer. This is especially true in B2B fashion such as PR where the confidence of clients is influenced by the interactions they have with the PR agency's staff. Many consumers stay loyal to the same hairdresser/stylist for a long time because of their relationship and the trust they have in the person. It is common for hairstylists to take customers with them when moving from one salon to another. Retailers who employ staff to sell to consumers, handle customer complaints, process telephone orders and deliver many other services are dependent on the performance of those people to reinforce the brand values and image.

Process

Process refers to the steps or service events that comprise the service offer. In general the fewer steps there are in a service, the more standardised it is. For example, a market stall only has browse and pay elements in what it provides. There are no changing rooms, alterations or any other service facilities, and cash is generally the only means of payment. In contrast, a shopping experience at a fashion department store offers many steps that can be selected and thus customised by consumers during each visit. These include cafés and bars, product demonstrations, personal shopping services, style advisers, personal makeovers, cash dispensers and other banking facilities, internet access, toilet and baby-changing facilities and relaxation areas for non-shopping partners (usually male-oriented).

Physical evidence

This refers to all the tangible cues that customers can use to inform their perceptions about the quality of a service. It normally refers to the physical infrastructure through which the business operates, such as the store, catalogue or website, and all sensory communications, including brand advertising, visual merchandising, promotional material and staff. Fashion businesses need to be clear about sending consistent messages to their customers which match the Physical evidence with the positioning of the service.

Service quality and gap analysis

Fashion businesses need to understand how customers evaluate the quality of their product and service offer. In the case of products there are tangible cues that customers (B2B or B2C) can use to evaluate quality. These include fabric, fit, finishing, trims, fashion design and many other aspects of a fashion product. However services do not possess the same tangible cues and as a result are evaluated differently.

Service quality can be defined as the matching of the customers' expectations and their perceptions (Zeithaml, 2000). Where a gap exists between what a customer expected from a service experience and what they perceived to occur, there is poor service quality. Where perceptions exceed expectations there is good service quality. This is part of the Service Gap Analysis model (Zeithaml, 2001), which states that in order for an organisation to close the quality gap, referred to as Gap 5, there are four other gaps that need to be closed first. These four gaps contribute to keeping Gap 5 open and are listed below:

- **Gap 1** – the gap between customers' expectations and management's perceptions of those expectations;
- **Gap 2** – the gap between the management's perceptions and the service delivery standards created;
- **Gap 3** – the gap between the service delivery standards created and the service delivery;
- **Gap 4** – the gap between service delivery and the external communications of the organisation;
- **Gap 5** – the gap between customers' expectations and their perceptions.

Customers' expectations are believed to be formed from their past experiences, personal needs, word-of-mouth referral (of others) and the external communications of organisations such as brands. The model has many practical applications in the evaluation of the service quality delivered by fashion retailers and other fashion businesses.

Blueprinting

The term 'blueprinting', typically associated with architectural design, can also refer to the planning and design of a service process. Services, like products, can be broken down into constituent parts and those parts can be engineered. In this context, blueprinting refers to the systematic planning of the service and assumes that a service comprises a series of steps or events which are service encounters between an organisation and customers.

Service events occur in a linear sequence following needs such as searching for a product, evaluating it, making a purchase, and so on, but each requires resourcing by the service provider. When applied to a common example such as a retail experience, it is also necessary to build in potential variability along the linear steps. For example, if a customer enters a store and seeks information about fashion products they wish to buy, the retailer can provide this in different ways. The simplest and cheapest way would probably be through signage. However, customers may have more complex search needs that they want addressing as they enter and, in that case, staff would be a more effective way to resolve the problem. Some retailers supplement this with a 'meet and greet' service. Department stores provide a range of information that includes information points that are staffed, signage and 'meet and greet' staff at key entrances, since the range of products is very diverse and covers a wide area.

A service can therefore be regarded as a process of linear steps with potential variability at each stage. The manipulation of the number and variability of the steps or events in the service affects the quality and the standardisation or customisation of the service provision.

Fashion retailers can increase the number of service events or steps in their provision to increase sales value and market penetration. For example, a fashion retailer may add an in-house alteration service/personal shopping/a store card/ gift vouchers/wedding lists to generate more sales revenue and to improve the service offer for customers.

It is possible to build in a specific customer experience that will appeal to a target market. The planning process can also identify at which points in the process 'moments-of-truth' interactions with customers are likely to occur.

Figure 7.4 shows the typical generic stages of a fashion retail service blueprint.

Fashion logistics and distribution

It is important to realise that in the UK there are estimated to be over thirty thousand retail outlets selling clothing and footwear at different levels of the market. Despite being relatively small the UK has a complex and densely packed retail infrastructure. Fashion retailing is required to turn its stock over much faster than ever before as the demand for fast fashion gathers momentum. This in turn has driven the development of faster and more efficient merchandise logistics and distribution systems.

Most of the large fashion retail organisations in the UK have fully automated DCs into which suppliers deliver stock and from which the retailer sends out the right level of stock to individual retail outlets. Having the DC in the right place is again an essential part of marketing decision-making. These sophisticated DCs receive stock, store it briefly and then pick the exact quantity by style, size and colour to be distributed to outlets all over the UK.

Specially designed lorries or wagons (as they are now commonly called) undertake regular store deliveries. Each part of the UK will have a predetermined number of stores and the most efficient route for the delivery will be computer-designated before the driver sets off on the delivery round. Most outlets will have prescribed numbers of weekly deliveries, although these may be increased or decreased in line with seasonal demand. No business can afford to send vehicles on long journeys to make deliveries of little value – it simply does not make economic sense.

Computer-assisted routing and satellite navigation and truck location systems enable logistics and distribution managers to keep their delivery resources working to the most effective level. Getting the right product to the right place at the right time is an essential part of fashion logistics. DCs were once known as warehouses, although this term is now rarely used, as fashion should be received and sent out as quickly as possible if it is to have the greatest impact upon the consumer. Fashion left in warehouses for a long period of time rapidly becomes unfashionable! The name of the game is to move stock as quickly as possible into the DC and then to distribute it in the most effective and efficient way to the retail

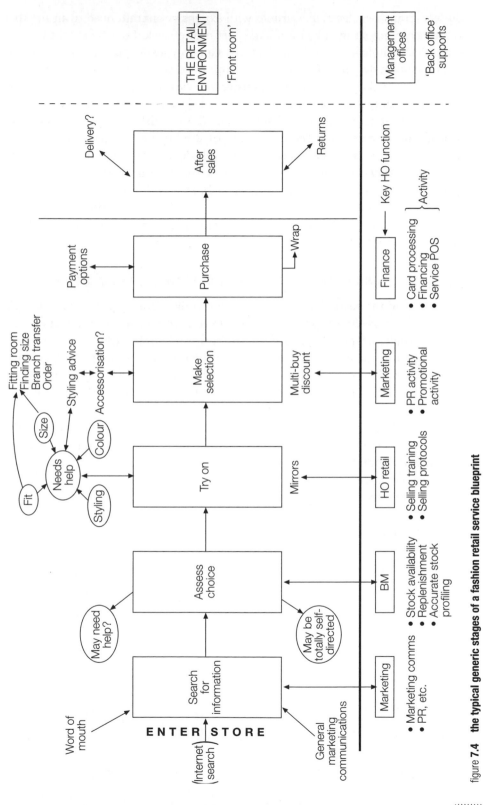

figure **7.4 the typical generic stages of a fashion retail service blueprint**

outlets. Transport fleets, like airlines with expensive aircraft, need to ensure that vehicles are not sitting idle for a large part of the week. Logistic executives will often deliberately have a vehicle fleet that can only just cope with average levels of distribution demand. They prefer to employ extra capacity from external fleet owners rather than investing in expensive vehicles that spend their time sitting idle and are only occasionally used to cope with peak capacity demands.

The cost-effectiveness of a fashion business's logistics operation can have a profound impact upon the net profits of the business. Most larger fashion organisations have a well-managed and well-developed operation where one senior manager or director oversees both the DC and the transport fleet. Good logistics is especially vital for fast-fashion brands and retailers. The need for fashion marketers to understand the limitations and abilities of fashion logistics divisions and suppliers is essential when planning virtually any form of marketing activity.

Supply chain management issues related to fashion marketing

In the fashion industry the generic process of distributing products to people is referred to as the supply chain. Fashion marketers need to understand the issues, problems and complexities of the supply chain in order to make timely and logical decisions when planning or undertaking any marketing activity. With such a high proportion of fashion merchandise now coming from abroad, failing to get the timing of the marketing right can be an expensive matter.

Whilst supply chain management is a separate discipline from fashion marketing, there are clear overlaps with regard to many issues such as the selection and management of channels of distribution. A fashion garment may well involve many separate processes/stages before it reaches the consumer, with certain stages being geographically separated. In the case of a printed T-shirt, for example:

1 yarn manufactuer
   ↓
2 fabric knitter
   ↓
3 textile dyer and finisher
   ↓
4 garment maker
   ↓
5 textile/garment printer
   ↓
6 wholesaler
   ↓
7 retailer
   ↓
8 consumer

(*Note*: the number of stages involved varies according to garment type and also according to the type of retail channel involved.) There are many different options that are dependent upon the business models of those fashion companies involved. Some larger companies such as Inditex (Zara) prefer to be vertically integrated in order to control product design quality and costs and the speed of products to market.

In general, within any industry, the shorter the supply chain the more efficiently and effectively the product gets to market. The ultimate short supply chain would be for a clothing factory to deliver directly to its own shop(s), removing the need for any decision-making delays by middlemen such as wholesalers and agents. With intermediaries, there are the added problems of time delays in decision-making, potential communication confusion and increased prices as a result of commission. In today's hypercompetitive fashion marketing environment, fast delivery and keen prices are essential ingredients of successful fashion marketing. To this end, nearly all large fashion retail chains are now dealing direct with suppliers to cut out the middlemen. This enables rapid communications, fast decision-making and a greater ability to bring fast fashion to the market at competitive prices.

It is important for readers to realise that the structure of each nation's clothing and textile supply chain varies. Usually it is the result of economic and historic forces; there is no one global model. The UK fashion supply chain is currently typified as having:

▸ a large number of national clothing retail chains which dominate the sector and a decreasing number of independents and small chains;
▸ a decreasing number of textile and garment manufacturers, which has resulted in a high dependence upon imported fabrics and garments.

In other European countries such as France and Italy the situation is very different, with relatively high numbers of independent retailers and a substantial manufacturing sector compared to that of the UK. Nevertheless, all developed economies are likely to decrease their manufacturing bases as a result of increasing global competition and the removal of a majority of trade barriers following changes to the MFA. It is likely that the current UK supply chain mode, with its high dependency on cheap overseas production, will be replicated in a majority of the developed, high-cost countries as a result of low-cost producers flooding their once-protected markets.

Concluding comments on the Place element

As consumers become more empowered and knowledgeable and as product costs decrease at the same time as conventional retail operational costs increase, the shape and functions of the supply chain and its constituent players will alter accordingly.

Traffic congestion and atmospheric pollution are now putting a question mark over the long-term sense of using the motor car for shopping. Add to this the increasing likelihood of more congestion charging and road pricing and fashion marketers of the future may not be able to rely totally upon the car-borne customer. The increasing use of the Internet for fashion shopping may be an obvious byproduct of global traffic congestion.

It is possible that improved internet speeds, better picture quality and reduced telecommunication costs will one day fundamentally change the way in which the majority of us shop for clothes. As will be discussed in chapter 9, the increasing importance of eBay in the trading of scarce and rare fashion items may be an important wake-up call to all conventional fashion businesses. There are very few differences between buying clothing from catalogues or from the computer screen – mail order once took a large market share of the clothing market. Internet retailing might do the same in the future.

branding in fashion and luxury

Branding remains the vital marketing tool to differentiate and attract consumers at all levels in global markets.

Alison Sachs, Managing Director, Swarovski

Introduction

This chapter aims to explain the underpinning theory concerned with branding and to discuss the subject in the context of contemporary fashion business. The global fashion industry comprises many different kinds of business activity, which can be conveniently grouped into the categories of B2B, B2C and, more recently, C2C. It is important to realise that companies and organisations in all categories use branding, although objectives and strategies vary according to the differing needs of business customers and consumers. For example, FMCG brands need to achieve high levels of brand recognition for their products, since they target consumers in competitive mass markets and do not control the POSs (run by retailers). Consequently, their marketing utilises packaging design, television advertising and incentives to influence consumers. Conversely, a niche web-based fashion business will primarily use online marketing and PR to achieve its brand positioning.

One word – two meanings

The word 'brand' generally has two different applications. The first and more obvious is the reference to a recognisable identity, name, logo or other symbol which acts as a means of communication between organisations and consumers. For example, we all recognise the word 'Coke' and understand that it represents a brand of cola. The second application refers to a particular business model, in which a company creates desirable products and utilises third-party channels to distribute them. It is able to do so since it invests in design product quality and communication as opposed to rebuilding. However, in recent years the distinction between the business models of brands and retailers has become less obvious, as many retailers have themselves become brands and most brands now have some retail presence in major shopping locations, or online. Brands, which have extended their distribution into retailing, are at risk of increasing their cost bases.

B2B branding

The approach to branding may be different when a company is selling to another business from the approach used when selling to a consumer. For example, a PR agency works to achieve publicity in various media for their retailer or other fashion brand clients. In the B2B fashion market there are many marketing services companies and specialist PR agencies such as Halpern, Modus and Red. Each has a distinctive brand positioning, a good reputation within the industry and is well known to its market, which includes fashion retailers and other brands. PR agencies vary dramatically in size: some may have only a few staff; others may have hundreds.

The attributes that fashion customers, or clients, seek from a PR agency are integrally connected to the outcome of PR activity – specifically publicity. Attributes, which are likely to feature as part of an agency's brand image, therefore, are performance-related and concerned with reputation and reliability. Customers value quality and reliability in the service provided, as opposed to conspicuous image. It is unlikely that the end-user fashion consumers, who buy the clients' products, would know of the PR agency involved.

Similarly, most contract-clothing manufacturers do not brand themselves to consumers, since their market is primarily the fashion retailer brands. The products made for own-brand fashion retailers are sold to consumers with the retailers' brand logo on them and through the retailers' own stores. The manufacturers' approach to branding will therefore focus on the needs and requirements of the retailer customers that they sell to, in particular buyers who place orders. As such, the brand attributes and values that manufacturers wish to communicate are more concerned with technical performance and service.

Some small designer companies believe that they cannot brand because they do not have the financial resources to do so. However, a number of designers have branded themselves in conjunction with a major retailer brand. This includes the new generation of designers at Top Shop.

B2C branding

Brands selling to consumers face more complex and competitive markets in which to brand themselves. Consumers are more numerous and diverse, and likely to be less loyal than the B2B customers. Whilst the brand attributes desired by consumers will also include technical competence and reliability, fashion consumers frequently demand a 'badge' that can be worn conspicuously to make a statement about their identity. Further, fashion markets are subject to fast-moving changes that directly impact on consumers' tastes and the decisions they make.

The terms 'brand' and 'branding'

Rather like marketing and merchandising, the term 'brand' is used in fashion to mean different things. Some observers consider it to refer only to high-end, established designer products. In fact, the term can be applied to any company or product which possesses a distinctive identity that communicates meaning and values to its customers. Ultimately the central aims of a brand are to differentiate it from its competitors and to convey meaning to influence customers' buying behaviour. The term 'branding' is used to refer to the process of developing and maintaining all aspects of a brand. Branding can principally be described as a process whereby a name and a reputation are attached to something or someone.

What is a brand?

Traditionally brands have been design and manufacturing businesses that needed to communicate with consumers through advertising, since the companies did not own and operate stores and therefore did not control the POS. Consumers are very influenced by the POS environment and so manufacturers' brands need to influence consumers before they enter the retailers' stores. Consequently, such businesses needed to persuade retailers (stockists) to stock their products while simultaneously persuading consumers to seek out those products. Branding therefore is a critical means of communicating with consumers before the POS, which is often controlled by a third-party retailer/stockist.

In the 1970s and early 1980s branding was largely product-focused and a tool used mainly by manufacturers. Some see a brand as a product which provides both functional benefits and added values that some consumers are prepared to pay for. Certainly there are famous products that are often prefixed by their brand name, such as Kellogg's cornflakes, Heinz beans, Levi's jeans, Louis Vuitton luggage, Barbour jackets, Swatch watches, Kangol berets, Burberry raincoats and CK underwear. Occasionally, an innovative product is directly linked to its designer's name and the two subsequently become interchangeable, as with the Macintosh, the Dyson and the Apple Mac.

However, a brand is typically much more than a product and is normally the name of a company, organisation or individual. As an intangible idea, a brand is not confined to the physical limitations of products that become old-fashioned, worn-out or broken but can be revived and reshaped in the minds of consumers. As Randall (1997) observes, 'A brand, then, has an existence separate from an actual product or service: it has a life of its own.'

Methods of expressing a brand

The ways in which a brand can physically manifest itself are complex. Some of the key techniques used are described below:

- **House or brand colour** – M&S, for example, has consistently used shades of green as its house logo/typeface colour. Selfridges has cleverly conveyed yellow through the use of its carrier bags.
- **House or brand shape** – the perfume bottles for Chanel No. 5 have retained a distinctive shape. Also the Diane von Furstenberg wrap dress is the designer's signature style and has taken on a generic/iconic status.
- **House or brand logo** – examples of this are the Nike swoosh and the Chanel double C. Logos will often take on board the house colour as reinforcement.

House or brand typeface – most brands try to use a standard typeface on all forms of corporate communication, such as shop fascias, websites, letterheads and vehicle livery.

How is branding physically applied?

The main opportunities for the physical manifestation of branding are as follows:

1 **On the outside or inside of the garment/product** – all fashion items generally have a branded label attached to the inside of the product. Some will also usually carry information about the fabric content, size, care and, sometimes, country of origin. Brand logos attached to the outside of garments are often highly prized by certain cultures and consumer subgroups.
2 **Packaging when the garment is sold** – e.g. bags, suit carriers, wrapping paper and till receipts.
3 **Printed communications** – store display cards, brochures, letter heads, window cards, price tickets, adverts, handbills, flyers, window stickers and nearly all items associated with visual merchandising.
4 **Transport** – on brands' own vehicles and any paid form of transport advertising on taxis, trains, and aircraft, for example the Tommy Hilfiger airship.
5 **All advertising and publicity** – all visual advertising communications and media will take the opportunity to show the brand identity to a greater or lesser extent, again as a reinforcing agent. Web 2.0 provides brands with more opportunities to engage consumers with high-quality AV and interactive software. Ambient advertising being is increasingly used – the Nike swoosh, for example, is often painted on to sports pitches so that the camera following the game will show the brand during the match.
6 **Personal** – sales staff will often have to wear the brand products in retail outlets as part of their contract. There have also been examples of

individuals with brand tattoos on exposed parts of the body – for which they receive a fee.

7 **Sound** – many brands have used distinctive jingles in advertising and for in-store sound systems – many brands now use pop or classical music to reinforce brand associations, as part of experiential marketing.

8 **Retail outlets** – stores, visual merchandising, websites and catalogues influence consumers when shopping.

Brands are forever seeking new ways to keep their target consumers continually exposed to physical manifestations of the brand, to ensure recall, reinforce brand awareness and build brand integrity and value.

What's in a name?

The brand name is arguably the most significant part of a brand. It is the hook on to which customers attach all their knowledge, experiences and perceptions of a particular company. It is also a trigger for consumers to screen in, and receive branded communications – it can be a message in itself. For example, the brand name Chanel communicates a message of exclusive luxury, whereas Fubu conveys a message of 'edgy', urban street fashion.

Furthermore, a company name is the one element of a brand that is very unlikely to change over a significant period of time. Consequently, the name evolves to be a major asset as it becomes a generator of sales, focus of goodwill and symbol for a host of differentiated customer benefits. In contrast, other aspects of a fashion company's branding, such as marketing campaigns, packaging and product designs, may change seasonally.

The name: refers to the company or product name that is used to articulate the brand. Most brand names refer to the company and many choose to express their name through initials, such as DKNY, M&S, ASOS and FT (*Financial Times*). Where the generic market positioning of a company is inconsistent with a desired fashion statement, then a subbrand is sometimes created to represent the product category – Sainsbury's, for example, is a leading UK grocery brand that has no fashion identity and so has used the initials TU to launch a fashion clothing range. TU was created after a great deal of research and is believed to be edgy and to have an international flavour. Frequently a brand that has been quiet for some time will be refreshed through the new associations made with the name. Lanvin is an example of an old-fashioned house that has been successfully revived and given a new more modern feel.

A logo is another expression of a company's brand name, for example the LV logo to represent Louis Vuitton. It is likely to refer to a company that is already a brand, as it needs an existing identity to reference in order for the logo to have symbolic value. Sometimes a moniker can replace initials, for example FCUK instead of FC. The rock star Prince once attempted to rename himself as a sign, which presented problems for broadcasters who were forced to refer to him as 'formerly known as'. Perhaps unsurprisingly, the rock star reverted to his original name 'Prince'.

Marks & Spencer have moved away from using their full name to using the initials M&S. This is in recognition of the fact that their customers tend to shorten the name when referring to the company and its products. A logo tends to run in parallel with a company name.

- A **signature** is often used in fashion and luxury to reference a distinctive designer who may not have the size or level of recognition to be a significant brand. Designers at Debenhams would be a good example, as they are specific to the store and do not have a global reputation. However, some market analysts also refer to the designer label Jil Sander as a signature as opposed to a global brand, in part because of its unique identity and because it is relatively small.
- A **unique product attribute**, for example the Burberry check and Pucci prints. A distinctive product attribute inevitably has the visible capability to convey brand image and values, but is more likely to do so through the evolution of a company's history rather than as a planned tactic such as a logo. In the examples of Pucci, Laura Ashley and Burberry, the distinctive fabrics are a feature of their heritage. Burberry has been very successful at using the check to revitalise its brand, although the subsequent adoption of the check by certain unsuitable consumer groups has proved difficult for the brand in the UK. A successful brand such as Burberry is able to use its heritage to move the brand concept forward to engage with consumers in new ways.

Colour and sound

At a simplistic level, a brand may be explained as a recognisable name, sign, product or service that is distinctive, possesses an identity and has meaning and value for its customers. The name will frequently refer to a company which sells products or services. However, there may be more than one manifestation of a brand name: it may be recognised visually by written words, a symbol and even a colour.

Orange launched its advertising in the 1990s with a teaser campaign displaying orange poster boards with just a name. This raised a great deal of public curiosity about something new that was orange, raising an awareness of the new product and service in advance of its launch. M&S uses its traditional green, occasionally varying the shade, Per Una is pink, Selfridges is a strong canary yellow and Monsoon is a distinctive plum colour.

Some companies also invest in audio branding to help strengthen their integrated marketing communications by enabling them to be recognised on broadcast media (radio and television) as well as visual media. Intel and Microsoft both possess very distinctive tunes that are used in conjunction with their logos when broadcast across audiovisual media such as television, cinema and the Internet. The tunes can aid recall of the brands and brand recognition in a single channel medium such as radio, while the images work to the same end in purely visual media such as print and outdoor posters.

Many people still associate Levi's with Marvin Gaye's 'I Heard it Through the Grapevine' following the ground-breaking Levi's advertising of the 1980s that featured Nick Kamen. In fact there was a period in the early 1990s when Levi's used the music of edgy pop/rock groups such as the Clash ('Should I Stay or Should I Go?') and Babylon Zoo ('Space Man') in television and cinema advertising. The association enabled it to inject a cool, edgy personality into its brand name, appeal to a particular market, and be linked to those songs in the future.

Brand positioning

The positioning of a brand in a market segment is normally an outcome of a company's marketing strategy. Market positioning is covered in chapter 3 and the same principles apply. Brand positioning in fashion is increasingly based on aspirational lifestyles and personalities which are designed to appeal to the target market. A brand image and message must make sense to the customers, who seek reassurance that it is relevant to their needs and aspirations. In all business sectors, brands are not static and move position as a result of external competitive activity. For example H&M, Mango and Zara entered the UK market as fast-fashion brands and repositioned many UK retailers who were slow to respond to fashion change.

A company's brand positioning may shift slightly from its original one through co-branding. Co-branding describes the strategic link between two operating brands that believe a synergy develops from a collaboration. The collaboration enables them to achieve reciprocal benefits from the association of their brands and is designed to advance the strategic interests of the two participating brands. Examples of co-branding in fashion include Armani and Mercedes and the various collaborations between H&M and various fashion designers. Karl Lagerfeld, who is best known for his work at Chanel and also for Fendi (LVMH Group), designed an exclusive autumn collection for H&M. The collection proved to be highly successful, increasing H&M's November sales by 24%, better than analysts' expectations of 19%. Since then H&M's collaborations with Stella McCartney, Madonna, Viktor & Rolf and Robert Cavalli have been successful in generating customer traffic and sales and improving brand positioning.

In the 1990s many businesses shifted the emphasis of their branding away from a particular product and more on to their company name. This is especially true of fashion retailers, who were quite unsophisticated in their image marketing throughout the 1970s and 1980s. Today, almost all fashion retailers have some kind of branded market position. Those who do not will probably find it difficult to survive as consumers struggle to understand what they represent and where those businesses sit in relation to competitors. In a very competitive and highly brand-conscious market there is a potential divide between the brand and the bland.

CASE STUDY

FCUK

In 1997 French Connection (FC), a hitherto undynamic womenswear fashion label, underwent a transformation into an international fashion brand. The change centred on the introduction of the (now well-known but still controversial) FCUK logo, which plays on the company's initials. The use of such a controversial logo ensured huge publicity and raised the company's profile internationally. The obvious pun on an expletive provided the company with a new image that was regarded as 'cool' for a number of years because it was rebellious, edgy and cheeky. Such associations are a critical aspect of the brand's contemporary identity, which initially enabled it to be easily identifiable with a younger, urban and trendy segment. The FCUK logo embraces both sexual and humorous references, giving the brand a wide scope in its marketing communications. Through focusing the branding on a logo as opposed to a product, the company has been able to extend into a much broader range of products and has secured access to retail space beyond its own stores. It has, for example, branded toiletries and cosmetics in the Boots retailer chain.

In the primary UK market, the novelty value of FCUK has almost totally gone and consequently the cheeky logo which was originally an asset is now a symbol of a 'has-been' idea that has limited scope for reinvention. It is interesting to note how quickly a once 'in' brand can lose its edge and as a consequence, lose customer loyalty and market share, ultimately becoming less profitable.

FC BRANDING AND PRICE

At its peak the FCUK brand was able to command higher prices than its diect competitors as result of the 'must-have' nature of the brand. As trading became more difficult, the company became less able to sustain those high prices. The price problem was summed up by Iain McDonald, retail analyst for Numis Securities, who said in 2005, 'French Connection has failed to adapt to the changing price perceptions within the UK clothing market. It is neither cheap enough to compete with the likes of Zara, H&M and Top Shop, nor is it distinctive enough to command the same premium as someone like Ted Baker'. In analysts' briefings Stephen Marks, the founder of FC, has repeatedly denied that price is a problem for the brand, blaming external trading conditions or inappropriate styling or merchandising deficiencies. However, as one FC wholesale stockist, Ian Snow, wrote in *Drapers Record* (2 March 1996), 'There is more competition from people who are cheaper but who are offering the same quality. You have got to be able to offer very good design and exclusive fabrics to make people pay more.' Here is a clear sign that, despite the historic power of the FCUK brand, if the product is not what consumers want, price can become a key marketing issue. Branding is not an automatic route to obtaining high prices.

FLAGSHIP STORES AND FC

Stephen Marks's FCUK flagship store in Regent Street, London opened in 2004 and it was not long before the company took its flagship-store strategy across the Atlantic, and opened a major Nicole Farhi store (an important subbrand in the FC stable) in New York in 2001. Here the emphasis is clearly on the marketing impact of the new megastore. The 2002 Annual Report states, 'The flagship Nicole Farhi store in New York has had a significant impact on the global awareness of the brand.' However, building brand flagships can prove expensive. As early as 2000, Alison Clements wrote of the Oxford Street store, 'While Nike Town is largely a temple for the brand, French Connection must make its flagship work commercially.' Unlike many of the world's megabrands, that open flagships which are not always commercially viable but which play an important role in promoting the image of the company, the FC brand's UK flagships did not really appear to be sufficiently different or ground-breaking to restore the brand's once near-iconic status. The FC stores frequently used large graphics and advertising in the windows to reinforce the brand's fashion positioning. One such included the strapline 'Apparently there are more important things in fashion, Yeah, right.' The statement communicates the point that those in the know understand that fashion is important. It does this using a tone that is consistent with a youth market.

FC AND GIMMICKS – A DOUBTFUL INTERNATIONAL BRAND BENEFIT

Whilst the original FCUK logo had immediate appeal to streetwise youngsters in the UK, it is doubtful that the English pun central to the slogan was always understood or appreciated in the company's increasingly important overseas markets – especially the American 'Bible Belt'. As Ian Forth, Account Director at the DDB advertising agency in London, wrote, 'I am not sure whether the FCUK branding works well overseas. Anything that really strikes a culturally resonant chord often doesn't travel well' (Forth, 2004). Here is a clear example of a cultural brand divergence, caused as a result of using a local/national brand attribute that will not easily be understood in another country.

FC is a classic example of a once-powerful brand that appears to have lost direction as a result of consumer brand perceptions changing negatively in relatively short period of time. The future success of FC will depend very much upon good brand management and a good product.

Brand extensions

A simple way for a branded company to grow sales is through brand extensions. In fact most new products are launched as brand extensions. Companies can develop new products within the perceived boundaries of their existing brand. Boundaries exist in consumers' minds about the credibility of a brand selling particular products. For example, it is highly unlikely that the Laura Ashley brand would be able to sell urban streetwear to teenagers because it lacks the right credibility. However, certain brands are able to sell a much wider range of products than others because their name represents an idea or philosophy which is communicated through the brand image and values. Virgin is an example of a global brand originally centred on the personality of Richard Branson, who is known for his innovative approach and entrepreneurial attitude. Through branding their name around a concept or idea, companies are able to develop and sell a much wider range of products that benefit from the same brand association. These are normally referred to as brand extensions and enable companies to increase sales more easily. Through the trend in lifestyle retailing in the late 1990s many fashion brands have extended their ranges well beyond clothing, footwear and accessories. It has been common for many years for haute couture designer brands to sell brand extensions, typically in the perfume, cosmetics and beauty product categories. Celebrity brands such as Jordan and Kylie have followed these same principles.

CASE STUDY

GIORGIO ARMANI

Giorgio Armani and Sergio Galeotti founded the Giorgio Armani SpA business in 1975. The company now has an annual turnover of €1.63 billion and is one of the best-known luxury brands in the world. It currently sees itself as 'an independently managed world leader in the fashion and luxury goods sector' (Sishy, 2004). The business operates through both wholesale and retail channels, accessing a retail network of some 325 stores worldwide, of which approximately 111 are group-owned stores. In common with many other fashion and luxury brands, Giorgio Armani sees stores as crucial to managing the customer experience and brand perceptions. The stores bring the various brands to life in the most complete and representative way, providing a direct interaction with Armani customers in every corner of the world. It is currently the only luxury brand that sells across all market levels, from couture with Privè to mass market with Armani Jeans.

Throughout the years the brand has grown to become global as a result of innovative product developments, brand extensions, strategic licensing agreements and joint ventures. Key licensing agreements include those with L'Oréal (1980) and Luxottica Group SpA (1988). Armani also has a franchise agreement with Club 21.

In contrast to many other luxury-brand groups, including Gucci, LVMH and Prada, Armani has preferred to grow organically instead of by acquisition. It has funded the growth internally as opposed to financing by debt and has remained independent rather than being publicly quoted or part of a conglomerate. This independence has enabled Giorgio Armani, the designer, to retain control of the direction and pace of growth of the company and brand. All too often a brand that becomes part of a conglomerate has to adjust its business and marketing strategies to suit the performance requirements of the parent company.

The company has a strong brand name which has a high level of integrity associated with it. This has enabled the business to maximise the name's potential by extending the brand into new product areas, including shoes, accessories and jeans, and new markets such as Armani Junior and the Casa homeware business. In addition to his clear business strategy, Giorgio Armani has created and maintained designs with an individual style and look. As a designer he firmly believes in the importance of pursuing his own ideas and creative vision, and ignoring what others are doing: 'above all I learned not to listen to other people' (source) This powerful and individual identity is what lies at the heart of the Giorgio Armani brand and underpins its integrity. Everything designed by the brand is approved personally by Giorgio Armani. It is of course hard to be too individual when in the fashion business. Ultimately fashion follows a pattern of development and a set of rules. Arguably the most important rule is to be broadly in line with the zeitgeist and uniformly agreed fundamentals of a fashion season. Otherwise a brand risks losing customers (both boutiques and consumers) and press coverage. This point is not lost on Giorgio Armani, who commented, 'In the work of fashion, if you don't follow the trends the press can ignore you. You are supposed to be yourself, yet at the same time follow the trends.'

When customers buy a product from a designer brand such as Armani, they are not buying just the product itself but also the whole package of benefits which the company has carefully built into its image and brand name. Such benefits include status within a reference group, a sense of achievement through ownership, product quality, heritage, association with a particular lifestyle, and so on. Giorgio Armani carefully creates products that people want; when asked about contemporary fashion he commented, 'To me, you shouldn't wear anything that defines you in a way that does not match your personality. It has to do with attitude, with freedom to adapt what you are wearing to your needs. It's not about wearing something that looks like it doesn't belong to you, either psychologically or physically.' Here is a clear example of a brand that bestows a raft of benefits, any of which can be assumed by the wearer to suit his/her own personality. Brands, like people, have personalities – often they closely relate to those of the brand originator.

What Giorgio Armani has achieved is a brand that is aspirational and in many ways somewhat understated – having a brand without formulaic limitations enables the fashion marketer to focus on a much wider variety of brand attributes when necessary. Bling and obviously ostentatious brands are too easily recognisable and the consumer may eventually tire of them. Brands with understated class will normally win in the longer term.

What makes up a brand?

There are various models and ideas about what actually constitutes a brand and how it is represented. In a practical sense there needs to be a name with which customers can associate and a product or service which they desire.

However, as the terms 'brand' and 'branding' have ever-widening applications, from political parties (e.g. New Labour) to individuals (e.g. Kylie Minogue), the precise ingredients will vary according to category.

Brand models and theory

Although the concept of a brand is simple and may seem commonplace from our perspective as consumers, theoretical models are helpful in explaining the complex elements involved.

Kapferer

In a business context a brand is a commercial name that sells products and services to customers. Kapferer (1992) refers to six ingredients or dimensions of a brand, which are:

- physique;
- personality;
- culture;
- relationship;
- reflection;
- self-image.

Levitt

Levitt's model (1962) helps explain how a brand can be understood by customers at different levels. In essence, it implies that all brands can be understood at the generic and expected levels, but that customers' engagement with a brand at the augmented and potential levels is harder to achieve.

The four levels are explained below:

- **Generic level** – consumers have an understanding of a brand in relation to the scope of its business activities and to its products, for example supermarket fashion brands such as George at ASDA.
- **Expected level** – there is a belief that the quality offered by the brand is acceptable and competitive. The brand may therefore become a cue for reliability, for example, M&S.
- **Augmented level** – the brand possess symbolic value and status. Gucci's name, heritage and reputation, for example, make it a globally recognised brand.
- **Potential level** – the brand aims to achieve brand loyalty from its customers though its superior benefits and unique positioning, for example, Bottega Veneta.

The model enables fashion marketers clearly to understand how consumers engage with a brand and what is essential when devising and planning brand-marketing strategies.

Interbrand

Interbrand, a leading global branding consultancy, believes that a brand is a synthesis of the physical, aesthetic, rational and emotional. Interbrand also identifies the following elements that combine to create a total impression of a brand (Clifton, 2003):

- products;
- service;
- name;
- packaging;
- advertising;
- direct mail;
- corporate identity and design;
- users;
- public relations;
- websites;
- company reputation;
- staff;
- history;
- promotions;
- sponsorship;
- environment;
- pricing.

While this may appear to be an exhaustive list, in fashion it is possible to add more, including store windows and runway shows, both of which have a considerable impact on the brand positioning and image of a fashion retailer or designer. What is evident from the Interbrand list is that virtually everything a brand does impacts on its brand image and reputation.

Although the three theoretical models provide differing views of brand components, they are helpful as general guidance – each brand and marketing situation requires an individual emphasis and approach.

Measuring brand performance

Ultimately the best method of measuring the performance of a brand is through sales and profit. However, other aspects of branding sometimes require measurement.

The brand asset evaluator is a sophisticated means of measuring brand value. It was developed by Young & Rubicam and evaluates differentiation, relevance, esteem and knowledge. Readers are encouraged to research this and consider its potential. However, fashion business models, particularly those operating online, are changing so much that new methods of measuring brand performance will undoubtedly be required.

One-word brand equity

Successful brands have always depended on simple and clear propositions, with marketers and advertising agencies endeavouring to summarise a brand concept as concisely as possible. Recently some within marketing have been debating the benefits of 'one-word-brand-equity' arising from the success of brands with one-word names. The issue is very much influenced by the huge global success of internet brands such as Amazon, eBay and Google. The latter has even given rise to a verb – to google, reflecting the unique way in which consumers relate to it as a brand. Advocates of one-word branding believe that by effectively taking ownership of a word, a brand will more easily take root in the consumer's mind. Further, the brand is able to communicate more easily using different media channels – which is very useful in a world where the media are very fragmented.

Brand image and values

Brand image refers to a particular mental picture and set of feelings that consumers have about a brand. The image is a composite of all that the consumer understands and experiences with regard to that brand and can usually be summed up in one word, for example 'cheeky' in the case of FCUK. It evolves over time as marketing communications and other activities undertaken by the company impact on consumers. Equally, all the experiences that consumers have of a brand impact on their perception of it. It is crucial in fashion to assign values, for example cool, trendy and exclusive to differentiate businesses. Sometimes a company may state a desire to change its image through advertising or other IMC, although this is unlikely to have a significant effect in the short term. Changing an existing image can take many years and requires all elements of the marketing mix to be focused on the same objective in a consistent manner.

The term 'brand values' normally refers to those values and philosophies held by a brand which are used to differentiate that brand from its competitors. For example, The Body Shop differentiated itself for many years by using socially responsible suppliers and ingredients. Companies in many industry sectors believe that it is increasingly significant for them to address CSR. However, it is not certain that many brands view CSR as a critical component of the brand values that consumers are seeking in fashion and luxury products. For example, real fur has been back in fashion for a number of seasons and has had the backing of several fashion editors. Equally, there is uncertainty about the eco-credentials of 'natural' fibres in fashion clothing, as treatments in crop production, fabric development and finishing and garment care are often less environmentally friendly than those required for some synthetic fibres.

Bogus brands

As a separate issue from the (illegal) counterfeiting of desirable fashion and luxury brands, there exists a market for 'bogus brands'. These are imitation brands that use names which reference particular national stereotypes, affording them a perceived quality and design status. In the UK such bogus brands may include UK-sourced fashion products that have names ending in ita, ani, ini or icci, which unsuspecting consumers believe are Italian in origin. Such brands are more often found at the value end of the market or in independent boutiques. Similarly, a name that includes London, New York, Milan or Paris may be falsely associated with the fashion status of that city. This is not solely a UK phenomenon, as many Asian countries also produce versions of Western brands, using words 'inspired' by traditionally English, French and Italian names. English-sounding brand names also enjoy considerable success in India.

Why bother branding?

In our current brand-conscious society people are less and less interested in generic products that offer purely functional benefits; they desire branded products and experiences that deliver meaning, image and emotional benefits over and above the expected product benefits. As competition has increased and the market for fashion clothing and accessories has become saturated so it has become more difficult for consumers to differentiate one fashion product from another purely on the basis of the quality of the products; consumers need something else to signify relevance or desirability in a product and generally the differentiating factor is either the price or the brand name.

In the past there was a clear distinction between clothing as a commodity and clothing as fashion. Fashion tended to be associated with designer names, and UK clothing was bought by the masses from reputable retailers such as Marks & Spencer, British Homes Stores and C&A. However, as business and consumers have become more sophisticated so branding has lifted most clothing from a commodity purchase into a brand purchase. Those businesses that had the vision to see this repositioned themselves, for example British Home Stores became BhS.

There are many brands that are marketed in many different types of consumer market – fashion is no different. Far from being restricted to clothing and a limited range of accessories, the fashion market now includes beauty products, cosmetics, perfumes, sunglasses, mobile phones, iPods, trainers, small leather goods, shoes and many other items. This has led to a greater need for differentiating on the part of fashion companies.

The growth of experiential retailing is a response partly to intensive competition and partly to the fact that consumers can be very influenced by their shopping experience in the store environment or at the POS. Flagship stores, epicentre stores and guerrilla stores are all methods of conveying a richer brand experience to consumers. As the proportion of UK consumer spending on clothing, furniture and food is expected to drop in the future, so the spending on leisure is expected to increase. Flagship stores operated by brands such as Adidas and Nike already blur the distinctions between fashion and leisure. These are as much interactive sensory experiences as they are locations at which to buy sportswear clothing.

The move towards a greater emphasis on the overall brand experience in stores illustrates a shift in the emphasis of branding to affect customers emotionally: 'A consumer's relationship to a brand is as much to do with what it makes him feel as to how it performs' (Olins, 2003). If customers feel good about a brand they are more likely to spend money on it, return to it and, more especially, recommend it to others.

Benefits of branding

In 1960 the influential marketing writer, Theodore Levitt, wrote a seminal paper in the *Harvard Business Review* entitled 'Marketing Myopia'. In it he made the profound point that consumers who buy $1/4$-inch drills actually need $1/4$-inch holes. In other words, consumers seek the benefits of the products that they buy. For many fashion consumers, owning and displaying the brand is the main point of, or benefit supplied by, the clothing and accessories.

In fashion the benefits sought from the products that an individual buys tend to relate to how that individual will be seen by others. Fashion is highly visible when worn, making it the perfect vehicle for an individual to convey an image to others. This makes it very attractive for fashion companies to develop a brand since their products are designed to be conspicuous.

Fashion is also highly disposable and by its very definition has a limited life span, meaning that consumers buy regularly and that there is the potential for a great deal of repeat purchasing. Fashion is about 'now' and 'fitting in', hence the terms 'in fashion' and 'fashionable'. As consumers have become more sophisticated, so they also want to stand out. This can be achieved by developing a personal style within the context of a fashion season.

Benefits of branding to a business

Branding:

- provides a visual cue to convey meaning and messages to consumers;
- directs customers' buying behaviour;
- differentiates a company from its competitors and acts as a means of positioning;
- facilitates additional product benefits by representing an image and providing status;
- enables a company to develop and sell brand extensions;
- secures future income streams so long as the brand is credible and relevant;
- provides brand equity to the company.

Benefits to customers of branding

Branding:

- reduces the complexity and level of involvement in purchase decision-making as brands represent appropriate choices;
- delivers consistency and reliability in the product benefits;
- provides status and other image benefits conferred by the brand through conspicuous association with it.

How do brands work?

Interbrand has identified what it refers to as 'five portals to a consumer's mind'. In essence these are ways in which a consumer can relate to a brand and they provide useful indicators of how to communicate a brand message to consumers. Each point gives a reason why a customer prefers a specific brand over others:

- **benefits and promises** – it offers a compelling reason to buy;
- **norms and values** – it resolves an inner conflict with their norms and values;
- **perceptions and programmes** – perception and behaviour programmes point to it (the brand) as a logical choice;
- **identity and self-expression** – it expresses their (desired) character and identity;
- **emotions and love** – they love the brand.

Brand loyalty

Brand loyalty refers to the deliberate and sustained customer preference for one brand's products over other brands' products. It is a key reason for companies to brand themselves in a competitive market. The extent to which customer brand loyalty can be achieved may be affected by many factors including the type of market, intangible benefits, competition and the subsequent risk (of dissatisfaction) to customers of brand-switching. The emergence of fast fashion in the 1990s raised customers' expectations about the speed of change and the accessibility of the latest looks. Fashion and clothing brands are expected to provide products that reflect the latest fad or trend in a way that is relevant to their customers.

Although young women's fashion is the most trend-sensitive, middle-market brands also need to keep pace with contemporary looks and deliver an appropriate interpretation for their customers. Fashion brands need to be innovative and on-trend to remain desirable and even then it is very likely that a consumer will buy other brands. As the fashion media have educated mass-market consumers about styling, so it is normal for a woman to wear an outfit comprising two or three different brands; the days of everyone wearing, or at least owning, a pair of Levi's jeans or M&S knickers appear to have gone. Today a consumer is likely to shop at an 'evoked set', or select group, of brands that she believes will best meet her needs for individual product categories.

How do you measure brand loyalty?

Interestingly, research undertaken by the authors for this book indicates that almost no fashion brand could clearly define in quantitative terms what they meant by a loyal customer. Brands accumulate a great deal of information about their customers but don't appear to use it to define a loyalty benchmark.

Parameters that many fashion brands could use to define a loyal customer include:

- the length of association with the brand (historically);
- the number of store/site visits (by the consumer) per month or other specified period of time;
- the average spend;
- the frequency of purchase;
- the ownership of a store card;
- the response to direct marketing promotions;
- the word-of-mouth referral schemes.

In order to define what makes a loyal customer, brands should monitor these parameters on a regular basis. Few fashion brands appear to have formalised lifetime value. Chris Anderson's book *The Long Tail* (2006) writes about the impact of endless choice creating unlimited demand. If this is the case, and it seems that e-commerce and other shopping technologies are facilitating an ever-widening choice (via niche suppliers), then it seems likely that brand loyalty will be affected as consumers are constantly tempted to try the next new thing.

Relationship marketing

In the 1990s relationship marketing emerged as a mainstream dimension of marketing thinking and practice. It was linked to a debate about methods of increasing customer retention and so-called 'loyalty marketing'. The latter refers to an incentive-driven approach to increase repeat purchasing by customers using the now familiar reward schemes or points cards. This drive is discussed in more detail in chapter 6, and is widely believed to have had little direct impact on actual customer loyalty. Loyalty marketing programmes can increase the number of customer transactions at a cost, but should not be confused with relationship marketing or brand loyalty.

Relationship marketing is a strategic approach used by a company to retain customers through the delivery of real value and quality products and services that are differentiated from competitors. It is believed that companies are better able to achieve this through a high commitment to meeting customers' expectations, service provision and a continuous dialogue with customers over their needs and wants.

Some argue that conventional marketing is focused on achieving market share by winning new customers without addressing the issue of customer retention. They refer to the difference in approach between a 'transactional' focus where the business is more interested in achieving many single repeat transactions and a 'relationship' focus where each customer is an investment and has a lifetime value. However, a relationship approach is more consistent with one that can achieve brand loyalty among consumers. When handled correctly by a brand, anonymous consumers may be turned into known individuals who became advocates for that brand.

Categories of fashion brands

The global fashion market is a complex and disparate one, containing many different categories of fashion business. The products of mass-market fashion brands are mostly bought and used by people who have little interest in the heritage or structure of the brand's business. There are, however, so many different types of fashion brand, in the broadest sense of the term, that it is useful to group them to understand their place in the market. By categorising brands some clear differences emerge:

- **Designer brand** – established or rising major designer whose signature personality is the key attraction and who is mainly associated with fashion, for example Paul Smith, Armani, Prada. There maybe some crossover with luxury brands. However, it is worth drawing a distinction between living designers whose name is the brand and luxury brands which have new designers continuing a legendary name.
- **Luxury brand** – a heritage global brand, such as Chanel, Bulgari, Gucci or Hermès, that is focused on exclusive fashion and/or luxury goods, is expensive and is coveted by consumers.
- **Fashion brand** – the business is primarily design- and production-led and wholesales/franchises/licenses its products but has some retailing, for example FCUK, Levi's and Nike.
- **Retailer (own) brand** – does not normally manufacture but designs and sources its own products through its retail network, which may comprise own stores, concessions, e-commerce and catalogues, for example Next, Topshop, Oasis and Warehouse.
- **Retailer's subbrand** – a brand owned by a retailer that is normally sold exclusively within the retailer's own stores, for example Per Una (M&S), George (Asda), Florence & Fred (Tesco).

However, there is no uniform definition of or approach to categorising fashion brands, designers and retailers.

The categories of fashion companies in table 8.1, used by WF, illustrate the different ways in which fashion businesses are viewed. For instance, many of

table **8.1** categories of fashion retailers and brands

Menswear

Clothing Multiples	Sports Shops	General Stores	Department Stores	Supermarkets	Discounters
Next	JJB Sports	M&S	Debenhams	Asda (George)	Matalan
Burtons		Littlewoods	House of Fraser	Tesco *	TK Maxx
River Island		BhS	John Lewis		Primark
Ciro Citterio					Peacocks
Topman					The Officers Club
Moss Bros					

Womenswear

Clothing multiples	Clothing multiples	General stores	Department stores
Arcadia Group:	Bay Trading	BhS	Debenhams
Dorothy Perkins	Coast	M&S	
Evans	Etam		
Topshop	Gap		
Miss Selfridge	H&M		
Wallis	Monsoon		
Rubicon:	New Look		
Principles	Next		
Warehouse	Oasis		
	River Island		

*Tesco retail their own brand 'Florence & Fred' and the US brand 'Cherokee'

the companies listed in the clothing multiples category would certainly see themselves either as a brand (e.g. Gap) or as a retailer brand (e.g. Topman).

Topshop is listed as a clothing multiple, which, although technically accurate since it operates multiple retail outlets of fashion clothing, does not really distinguish it sufficiently from other less powerful retailer brands such as Bay Trading and Morgan. Although Topshop is a national fashion retailer, it is also now a globally recognised fashion retail brand. This is because of the recent Kate Moss collaboration and the fact that it shows its Unique range at LFW. It has stores in foreign markets and is positioned as one of the main directional high-street fashion retailers in the UK. Many would also argue that Debenhams has a clearer fashion positioning than JLP, following its strategy to co-brand with designers such as Jasper Conran and John Rocha.

Ownbrands

To some people the term 'brand' has a more colloquial interpretation, referencing businesses whose products or services are considered very desirable. Typically, such products are broadly distributed by branded companies through retailers who seek to stock and sell popular products. The traditional relationship between a brand and a retailer has existed for many years in the grocery sector. Large multinational manufacturing groups such as Unilever, Procter & Gamble (now merged with Gillette) and Colgate-Palmolive design, produce and 'market' heavily branded products to supermarkets/grocery retailers such as Tesco. The branding strategy for their products is to create desire in consumers so that retailers will stock the products on their shelves. This distinction between the grocery manufacturers and the retailers illustrates the different business models – whilst retailers invest in stores, manufacturers invest in brands.

Supermarkets were originally only retailers of branded products but have subsequently evolved into a mixed economy of selling manufacturers' brands and own brands. Own-brand grocery products were initially considered to be inferior to manufacturers' brands and were positioned as value items targeting consumers who sought lower-priced goods. Own brands were created as a product response to more accurate segmentation of the consumers coming into retailers' stores. With the development of supermarkets' branding, 'own label' soon became own brand as product quality and packaging competed well with manufacturers' brands. Retailers are, after all, are in a strong position to develop their own brands as they have a regular flow of customers into their stores.

The term 'own label' has now largely been replaced by that of 'own brand' as supermarkets themselves have become branded retailers. Through developing their own distinctive and clear brand identities, supermarkets such as Tesco and ASDA have been able to increase sales by developing their product offers in non-food/FMCG areas such as clothing, home goods and white goods.

ASDA is also a good example of how a grocery retailer has been able to use its huge captive customer flow to sell non-food products. By employing fashion entrepreneur and designer George Davies, ASDA steadily developed its George range into a credible clothing brand over many years. The range has subsequently emerged as a leading value-fashion clothing brand within the UK and sells well in the US through Wal-Mart outlets.

The fashion industry demonstrates similar relationships, for example between retailers, including department stores and fashion boutiques, and manufacturers of fashion designer labels and brands. In this case, the term 'manufacturer' refers to brands both designing and producing top-end fashion or those making mass-market fashion products such as jeans.

Own labels

The term 'own label' is not as commonly used today as it was even ten years ago. It refers to retailer own label and the products that retailers design and manufacture under their own name. Initially associated with grocery retailers, the term has transferred over to fashion stores. Some examples are shown in table 8.2.

Fashion retailers have subsequently developed their own-brand concepts in different ways according to their heritage and market position.

table **8.2** **fashion retailers and their own labels**

Fashion retailer	Label
Top Shop	Moto
House of Fraser	Linea
Marks & Spencer	Per Una, Blue Harbour, Autograph
New Look	915

In the 1980s the former Burton Group (forerunner of today's Arcadia Group), experimented with various retailer brands. New retail brand formats were developed and these included Hutton (menswear), Radius (menswear), and Lady B. Lady B branded itself using a logo featuring an image of a woman with a bee obscuring her eye. Whilst this might seem incredibly unlikely, given the sophistication of modern consumers, it is illustrative of the excesses of the pioneering stage that fashion retail branding was going through in the late 1980s.

Fashion retailers have become smarter about the selection of sub-brand/own brand names. In the past seemingly little attention was given to the 'sexiness' and sophistication of the own-brand concepts, as illustrated by the examples of defunct brands shown in table 8.3.

Creativity and innovation are very important in successful branding and table 8.4 lists innovators of fashion brands in the UK.

Overbranding?

Some believe that people's daily lives are now too dominated by branded goods and brand names, a view that is supported by the immense choice available to consumers across all product categories. The evolution of lifestyle marketing to identify and satisfy consumers' 'related product needs' has been a major driver behind brand extensions. Fashion businesses have extended ranges well beyond the normal accessories associated with fashion clothing, into home products and electronic accessories such as mobile phones and iPods.

The trend towards 'anti-branding' means that companies need to be thoughtful about their approach and the message and image communicated to their target market. In the same way that Levi's anti-fit jeans are simply a baggy fit on the consumer, so anti-brand companies are simply projecting a differently branded message. New methods of communicating to consumers

table **8.3** **deleted retailer own brands**

Retailer	Brand
Burton	Mr Burt (young men's fashion, 1960s–1970s)
Debenhams	Debroyal (1960s 1970s)
C&A	Jinglers (men's casual wear, 1970s–1980s)
British Home Stores*	Prova (1960s–1970s)

* Repositioned by Philip Green as BhS

table **8.4**   **innovators of fashion brands in the UK**

Company name/brand	Category
Marks & Spencer (1930s)	Original mass-market fashion and clothing retailer
Dickins & Jones (1930s)	Original fashion department store (London's most fashionable department store for several decades)
C&A (1930s)	First overseas family clothing retailer to succeed in UK
Carnaby Street and the King's Road (1960s)	Original destination locations for young fashion
Biba (1960s)	Original womenswear fashion and lifestyle brand
Jean Jeanie (1970s)	Original denim-led retailer (mainly own brand)
Miss Selfridge (1970s)	Original multiple fashion retailer to extend the brand into cosmetics
Laura Ashley (1970s)	Original mass-market combined fashion and home furnishings brand
Richard Shops (1970s)	Innovative high-street fashion retailer using TV advertising
Warehouse (1970s)	Original design-led multiple fashion retailer (Jeff Banks)
Tie Rack (1970s)	Original niche fashion accessories retailer
Benetton (1970s)	First overseas multiple fashion retailer brand to become mass-market in the UK
French Connection (1970s/1980s)	Original wholesale fashion brand to diversify successfully into retailing
Next (1980s)	Original lifestyle and coordinated high-street fashion retailer focusing on working women. Innovative catalogue
Olympus Sports (1980s)	Original multiple fashion retailer specialising in sportswear
Katharine Hamnett (1980s)	Original fashion designer concerned with ethics in fashion
New Look (1990s)	Original fashion discount retailer
George (Asda) (1990s)	Original supermarket fashion own brand
Burberry (1990s)	First proponent of 'accessible luxury fashion' in UK
WGSN.com (1990s)	First 'pure-play' online global trend and style information provider
Zara (1990s)	Original overseas retailer brand to introduce fast fashion on the high street
Net-A-Porter	First online retailer dedicated to selling luxury fashion

through guerrilla marketing are really only creative and often extraordinary approaches to branding. This is discussed further in the next chapter.

Ironically the book *No Logo* by Naomi Klein (2000), which is an influential text on the issues of global commerce and 'one-size-doesn't-fit-all' branding, is internationally recognised. It too could be argued to represent a brand in the field of literature on social responsibility in global business.

A newly evolving consumer response to bad brand behaviour is termed 'brandalism'. Tempting though it may be for some to dismiss the term as a fad or an example of marketing jargon, it refers to a growing trend towards individuals challenging large corporate brands.

Luxury brands

Much of the branding theory covered in this chapter applies to the luxury goods industry. There are some issues which are specific to the luxury industry and which warrant inclusion here.

table **8.5**   luxury-goods market – product categories

Product category	% contribution (approx.)
Leather goods	33
Watches and jewellery	30
Apparel	10
Perfume and other goods	27

source: Yamaguchi, 2007

Until the 1990s the global luxury-goods industry was a relatively niche one, focused on very wealthy and sophisticated consumers. Luxury businesses were small by comparison with mass-market fashion brands and lacked significant brand equity. In the 1980s Louis Vuitton was a small luxury company. Today it is the largest multi-brand group with a market capital of approximately €$35 billion. Throughout the mid–late 1990's a sea change occurred in the industry and many old luxury houses were resurrected by powerful and emerging multi-brand groups such as LVMH and Gucci Group NV.

Many iconic brands of luxury goods, including Gucci, Louis Vuitton and Prada, began as leather-goods businesses. In common with others they have grown into fashion brands with diversified product portfolios. Towards the end of the late 1990s luxury-brand management had almost become formulaic, using image communication, directly operated stores and runway shows to reposition heritage brands as modern-day cultural symbols of success. Designers who were previously not known to the average consumer have become household names.

The repositioning of the houses into dynamic luxury brands has typically been based around a strong, new fashion identity. Fashion has provided the portal for the brand to travel from an old world defined by its heritage into a new one where its heritage becomes redefined. Louis Vuitton, Gucci and Prada – which were all originally leather-goods businesses – have become new, iconic fashion names in their own right. They also represent three of the four most significant multi-brand luxury groups in the world; the other (and the second largest) is Richemont.

Ironically, the fashion clothing paraded down the runways at both RTW and couture fashion weeks represents a relatively small part of the luxury goods market compared with other product categories (see table 8.5).

Terms such as brand DNA, dynasty and heritage have all been used by these companies and their brands to reference an original design philosophy that could be reinterpreted and made contemporary by new designers and marketers. Many other brands that have undergone rediscovery and repositioning were in fact fashion icons in their own right, including Balenciaga, Yves Saint Laurent, Givenchy and Christian Dior.

This broadening of the appeal has been described as making luxury accessible or democratised. As Tom Ford recently pointed out, 'Luxury has gone from being hard to find to hard to miss' (Jackson, 2007). The strategies used to achieve this involve integrated brand management as articulated by Umberto Angeloni, ex-CEO of the Bironi Group:

In the last 10 years we have witnessed the explosive growth of many brands. This has been fuelled by the accelerated creation of new wealth (during 1999 in the USA alone there were 1,200 new millionaires daily) and its consumeristic, status-motivated nature. During this period it seemed that to 'establish' a global brand was a relatively simple exercise: the hiring of a 'star designer', the staging of pharaonic fashion shows in Milan or Paris, celebrity dressing, the funding of massive advertising budgets (only ten years ago 4% of sales was the industry standard, while today it is closer to 10%) with subsequent abundant editorials, and the opening of a seemingly endless string of retail boutiques in every corner of the world. (Angeloni, 2001).

Luxury fashion brands which bear the name of their original designer are listed below:

- Giorgio Armani
- Ralph Lauren
- Dolce & Gabbana
- Prada and Miu Miu
- Donna Karan
- Versace
- Stella McCartney
- Jil Sander
- Helmut Lang

Some analysts refer to Jil Sander and Helmut Lang as signatures rather than brands. In both cases the originating designer whose name and individual identity is synonymous with the signature label left the company in early 2005.

Whilst there are still many luxury fashion businesses that employ 'star' designers to drive the creative direction of their brands, including Louis Vuitton (Marc Jacobs), the industry has moved away from this. Some luxury brands are prepared to wait months before finding the right designer, such as Chloé, which recently appointed Paulo Melim Andersson following the departure of the hugely successful Phoebe Filo. Table 8.6 lists luxury fashion brands which employ star designers.

Table 8.7 lists luxury fashion brands which employ successful designers who have yet to become household names.

table **8.6** **luxury fashion brands employing star designers**

Iconic brand	Star designer
Christian Dior	John Galliano
Hermès	John Paul Gaultier
Chanel	Karl Lagerfeld
Louis Vuitton	Marc Jacobs

table **8.7** **luxury fashion brands employing successful designers**

Iconic brand	Designer
Givenchy	Richard Tisci
Gucci	Frida Giannini
Yves Saint Laurent	Stefano Pilati
Balenciaga	Nicolas Ghesquière
Burberry	Christopher Bailey
Lanvin	Albert Elbaz
Chloé	Paulo Melim Andersson

In luxury, branding is critical since image and status are important benefits for consumers. Two key brand management issues for luxury brands are product integrity and directly operated store distribution.

Product integrity

For many consumers the artisan quality of a luxury product is what distinguishes it from the mass market. This is typically linked to the perceptions about national identity and the country of manufacture. This issue of 'made-in' is especially important to consumers from emerging markets who may need the reassurance of a brand's heritage to understand its value. 'Made in Italy' is considered key for both Valentino and Gucci as consumers buy the name and the history of the name. Many argue that creativity and the ability or 'know-how' associated with innovation and craftsmanship are the real critical success factors that underpin product integrity within the luxury market. Umberto Angeloni of Brioni argues that the 'making factor is a major component in the brand and a basic element of the dream factor.' He also believes that moving production could affect product integrity, which is an important element of a legendary brand: 'If you forget the brand you are no longer legendary' (Jackson, 2005). Product integrity is undermined by counterfeiting, which is a huge global problem. Although many consumers are deceived into buying fakes, others see no harm in buying what they regard to be a cheap version. Bernard Arnault of LVMH has recently commented that the industry must now tackle this problem and make it socially unacceptable to own fakes.

Directly operated store distribution

Most luxury brands have moved away from licensing and franchising as channels of distribution in favour of own stores. These are often large, exotic flagship stores that are used as much for brand management as they are for generating sales. Gucci now generates 70% of its sales revenues through a global network of more than two hundred directly operated stores and regards them as the cornerstone of its strategy. Its flagship store in Ginza, Tokyo delivers exceptional levels of service and the selling price of its goods is 20% higher than the average for the Japanese market.

Concluding thoughts

There are many definitions of the term 'brand' all of which refer to the need to be recognisable, differentiated and have meaning to customers. In fashion, whilst all these factors are important, a fashion brand is also something that customers want to be associated with through the conspicuous use (or wearing) of its products. This is not a dimension that all brands share. For example, most household goods (from FMCG to electrical) are branded, but the significance of the brand names is primarily associated with product quality, reliability and performance, as opposed to conspicuous 'badge-wearing'. Other product categories are also conspicuous (e.g. cars and alcohol) and are subject to similar 'fashion' trends, but badge-wearing will always be an essential characteristic of fashion products. Even the recent 'don't flaunt it' message from some luxury brands is a positioning statement to reassure their wealthy customers that there is still a cachet attached to ownership of the products.

'For a brand to succeed it has to reflect the needs and the desires of a generation at a particular point in time. It has to be of the moment, but with eternal values that will always be recognized' (Menkes, 2001).

new approaches to fashion marketing

We are witnessing a profound consumer communications revolution, with a declining sense of trust in advertising as the best source for information about products and services: this challenges brands to create new channels of communications. Media is the new creativity

Ben Richards – Director, Naked Communications

Introduction

This chapter aims to inform readers about the relatively new approaches to marketing that have emerged in the US and Europe since the late 1990s. Much traditional marketing theory stems from American academics and practitioners from the 1950s onwards and was developed in a world where markets were more homogenous and less competitive.

Today each new generation of consumers is exposed to commercial influences, advances in technologies, social attitudes and lifestyles that are often fundamentally different from those experienced by the previous generation. This is making conventional approaches to marketing less effective as consumers are more informed about products, brands and prices and are generally cynical about the marketing messages communicated by large corporations. Further, as technologies evolve and societies become more socially and culturally diverse, so people's values, attitudes, lifestyles and media viewing and consumption habits are changing and becoming increasingly fragmented. The social networks which have developed as a result of the Internet revolution have enabled people to become connected irrespective of geographical location. The benefits of connectivity are now enhanced by mobile provision, enabling people to engage with the Internet more flexibly and spontaneously.

Greater market fragmentation in terms of both supply (branded competition) and consumer demand means that PLCs are likely to become shorter and product styles are likely to change faster in many sectors but especially in fashion. Fashion is traditionally defined by change and now change occurs more quickly.

New approaches to communication

Advertising was the dominant method of communication for influencing mass-market consumer demand throughout the twentieth century. It is traditionally regarded as an effective means of raising awareness and influencing the attitudes of consumers. In general terms, brands rely more on advertising than do retailers (who use stores to communicate as well as to distribute) and luxury brands spend proportionately more than mass-market brands. However, the value and relevance of single-way communication, from brand to customer, is considered by many marketers to be limited when compared with more interactive, experiential, and customised communications. New media technologies have paved the way for more user-centred, interactive and flexible forms of communication such as blogs, wikis and social networks, which encourage and facilitate the uploading of user-generated content. Fashion and celebrity, in particular, are subjects that easily transfer to the webpage from hard copy. Why bother reading a hard-copy magazine when the interesting information you seek is also available (without the adverts) via mobile wi-fi access on a specialist website which is updated daily? Further, why not log on to a social network site where large numbers of like-minded people can discuss topics of shared interest instantly? A hard-copy magazine lacks the benefits of instant interactivity, which are important for many younger consumers.

A key issue for marketers is to recognise not only that today's connected consumers have the ability to do this but also that today's teens and pre-teens are very likely to grow up using improved versions of such technologies as their primary means of communication in the future. Fashion brands are facing the challenge of communicating with today's technology converts (who have at least grown up with hard-copy media) and tomorrow's 'techno' generation.

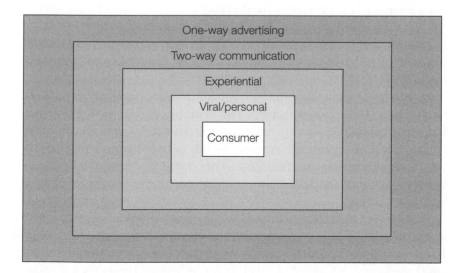

figure **9.1** **wrapping the consumer in layers (1)**

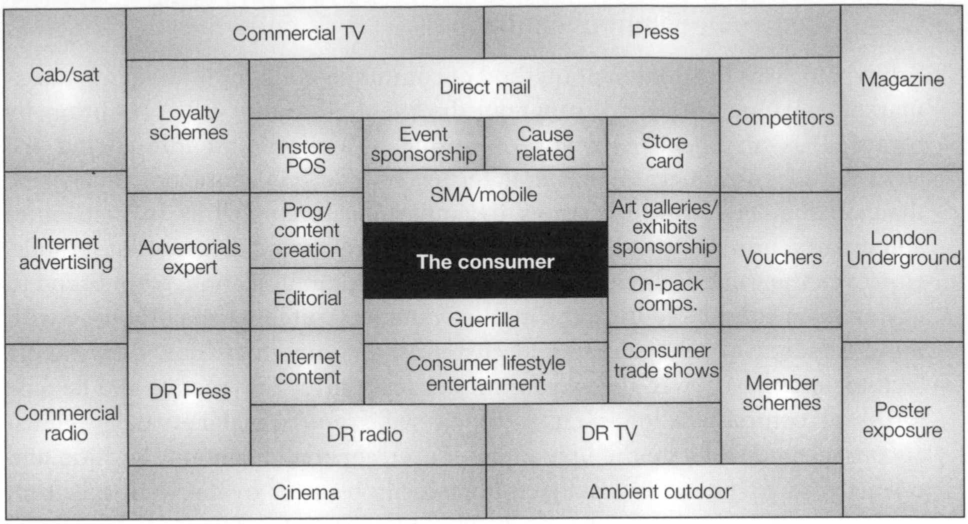
Commercial TV
Press
Cab/sat
Magazine
Direct mail
Loyalty schemes
Competitors
Instore POS
Event sponsorship
Cause related
Store card
SMA/mobile
Prog/ content creation
Art galleries/ exhibits sponsorship
Internet advertising
Advertorials expert
The consumer
Vouchers
London Underground
Editorial
On-pack comps.
Guerrilla
Internet content
Consumer lifestyle entertainment
Consumer trade shows
DR Press
Member schemes
Commercial radio
DR radio
DR TV
Poster exposure
Cinema
Ambient outdoor

figure **9.2** **wrapping the consumer in layers (2)**

Methods of communicating with consumers

The models created by Naked Communications (figures 9.1 and 9.2) illustrate a multi-faceted, layered approach to communication with consumers. Each layer involves a different level of interaction with the audience, beginning with the single-way advertising (all media) in which consumers simply receive messages. Single-way advertising, from brand to consumer, is a 'scatter-gun' approach to communication normally associated with mass markets. FMCG brands advertise in this way, using media such as television to target a mass consumer market. The somewhat dictatorial approach of advertising contrasts sharply with the other methods illustrated in figure 9.1, which involve varying degrees of consumer participation. In general terms the more consumers participate and are engaged, the greater the impact of the communication upon them.

In addition to variation in the levels of interaction, the methods also vary in the credibility of their impact. For example, a viral SMS campaign often has more credibility for consumers since the message is communicated via friends and colleagues. An example of this is the Dove 'outrage' self-esteem viral campaign run via YouTube. This word of mouth is distinct from branded advertising, which is typically seen by consumers as corporate selling.

In Figure 9.2 the different marketing communications methods are positioned at varying distances from the centre, representing the levels of interaction and customer closeness: the closer they are to the consumer the greater the impact. Viral marketing, which often involves an individual receiving a message from a friend or other close contact (reference group), is believed to have a greater impact than single-line methods of communication. In summary, marketing communications are moving from broadcasting, where it is hoped that a message will get through, to 'uni-casting' to individuals.

The changing world of communications

The term 'marketing communications' has always been broader than advertising, encompassing PR, visual merchandising, packaging, events management and many other communicative activities designed to raise awareness and influence customers' attitudes. The emergence of experiential marketing and 'retailment' in the late 1990s extended the methods used to influence consumers to include various in-store or retail-based experiences. Such developments recognised the fact that consumers are very easily influenced at the POS. Store design, ambience and layout are now critical success factors for many fashion retailers and fashion and luxury brands. In fact the Place element of the marketing mix is often as important as the Product element for many flagship and department stores, especially when they carry the same brands as their competitors. The huge investment that some brands have made in their limited retail networks, mostly comprising flagship stores, has necessitated greater creativity in store design. Some might argue that as much if not more creativity now goes into the design and marketing of stores as goes into the products sold in them. In fact, stores have been described as adverts with walls. As brands and retailer brands compete for customers in densely packed retail locations, it becomes more important for stores to stand out and be innovative.

The changing role of stores has meant that they are now:

- a brand communication vehicle in a busy shopping location;
- an advert to direct consumers to other channels such as websites;
- a location to deliver entertainment and sensory experiences to consumers.

However, cyberspace is likely to be the next battleground for brands as consumers move spending from real-world stores to online virtual selling environments and websites. Creativity and innovation will still be critical success factors in engaging consumers but the retail infrastructure costs will be much lower.

The diminishing role of advertising

Advertising used to be considered the most influential marketing tool when communicating with consumers. It is able to convey a brand's message very powerfully to a relatively homogenous mass market via widely accessed media. In the UK the broadcast media used to comprise one or two commercial channels, which could command an audience of millions at peak viewing times, and a limited number of commercial radio stations. Now consumers have access to a large number of commercial television stations through satellite and cable technology and to many radio stations via digital radio – the most recent radios will deliver about seven thousand internet radio stations! Many baby boomers and Gen-X consumers will have their own favourite slogans recalled from the TV advertising of various FMCG products. Such a shared generational awareness and even fondness for these slogans is not common among Gen-Y and younger consumers as distinctive tribes view a fragmented media. Young people spend more time accessing the Internet (up to 23 hours a week) than watching television (Tech Tribe Report 2006). It would appear that the computer mouse has taken over from the TV remote control for many 16–25-year-olds. Many marketing professionals have doubts about the long-term future of mass-market advertising messages in print and broadcast media now that the way in which media is consumed is changing.

New media technologies

The term 'new media' has a wide application, referring to electronically and digitally driven technologies which allow users greater control and access than conventional media. Categories of new media include the Internet, mobile technologies (including iPods, mobile/cell phones and wi-fi PDAS/MDAS such as the BlackBerry), computer games and cable/satellite interactive television. The growth in the use of new media arises from the emergence of enabling technologies, which includes the digitalisation of data. Digital technology, such as metal or fibre-optic cables and or digital radio waves, allows the provider to push more information (data) into a narrow space. Digital radio waves are able to carry more information than analogue radio waves since there are more frequencies available and they are able to transmit accurately at speed and across distance. Developments in computer memory and processors are facilitating further applications. As gigabytes turn into terabytes then consumers have a vastly improved capacity on an increasingly smaller mobile device.

The use of the Internet

It is now common for fashion companies to operate their own websites. Sites are increasingly transaction-enabled, allowing fashion brands to become multi-channel distributors of their products. Some brands, such as Next, which have a heritage of store and catalogue operations, are already proficient multi-channel retailers. Next is achieving more growth from its remote channels than from its stores. Some fashion retailers are also considering the possibility of developing their e-commerce proposition to include animated virtual shopping using 'drag and display' outfits on digital mannequins.

The Internet has created new categories of business simply as a result of the benefits derived from online operation. For example, WGSN is an online fashion-style information company that exists largely as a result of its ability to deliver a wide range of information to a large network of clients instantly via its site. PRShots is a widely used B2B tool in fashion that allows journalists to log on to the site (PRShots.com) and upload JPEG images of brand look-book samples to use in the fashion features of newspapers and magazines. In fact the now iconic brands eBay, YouTube, Google and MySpace all exist only because the Internet enables them to. Interestingly, each of these brands has achieved global brand awareness and loyalty within a very short period of time. It seems that new brands may not need twenty or thirty years of trading to become established, as large brands have done in the past.

The proliferation of businesses that have taken advantage of the opportunities uniquely afforded by the Internet is being matched by the increase in its use by consumers. Surfing has progressed to game playing, the development and participation in different categories of online virtual communities, blogging and other types of user-generated content. Individuals who do not have a voice in the real world suddenly find that they do have a voice online in a virtual world or social network. The fact that the term '404' has entered the English language as slang for being clueless (or lacking knowledge) about something illustrates the extent to which the Internet is influencing people's lives. The number 404 refers to an error message (404 Not Found) which arises from a failed online search.

Affiliate marketing

This refers to a form of marketing in which a brand enters into a reciprocal arrangement with the owner of a website, providing financial reward for traffic channelled from the independent website to that of the brand. It is more commonly practised in America, where brands and retailers typically operate a sliding scale of rewards to website owners who demonstrably generate traffic to a brand's site. Two examples of fashion brands operating online affiliate programmes are Contessa and La Senza lingerie. The financial rewards vary for registered affiliates according to the level at which traffic from their site engages with a brand. This ranges from the lowest reward for a site hit or visit and increases according to how many pages an individual referral visits, whether or not they purchase a product and, if so, how much they spend.

Traditional methods of evaluating the effectiveness of a website, such as measuring the number of hits per page and click-through rates/the cost per click, may no longer be sophisticated enough to direct future marketing activity. Similarly, traffic-generating schemes, such as affiliate marketing programmes, are unlikely to persuade consumers of a brand's ability to meet their needs.

eBay

eBay is an established and now iconic online auction business. It warrants a specific mention in this chapter as it is facilitating a new market for fashion brands. eBay's capacity to trade anything at the push of a button is influencing the fashion retail process in a new way. Excess consumer demand for fashion products that arises from the selling out of limited edition products or hot-selling lines can now be satisfied through the resale of products on eBay. Recent examples of this include the Anya Hindmarch bag that originally retailed for £5 but resold on eBay for up to £200 after the huge press hype surrounding its conspicuous use by celebrities. In effect, the hype generated a viral word-of-mouth buzz, which developed its own momentum and increased sales accordingly. The same happened with elements of the Kate Moss range for Top Shop. These are more recent examples of a trend that goes back to at least 2004 when a dress (created for Tesco's Florence & Fred brand) sold a version of the green Chloé dress worn by Kylie Minogue to the Cannes Film Festival. The Chloé dress is reported to have retailed at up to £1400 whereas the Florence & Fred dress originally retailed at £45. However, the restricted number made meant that not all consumers could buy the Florence & Fred version and so a market began on eBay. The dress subsequently sold for over twice its retail price. This is not a unique incident and eBay is frequently used to buy and sell fashion products which are no longer available in the traditional market-place.

Fashion products are now routinely resold by consumers who, having bought limited-edition items as a short-term investment, make a profit from reselling them. In summary, eBay provides not only a new retail option for brands but also a facility for consumers who wish to trade in limited-edition fashion products. It has created a C2C market.

Multi-channel media

In any chapter dealing with new technology there is an inherent risk that the content will quickly date. However, there is a need to explain the context in which potential marketing tools such as viral marketing are operating. In the recent past, consumers had to buy different hardware to engage in the different entertainment media. For example, computer games were exclusively played out on consoles or specifically designed hardware such as the PlayStation PS3 and Xbox. Similarly, the Internet was originally accessed through PCs and then laptops. Now, however, merged providers and improved technologies enable people to use multi-channel media. Most mobile phones can now act as a telephone, SMS provider, camera and MP3 player, with newer versions capable of providing access to e-mail and, on some handsets, television and radio.

Each category of hardware is still improving, as we see with HDTV, flat-screen TVs, faster PCs, laptops, mobile digital assistants (MDAs) and new games consoles. Communications providers are also improving their offer with a number moving towards triple-play (television, telephone and broadband provision) or even quadruple-play (also has mobile provision). In the UK quadruple-play provision is now established with the combined providers such as Virgin, Telewest and NTL. As mobile technology develops, then quadruple-play provision is likely to expand. The launch of Apple's iPhone offers consumers the hardware to enjoy quadruple-play multi-channel media interaction.

New generations of technologies and communications companies will undoubtedly present further product and services innovations to consumers. For example, eBay has evolved from facilitating the simple exchange of products to being a lifestyle community in which many people earn a living by trading goods and services to other eBay users. This inherently innovative brand also owns Skype, which, having popularised computer-based web telephoning, is now extending its call services to new types of phones. The phones include a dual one that allows both Skype internet calls and traditional calls at low cost from a cordless handset.

Marketing implications

The nature of the new media and the ways in which they are being used provide consumers with opportunities to discover a wider range of brands and products and experience new services. The most obvious change is that consumers can now search and buy whilst on the move thanks to mobile connectivity. This is likely to increase the frequency of browsing and impulse purchasing. Many marketers believe that consumers are also likely to spend more on their credit cards when online compared to face-to-face purchasing situations where the physical transaction underlines the spending process more obviously.

Connectivity

Since the Internet pioneering days of the 1990s e-commerce is now fully entrenched in very many consumers' shopping behaviour. The dot-com crash of 2000 signalled that businesses and consumers were not 'on the same page' in terms of technology, know-how and understanding the (now clear) benefits of e-commerce. Subsequent improvements in technologies and websites, consumers' familiarity with the Internet and the mass-market adoption of broadband access at home have realigned consumers and businesses.

The effect is that electronic shopping now provides a real and significant threat to those retailers who are primarily reliant on bricks-and-mortar trading. Some businesses are more vulnerable to online retailers than others. DVDs and CDs are increasingly bought online by consumers. This is because the retail prices are generally lower and the choice is wider. In a double blow to specialist bricks-and-mortar music retailers such as HMV, consumers are also able to buy music via downloads, possibly leading to the end of CDs and DVDs altogether. The music industry has been almost turned on its head as a result of peer-to-peer file-sharing. The widespread online distribution of music was originated by Napster, whose technology paved the way for the 'legitimate' sale and downloading of music. As a result consumers are now able to download music tracks at cost via Apple's iTunes, Zune and Napster. Interestingly, the video application of iTunes also enables users to view other products such as feature films, extending the commercial threat beyond the music industry to entertainment more generally.

Consumers' use of the Internet now extends beyond random surfing and e-mail to include interactive entertainment, trading (on auction sites such as eBay) and social networking. This greater use of and reliance on technology and the Internet to facilitate work, entertainment and social networks is increasing the importance of connectivity for many people. For an increasing majority the ability to connect to anyone 24/7 via a mobile/cell phone and the Internet is now an expectation. It is no longer a novelty, a luxury or even particularly cutting-edge. Wireless access is common in many commercial, working and even home environments. The term 'consumer-to-consumer' (C2C) is an evolution from B2B and B2C. It refers to the significant number of individuals who buy and sell directly to each other. The middleman (retailer) is replaced by a business that facilitates a transaction.

Group-buying

Letsbuyit.com is a site that was ahead of its time when it originally provided the opportunity and infrastructure for consumers to collaborate and buy online as a group. Today, in its current format, the site provides a 'co-buying' service, which it described as 'co-operative shopping for the 21st century ... a really simple way of getting better value by bringing people together via the Internet'. Undoubtedly this concept of group bulk purchasing for individual gain will flourish as more people adapt and increase their use of the Internet. Ironically, co-operative buying is not a new concept. Co-op retailing has existed for many years in a number of countries including the UK, Europe America and Japan. The pioneers of this form of trading were a small group of weavers from Rochdale in England, who started the first modern co-operative business in 1844. Their poor working conditions and low wages forced them to pool their resources to buy basic goods at cheaper prices. Interestingly, a number of Victorian ideas are re-emerging, including the building of homes by modern supermarkets to house their workers. Such ideas are often represented as being a new concept!

Social networking sites

The term 'social networking sites' refers to websites that facilitate communication, networking and user-generated content. Communities of people are connected through various social activities, including posting and viewing videos, pictures and written messages through blogs or instant messaging. Three of the most popular sites include YouTube, MySpace and Facebook. MySpace is arguably the best known of the three (at the time of writing this book) and is used for dating, making friends, professional networking and sharing other interests.

The social networking sites MySpace and Bebo are now the fifth and sixth biggest online brands in terms of webpages viewed, according to research from Nielsen/NetRatings (2006). As an example of traffic flows, the research shows that MySpace attracted 2.84 million visitors in April 2006, compared with 2.16 million to Bebo. A significant issue for brands and other business trying to cash in on this phenomenon is how to 'monetise' involvement with people on the sites. A fundamental marketing issue in the future is likely to be the problem of how to make money out of activities where people (potential consumers) are in charge. There are already strong debates about the potential damage to the credibility of sites that accept corporate advertising or sponsorship.

On a smaller scale, many brands, ranging from mobile/cell phones to cars, use simple social networks to enable greater brand involvement with and among their customers. Typically the sites offer consumers the opportunity to comment on and discuss their favourite products. In many cases the consumers are advocates of a particular product and can spread communications virally and more effectively than the brand itself. Any criticism can be evaluated and, where objective, can be a useful source of market research.

Marketing implications

Social network advertising and sponsorship is likely to grow significantly in the future as sites generate millions of hits per month and have distinctive memberships. There are clear benefits to be gained from operating site-based online consumer communities for fashion brands that wish to nurture relationships with their customer. Brands may be able to research the attitudes and opinions of members of the sites. Positive and negative commentary can be examined and used by brands to inform, plan and develop further marketing activities. Third-party C2C endorsements from consumer advocates of brands are likely to be more effective at influencing attitudes and behaviour than direct brand communications. Sites such as Stylehive.com already provide a forum for 'shopaholics' to share information about their experiences.

However, it is probable that at some point in the near future more thorough and systematic 'product review' sites will emerge on a scale similar to that of MySpace. They could provide members with shared product experiences and candid views and commentary on brands and products.

Avatar marketing

This new form of marketing has arisen as a result of the success of in-game communication where a brand's logo features in the content of a computer game, either console-based or online. An online game may also be referred to as a massive multiplayer online role-playing game (MMOPG). A developing trend in gaming is 'social impact games'. They are created with the intention of conveying a social message through entertainment. A development in gaming is the virtual social space or 'being space' where people can socialise using a virtual identity called an avatar. An avatar is essentially a computer icon that represents a virtual person with an identity created by its owner-user. Entertainment using virtual communities has proliferated over the last few years, with Habbo Hotel being popular among teens and younger adults. Habbo Hotel is a multi-dimensional virtual hang-out and game community for teens. The hotels exist in virtual reality but are customised around different countries just as real hotels would be. The user's Habbo (avatar) can engage in many social activities with others, using themed areas in the hotels such as bars. Real-world brands including Sprite and L'Oréal recognise the significance of in-game branding as both make a point of having brand presences in virtual worlds.

Second Life (SL)

A step up from the Habbo concept is the virtual world of Second Life (SL). It is worthy of a separate and specific mention since it is a much more sophisticated phenomenon than the online game or virtual meeting space. It is not only a 3D visual networking site, but also an alternative lifestyle and a digital world in which the virtual 'residents' exist by creating and manipulating avatars. SL is a hybrid, combining elements of gaming, social networking and e-commerce. Avatars that are created and styled by their real-world owners represent residents, who have the opportunity to convey a separate self-image and identity using the appearance of the avatar.

In the virtual world of SL, residents earn and spend money. The exchange rate of approximately two hundred and seventy-five Linden dollars to one US dollar facilitates a real exchange of value between the virtual world and the real world for businesses. A number of fashion brands have traded in the virtual world, with American Apparel arguably being the most dominant early on and Armani opening a version of its Milan flagship store in 2007.

Marketing implications

The most obvious implication for marketers operating within the virtual environment is branding. Brands can market real-world products to an entirely new market of real consumers via a virtual world in which there is much less (if any) competition. Methods may include the provision of branded products used by avatars through to the communication and branded retailing of avatar products within a virtual world.

The real person who owns and uses the avatar character can choose a completely different self-image (an alter ego) through the avatar. This may mean that people engage with a different set of brands using the avatar than they would normally do in the real world.

Kate Moss

The authors have decided to include a section on the fashion model, celebrity and opinion leader Kate Moss to illustrate her significance as an influence on the demand for fashion products. Moss has an ability to be in the forefront of new trends, either through starting them herself or through being associated with others who start them. For example, in 2006 she was pictured in the press carrying a special-edition charity bag designed for and sold by the UK retailer Superdrug. The bag retailed at £2.99 and was designed to celebrate the thirtieth anniversary of the Prince's Trust, a UK charity. It sold in large numbers following the publicity generated by pictures of Kate Moss carrying it.

The name Kate Moss has grown to become a brand that others associate with as much for who she is as for her model looks. The unique impact she has on fashion is partly a result of her success as a model and partly a result of the media personality that she has created. From the early days of her 'heroin chic' look she has been surrounded by controversy. The controversial association with drugs became a big issue in 2006 as allegations of drug use in her personal life threatened to end her modelling career. The brands for which she modelled did not want to be associated in any way with a drugs-related scandal. However, since then Moss has resumed her modelling career with great success, adding another dimension of 'survivability' to her ever-widening set of brand attributes.

As a fashion model she has enjoyed a longer career than most of her peers and has managed to model successfully for a wide range of designers and brands. Unusually her modelling stretches across a diversity of brands and sectors. Clients range from luxury fashion brands such as Chanel, Gucci and Christian Dior to mass-market consumer goods including Virgin mobile and Rimmel cosmetics. The styling and attitude conveyed in the 'Rimmel London' advertising clearly drew from her own London background and bought a sense of her personality to the brand, making it 'edgier' than its competitors.

In addition to the controversy surrounding her private life, Moss's brand image is enhanced through the innovative projects with which she becomes involved. Her recent participation in the Agent Provocateur 'Dreams of Miss X' campaign is a good example. The lingerie brand created four mini-films themed around the erotic dreams of agent Miss X acted by Kate Moss wearing Agent Provocateur products. The films are light on plot but heavy on sensual atmospherics, with Moss modelling the lingerie products to great effect. Inevitably the series attracted great consumer and media interest, which was boosted by press reports of the Agent Provocateur site crashing owing to excessive demand.

A further morphing of Kate Moss's career took place as a result of her design collaboration with Top Shop. Top Shop's launch of the exclusive KM range of clothing, which has the design 'handwriting' of Moss, was carefully managed to maximise press and hype among consumers and the media. The range was inspired by her own favourite clothes and as such was criticised for lacking originality. It was supported by an innovative communications campaign which featured the release of a podcast showing Moss working with buyers and designers within Top Shop. The podcast was available both on a site dedicated to the partnership and also via YouTube and iTunes. However, it remains to be seen whether an individual such as Kate Moss can continue to reinvent herself and so sustain consumers' interest in her as a brand.

Guerrilla marketing

Sophisticated, time-poor and technology-enabled consumers, with short attention spans, are driving many brands to adopt unconventional communication methods to connect with their customers. The need to use unconventional marketing methods also arises from a belief that many modern consumers, the young in particular, are extremely cynical of branded advertising and other corporate communications. Marc Gobé (2001) reinforced the importance of brands doing something different from the norm when he stated, 'For some brands, what works best is to use guerrilla marketing as a way of exploring the creative possibilities for brand contact.' This is especially true for fashion, which is a creative industry. Consumers expect and get new designs in their fashion products but very often have to put up with brands using tired old formulas to try and gain their attention and secure their interest and their money. Saturation in marketing communications today means that advertising in a magazine is unlikely to generate much more of a reaction than the flick of a page from an increasing number of younger consumers. It is ironic that brands seem to appreciate the importance of adding value to their products but often fail to understand the importance of adding excitement to their communications.

What is guerrilla marketing?

Guerrilla marketing describes various unconventional means of pursuing conventional marketing communications goals. It is highly targeted and utilises innovative and creative ideas to generate excitement and word-of-mouth communication via targeted networks of people. Campaigns are designed to be unusual and attention-grabbing while delivering intelligent and stimulating messages. Guerrilla campaigns frequently aim to secure significant PR as a promotional output of their innovative marketing activities.

Guerrilla marketing campaigns are normally:

- creative, innovative and attention-grabbing;
- relatively inexpensive to implement;
- perishable – of limited duration;
- targeted at a specific segment;
- part of a coherent communications and brand strategy;
- intended to stimulate action by consumers;
- designed to generate publicity as part of an integrated communications strategy.

Such campaigns are designed to raise awareness and generate consumer activity in a similar way to conventional communications but are better able to do so since they stand out from the vast array of conventional advertising which swamps the media.

Guerilla communications techniques

There is a wide range of methods that brands use in guerrilla campaigns. To some extent the methods may evolve according to the specific nature of a market. For example, a sportswear brand will utilise different concepts and cultural references from a formal outerwear brand.

Guerrilla communications techniques vary and include:

- flyposting of adverts;
- pavement painting;

- hijacking street furniture;
- buzz marketing;
- viral marketing (typically by SMS or e-mail);
- street theatre and performance art;
- innovative vehicles driving around selected locations;
- flash mobs;
- droplifting.

A flash mob refers to a group of people who self-organise around instructions normally conveyed by a website and who collectively engage in some specifically agreed activity for a brief period of time. Examples of flash mobs include people meeting at railway stations to dance silently on the spot listening to music on iPods or other MP3 players. There are clear guerrilla marketing applications of this sort of collective behaviour for brands. Indeed one can argue that flash mobs are modern versions of the 'happenings' in the 1960s.

Drop-lifting, or reverse shoplifting, refers to the placement of products into retail outlets without their knowledge or consent. Although most commonly associated with performance art, droplifting also has the potential to be an innovative method of brand communication.

Sometimes guerrilla marketing verges on the illegal – especially when flyposting is involved. However, the relatively small fines given for flyposting are often outweighed by the huge financial rewards potentially created by the guerrilla-marketing tactic employed. Other ideas for guerrilla marketing include the leaving of strategically placed cards in clubs and restaurants or at concerts/gigs or other public places likely to be frequented by the consumer group to be targeted. The marketing communications objective may be simply to raise awareness, or possibly direct targeted consumers to act in a particular way. However, once the message or communication has been seeded using guerrilla-marketing tactics, the level and calibre of word-of-mouth communication that it then creates is difficult to measure.

Why are they needed?

This sort of innovative communication/promotion technique is increasingly popular since it is much more personal and original than a large national advertising campaign. This small-scale and very individual type of marketing communication has the ability to achieve prominence and credibility because it is unusual and therefore more likely to be remembered by the consumer.

Guerrilla (or 'pop-up') stores

Stores, in their various forms, have been famously referred to both as adverts with walls and as cathedrals of consumption. Since the mid-1990s the directly operated store (DOS) format has been the preferred channel of distribution for many fashion and luxury brands operating in competitive global retail markets. This trend is explained by the fact that brands belive that it is important to manage and control the customer shopping experience at the POS. The convergence of 'mass-to-class' and 'class-to-mass' has stimulated the growth in 'accessible luxury' and smarter mass-market retailer brands. A consequence of this is that more brands are competing for consumers and are using store design as a means of conveying a strong brand statement.

However, a high degree of homogeneity has evolved within retail locations and many stores look and feel very similar to each other with the result that the shopping experience often has insufficient differentiation between brands. The UK has a particular problem with cloned high streets and this is an issue that has been discussed at government level. Ironically a different problem exists in new shopping locations such as Dubai, where brand adjacencies do not always fit with the intended market positioning of those brands. This typically arises through a lack of familiarity with Western brands on the part of the host retail locations.

Guerrilla stores are a solution to the problem of how brands can differentiate themselves from their competitors. The basic idea is to grab the attention of consumers and attract them into the stores, which are usually open for a limited period of time. The temporary nature of the outlet quickly generates word of mouth, attracting the media and high levels of publicity. The speed with which guerrilla stores come and go helps to create a sense of freshness, surprise and exclusivity for the brands involved. Guerrilla stores are often referred to as pop-up stores owing to the speed with which they open and then close down. The suddenness of the arrival and the equally fast departure helps generate excitement among the press and consumers, ensuring high levels of publicity for the participating brand.

Characteristics of guerrilla stores

Some features common to this type of promotion outlet are described below:

- Products are normally different from the brand's mainstream ranges. For example, they may include limited editions, products from new designers and unusual packaging or discounted pricing.
- They take advantage of low-cost rents and short leases.
- The location is important: commonly high-traffic or very trendy areas.
- The shopping experience is different from the mainstream with more emphasis on atmosphere – like an exhibition more than a service.
- Store openings are often communicated to a network of opinion leaders.
- The products and stores are not normally intended for the mass market but are selected to appeal to opinion leaders who become advocates of the brand.

Some websites such as superfuture.com provide details about the opening of new stores, including guerrilla stores.

The implications of guerilla stores

Guerrilla or 'pop-up' stores represent a powerful branding operation and a tool to combat the consumer inertia which arises from boring-looking stores and predictable shopping experiences.

Viral marketing

Viral marketing is closely related to guerrilla marketing in that it uses word of mouth to communicate messages. Word of mouth, or word of mouse, operates through a social network and often uses e-mail and/or SMS texting. An important feature is that the individual, unconnected with the brand, passes on a message unprompted by the brand. This is a further example of the increasing involvement of consumers in brand communications.

In 2006 a number of videos were uploaded to the Internet which were recordings of what happens when Mentos mints are combined with Diet Coke. One video in particular showed what appeared to be a choreographed experiment which resulted in a fountain-like explosive akin to a firework. The novelty of this sparked a word-of-mouse explosion of interest in the video that was picked up by the media. Media attention increased awareness and so momentum grew, resulting in a viral communication of the experiment all over the world. The value of this 'citizen marketing' was exploited further by Mentos, who subsequently organised a competition through YouTube to create the word's biggest soda geyser.

Brand hijacking

The proliferation of brands as a result of increased consumer wealth in Western economies has resulted in an extremely crowded and competitive market-place. The inevitable increase in marketing communications has diluted the power of advertising to excite and influence consumers. In summary there are too many adverts making too much 'noise' for any to be really successful. Brands have been forced to consider other more creative methods of raising awareness and influencing customers' attitudes.

Coupled with this problem is the fact that the oversupply and overexposure of branded products means that many brands have become diluted and are in danger of losing their status as acceptable symbols of cool. In the future it is very probable that consumers living in mature, developed economies are less likely to regard high-profile branded goods as symbols of status. Overall this means that brands need to think differently about what status is and how consumers are choosing to define it. By the same token, brands need to think differently about how consumers will discover and interpret their brand communications and to recognise that many consumers will want to get involved on some level. This notion of consumers exerting control over brands and their development is an important one. Brand managers have understood for some time that consumers form quite emotional links to the brands they adopt and feel a sense of belonging or even ownership. Even at the level of Marks & Spencer, consumer research indicated a strength of feeling that resulted in the slogan 'Your M&S'. To some degree this is the background to the term 'brand hijack'.

Brand hijack, coined by Alex Wipperfürth, refers to a scenario where consumers are encouraged to collaborate in the image and communications of a brand at its inception and during its evolution. It is not so much a hijack as a carefully brand-orchestrated mobilisation of selected consumers who are encouraged to act as brand ambassadors or advocates. On the face of it, the brand appears to benefit from grass-roots and impartial consumer enthusiasm, which, as we all know, is worth more to a company than brand-sponsored advertising. However, despite the somewhat Machiavellian approach, the brand still needs a big idea to sell to consumers. In this respect the old rules of marketing, which require differentiation and a gap in the market, still apply. A key element in successful hijacking is enabling consumers to co-create brand content in communications. This is of course more easily facilitated by the user of social-networking and internet-based viral campaigns. Wipperfürth argues that it is better to 'hire your audience' than a cool hunter.

Although Wipperfürth's use of the term 'brand hijack' refers specifically to a series of orchestrated marketing activities, readers should appreciate that brands are vulnerable to a more conventional and unplanned hijack. A good example of this is the Burberry brand, which has suffered from a very specific problem in the UK. The trademark check that is an integral part of its brand identity was adopted by football hooligans and subsequently by a broader group collectively but lazily referred to as chavs. This association conflicts with the refined, classic, luxury image that Burberry cultivated to reposition its image. To a large degree the hijack is a result of Burberry's success as more consumers have bought into the repositioned brand and its cool image. However, like all brands, Burberry is unable to stop individuals buying and wearing its products and equally unable to stop photographs of people wearing the brand's products from appearing in the media.

Conclusion

With about one billion people throughout the world now online, there are more opportunities for people to connect and interact with each other than ever before. The collective, 'top-down' culture of the past is rapidly being replaced by more fragmented, colloquial and diverse communities that increasingly engage via online channels (fixed and mobile). This enormous global forum is fundamentally shifting the balance of power away from brands to consumers. Consumers have access to more information, more choice and more brands than ever before.

In the past marketers had targeted relatively passive, homogenous and well-defined customer segments. Now it is consumers who are in a position to target brands, making selections from conventional stores within national markets and from online brands unrestricted by geographical boundaries.

Brands are not simply assimilated into consumers' minds through advertising as they were in the past. The brand communications via the new media are increasingly being influenced by the consumers themselves.

strategic and tactical planning in fashion marketing

Fashion businesses operate in a constantly changing global business environment. Fast change requires both strategic and tactical planning, which must be implemented creatively and with effective management controls.

June Lawlor – Director of Womenswear, Accessories and Beauty, House of Fraser

Introduction and context

The aims of this chapter are to explain the strategic role of marketing within a fashion organisation and to examine the relationship between strategic and operational fashion marketing theory. By now readers will appreciate that the term 'marketing' is a very overused word and is frequently misunderstood. To many in fashion, marketing refers to the function of marketing communications, which is the role responsible for promoting a business, brand, product or service. As such the term is also often interchangeable with PR for many fashion retailers and brands.

However, the scope of marketing as both a business and an academic discipline is much wider. Non-fashion businesses such as the grocery and supermarket brands have often led the way in new marketing strategies, tactics and activities. FMCG brands in particular have long since adopted a marketing orientation to their businesses in which products are developed and tested with consumers' input at regular stages. In food, for example, taste tests and consumers' views on packaging are integral to new product development. This is in stark contrast to fashion, which dictates the available choices each season. Interestingly, some fashion retailer brands have developed brand departments within their organisations to manage the strategic process of positioning more as a brand than as a simple retailer. Supermarkets and FMCG brands have also been more sophisticated in their use of sales promotions than fashion retailers. They use a wider range of sales promotions, including self-liquidating offers, in/on-pack giveaways and coupons, competitions and banded packs. Traditionally, fashion retailers and other brands have predominantly relied on discounting prices in the annual sales. In recent years fashion brands have begun to adopt more sophisticated sales promotion techniques, mirroring the activities of FMCG brands and supermarkets.

Terminology

It is important to be clear about terminology, since words such as discount, value, brand, and subbrand may be used casually to reference types of fashion business which are in fact following completely different strategies. The category often referred to as discount may include supermarkets, value retailers and off-price retailers, all of which are in fact using different generic strategies.

Since the mid-1990s the fashion retail sector has seen the emergence of new price-differentiated formats that include value (Primark), discount (MK1) and off-price retailers (TK/TJ Maxx). In contrast to these kinds of businesses, other fashion retailers reduce the prices of selected lines tactically at points during the season. In so doing, they are able to provide a higher-quality offer, which can normally carry a premium retail price. However, readers should note that downward price pressure in the market generally means that it is more difficult for these retailer brands to sustain full prices, and thus full margin, for long periods within a season. The length of the period within which to sell at full price is increasingly being exasperated by the effects of fast fashion.

Similarly, the word 'brand' is more often used to refer to designer or higher-end fashion businesses when in fact it includes a much wider portfolio of companies, including middle- and mass-market retailers. Zara, Mango and River Island, for example, have become desirable names associated with fashion-cool status and are fashion brands. To some degree PR helps retailers to achieve this position. For example Chelsy Davy, girlfriend of Prince Harry, was photographed wearing a Warehouse dress on a night out. This is not new, of course, since there are many examples of A-list celebrities wearing the products of mass-market brands – Madonna was photographed wearing a Gap sweater in the mid-1990s.

Branded fashion retailers who have introduced subbrands also use the term 'brand' in a strategic context. Although this has been discussed in chapter 8, it is important for readers to reflect upon the significance of subbrands in the strategic planning of fashion retailer brands.

Strategy

Strategy is also a word that has many different interpretations, depending on its use. Most commonly it refers to the formulation of planned activities in which resources are used to achieve objectives. In business a strategy is normally contextualised by the need to be competitive since the often unspoken but underlying imperative for any commercial organisations is to remain in business through making a profit.

There is an implied understanding that a strategy is a long-term plan, as opposed to a tactic, which is short-term and operational. In business theory it is usual to consider both a corporate and a business strategy for an organisation. This enables an organisation to make decisions about objectives, resource allocation and timeframes according to the different needs within that organisation. For example, many larger corporations own and manage brands that are all different. The parent corporation needs to consider an appropriate strategy for its own survival and then separate strategies for the brands that it operates. The brands owned by a parent organisation are typically referred to as strategic business units (SBUs). Parent companies such as Inditex, which owns Zara and Massimo Dutti among others, and Arcadia Group, whose portfolio includes Top Shop and Miss Selfridge, will make decisions about resource allocation according to the strategic objectives that are set for the SBUs. The brands are likely to face varying levels of competition according to their market position (including geographical), different product life and fashion cycles and be at differing stages of business development (the structure of the distribution network and so on). A useful model to analyse a portfolio of different brands is the BCG matrix, which is discussed later in the chapter.

The fickle nature of fashion

Any business strategy needs to plan for both success and failure if a brand is to survive the unexpected. Fashion is particularly vulnerable to changes, which are outside the direct control of a company and which can arise suddenly. For example, unseasonable weather can wreak havoc with the demand for clothing and accessories, as we have seen during the recent wet summers and mild winters. To some extent the fashion industry is well positioned to deal with sudden changes since fashion is all about change. However, the trend is for change to occur faster and the successful brands of the future will be those which are best capable of responding quickly and effectively to unexpected change.

This chapter is not intended to provide a mini-guide to corporate strategy but to explain the important strategic processes and thinking required for fashion businesses to succeed. Readers should supplement this chapter by research into the subject of corporate strategy where a number of models and theories are considered further.

Much writing and thinking on business strategy goes back to the 1950s and 1960s, from writers such as Levitt and Ansoff and, more recently, Johnson and Scholes, Porter and Lynch.

Strategy-tactics flow model – the Strat-Tact (ST) Model

One of the problems of understanding strategy is integrating different but important tools, models and frameworks in a holistic manner. Many theoretical marketing books, whilst describing and explaining the analytical tools in isolation, often fail to inform readers how and in what sequence to plan and how to put analytical frameworks and tools to their best use. As a solution, the authors have created the following top-down and bottom-up Strategy-Tactics or Strat-Tact / ST-flow model. It clearly sets out the sequence in which brands should plan, make and implement decisions that span the strategic through to the operational. Like

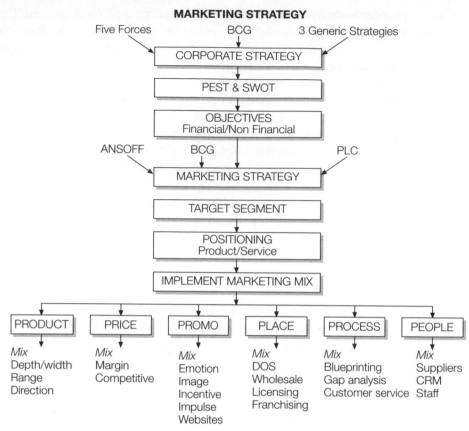

MARKETING STRATEGY

Five Forces · BCG · 3 Generic Strategies

CORPORATE STRATEGY

PEST & SWOT

OBJECTIVES
Financial/Non Financial

ANSOFF · BCG · PLC

MARKETING STRATEGY

TARGET SEGMENT

POSITIONING
Product/Service

IMPLEMENT MARKETING MIX

PRODUCT	PRICE	PROMO	PLACE	PROCESS	PEOPLE
Mix Depth/width Range Direction	*Mix* Margin Competitive	*Mix* Emotion Image Incentive Impulse Websites	*Mix* DOS Wholesale Licensing Franchising	*Mix* Blueprinting Gap analysis Customer service	*Mix* Suppliers CRM Staff

figure **10.1**   Stratmodel A and Stratmodel B

many models it acts as a guide or checklist of things to remember when planning and helps explain the relationship between long- and short-term requirements.

Top down or bottom up?

It is advisable to consider a strategy both from the top down (strategic to tactical) and from the bottom up (tactical to strategic). Each can offer an important perspective on planning and enable fashion managers to make balanced decisions. A top-down approach is influenced by longer-term, 'big-picture' considerations whereas tactical is concerned with how best to implement decisions.

Fashion shops carry huge numbers of fast-changing styles, colours and sizes, making low-level or 'bottom-up' planning incredibly complex. Every garment type will have many subcategories, all of which have to be planned in detail if they are to fit accurately and logically to the varying types and sizes of outlet. These plans are usually created by numbers of units per style/size/colour.

At the other end of the scale, owners and/or executives in fashion organisations have to develop overall or 'top-down' financial plans which clearly show the expected levels of sales and profitability that the organisation plans to make over a period of time. Most fashion organisations undertake overall top-down financial planning several years in advance, although the low-level bottom-up unit plans are developed closer to the season to coincide with the buying lead times of the product(s) involved. In weather forecasting, the most accurate and detailed weather forecasts are those with the shortest range. Similarly detailed planning with regard to unit sales is best left to the last possible moment. Fashion, like the weather, is notoriously changeable.

A gap in the market

Most businesses begin by someone identifying a gap in the market for a product or service and having a vision of what the new business might be which would fill such a gap. This stimulus often arises out of a need that is not being addressed commercially or from poor-quality existing provision in a market, which leads someone to believe that they can do better. All businesses generally start with a vision as to what the company will be about. Often it is this entrepreneurial ingredient that is the most important part of business success, an ingredient that is hard to find, analyse and understand.

Once an initial idea is conceived, a vision is developed to articulate more clearly the rationale and scope of the business. A mission statement may also evolve to explain to both internal and external customers (staff and customers) what the business stands for, what business activities are involved and how the business is different from its competitors.

Mission statements

Some companies articulate their business intentions through their general approach to trading; others provide a mission statement. The decision by an organisation to formalise this type of statement is more common in American business thinking. The lack of a formal statement, however, does not necessarily mean that a business will fail.

The business mission may also be expressed in the broader terms of corporate goals, for example to be the biggest and the best or simply to have an ethos or integrity. There is an increasing public interest in CSR, which is often embodied in the underlying ethos of a brand and the way in which it undertakes trade. For example, Stella McCartney clearly aligns her personal vegetarian lifestyle and views on animal cruelty to the brand values of her fashion house. The People Tree and TRAID (Textile Recycling for Aid and International Development) share a common vision about integrating Fairtrade and environmental policies into their business strategies.

The People Tree describes itself as the pioneer of Fairtrade and ecological fashion and states that it is possible to wear stylish, exciting and affordable fashion at the same time as respecting people and the planet. It lists two sets of policies that make a clear distinction between the issues of Fairtrade and ecological fashion (see Table 10.1).

It is interesting to note that the lists do not contain anything controversial and in fact identify many practices that one might reasonably expect all fashion

table **10.1**   People Tree's policies

People Tree's Fairtrade policy	People Tree's eco-policy
To pay producers fair prices	To promote natural and organic cotton farming
To make advance payments when needed	To avoid using damaging chemicals
To promote traditional skills	To use natural, recycled and biodegradable substances where possible
To promote rural development	To recycle where possible
To operate with transparency	To protect water supplies and forests

source: www.peopletree.com

companies to employ as a matter of course. However, most items on the lists are not recognised by the authors as being associated with leading fashion brands – retailer or otherwise. Philippe Starck recently predicted that sales will in the future come from 'products that deserve to exist', adding 'We must ask to pay the proper price and stop the slaves' (Jackson, 2007).

Examples of some other fashion companies' mission statements are shown below:

- At Gap Inc. we never stop moving. It takes thousands of passionate, dedicated and talented employees around the world to deliver the merchandise and shopping experience our customers expect and deserve.
- Richemont is committed to maintaining the uniqueness and individuality of each of its brands. We believe in strength through diversity.

Richemont is the second largest luxury goods conglomerate after LVMH.

Personal involvement

At the high end of fashion, the entrepreneurial spark, which is initially responsible for launching a business, is often linked to an individual's personality, values and set of skills. This is why fashion companies which start up under the control of a dominant individual sometimes achieve limited growth. Growth frequently involves a complex set of skills and knowledge that is different from that needed to begin a business. For example, many fashion brands can only expand by moving into international markets and diversifying their business activities, both of which involve significant new challenges.

Two examples of designer-/owner-dominated brands are Prada Group (Miuccia Prada) and French Connection (FC) (Stephen Marks). Although hugely successful in terms of brand equity, both Prada and FC have experienced business difficulties linked to the strategic decisions they have taken. FC appears to have had no post-FCUK strategy to deal with the inevitable loss of interest that followed the huge hype around the controversial brand positioning of FCUK. Prada became a silent conglomerate through the acquisition of a number of smaller, prestige signature brands, including Helmut Lang, Jil Sander and Church's shoes, but then divested itself of them following the poor financial performance of the Prada Group. Now approximately 99% of Prada's revenues is derived from the two brands Prada and Miu Miu. Miuccia Prada exerts great influence over the brands' image as the person responsible for the creative direction of the businesses. The cutting-edge brand identity is augmented by her eccentric personality. Similarly, Stephen Marks is the driving force behind FC.

The dominant entrepreneur may not necessarily be a designer. There are many examples of such individuals who have saved ailing corporations or launched new businesses. In the 1980s Sir Ralph Halpern presided over the creation of the Burton Group, which encompassed mainly fashion retailers which were ailing but were turned around. The Burton Group was hugely influential on UK fashion business practices and was the forerunner of today's Arcadia Group. Interestingly, another business entrepreneur took over the Arcadia Group and focused considerable attention on developing the Topshop retailer brand, in particular positioning it in the designer RTW market at LFW, through the Unique collection, and expanding into the lucrative American market via a range carrying Kate Moss's name and sold through a concession in Barney's department store.

Designers and managers

The majority of luxury brands are a successful blend of creativity and strategic management. The brands place enormous importance on innovation and creativity in design and employ leading designers to direct product and image strategy. In other words, the role and importance of the designer, creator or artist is at least as important as that of the management. This is in stark contrast to the majority of fashion retailer brands, which are directed by buyers, operate to a more restricted brief and have designers who are largely anonymous.

At the high end of the market, commentators have observed that the relationship between the manager and the creator is crucial to the success of the luxury brand or fashion house. Table 10.2 shows some examples of the creator–manager partnerships that have been central to the commercial success of famous fashion and luxury brands.

Such partnerships require mutual respect, trust and appreciation for them to be successful. Although Gucci Group is no longer under the direction of Ford and De Sole, the current CEO, Mark Lee, has a very strong belief in the ability of, and works closely with, Frida Giannini, Gucci's creative director.

table **10.2   examples of creator–manager partnerships**

Brand	Creator	Manager
Armani	Giorgio Armani	Sergio Galleoti
Chanel	Karl Lagerfeld	Alain Wertheimer
Christian Dior	Christian Dior	Jacques Rouet
Donna Karan	Donna Karan	Stephen Weiss
Ralph Lauren	Ralph Lauren	Peter Straum
Prada	Miuccia Prada	Patrizio Bertelli
Valentino	Garavanni Giammetti	Giancarlo Giammetti
Gucci Group	Tom Ford	Domenico De Sole

LVMH is also an interesting example of a conglomerate. It is overseen by the entrepreneurial Bernard Arnault and has a host of exceptionally talented, famous and very different designers/creative directors including John Galliano, Marc Jacobs and Karl Lagerfeld, all of whom Arnault has to manage to some degree.

It is unlikely, even in the mass-market fashion sector, that a charismatic one-man band will be truly successful in the long term.

Internal corporate politicking

A very significant and frequently underrepresented subject in business writing is the impact of politics on a fashion organisation's corporate and business strategies. This may take many forms, including the following:

- M&A (merger and acquisition) activity resulting in the new parent company's decisions to rationalise or impose strategies on newly acquired brands.
- Nepotism or poor selection of staff, which may be self-perpetuating and is often a criticism of family-run brands.
- The appointment of a new CEO with a short-term personal career agenda to implement change for change's sake and to achieve some quick-fix results before moving on.
- The lucky career executive who benefits from 'Buggins's turn' and/or a lack of available alternative applicants but who may not necessarily be the most suitable appointment.

In truth the performance of some senior executives may benefit from a marketing momentum created by the strategic work undertaken by a predecessor. It may take several years to realise the benefits of and evaluate some major strategic decisions, such as repositioning a brand or moving into or withdrawing from international markets.

Competing in markets – strategy at a corporate level

The term 'corporate strategy' typically applies to large organisations where strategic planning is complex because of the size and scale of the company (which is more likely to be in multiple or global markets). However, most of the fundamental concepts and philosophies also apply to small businesses. For example, a small fashion boutique needs to be focused on its business purpose (mission) and decide how it intends to be different and compete in a particular market-place (generic strategy).

Key questions arise for a small fashion business, just as for a large corporation, such as 'Why will a customer buy from our boutique?' This question simply relates to decisions that the boutique owner must make about the type of product and service provision required to attract customers. This might involve issues of differentiation by location, product range, price positioning, service and many other variables.

Generic strategies

The most fundamental strategic decision made by a commercial organisation is concerned with establishing the basis upon which it intends to compete, develop and sustain a competitive advantage and outperform competitors.

Since the main aim of a business is to continue and hopefully to grow, one can say that a key aim of any business strategy is to establish and maintain a sustainable competitive advantage. Possessing a competitive advantage is all very well but is of no use if it can be easily copied, and so it is crucial for a fashion business to determine how the advantage can be sustained over time.

At this generic strategic level the prevailing wisdom adopts Michael Porter's view that there are three strategic choices: cost leadership, differentiation and focus. There have been debates about whether or not they are mutually exclusive, which probably reflect trends in business activities and cycles since the 1970s. Business in the twenty-first century is vastly different in terms of flexibility, speed of change and globalisation. Consequently, business models need to be different and are less likely to stay neatly in one or another specific category for very long. Strategies need to be continually reviewed and may require either a small or a seismic change – this is where continuous marketing research pays dividends.

The three main generic strategic options are cost leadership, differentiation and focus, and these are discussed below.

Cost leadership

This is where the business achieves an advantage over competitors through being the lowest-cost operator. It may achieve this through keeping operating costs and product costs as low as possible. As the lowest-cost operator it may choose to achieve a higher margin through competitive retail pricing or gain market share by offering the cheapest retail prices in a market. As businesses operate globally it is not always clear which one is the cost leader in any particular market. For example M&S is the largest clothing retailer in the UK but looks pretty small when compared to some American clothing companies such as The Limited. Interestingly Asda Wal-Mart's fashion retailer brand, 'George', may only have a small market share in the UK market (approximately 3%), but sells throughout America, making it potentially a more significant global competitor.

Brands may be able to achieve cost leadership at category level if they have sufficient market share. In the 1990s M&S had a dominant market position in the product categories of lingerie and underwear (around 30% by value). They chose not to be the cheapest retailer in the category, pursuing a differentiation strategy with a higher margin. As a consequence, La Senza was able to enter the market and establish a firm brand position. It is likely that M&S could have seen them off using their market dominance to deliver lower retail prices.

Differentiation

Since, in theory, there can only be one lowest-cost business in a market, others have to compete on the basis of something different from CP. The vast majority of fashion brands compete using some form of differentiation typically associated with design, branding, service, fashion status and desirability. Since fashion is principally about change, it is unsurprising that trends often emerge on the basis of differentiation linked to what is considered to be cool at that time. Some trends may last a long time, for example urban street sportswear, while others, such as bling, may disappear more quickly. Interestingly, globalisation means that a trend which is expiring in a Western fashion market could easily take off in an emerging market. The current general concern for the environment has spawned a variety of differentiation possibilities that include:

- products made using Fairtrade principles (with regard to materials and manufacturing);
- products made from eco-friendly textiles and low-level carbon-footprint manufacturing;
- products made from recycled fabric (obtained from unwanted clothing and other items).

Focus

This is a strategy of focusing on a particular market segment using either low cost or some form of differentiation as a way of achieving competitive advantage. A focus strategy is normally one of specialisation and frequently involves service businesses in the fashion industry such as the online fashion-trend prediction business WGSN.com. The term also refers to businesses that operate in a niche market, such as specialist fashion boutiques, suppliers of outsize clothing and manufacturers of hi-tech clothing.

Some fashion businesses are highly focused on one or a few categories, while others focus on a very specific level of the market. Many famous international brands such as Burberry (the Burberry trench coat), Dunhill (smokers' requisites) and Mont Blanc (fine writing instruments) originally built their businesses principally around one product or product grouping. In the world of global competition and fast-changing consumer tastes, most international brands have had to diversify their product offer, in order to maintain their market position. The danger of focus is that a business may limit itself to a product or service that goes out of fashion then find it too late or too difficult to diversify, as in the case of the Sock Shop.

The need for using a combined strategy

In reality most businesses will use a combination of the generic strategies described above, in order to take advantage of differing market opportunities as they arise.

Distinctive competence

Distinctive competence refers to the unique set of characteristics that a company possesses relative to competitors in the market. A fashion brand should base a strategy around its distinctive competence in order to achieve a clear and sustainable market position. Some of the critical success factors for a fashion business are listed below:

- clear market position and brand USP;
- patents and copyrights;
- quality products;
- design and managerial talent;
- experienced management;
- an effective distribution network;
- a desirable/cool brand image;
- supply-chain efficiency and relationships;
- vertical integration capability/speed to market;
- financial stability;
- good store site portfolio and freeholds;
- modern IT systems;
- broad geographical coverage.

There is a clear relationship between the distinctive competence and critical success factors of a fashion business.

Matalan, one of the original UK discounters, built its business on the premise that out-of-town locations would be better in terms of cheaper rentals and easy customer access, in line with the trend for out-of-town shopping centres. However, the arrival of the Irish Primark discount chain on British high streets has proved more popular with consumers, who see it as a better and more conveniently accessed product. M&S once boasted that 99% of its products were made in the UK, and for many years enjoyed market dominance as a result of having an efficient supply chain. Latterly, as UK production costs became uncompetitive, M&S, like most other retailers, have turned to foreign product sourcing. In these examples we see a migration of strategy to meet new market conditions.

There is a vast literature on strategy, some with formulaic views, some more laissez-faire. Lynch's support for emerging strategies may not be best suited to the fashion industry, where marketing planning may require long lead times in areas such as shop acquisition (Lynch and Kordis, 1998). However in other areas of fashion marketing – such as the product sourcing of fast fashion, where production moves rapidly and geographically – Lynch's ideas would seem to have credence.

Whatever strategy is utilised, in general it is essential to be ahead of the market and to be proactive rather than reactive. Businesses never stand still; they either move forwards and grow or they slide backwards and decline. Late alterations in strategy to market changes invariably have less impact than if they were done with the business in control.

The macro marketing environment

All organisations operate in market-places that are affected by forces outside their control. This trading environment can be analysed at a macro level using various versions of a model generally known as PEST (Political Social, Economic and Technological). The acronym is a simple checklist of variables that impact on all commercial organisations. Variations on PEST include PESTC (includes Competition), PESTL (includes Legal), and so on. There are endless variations according to the elements that fashion managers consider to be most likely to impact on their businesses. For example, the legal variable would be a good factor for own-brand fashion retailers to consider now that designers and luxury brands have become more successful in challenging infringements of copyright on their designs. Recent cases involving Chloé and Jimmy Choo designer brands against a selection of mass-market fashion retailers have resulted in some high-profile fines for the retailers. This sends an important signal to those fashion retailer brands which are careless in the way they design popular versions of clothing and accessories sold by luxury brands and high-end designers.

Political forces

Direct forces

In certain countries, such as France and Italy, the fashion industry is strongly economically supported, both directly and indirectly by government-provided finance. In other countries the fashion industry is not seen as being of economic significance, and this would appear to be the case in the UK. Throughout history, textiles and garments have enjoyed a level of protectionism not enjoyed by other important products. It is suggested that the strategic significance of clothing as an essential for life may have contributed to the levels of protectionism enjoyed by producers in the developed world. Developed economies started to form an international trade organisation in 1947, but as a stopgap measure to avoid massive and quick disruption of their economies by cheap developing countries, they created and signed the GATT. The MFA under GATT controlled the amount of merchandise by category that developing countries could ship to developed countries. Each year quotas were set – generally increasing year on year, but aimed at allowing the textile and garment industries in the developed world time to diversify and focus on producing non-basic/more expensive products. The World Trade Organisation (WTO) became the successor to GATT in 1995 and since then we have seen the virtual removal of tariffs on the majority of textiles and garments throughout the developed world. This shows how politics has been very influential historically in the protection of fashion-related industries, although now, with the removal of trade barriers and quotas, political influence in trade protectionism issues is minimal.

Indirect forces

In some countries there is much more legal control over fashion marketing activity than in others. In France, for example, the start and duration of the biannual sales is legally controlled, whereas in the UK it is not. In the UK there are many legal statutes controlling the sale and marketing of fashion products, as well as the way in which they are promoted. Certain elements of marketing come under the control of voluntary codes, which are not policed by the legislature but are instead controlled and censured by the industry's own lead bodies, such as the Advertising Standards Authority. It would be almost impossible to list all the statutes and voluntary codes that affect the marketing of fashion in the UK. It is estimated that there are over two hundred statutes that impact generally upon marketing consumer goods. *Note*: Readers would be best referred to the lead marketing bodies and associations, or expert legal advice in the country in question, if in any doubt about the legality of a local marketing issue.

Economic forces

The size, level of growth and general state of an economy can have a direct bearing on how much fashion is bought by the population of that country. How evenly a nation's wealth is spread among its different social classes can have a huge impact on its fashion market. Younger age groups spend far more on fashion than older ones, and women spend twice as much on clothes per annum than men. Levels of unemployment and the housing market are two of the key factors which affect consumer confidence. During economic downturns, fashion can often suffer as a result of people's decision to hold off purchasing. The easy availability of credit and modern students' acceptance of debt are encouraging young consumers to spend rather than save. During the past decade the UK has enjoyed much greater economic prosperity than many other European countries. However, the recent global credit crunch has ended this.

Socio-cultural forces

Changing social structures (e.g. more women going to work) and demographic changes (e.g. an ageing population) can have a profound effect upon the type and level of fashion consumption. Western society is currently enjoying unprecedented levels of personal wealth, although it now appears that there is a growing divide between the rich and the poor. Poverty is still increasing, and it is estimated that one child in every four/five is being brought up in poverty. It is important for marketers to be aware of wealth distribution across the social divide and also geographically. The growing ethnic communities in certain parts of the UK are creating new demand patterns for retailers. In some areas with a large Asian population, clothes need to be made available in smaller sizes; if there is a predominance of Caribbeans, the opposite is true. Despite what is known as the homogenisation or internationalisation of fashion, many ethnic or cultural subgroups are not catered for by mainstream fashion. The fashion marketer should be fully aware of the location of these subgroups and of their needs and wants. These subgroups may be wealthy. The growing gay community is often wealthier than the heterosexual majority – the 'Pink Pound', as it has been dubbed, is a valuable segment of the UK fashion market. Children are maturing earlier, mainly as a result of improved diet and health facilities, and are entering the consumer arena at an ever-younger age; children as young as five or six are now demanding the latest trends, styles and brands from their distraught parents.

Technological forces

There are many technological advances that have historically and will in the future change the way in which we select fashion. Home shopping via digital TV and the Internet may well reduce the market demand for traditional retailers, especially as picture definition, transaction security and download speeds improve. The speed of data transmission, the complexity of what needs to be analysed and the speed at which it can be interpreted by fashion buyers and merchandise planners are critical for competitive success in today's crowded high streets. Speed is of the essence in all fashion businesses, with technology now vitally important in the decision-making processes. Marketers need to keep abreast of technological developments if they are to ensure that their business is delivering the best and fastest decisions. Garment and textile manufacturing is continually developing and improving, meaning that those who embrace technology first will enjoy at least a temporarily sustainable competitive advantage. Sometimes the advantage is more sustainable if copyrighting or patenting has been possible. Virtual flagship stores can now be found online.

Other factors and driving forces

Although there are four major headings in PEST there are a few individual forces, which are worth separate comment (although they could easily be fitted in under a relevant PEST headings):

- **Fast fashion** – continues to exert an influence beyond those brands that engage in this style of trading. Consumers' expectations across other sectors, including luxury, are for more frequent and faster change. In 2005 Robert Polet, CEO of the Gucci Group, commented, 'Consumers are being educated by fast fashion retailers . . . with new products changing, creating a fast shopping rhythm' (Jackson, 2005).
- **Increasing foreign travel** – with an increasingly wealthy world population, higher levels of foreign travel and cross-cultural contact are the norm. This has been one of the greatest drivers of the globalisation of fashion.
- **Increasing concern about the environmental impact of fashion** – like most other human activities, the international fashion industry is under scrutiny with regard to the pollution it produces. There are now many organisations and interest groups monitoring all aspects of the fashion

supply chain. Fashion marketers may well be called to account on issues such as carbon emissions and polluting practices.

- **Increasing ethical concerns** – as more clothes and textiles are being produced in the developing world, high-street retailers are regularly coming under the spotlight for using cheap or slave labour. Many retailers have signed the ETI (see www.ethicaltrade.org) which is concerned with worker's conditions, pay and rights, and other issues relating to CSR. Groups such as Labour Behind the Label (see www.labourbehindthelabel) are actively lobbying retailers and government to stop international worker exploitation. Again, this is all of great significance to those trying to manage marketing activities

How to use PEST analysis effectively in fashion marketing

PEST analysis is a vital activity undertaken ahead of the development of any marketing strategy. The good marketer will be continuously scanning formal and informal sources of relevant information – which requires an analytical and enquiring mind. It is a very important part of the intellectual marketing process, and successful PEST analysis is the essential foundation of all good marketing plans, strategies and tactics. The only way to ensure that the marketing organisation and the individual are aware of all the key issues and problems is through a continual 'scanning' of all information and indicators available in the overall marketing environment. Once a key issue has been isolated, the marketing planner must write it up as a short bullet-point descriptor, for example:

- **Increasing interest in fashion retailing CSR by UK consumers** – Any venture considering opening in the UK should be certain that it has a clear and concise CSR policy, which is being/can be formally controlled and measured.

With clearly defined PEST bullet points like the one shown, the marketer is then able to rank and weight them under each of the PEST headings, making it easier to plan what marketing actions and activities will have the greatest short-term and long-term impact. PEST analysis is usually best undertaken in a team situation, to avoid personal bias and to obtain maximum objectivity.

Porter's Five Forces model (1980)

Porter's Five Forces (Porter, 1980) is a model that helps marketers to analyse the competitive environment. It is still very relevant today. The model identifies five major forces that are continually impacting upon the organisation, and seems ideally suited to the highly competitive fashion industry. These forces are:

- the level of bargaining power of suppliers;
- the level of bargaining power of both business and consumer buyers;
- threat of entry into the market by new entrants;

- threat of substitutes coming into the market;
- the general level of competitive rivalry within the total market-place.

Shown below, in figure 10.2, is the authors' view of Porter's model as applied to the fashion industry

Some forces have a much greater significance in the case of the fashion industry than in the case of general merchandise. The huge conglomeration of large international store groups, for example, have incredibly strong bargaining power over suppliers. It has been reported over recent years that many large international retail operators have, as a result of their huge buying power, simply imposed price reductions across the board upon their suppliers, without discussion. Anecdotally most suppliers have accepted this without argument for fear of later retribution. It is doubtful whether such aggressive price-reducing edicts, imposed by powerful buying groups, can ever guarantee long-term strategic success. All businesses need to make a profit. If there is a belief that prices are too high, therefore, the first question to ask is why the organisation has agreed to pay such high prices in the first place. Perhaps the buyers need replacing! Suppliers may respond in many ways, for example looking for other buyers or cutting corners in cloth and manufacturing quality in an endeavour to make up lost profit. This whole issue is a sensitive one. There are very few long-term gains to be made by potentially alienating your supply base; good suppliers are always in short supply. In most interpretations of Porter's model it should be carefully noted that the bargaining power of the retail buyer is the sum of the total bargaining power of their customers. It is therefore essential that retail fashion buyers ensure that their ranges really do reflect the total needs and wants of their targeted customers, often termed as derived consumer demand.

In the context of UK fashion retailing, the threat of new entrants always exists. It may come from global competitors such as Mango, Zara, Abercrombie

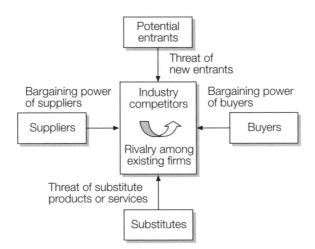

figure **10.2   the Porter Five Forces model in a fashion perspective**

& Fitch and H&M, all of which derive a significant part of their sales from overseas and internet trading. However, even with huge amounts of capital at their disposal, these foreign competitors will find it difficult to acquire good retail sites in most major UK towns and cities as they are already taken by the major UK-owned retail groups. This combined with the slow-down in the development of regional and local out-of-town shopping centres, means that organic growth is likely to be slow as a result of having to go through the process of vacant site acquisition. Wal-Mart, the world's largest US-owned retail giant, realising the problem of market entry into the UK, acquired ASDA, an existing UK retail business, rather than trying to acquire sites. The UK is a mature and highly competitive market, which has proven a difficult challenge for many foreign fashion businesses. The huge pressure now being put upon the middle-market retailers by supermarkets and discounters may potentially open up opportunities for foreign entrants in the future.

The Boston Consulting Group growth–share matrix

Originally developed in the 1970s, this has become a well-proven analytical tool to help organisations make decisions about their future potential (% annual market growth rate) and also their relative competitive position (% market share). It can be used in several ways in the fashion industry to help both large and small businesses, although, at its inception, it was intended to be an analytical tool to help large corporations, consisting of several different types of business, to analyse and understand the current situation pertaining to all their businesses. From this they would be able to assess the strength of each to help and support strategic corporate decision-making. The Boston Consulting Group (BCG) matrix is in a four-box quadrant layout, as shown in figure 10.3.

The horizontal axis is expressed as the market share of the business compared to that of the market leader, whilst the vertical axis shows the average annual growth rate of the market that the business is operating in. It is divided into four quadrants called stars, question marks, cash cows and dogs, which explain how the business(es) stand(s) relative to the market leader:

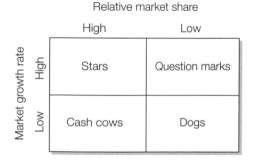

figure **10.3** **the BCG growth–share matrix**

- **Stars** – successful question marks tend to move into the star category, and stars are market leaders in high-growth markets. They are generally expensive in terms of the promotional expenditure required to keep them ahead of the competition, but hopefully will one day become cash cows.
- **Question marks** – those businesses (or parts of a business) that are operating in high-growth markets, but enjoy a relatively small market share. Generally businesses start off in this quadrant, but if they are to increase their market share, they often require a high level of investment to catch up with the market leader.
- **Cash cows** operate in a market where growth rates are less than 10% per annum but still retain a relatively large market share. As the name suggests, they do produce a great deal of cash. It is probably an unexciting business, but as a market leader it enjoys economies of scale. However, should it start losing market share, it might have a negative impact upon the overall viability of the organisation. In a portfolio, cash may be used to invest in brands that are at different stages of development.
- **Dogs** generally have a small share in a low-growth market. Often they run at a loss and valuable management resources can be used up trying to keep them afloat. The decision about whether or not to close them down to mitigate future losses is usually high on the agenda.

With each of the categories described, it is essential to decide on one of four key options when planning the strategy, investment level and business objectives. These four key options are described below.

How to use the BCG growth–share matrix for marketing planning

A fashion conglomerate may face a number of options relating to its SBUs. For example, it can build up or hold and stabilise the market share, close the SBUs down, sell them off or simply use them as source of cash without worrying about the consequences. The latter option is particularly relevant for weaker cash cows that may be heading quickly towards dog status. The ways in which the matrix was originally intended to be used were mainly focused on large industrial conglomerates, but it can easily be adapted to be a tool in the fashion industry to analyse the individual performance of garment types being sold within the business. If the performance of any fashion retailer's garments were to be placed on to the matrix, it would soon become evident that certain garment types were performing better than others. The matrix would in this instance immediately allow management to identify the strong and the weak, thus enabling them to devise strategies to deal with/improve the weak, whilst at the same time more fully potentialising the winners. This matrix is an important, practical and transparent analytical tool that is easy to use in the fashion context. It does not give answers about what strategy to develop, but simply acts as a guide to what is happening at a particular time. It is not a forecasting tool in any sense.

After undertaking the PEST analysis, which is generally written in the form of a bullet-pointed report, indicating clearly *what* forces are relevant and *how* they are likely to impact upon the organisation, it is now important to identify any *opportunities* or *threats* that the organisation is likely to be faced with, which might significantly impact upon the trading potential of the organisation. In general, threats are usually outside the control of the organisation. The 9/11 terrorist incident at the Twin Towers in New York in 2001, for example, had a detrimental effect upon tourism and impacted badly upon the luxury goods industry as a result of the reduced number of people flying. Threats can come from many quarters, although in the fashion trade the universal threat always includes fiercer competition. Often, as a result of unplanned external situations, opportunities arise that enable an organisation to develop their business in a way not previously considered. It is useful for all fashion businesses formally to undertake a regular and detailed opportunities and threats audit, being careful to rank and weight each one to ensure that the business considers the most important opportunities and, at the same time, creates detailed contingency plans to counter what are perceived to be the more important threats. Well-organised fashion marketers will be regularly assessing these opportunities and threats in their marketing reviews. The marketing review process is dealt with later on in this chapter.

Analysing and auditing the internal environment SWOT

A SWOT (strengths, weaknesses, opportunities and threats) analysis is an essential part of developing marketing strategy. The four-box analytical tool helps marketers accurately to capture the internal strengths and weaknesses of the organisation and also to examine external threats and opportunities. The classic SWOT layout is shown in figure 10.4, generally completed using clear and individual bullet points for each issue – which should then be ranked in

INTERNAL

Strengths	Weakness
•	•
•	•
•	•
•	•

Opportunities	Threats
•	•
•	•
•	•
•	•

EXTERNAL

figure **10.4** **the classic SWOT analysis tool**

order of importance. (*Note*: This analysis is best undertaken in a team situation, to avoid total bias and to obtain maximum objectivity through shared group experiences and perceptions.)

Once the external environment has been fully investigated, it is then essential for the organisation to look inwards to analyse its own resources and its ability to work effectively within that environment. The four main business aspects that are normally analysed are the product acquisition/manufacturing, financial, marketing and organisational strengths.

Product acquisition/manufacturing strengths

In the fashion industry, the ability of the organisation to buy or sell the right fashion product is pivotal – nobody can market a fashion product that is perceived as being less than excellent. The fashion consumer is unforgiving of poor style, design, quality or value. Getting the fashion product wrong, as already described in chapter 4, is irrecoverable – bad product must be moved out of the business quickly (usually requiring a costly mark-down). All the issues relating to product manufacture and sourcing should be clearly measured, ranked and weighted to ensure that the business is dealing with efficient manufacturing resources. Most fashion retailers will monitor each supplier using key performance parameters, for example:

- the percentage of deliveries which are on time;
- the percentage of merchandise sold at full price rather than at discount;
- the percentage of merchandise returned with quality problems;
- the level and quality of design input.

Over time, the overall performance of suppliers can be measured to help with future strategic sourcing decisions. With good monitoring of the supply chain, there is no hiding place for a poor product source.

Financial strengths

All fashion organisations require working capital with which to buy stock, invest in capital projects and pay staff. The fundamental resource drivers are staff, stock and space, all of which have a cost. Despite the high levels of mark-up (the extent by which the CP is increased to arrive at the RSP), most international fashion retailers are only likely to retain a net profit of around 5–15% of sales. The fashion industry's demand for capital varies depending upon where a business is placed in the supply chain. Textile and yarn manufacture can be very capital-intensive, owing to the high cost of machinery, whereas garment manufacturing uses less capital, but more labour in terms of machinists. Fashion retailing can also be very capital-intensive, particularly if a fashion retailer actually owns stores. Nevertheless, to stock, staff and equip a fashion business is costly, particularly if that business is located in an expensive city-centre site. Many of the longer-established UK retailers such as House of Fraser, Debenhams and M&S used to own the majority of their valuable city-centre retail sites, but in recent years, they have sold these off to release capital that has been used to further develop and enlarge their business operations. Many financial experts judge capital tied up in a shop freehold to be dead capital that is best released for other more profitable activities. Whatever size or type of fashion business involved, it is essential to have working capital available. Unlike the erratic cash flow of some businesses, including manufacturers of capital goods such as textile machinery, fashion retailing has a fairly predictable cash-flow pattern. It is this ability to generate cash that has made retailers so attractive to private investors and capitalists. Once mainly quoted on the London Stock Exchange, many fashion businesses such as River Island, Arcadia, BhS, Debenhams and Jaeger are now owned privately. Whether private or public ownership of large fashion companies benefits the UK fashion industry remains to be seen. Having the right finance available is a critical success factor for all fashion organisations. Any shortage of working cash can often be survived by cutting corners, which can destroy the development of a long-term winning marketing strategy. The greed of owners and directors has been known to destroy once-successful fashion businesses.

Organisational strengths

In previous chapters, the 7 Ps of fashion marketing have been discussed at length, including the People element. All businesses rely heavily upon the talent, knowledge, vision, dedication and loyalty of the people that work for them. Many large, modern fashion businesses have developed from humble beginnings as a result of the entrepreneurial drive of one person (e.g. Simon Marks of M&S and Montague Burton of Burton Menswear). These natural instinctive marketers had a clear vision for their organisation, their name and vision living on long after they had gone. Successful organisations always regard their staff as a valuable resource, not as a cost. It is essential when undertaking an internal staff audit to consider the following staff attributes:

- length of service;
- historic performance levels – e.g. sales and profit success;
- skills and qualifications;
- personality traits;
- level of creativity;
- level of flexibility.

There are many other attributes that could be ascribed to staff working in different parts of an organisation. Many organisations fail to undertake a regular staff audit, or to create a succession plan. It is a well-known fact that fashion organisations are subject to a high level of staff turnover, particularly in the area of retail operations. Good staff are increasingly hard to find, despite the educational opportunities now available. Many larger fashion organisations go to great lengths to recruit and retain good staff, through a combination of high-quality training programmes and well-constructed incentive schemes. Money is not always the key driver of staff motivation. Understanding the best ways to motivate and retain staff is an essential part of the overall business and marketing strategies.

Marketing strengths

It is an essential part of any internal audit to take a closer look at the overall efficiency of the marketing operation. Again, a ranked and weighted table answering these main questions would help clarify strengths and weaknesses. It is important for the marketer to be able objectively to rank the organisation against its main competitors. It is often easy for businesses to overestimate their own effectiveness and efficiency, hence the need for an external reality check:

- What are the customer perceptions of the organisation over time?
- Does the company have a high market share, and is it increasing or decreasing?
- How efficient is the supply chain of the organisation compared to the competition?
- How innovative is the organisation – is it a fashion leader or follower?
- How well represented is the organisation both nationally and internationally?
- What competitive advantages does the organisation possess?
- How effective has previous marketing activity actually been?

During the internal audit, it is essential that the organisation seeks the required information from as many areas and levels of the business as possible. Too often the managers of fashion businesses have an undying faith in their own views and opinions, ignoring the reality that can be gleaned by talking regularly to staff at the customer interface. Blind executive self-belief has been the causative factor behind many collapsed fashion businesses!

Chapter 2 refers to the fundamental requirement for all fashion organisations to keep monitoring the marketing environment, both internally and externally. Fashion organisations can spend too much time scanning the external environment and fail to monitor their own internally generated marketing activities. All plans require action to be applied, hopefully with a positive benefit to both the short-term and long-term performance of the organisation. It is therefore necessary to monitor the effect of all marketing activity such as the level of press coverage generated as a result of PR initiatives. Consumers may change their views about a brand, but this is a slow process and generally does not happen overnight. The continual longitudinal monitoring of customer perceptions is a critical ingredient of good internal auditing. The past is usually no guide to the future.

Financial objectives and their planning

Very often the first key objectives of a fashion business are financial. Financial success is generally based on achieving the highest possible return on capital and effective cash flow management. During the financial planning process, executives will look at past performance as well as at marketing information about the business's current situation. Some of the main financial objectives are listed below:

- annual sales plan + % annual growth on the previous year;
- net profit retained after all expenses;
- annual % return on capital invested;
- annual cash flow being generated by the business;
- review of liquidity ratios to ensure that the overall level of indebtedness is not too high.

There are many other accounting ratios that are used by fashion companies during the early financial planning processes, such as stock-turn ratios (the speed at which stock comes into and is sold out of the business) and mark-down ratios (the level of price reductions needed to clear out old stock as a percentage of the overall annual sales). The very transient nature of fashion products makes stock planning and its associated ratios of great significance when planning final levels of profitability.

Again, there is no formulaic approach to financial planning but, needless to say, the organisation's ability to achieve the declared financial plan is normally critical to its long-term survival and development. Financial objectives translate to budgets, plans and targets.

Non-financial objectives and their planning

Although financial objectives tend to assume a high strategic significance, the fashion marketer now has to decide upon the non-financial objectives (including marketing-orientated) to support the overall financial planning process. Until the marketing-related objectives are established, it is unlikely that the finance element of the business will undertake detailed low-level, bottom-up planning to support the initial top-down overview. No money can be made unless products are sold. The integration of the financial and marketing plans by the organisation is an essential step if the whole organisation is going to move forward with confidence. The practicalities and workings of this process vary by organisation, although many companies favour the use of strategic-planning awaydays. At these, executives from all business disciplines are able to sell and buy into the overall corporate direction being planned for the business. Such planning meetings are normally so intense and detailed that they will be conducted away from the business, to ensure that day-to-day interruptions do not disrupt the intensive thought processes. Smaller businesses, whilst undertaking the same logical thought processes, usually do it in an informal way, often with the owner simply publishing the objectives for all to follow.

Non-financial objectives fall into two main categories: marketing objectives and marketing communications objectives, although marketing communications objectives will be dealt with later on in this chapter under the development of marketing strategy.

Objectives need to be measurable and so are normally quantifiable. Typical examples of marketing objectives are as follows:

- Increase the number of national fashion outlets to 100 from 90 in one year.
- Increase sales value by 10% on last year and unit volume sales by 15% as a result of new lower prices, thus increasing market share from 3% to 4%.
- Increase consumer awareness of a new fashion brand among women aged 16–24 from 60% to 70% over the next financial year.

Marketing objectives need to be specific and clear, and should indicate the time period over which they will be measured. It is important for them to be both realistic and challenging. It is usual for the most important ones to be at the top of the list. Most important of all is the need to ensure that everyone within the organisation agrees to them and feels that they can be achieved. Good financial planning in the first instance really helps the setting of sensible marketing objectives. The authors have, during their long careers in the fashion business, seen many examples of unrealistic financial and marketing objectives set by poorly informed management. Again, the need to understand what stage the organisation is at will make the whole planning process flow logically and easily.

Once the financial and marketing objectives have been agreed comes the critical stage of marketing strategy development. This is when the fashion marketer decides how the marketing mix will be manipulated and controlled most efficiently and effectively to achieve the planned financial and marketing objectives. The definitions of the key elements of the marketing mix have been described in detail in chapters 4 to 7. It is at this point of the strategic marketing planning process that fashion marketers ensure that the right product at the right price is distributed to the right place using the most effective and efficient marketing tools.

Marketing strategy?

The marketing strategy of a fashion business is the strategy that leads to the implementation of a marketing mix. Sometimes this fact becomes obscured by the specific use of the term 'marketing' to reference marketing communications. Marketing communications is in fact part of a marketing strategy.

Marketing communications objectives usually refer to how the communication should hopefully affect the mind of the target audience.

Typical marketing communications objectives might include:

- Promoting in the launch of a new flagship store, by creating 50% awareness of the target audience living within the local catchment area, one week before the opening.

- Repositioning a specific brand as an upmarket brand from being a mid-market brand over a two-year period.
- Changing 30% of the targeted consumer group's attitude from being neutral towards a brand to it becoming a 'must-have'.

There exist a number of models which are extremely useful in planning a strategy for developing the sales of products in markets (i.e. a marketing strategy). The key model is Ansoff's product/market matrix. However, before analysing the strategic options it is helpful to consider some related assumptions that include the following:

- Change is inevitable, especially in fashion, so it is better to plan for change than to react to it.
- Boundaries exist in the minds of consumers about the scope of products that a brand can sell credibly. For example, it is unlikely that Speedo swimwear would be a credible brand for bridal wear. This sets some boundaries for the development of products and brand extensions. However, supermarkets have been able to sell fashion products by understanding the hierarchy of benefits sought by consumers such as low price, value and convenience.
- There are varying levels of risk associated with the implementation of the various product/market options. Each option has an opportunity cost attached to its implementation.

Ansoff's matrix

The typical Ansoff's matrix is shown in figure 10.5. It is a simple four-box model aimed at helping the fashion marketer to plan the best strategic option.

Ansoff's product/market matrix or alternative directions for development model is an excellent matrix for helping fashion managers plan the options available to grow sales. Various versions exist of this model but all agree on the four principal options:

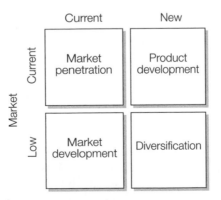

figure **10.5** **Ansoff's matrix**

- market penetration;
- market development;
- product development;
- diversification (related/unrelated).

Market penetration refers to the option of increasing sales through selling more of the same product to the same market. The interpretation requires a degree of common sense as the term 'same product' is ambiguous. In some industries even the most minor adjustment to a product can fundamentally alter it. For example, adjusting the sugar content of a brand of tinned baked beans effectively puts it into a new product category (healthy beans).

This is not necessarily the case in fashion where, for example, a 100%-cotton-jersey short-sleeve top may initially be manufactured in only two colour options but may be developed in another three for the next season. Since the product is the same in all respects (fabric, specification, fit, trim) other than colour, the marketer should regard the additional versions as the same product – especially if it generates a good profit margin per unit sale.

Other 'tactical marketing mix' methods of delivering on the marketing strategy of market penetration include:

- sales promotions (incentives to increase sales volumes and encourage link sales);
- advertising, PR and visual merchandising to raise additional awareness of and interest in products within the existing market;
- increased distribution within the target market (for example, opening more stores within the same country).

It is worth pointing out at this stage that the same consumer profile can be found in many different locations within the same country. For example, a retailer brand that distributes only in London is likely to find the same type of consumer in Manchester, Brighton, Glasgow and Leeds, albeit in differing numbers. A key role of segmentation is to determine where it is most profitable for a brand to open new stores, given the numbers of its target consumers. Opening stores within the same country, therefore, is market penetration.

However a point will be reached where the retailer has opened the optimum number of stores for the demand and to continue would saturate the market. Opportunities to grow sales then emerge from the remaining Ansoff options: product development, market development and diversification.

Product development

This involves growing sales through introducing new products to the same market. An example of undertaking product development would be launching new brand extensions. For example, if the macro analysis indicated that celebrity was still a strong fashion driver, then a brand might choose to develop a new range of products in partnership with a famous individual. The recent and continuing trend in celebrity perfumes illustrates just such product-level brand extensions.

Market development

In this case the fashion brand grows sales by entering new markets. Examples of this might include overseas expansion and selling to men as well as women.

Topshop's KM range is another example of the implementation of such a strategy, in which Topshop benefits from the association with Kate Moss's celebrity and global fashion-icon status. Strategically the KM range was used to sell in the difficult American market where her brand equity is greater than that of Topshop. The way in which the Promotion element complements this is the communication of a podcast showing Kate Moss working with the buying team for her range in Topshop. This podcast was available both via iTunes and on YouTube and appealed directly to the target market. Interestingly, items of the KM range also found their way into boutiques in New York's trendy Soho district.

The process of expanding into international markets is more complex and risky than expanding geographically within national boundaries. There are many reasons for this, which include the fact that the marketing-mix elements will need adjusting as a result of the differences in culture and language and also that the earnings in foreign currency will be subject to rate changes.

Both may have significant effects upon the profitability of the strategy, which is why brands should consider the opportunity costs of selecting one strategic option over another.

Diversification

This involves brands trading in new areas, typically with new products in new categories. Sometimes the diversification has a strategic logic since it is complementary to the existing business, as in the case of a retailer buying a manufacturer. Such vertical integration may be prompted as much for defensive reasons as by the drive to grow sales. Unrelated diversification describes a situation where a fashion brand moves into a completely unrelated area of business activity. Sometimes this can be stimulated by tempting profit opportunities.

In reality, most fashion brands engage in more than one option simultaneously. For example, it is common for a brand to continue market penetration whilst simultaneously entering international markets and launching new complementary products such as accessories.

The PLC model

This model suggest that all products and markets experience a finite life cycle. The model is particularly useful in the fashion industry where some fashions, such as a new celebrity look sold by Top Shop, can have a life of only a matter of weeks. Other fashion looks are more enduring – the male suit is a category that has been around for over a hundred years, although it is now worn much less than before. Understanding and estimating the current position of the product, brand or business on the PLC is vital in the development of strategy. Experience is essential as there is no formulaic way of determining this position. Readers are referred to chapter 4 for more detailed comment and explanation of the different types of fashion PLC.

STP

The STP process has been fully explained and discussed in chapter 3. It is now, at this point of strategy development, that the business has to be certain exactly which customer segment is going to be targeted and exactly what product is being offered to them, as well as where and how. This is a critical point in the whole marketing planning process. It is important to reiterate the point that if a fashion product or service is fundamentally wrong in terms of design or offer, then there is simply no possibility of it succeeding in the market-place no matter how well it is promoted, priced or positioned. The interpretive processes between the original concept through to the final purchase of a fashion product are critical. There is no formulaic methodology that can ensure that a designer/buyer brings the right product to market at the right time. Over time segment profiles can change and competition can require a brand to change its positioning.

The implementation and optimisation of the marketing mix

Once a marketing strategy is agreed, the most important and final process of the strategy development is to plan its implementation through the 7 Ps of the marketing mix. It is hard to be prescriptive about how each element of the marketing mix should best be used, owing to the huge number of variables faced in each fashion-marketing scenario. However, fashion managers need to establish the best means of utilising the elements to achieve sales targets across different markets.

The product element

It is important to remind readers that the decisions about the product market strategy, such as market developments, are actually made by designers and buyers. Fashion direction, product variety and volumes all impact on sales levels.

Branding of fashion products

The decision to be a brand or a retailer (brand) is a generic one since it determines the basis upon which a fashion company will compete in a market.

If branding is to be used to identify fashion products and augment benefits with fashion status linked to a particular identity, it usually requires different types of brand management. For example:

- **Corporate branding** – BhS only sells own-label merchandise over a wide range of fashion product types – with the exception of the Tammy brand which Philip Green acquired, having bought Etam.
- **Range branding** – M&S sells a range of its own brand and other subbrands such as Blue Harbour, Per Una and Autograph.
- **Individual brand names** – The Arcadia Group has individual businesses, each mainly selling their own brand of merchandise, for example Dorothy Perkins, Evans, Burton Menswear.

Branding is discussed extensively in chapter 8. The increasing consumer interest in brands has driven many own-brand fashion retailers to develop their own subbrands. Retailers prefer to create their own 'new' brands rather than stocking manufacturers' brands, as they usually generate higher margins. Brands have many advantages over non-branded merchandise, with branded clothing being far more significant for male purchasers than for females. It appears that UK men prefer the safety of buying into a brand, rather than trying to select a garment solely on its attributes and benefits. Possibly the male is a lazier shopper. Brands are more easily recognised by the consumer, also carrying a price premium for the brand owner or retailer. Branding adds value and allows differentiation in the crowded marketplace.

Developing new products

In the fashion industry the decisions relating to the product element of the marketing mix are undoubtedly the most important. Key issues include:

- product attributes – brand name, style, colour, size, quality, features and packaging;
- product benefits – these relate to image and performance (e.g. sports clothing would need to perform effectively under stress; evening dresses would need to enhance the body's contours);
- support services – personal style or shopping consultant, ease of exchange after purchase, etc.

To support these critical product decisions, portfolio analysis and PLC modelling should both be used. The PLC of a fashion product can range from a few weeks (Zara's key fashion lines) to many years (Levi's jeans). The fashion marketer must always be able to make an informed judgement about where an existing or proposed product is on the PLC curve. Different points on the curve require different forms of promotional support and expenditure.

The life-blood of fashion is NPD, which can come from either inside or outside a fashion organisation, or indeed a combination of the two. More retailers are now using in-house design departments and describing themselves as designer retailers. At higher market levels, design is often a key ingredient of the product, although, in general, well-designed fashion product is now being demanded at every level. Clothing is no longer seen as a commodity in the UK.

Fashion needs NPD at a much higher rate than other consumer products, as a result of the high level of (product) line change required. Product failure occurs to some extent at all market levels of UK fashion, although good marketing and merchandising management can help minimise its impact. The common reasons why fashion products fail can be summarised as follows:

- poor or outdated design;
- poor sizing or fit;
- unfashionable or irrelevant styles/prints/colour(s);
- poor positioning or in-store presentation;
- poor value or uncompetitive pricing;
- poor or non-existent consumer awareness of the product and/or its availability;
- hyperstrong competitive offer elsewhere.

Product failure is very often the result of a combination of these factors, although the apportionment of blame may prove difficult. Fashion product development is normally supported by the development of creative mood boards, to help those involved understand the style and direction of the range or brand for the season involved. A mood board will normally contain sketches, photographs, colour palettes and fabric and yarn swatches. It might also be supported by prototype samples.

Unfortunately, unlike other less changeable consumer products, the high speed of line introduction and change within the fashion industry means that test marketing is not normally a viable proposition. In the development of fashion marketing strategy, the need for the right product is mission-critical. This fundamental but obvious requirement is often overlooked by supposedly well-informed fashion businesses.

The price element

A detailed pricing schedule that clearly defines planned pricing in relation to competitors and the market in general is a normal starting point. Much secondary information is freely available in secondary sources such as Mintel. With price competition currently being an issue, continuous price surveillance is very important. Key price points will also be identified at this stage; especially the entry-level price. For retailers, prices will mainly be fixed. However, manufacturers, wholesalers and brands may well have prices that appeal to and are relative to different levels in the market. (*Note*: All pricing decisions are ultimately driven by the overall financial profit objectives of the business.) The pricing of fashion garments in a retail context is very much in the domain of the buyer and the merchandiser. It is very rarely solely a marketing-led decision in view of the fact that selling at the correct price level must generate enough margin for the business to survive and thrive. Chapter 5 deals with this key aspect of both strategic and tactical marketing planning.

The Promotional element

There is a wide variety of promotional tools that can be selected, but in general each level of the clothing market has certain tools that are appropriate. Lower-priced businesses will usually rely more heavily on sales promotions, whilst more upmarket fashion businesses may rely heavily upon advertising in glossy magazines. Whatever tools are chosen, the key is to achieve the best response for the money available. It is usual to define more clearly the marketing communications objectives, which generally revolve around the consumer or customer response. Typical marketing communications objectives were defined earlier on in this chapter, and it is important that they should align with the overall marketing objectives. Having well-defined marketing and marketing communications objectives (normally in a bullet-point format) are vital in ensuring that all marketing and marketing communications expenditure is used effectively and efficiently. Readers are referred to chapter 6 for a detailed review of the available methodologies and tools relevant to different types and levels of fashion business.

The Place element

It is important for certain fashion brands to be seen in certain retailers. Upmarket brands would not wish to see their brand values and integrity compromised by their product being sold in low-end outlets; an exclusive and limited distribution would be more appropriate. For fashion retailers themselves, the position and geographic spread of their chain will depend upon a wide range of variables, such as available sites, location of targeted market segments and competitors' sites. International fashion marketers also need to select the right countries and retail partners in which to sell their products. Fashion businesses may often choose to place their products through several channels of distribution, for example retail shops and the Internet. Marketing strategies will sometimes need to vary for different marketing channels and/or stages of the supply chain. Each distribution channel may need to make substantial adjustments to the marketing mix. The decisions about how fashion products get to market vary widely as result of geography, the structure of the supply chain, adaptability and, most importantly, customer expectations. The wide variety of options available are fully discussed in chapter 7.

The People element

Much of the fashion sold, in all types of business, involves the use of personal selling. The UK suffers from a culture where the personnel involved with the selling process are not generally very highly regarded. This is not the case in countries like the US and France, where selling and serving at the customer interface is much more valued. Personal selling is the front line of marketing, and many more fashion businesses are realising its huge significance. Increasing levels of self-service in fashion retailing are the result of retailers trying to cut costs. This has led to a general diminution of selling skills, which is now of great concern to fashion businesses. The service element of the marketing mix must be faced head-on in the development of a marketing strategy. High retail-staff turnover is a difficult but ever-present issue in modern UK fashion retailing. Good training, motivation and, more importantly, recognition of the importance of the selling role are critical factors that need to be addressed. Differentiation through improved service levels is increasingly important, especially across global fashion markets.

The Physical evidence element

In nearly all types of business the selling environment has gained significance, probably as a result of increasing levels of wealth, which have led to the higher environmental expectations of customers. Drab, run-down shops and showrooms and slow, unexciting websites are no longer acceptable. The total span of sensory stimulation needs to be addressed in the development of a good marketing mix. Attention to detail is again a great way to differentiate a business, in an industry where product-led innovation becomes harder to achieve as information flows and supply chains seem to become ever faster. Service is hard to copy and to produce more cheaply. The marketing of fashion is very much a 'touchy-feely', people-oriented business.

The Process element

The way in which customers are dealt with from beginning to end needs clear and focused attention when developing marketing strategy. This is of importance in both B2B and B2C marketing. However, within the B2B supply-chain context, the complexity of the transactions means that efficient process management is important. So much can go wrong between the original concept and the final delivery to the shop. The need for efficient supply chain management places a new onus on process management strategies, particularly as UK fashion businesses rely so heavily on imported product.

Why fashion businesses need to plan

The bulk of this chapter has been concerned with explaining and analysing theory and models that are important to strategic planning and implementation within fashion. A distinction must be made between strategic and tactical planning. Strategic planning normally covers a period of between three and five years. Timescales are obviously not the same in all industrial sectors, but three years is a common strategic timeframe for most fashion businesses. As fashion becomes ever more influenced by the success of so-called fast-fashion brands, there is pressure on fashion retailers and brands to respond more quickly to market changes. Tactical planning typically refers to the implementation of the marketing-mix elements of a fashion business. In this case the timeframe is commonly 12 months or less, and may even be as short as a few weeks when applied to mark-downs (sales promotions). Once a plan exists, it needs to be reviewed regularly. This is because the macro and trading environments in which fashion companies operate change very quickly.

In order to develop winning strategies, it is essential for a fashion organisation to plan effectively. Planning is defined as 'The process directed toward making today's decision with tomorrow in mind and a means of preparing for the future decisions so that they may be made rapidly, economically, and with as little disruption to the business as possible' (Warren 1966). Planning is an essential part of military strategy and is equally vital in the context of business.

Planning, implementing and controlling marketing activity

The tools and frameworks needed to develop and control the marketing mix have been explained and discussed at length throughout this chapter. No two businesses, brands or products will use the same ingredients of the marketing mix. The need to plan, implement and control all marketing activities is very important, if time, money and effort are not to be wasted.

The Planning stage

All good businesses undertake a hierarchy of planning – larger fashion companies will have complex planning calendars and protocols, while smaller companies may use a more ad hoc approach. Planning normally starts with corporate planning, moving on to business plans and, finally, product and marketing plans. In general, marketing planning is always subservient to the corporate plan. It is the development of a clear marketing strategy, with clear marketing and marketing communications objectives that will enable the fashion marketer to adjust the key elements of the marketing mix accordingly. In most organisations, the development of corporate plans is normally done in consultation with the marketing department. Figure 10.6 shows a simplistic view of the planning process used by fashion businesses.

Marketing plans will need to be written in normal report writing style, with proprietary software, such as Marketing Planning Pro, providing a very neat and easy way to produce logical and easy-to-read marketing plans, as well as providing logical sequencing. The proprietary software will possibly need some minor amendments when used in a fast-moving fashion context. Once the

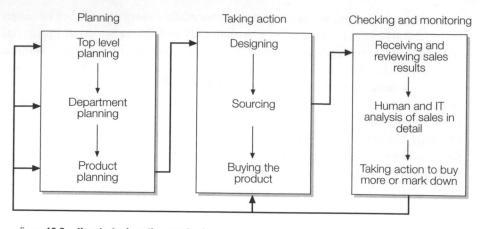

Planning	Taking action	Checking and monitoring
Top level planning	Designing	Receiving and reviewing sales results
Department planning	Sourcing	Human and IT analysis of sales in detail
Product planning	Buying the product	Taking action to buy more or mark down

figure **10.6** **the strategic action monitoring process**

source: adapted from Kotler and Armstrong (2006)

marketing plan has been written, it is normal for it to be formally presented to the main trading and commercial areas of the organisation, as it is essential to get senior management agreement to buy in and sign off – especially with senior management. Marketing activity always requires a budget, meaning that authorisation to spend will need to be agreed before the trading season being planned.

Implementation stage

Once a plan has been written and agreed, the detailed activities need to be implemented. The activities will often be undertaken by different business functions, so the plan – normally detailed with Gantt charts – will have an activity schedule showing who, what, when, why and how much and the anticipated/planned outcome of the activities. These action points and milestones will be picked up through good project/marketing management at regular trading/marketing meetings. A plan that is written and then put on the shelf and not regularly reviewed, referred to, discussed and acted upon is all but worthless. Undertaking any adjustments to the marketing mix without checking the planned objectives is a marketing crime. Regular review meetings will be needed to make changes to the proposed activities in line with trading performance and prevailing/anticipated market conditions. A marketing department that fails to communicate regularly across all functions of the business is simply not doing a good job.

The Control stage

As a result of the speed of change within fashion, most good international fashion businesses have huge amounts of sales data and information flowing in on an almost hourly basis. Fashion retailers probably receive, process and act upon sales data faster than any other type of business. Textile and garment manufacturers 'upstream' in the supply chain are normally well informed of trends by retailers, who share information via company intranets. This means that manufacturers are now having to react at similarly fast rates if they want to be suppliers of fast fashion.

Much of the response to marketing activity is undertaken by merchandise planners and buyers, who react and proactively send stocks into the supply chain to meet demand. The need to analyse sizes, colours, rates of sale and merchandise deliveries are achieved using merchandise planning and control systems. Such systems provide detailed information that is normally consolidated and fed back to marketers. This process allows the marketing department to be kept in the loop and to check that the marketing mix is working and that objectives are being achieved.

Day by day and week by week throughout the season efficient fashion businesses need to take corrective action to buy larger or smaller quantities of lines and to alter future delivery schedules to meet the anticipated demand. Once corrected, the loop is completed all over again as marketers and other trading functions check that changes have achieved the obejctive.

A final comment on strategy and planning

The best strategies and plans are those that are simple to understand and implement. Something too complex stands a greater chance of failure. To quote Warren Buffett, 'If you can't get your head around it don't put your money into it.' One of the other major dangers of any planning process is that once a plan is produced and implemented, the organisation often fails to continue to monitor how well it is performing against that plan. Very few businesses perform exactly to plan without the need to make small changes over time. Business is like sailing: the wind/economy changes and so the captain/manager has to make small alterations to arrive at the planned destination. The perfect plan that needs no changes has yet to be written; even with the best business planning, small adjustments will need to be made.

Despite the best corporate, business and marketing plan, businesses often suffer from the unexpected – both good and bad. The weather might be atrocious or, on the other hand, the business might happen to have selected the best designers, brands, styles and colours of the season. Planning, if not done thoughtfully, can act as a straitjacket to achievement and success. Good luck has always been the most uncontrollable but also the most wonderful part of fashion trading. The authors wish all readers the best of luck in their business activities.

Accessories: products that are designed to accompany items of clothing and so complete an overall 'look'. Usually intended to be decorative, common examples include bags, belts, scarves, hats, ties and costume jewellery, although the width of a range will vary among fashion retailers and brands. Accessory products enable some consumers to buy into more expensive fashion and luxury brands because prices tend to be affordable and represent the 'entry-level' point of a brand.

Actual product (benefits): the benefits offered by a product that are tangible and concerned specifically with its physical design characteristics and branding. The ownership of a particular brand can deliver the tangible benefit of status through conspicuous usage of the brand's products.

Adoption theory: a theory which explains the steps an individual goes through on the way to accepting or rejecting a new product, service or brand. Adoption refers to the stronger association that customers have with the brand over and above merely repeat purchases.

Advertising: any paid form of directed communication to customers which is conveyed through the media. In general terms brands are greater spenders on advertising than retailers since brands need to drive consumer traffic to (retail) stockists. Advertising costs normally include the production of the advert and the cost of media space. The luxury end of the global fashion market utilises print advertising more than the mass market. Advertising is increasingly moving online, away from traditional print and poster media.

Advertising Standards Authority: an independent regulator for advertisements, sales promotion and direct marketing in the UK.

Advertorial: an advert placed in the media, which is designed to appear as an objective editorial from the host publication. It is very text-driven and similar to a press release. The advertiser pays the media a fee for placing the advertorial in a similar way to that of an advert.

Affiliate marketing: a form of web-based marketing where a host site receives web traffic from numerous independent sites, which are known as affiliates. The host site remunerates the affiliates on a sliding scale of payment according to the level of engagement by the traffic with its site. Traffic is normally directed to the host site via an advertising banner on an affiliate's site. Asos.com and landsend.com are two fashion clothing retailers that have used affiliate marketing to develop their businesses.

Agent: any individual or organisation that acts an intermediary between manufacturer and customer. Agents are normally paid on a commission basis. A fashion brand may use an agent to access appropriate retailers in a foreign market.

Androgyny: a reference to the convergence of gender in society. Fashion has reflected the convergence in status and roles between men and women through clothing, accessories, make-up and hair styling. Iconic designers such as Yves Saint Laurent, with his 'le smoking' designs, and Paul Smith have made it popular for women to dress in sharply tailored trouser suits.

Aspirational group: any group or tribe which an individual aspires to belong to or associate with through the use and or ownership of specific brands, products or services.

Astroturfing: corporate communications masquerading as a consumer blog on a brand's website.

Atmospherics: any sensory stimulus used in stores or other selling environments to influence customer behaviour and perceptions positively.

Attitude: a person's relatively consistent positive or negative predisposition towards something. Fashion brands can position themselves using imagery that is consistent with the attitudes of a target market, for example understated, individual or rebellious. In fashion and youth culture, 'attitude' refers specifically to a no-nonsense, independent and assertive way of behaving which is consistent with a rebellious or anti-mainstream image.

Augmented product (benefits): the benefits offered by a product that are in addition to the core and actual benefits. Frequently they are intangible and service-related. In fashion this might involve service features that include 'no-questions' returns policies, home delivery, in-store styling advice, and so on.

Avatar (marketing): an avatar is a 3-D character that features in a computer-based environment created for games and virtual communities. They can be manipulated to act as people in various computer scenarios. Habbo Hotel and Secondlife are good examples of social network marketing that utilises avatars.

B2B: the term stands for 'business to business' and refers to commercial activity between businesses, as opposed to business selling to consumers. In fashion this could be illustrated by a fashion retailer buying products from manufacturers, or retaining a PR agency to undertake its public relations activity.

B2C: the term stands for 'business to consumer' and refers to any business activity with consumers.

Baby boomer: a term that refers to a person who was born in the period after the Second World War, between the years 1946 and 1964. They have experienced rock & roll, the 1960s, the sexual revolution, the focus on wealth and the concern with ageing and redefining 'old age'. They were the first 'teenage' generation to buy mass-market fashion from the high street.

Barcode: the coded tickets which are attached to products and which contain product and price information that can be read by till scanners. Radio-frequency information devices/tags are in the process of replacing barcode tickets.

BCG (Boston Consulting Group) matrix: Developed by the famous consulting group of the same name, this is an analytical quadrant-style matrix tool that can be used by an organisations to analyse, classify and understand its SBUs, brands or product groups in terms of their market growth rates and relative market share.

Behavioural segmentation *see* segmentation

Benchmarking: the standard adopted by any business within a market.

Benefit: something for which a customer will pay money. Normally referred to as a 'product benefit', it is the real reason why a customer will want to buy a product or service. Levitt observed that a customer buying a ¼-inch drill actually wanted a ¼-inch hole. Fashion products offer an extremely diverse range of benefits that are commonly linked by the conspicuousness of their use. Benefits can range from physiological (warm coat) to psychological (feelgood brand) and are generally packaged to form a USP, or competitive combination of benefits.

Blue cross (mark-down): not the name of a charity but a term commonly used for a short-term sale, usually mid-season, to stimulate sales and clear stock. Typically a blue-cross promotion lasts for a single day. It was originally devised by department stores, but now is adopted more widely by fashion multiple retailers. It is sometimes referred to as a 'one-day-spectacular' sale.

Branch: a single stand-alone outlet or shop of a retailer. A branch is designated with an individual number that denotes location and size and can be recognised by retail IT systems for delivery and transactional purposes.

Brand: a name, sign, symbol, sound, colour or design (or combination of these) that is distinctively identifiable, that represents a company or product and that has meaning to a customer. Some brands are worn as a badge by consumers in order to make a statement about themselves to others. The term 'brand' can also refer to a business model in which a company uses a wide range of distribution options including licensing, wholesaling, franchising and retailing. Over recent times, the traditional distinction between retailers (stockists) and brands has become blurred as retailers have branded themselves as brands and have increased their retail presence through flagship stores.

Brandalism: any direct or indirect action or reactionary behaviour undertaken by consumers against the branded messages from large companies. Usually motivated by a mismatch between a brand's promises and values and consumers' experiences of the brand.

Brand equity: the total value of a brand that includes all intangible and tangible assets. Intangibles include brand name, brand loyalty, perceived quality and brand associations.

Brand image: the visual image of a brand that a customer retains in his/her mind. It is the sum of all his/her experiences of the brand.

Brand loyalty: a state of customer loyalty that a brand hopes to achieve. A situation where a customer consistently prefers to buy one brand over another.

Brand span: the natural life span of a brand before it loses relevance and becomes less attractive to customers. There may be a number of contributing causes for the demise of a brand span, including increased and improved competition, changing expectations of customers and a lack of innovation and creativity from within the brand. Fashion brands are especially vulnerable to shortening brand span as fashion trends and competition demand faster change to an overall proposition.

Bricks and mortar (retailing): Retail distribution by stores, as opposed to catalogue or more particularly the Internet. The term has evolved to distinguish store retailing from e-commerce.

Buyer behaviour: the behaviour of customers when engaged in the buying process. Consumer buying theory uses different models of behaviour before, during and after purchase.

C2C: the term stands for 'consumer to consumer' and refers to the strongly developing methods of internet trading that enable consumers to deal directly with each other. eBay is a good example of a technology that enables C2C trading. It also takes in peer-to-peer exchange of digital music facilitated by brands such as Limewire.

Cash cow: low-growth, high market-share businesses or products which are established and successful. They are profit-generative and are used to support other businesses or products that are in need of investment. *See also* BCG matrix.

Catalogue retailing: a publication, such as a printed book or pamphlet, which features an itemised display of products for sale. The hard-copy publication typically includes visual and text-based data on the products for sale.

Historically, this form of retailing has been popular with consumers wishing to spread payments over time. Many catalogue brands have moved part or all of their offer online. Catalogue retailing experiences different patterns of consumer demand from store-based retailing, as demand quickly follows the catalogue issue before dropping off.

Category: sometimes called a product group, it is used to group related products together. It enables a fashion business to see how one type or group of lines is performing as a whole.

Category killer: a form of fashion business or product category that has a strong USP and competitive advantage, making it very difficult for others to compete effectively. It is common for the products to be sold at aggressively low prices.

Category management (cat man): the management of products within a specifically defined category enabling a more holistic 'business management' approach to individual products. The development of sophisticated microcategory management has been greatly enhanced through the emergence of powerful IT systems which provide significant analytical capabilities.

Cause-related marketing: a term that emerged into mainstream marketing in the 1990s. It refers to the collaboration between a brand and a charity (or other not-for-profit organisation) to achieve similar mutually beneficial marketing objectives. It is most commonly associated with PR in fashion marketing.

Celebrity marketing: marketing communications centred on the fame and personality of a celebrity. It works on the assumption that consumers' interest is increased as a result of the brand's association with a celebrity. It is likely that this form is on the decline as consumers experience celebrity overload.

Charity shops: originated by Oxfam in the late 1940s, they mainly sell donated second-hand or recycled products. There are currently in the region of 7,000 of these shops in the UK, run by various charities, generating £100 million profit in 2008.

Citizen journalism: contributions by individuals to new media where members of the public collect, report and disseminate news, information and opinions. This is facilitated by the mobile technologies and Internet which are available to the average person.

Closed questions: the term is used in both market research and personal selling. In market research it refers to a form of question used in surveys where all possible answers are available to respondents. Closed questions are typically seeking answers such as yes or no, strongly agree or disagree, and a descriptor on a bipolar scale. In a selling situation closed questions are designed to close the sale, for example, 'How would you like to pay?' or 'Which one would you like to buy?'

CMT (cut, make and trim): generally used in the production of garments when the fabric and trimmings are purchased by one party and then sent to a manufacturer who charges a fee for making them up.

Co-branding: the practice of using two recognisable brands together on one product or service. In fashion it is commonly illustrated by the commercial partnerships or agreements between retailers and designers, such as ALR at Oasis and Jasper Conran et al. at Debenhams.

Cognitive dissonance: the theory that consumers act to reduce tension or discomfort that arises as a result of conflicting information. For example, if a consumer has paid a high price for a product he/she will expect a high level of service and aftercare to accompany it. Fashion brands need to develop strategies to combat dissonance in their customers.

Competitive advantage: this refers to an advantage that a business has over competitors in a market. The advantage will normally be a unique and differentiated one that enables a fashion business to sustain a USP which is attractive to customers. Bases for competitive advantage in fashion are often linked with innovation, original product design, economies of scale, low retail price, brand identity and personality, speed to market, experiential retailing, luxury heritage and designer name. Fashion businesses need to be aware that a competitive advantage does not last forever, as competitors improve.

Competitive shopping: the process of monitoring competitors' product offer in store with a view to informing operational buying, merchandising and marketing decision-making. It is structured primary maketing research.

Competitor analysis: a systematic audit of direct and indirect competition associated with the planning and development of strategies and tactics.

Concept testing: a marketing research test, where members of a target audience are shown potential new products, services, ideas or concepts, in order to gauge their initial response, prior to further development or launch. It is a risk-minimalisation process.

Confusion pricing: a form of pricing where retailers do not present the full and total price of a product to a customer in one figure. The price tag of a product will normally be supplemented with further costs, making it difficult for a consumer to judge and compare its price with those of comparable products. The customer is unable clearly to understand the real price of a product and the value that it represents, as in the case of special deals on link sales of co-ordinated clothing. In some markets the presentation of sales by percentage alone may be confusing – for example, 70% off as opposed to a clearly marked new price.

Consumer: the end-user of a product. In fashion, the consumer refers to the person who buys and uses (wears) fashion clothing, accessories and related products.

Consumer buying behaviour *see* buyer behaviour.

Consumerism: a generic word encompassing all aspects and processes of consumer buying behaviour. It also refers to a social and cultural change in purchasing and consuming products and services.

Consumer product: a product that is bought or acquired for consumers' end use. It usually refers to everyday and low-priced items.

Consumer promotion: any type of sale promotional activity, aimed specifically at consumers to encourage them to try or purchase a product or service.

Concession: a formalised business arrangement whereby a manufacturer, brand owner or other retail business is enabled to trade its brand on a percentage commission basis inside another retailer's business.

Continuity lines: generally a more basic, less fashionable product that is expected to be in stock throughout the trading year, for example, basic white underwear.

Continuous panel: a specified panel of respondents who collectively participate in a longitudinal survey from which data are collected on a frequent basis.

Contract: normally a formal written agreement between individuals/business entities that outlines full and specific details of a commercial order for products and/or services.

Contract manufacturing: a manufacturing relationship, when a manufacturer makes products to the specification requirement of another individual or organisation, normally under that organisation's brand name.

Cool hunter: an individual who specifically seeks out new trends for fashion businesses and brands to guide or incorporate into their product offer and communications. Typically associated with the younger end of branded markets, the information may be gleaned from a wide range of global sources.

Copy testing: a method of testing how well an advert is likely to communicate with its targeted audience. This is normally undertaken before the full development of the advert and the associated campaign.

Core product *see* augmented product (benefits)

Corporate identity: an amalgam of all the tangible and intangible symbols, images, ideas and other manifestations that are deliberately communicated by an organisation to its many different publics. Ultimately it is the visual representation of an organisation's corporate personality.

Cost: the price at which an organisation purchases a product or service. A mark-up is then added to achieve a selling price, or profit in readiness for its onward resale to another stage of the fashion supply chain.

Cost, insurance and freight (CIF): the terms of the contract are such that the seller pays for all costs and freight and marine insurance to a named port. It refers to orders where goods are shipped by sea or inland waterway.

Coupon: a sales promotional tool in the form of a certificate of entitlement that enables a consumer to claim a cash discount on purchase, or some other benefit.

Couture (haute couture): the very exclusive French handmade dress industry based in Paris. The couture business is seen to be a loss leader for a number of luxury brands, but is retained because it creates an exclusive brand positioning. Couture is used by some houses to engage the fashion press in a debate about fashion and creativity and so obtain valuable PR.

Covermount: a free gift attached to the cover of a magazine, for example a beach bag attached to the cover of a summer edition of a women's glossy magazine.

Critical path: a schedule of key dates used in the planning and implementation of an event, season or other defined commercial situation such as a marketing campaign. It is used to identify priorities and monitor progress over the period leading to a deadline.

Critical success factors (CSFs): the key elements that determine success in a particular business. For example, in a fashion company, interpretation of fashion trends, product design and quality, price, speed to market and location of distribution are common CSFs.

CSR (corporate social responsibility): a catch-all term used to refer to an organisation's responsibility to conduct their activities in ways which are legal and socially acceptable. Most large organisations have a specific function dedicated to ensuring compliance with an ever-changing and complex social and cultural agenda that is driven sometimes by national and global politics. Elements that may feature within the scope of CSR include concerns over the sustainability of resources, ethical practices relating to employment, working conditions and the exploitation of people, animals and the environment.

Culture: the attitudes, values, standards and behaviours of a group that are often defined by nationality.

Customer: an individual who buys or uses a product or service in either a B2C or B2B situation.

Customer-centric marketing: marketing that puts the customer at the centre of all business planning and activities.

Customer database: a well-organised electronic or paper-based list of customer or prospects which details much useful information about their lives and circumstances and any information on their purchasing behaviour. This helps better targeting of future marketing activity.

Customer relationship management (CRM): the deliberate and sustained effort of an organisation to create a lasting and valuable two-way relationship with a customer.

Customer satisfaction/delight: basic customer satisfaction is the minimum level that all customers expect in any marketing transaction, while customer delight is achieved when expectations of a product and/or service are exceeded far beyond any known or normal expectation.

Customer value: the overall value of a customer to a business. This is often referred to as customer lifetime value and can be calculated as the average spend over a period of time. It may also refer to customers' perception of the extent to which a product or service has delivered value for them.

DC (distribution centre): a centre to which fashion products are delivered before being sorted, rebagged and distributed to stores. DCs have replaced warehouses for most fashion companies, as they want stock levels to be kept to a minimum.

Decider: the person who actually makes the buying decision, often not the buyer or purchaser. This applies to both B2C and B2B.

Demarketing: activities intended to cool or reduce the demand for a product or service in line with production capacity. Demarketing tactics may include raising prices, reducing image communications or promotion activities and/or restricting the supply of specific products.

Demographics: selected population characteristics used by organisations to describe markets or groups of people. Most commonly used in marketing as supplementary data to define and profile a specific target market. Demographic characteristics include gender, age, race, income, occupation, educational attainment, disabilities, mobility (e.g. travel time to work), home ownership and location.

Department store: a retail organisation which specialises in selling a wide range of products and services. They are distinguished from mixed or variety retailers by the much wider range of stock carried.

Descriptive research: research which describes characteristics and/or data about a specific population through addressing factual questions – who, what, when and how. The basic reason for undertaking this type of research is to establish the cause of something that is happening.

Differentiation: a generic strategy based upon being different from the competition. In fashion, most brands are differentiators and justify their existence by being different from other brands through a range of factors that include design, style, image, status, location, trend association, product quality, exclusivity and provenance, price, convenience, service and customer shopping experience.

Direct competition: a direct rival to a retailer or brand that is competing in the same market segment.

Direct mail *see* direct marketing

Direct marketing: direct communication by an organisation with actual or targeted potential customers. Methods include mailshot advertising (print and e-mail) and cold-calling to people's homes.

Direct response television (DRTV): television advertising that is designed to raise awareness and generate a specific response to the advertising message. The response usually desired by the advertiser is a phone call or e-mail from the viewer to the freephone number/web address featured in the TV advert.

Discount: a reduction in the selling price, usually shown as % discount or value reduction.

Discount store: a store that sells products at a very low price on a regular basis. Discount stores selling brands are often referred to as 'off-price' stores.

Distribution: the process of making products and services available to customers.

Distribution channel: a specific method of selling products and services to customers. The term normally refers to retailing (including e-commerce), wholesaling, franchising and licensing. All are commonly used by fashion brands. Brands may use intensive or selective distribution strategies according to market demand and positioning.

Dogs see BCG

DOSs (directly operated stores): stores which are owned and operated by brands as part of a channel distribution strategy. They are also referred to as mono-brand stores. They include large flagship stores located in prestigious locations, which act as a vehicle for communicating the brand experience to consumers. Many luxury brands shifted the emphasis of their distribution strategy away from licensing, franchising and wholesaling to DOSs in order to regain greater control over their branding.

Drive time: a term used to refer to the average time taken for consumers to drive from home to a retail location.

Drop lifting: the guerrilla marketing activity that involves a marketer unexpectedly placing products in a retail location, with the intention of generally surprising and exciting a new audience and so promoting that product.

EAC (equivalent advertising cost): a means of comparing the amount of column inches/centimetres of editorial or press coverage obtained by PR activity, with the equivalent media cost of advertising in that same amount of space.

EDI (electronic data interchange): this refers to networked electronic flows of information such as sales data or delivery information.

EFTPoS (electronic fund transfer point of sale): this refers to the capability of operating debit and credit cards in retailing.

Elasticity of demand: a theory explaining the relationship between changes in price and demand. When demand is 'elastic' a change in price creates a proportionally greater change in demand. So a (percentage) price increase creates a greater (percentage) fall in demand and vice versa. Where the calculation of the PED formula is greater than 1, demand is elastic and where it is less than 1, demand is inelastic.

Emotional marketing: a term coined by Marc Gobé which refers to a shift in marketing thinking, enabling consumers to connect emotionally with a brand.

Ethical marketing: refers to a marketing approach that places equal emphasis on ensuring organisations comply with standards that are in accord with generally agreed social values and attitudes. The CSR function will typically oversee the wide range of issues that could fall into this general area. There is no consensus as to what ethics in fashion specifically refers to and the concept can apply to the exploitation of people (low wages, working conditions, fair trade, child labour, the sexualisation of children in fashion, size zero models), the environment (issues of sustainability in production, use of natural resources, recycling) and animals (PETA). The lack of consensus means that there is no nationally or globally agreed approach to the subject.

Executive summary: typically the first page of a business report that provides an overall summary of the key points, including any headline figures and conclusions.

Experiential marketing: marketing techniques used by brands to engage consumers using face-to-face, interactive and sensory activities. They are intended to affect consumers emotionally, encouraging co-creation, greater spend and increasing the likelihood of brand loyalty. Experiential marketing is typically creative and engaging, but less abstract and spontaneous than guerrilla marketing.

External assessment: an audit of the macro trading environment undertaken to help an organisation make commercial decisions. A number of models exist, including the variations on PEST (see chapter 10).

Factory outlet: a distribution channel located usually (but not always) at manufacturing facilities and used to sell end-of-line products. The products are usually sold at a significant discount.

Fads: the short-term trend-driven demand for products.

Family life cycle (SAGACITY): a method of segmentation based on a theory of the family life cycle. It suggests that consumers have different spending priorities according to the variable family responsibilities over a lifetime.

Fashion: normally defined as the current style of dressing or appearance that is adopted by a majority of people at a particular time. Mass adoption is a key characteristic, hence the terms 'fashionable' and 'in fashion' (implying a majority consensus). Fashion is in part defined by its inevitable demise, as it survives through constantly changing. Fashion is different from style, which tends to be about individual expression.

Fashionability: a term used, mostly in buying, to reference the level of 'fashion' in the design of a product.

Fashion buyer: the function that decides on the fashion products to be sold by a brand or retailer. There are two main categories that operate within clothing markets. Brand buyer refers to the role associated with boutiques and most department stores, where the job is centred on selecting branded products to stocked for sale to consumers. The second and more complex role is that of an own-brand buyer.

Fashion cycle: the notion that fashion follows a cyclical pattern over time. Retro design trends are evidence of recycling and updating previous ideas.

Fashion forecasting: also known as trend prediction, it is the art of interpreting a range of qualitative style, design, cultural, social and technological information to predict future trends in style, product and fashion design.

Fashion lead time: the time between supply and delivery. In fashion buying it normally refers to the time between placing an order and receiving delivery into a distribution centre. Lead times vary hugely according to the type of fashion brand. However, the influence of fast fashion means that many mass-market retailer brands produce new collections every six weeks. Lead times may be as low as two weeks if sourced in a domestic market.

Fashion merchandiser: the operational role in retailing that parallels buying. Merchandising is concerned with range planning and control of stock flow into and around the business with the aim of maximising margin.

Fashion trend: a seasonal fashion theme that can be interpreted through the design and style of a product. Trends may emerge from a wide variety of sources, although the sequence of textile, product and fashion week shows contribute to a broad set of fashion looks for a season.

Fashion weeks: defined periods in the annual fashion calendar in which designers showcase seasonal fashion collections in a number of international cities (New York, London, Milan and Paris being the most influential).

Fast fashion: a term that refers to the ever-increasing speed with which some fashion retailers change their products. It is closely linked to the product design and supply concept of 'once it's gone, it's gone' that is adopted by retailers such as Zara.

Fixed costs: costs that do not vary with output and which normally include rent, wages and utilities.

Flagship store: the top store in its class. Well-discussed notions of the term 'flagship' include ideas of superiority, communication and innovation. The term, derived from naval usage to describe a superior ship often carrying the admiral of the fleet, crosses into retailing by signifying a brand's best store.

Flash mob: an organised meeting of a group of people to achieve a specified objective. The objectives are often quite random and esoteric, leading to considerable public interest and press coverage. Closely linked to the concept of 1960s' 'happenings' (see chapter 9).

FMCG (fast-moving consumer goods): refers to a sector of branded products that includes grocery and other household goods. Such products sell in large volumes every week.

FOB (free on board): the terms under which an order is made with a supplier or manufacturer. It means that the CP agreed only includes transport costs to a vessel at a port in the manufacturer's country.

Focus group: a small number of respondents who are selected to participate in qualitative market research. The respondents are interviewed in depth typically for a period of 45–60 minutes in order to understand the deeper issues that underpin more superficial responses. It is common for 10–12 focus groups to be required for the results to be useful.

Fragmentation (line or style): the break-up of a particular style into SKUs that no longer reflect a complete size or colour scale. Fragmented stock refers to product styles, which are left in sizes and/or colours that are unpopular and hard to sell.

Fragmentation (media): a very wide choice of media, meaning that each medium is seen by fewer consumers.

Franchising: a method of retailing that involves licensing an individual or company to sell a brand's own products as though it were the brand itself. To all intents it is the brand operating, since the consumer will see no discernible difference.

Fulfilment: the term used to describe the successful delivery of a remote transaction to a consumer.

Gen-X (Generation X): the term used to define the generation of people born between 1965 and 1979.

Gen-Y (Generation Y): the term used to define the generation of people born between 1980 and 1984.

Geo-demographics: a segmentation variable that mixes demographic information with geographical location data. It is critically important to the location of (physical) retail outlets.

Gift with purchase: a sales promotion involving the provision of a free gift to consumers when they spend above a certain amount of money or buy a specific product.

Globalisation: the general term referring to the broadening of international business, communication, culture, movement of people and diffusion of technologies.

Grey market/parallel importing: the terms refer to the trade of products which, although legal themselves (i.e. not counterfeit), are not authorised by the brands. They refer in essence to an unauthorised distribution of branded stock that may arise from excess production from licensed manufacturers.

Gross margin: the difference between the CP and RSP of a product as expressed as a percentage of the selling price.

Guerrilla marketing: a way of using non-traditional activities to persuade consumers to engage with a brand by involving and engaging them with more usual marketing activities, as opposed to traditional marketing approaches.

Heritage: refers to the history and reputation of a business or brand. This is critically important to brands in the luxury-goods sector, since heritage is integrally linked to the brand narrative and artisan quality of the products.

High street: term referring to a central shopping location in a UK town or city. Traditionally, shops are located around a central thoroughfare. This is still the case for many provincial towns and cities in the UK, although out-of-town shopping malls have become an important competitor. In the US the term 'Main Street' is used.

Home shopping: refers to retailing which enables consumers to buy products remotely (from stores) via a catalogue, television (teleshopping) or a transactional website.

Horizontal integration: refers to a type of business structure, management and control. It is a strategy used to sell products in many different markets.

Infomercial: a broadcast commercial that is longer and more factually informative than a normal TV advert.

Information jockey: someone who is capable of finding and interpreting meanings and drawing conclusions from a large amount of data within the organisation.

Independent retailers: small, owner-operated retailers that normally sell branded products.

Indirect competition: competition that impinges on a brand's sales, but less obviously so than a direct competitor. Any product that competes for discretionary spending can be considered indirect competition. For example, expenditure on mobile phones among teenagers reduces the amount of personal disposable income they have to spend on fashion products. UK supermarkets have gradually extended their non-food offer to include own-brand fashion products. In the early stages this would have been indirect competition to fashion brands. However, brands such as George and Florence and Fred are now direct competitors to many lower-priced fashion retailer brands.

Innovation: refers most commonly in fashion to new developments in design, both textile and product. Can also refer to marketing communications, retailing and media developments that are new and different.

Intensive distribution *see* distribution

Internal audit: an internal assessment of an organisation's strengths and weaknesses.

Internal marketing: internal communications within an organisation to ensure that an organisation's message and strategies are being implemented by all.

Jobber: the function which buys and distributes end-of-line terminal stock obtained from fabric suppliers and fashion retailers and brands.

Joint venture: the strategic partnership of two organisations in a new market. Such partnerships are increasingly important for Western brands intending to enter and operate in emerging markets such as India and Dubai.

Kickback: this means a bribe. Also colloquially known as a 'bung'.

KPI (key performance indicator): a measure of business performance such as sales, market share and profitability.

KVI: Key value item.

Knocking copy: refers to advertising copy, which attacks a competitor's product or brand.

Lead time *see* fashion lead time

Licensing: the business strategy employed when a brand authorises another business (licensee) to design, make and distribute products using the brand's name. The brand (licensor) receives royalties from the licensee, while simultaneously achieving wide market coverage at very low or nil cost. Some specialist product categories such as eyewear and perfumes require brands to use licensees when they do not have adequate product competency.

Lifestyle: a general description of how an individual or a group of people chooses to live.

Lifetime value: the potential earnings of a business from a customer based on forward calculations of current sales turnover (from that customer) throughout their life.

Like-for-like (LFL): refers to comparative sales figures. Like-for-like sales means this year's sales compared with sales from an equivalent distribution network (usually expressed in the number of outlets) in a previous period (normally a week/year).

Line: the general term used to describe an individual product, which may be available in several sizes and colours. Individual lines are normally given a unique line number to help product identification in the computerised merchandise planning system.

Loyalty marketing: refers to incentive-based schemes, including reward points, which were originally intended to achieve customer loyalty by securing repeat purchase. However, repeat purchase does not equate to loyalty, especially if customers perceive superior incentives are available elsewhere. Loyalty is not something that businesses can scheme to obtain, since it is an emotional disposition. Customer loyalty is typically achieved where the package of benefits provided by a brand is consistently better than those of the competitors. Further, too few brands have a clear idea of what customer loyalty means in terms of average spend or lifetime value.

Luxe: a shortened version of luxury.

Luxury brand: a brand that designs, makes and distributes luxury goods. Characteristics of a luxury brand include global recognition, exclusivity, artisan heritage and reputation for quality, immaculate service and premium prices.

Luxury goods: refers to products at the high end of a market and often associated with fashion. However, luxury goods include a very wide range of products from fashion clothing and accessories (including watches and jewellery) to wines and spirits, cars and even shotguns (as sold by Purdey).

Mark-down: the money spent on discounts to reduce retail prices with the aim of selling stock. Essentially it uses potential profit to clear old stock.

Mark-up: a measure of profit as a percentage of a CP. A mark-up is added to a CP to achieve a RSP. Retail buyers need to know their brand's mark-up in order to negotiate CPs with suppliers.

Market: any group of people, comprising buyers and sellers, who wish to trade. In fashion a market typically refers to a customer segment.

Market development: refers to a strategy in which a business increases sales by expanding its market into a new segment. This is commonly achieved through international expansion.

Market follower: a business that follows the marketing strategies of another.

Market leader: a brand which is at the forefront of its market, having the largest market share and highest levels of brand awareness.

Market penetration: refers to a strategy in which a business increases sales by expanding its market within the existing segment.

Market positioning: the position that a brand is perceived to hold in a market compared with competitors. Although brands plan to achieve a specific position (often located by price, design and quality), it is ultimately a customer's perceptions of a brand's positioning that matters. All too often there is a gap between the position that a brand thinks it holds compared with how customers perceive the brand to be positioned.

Market research: the specific process of researching a particular market using qualitative and/or quantitative techniques. This typically refers to primary research.

Market segmentation: refers to the process of identifying a subdivision of a wider market in order to target it effectively with a marketing mix. As such the market segment needs to be sufficiently homogenous to respond to a single integrated marketing mix. It also needs to be sufficiently capable of delivering sales over time. Chapter 3 deals with market segmentation in detail.

Marketing budget: the budget spent on marketing activity, which is normally focused on marketing communications (promotion), usually over a specified period.

Marketing communications (Mark Coms): the marketing activities associated with promotion (in the marketing mix). See chapter 6.

Marketing manager: the operational role responsible for implementing some or all of the marketing mix. In fashion, the marketing manager typically has the responsibility for implementing only marketing communications. Product, Price and Place (of distribution) are the responsibilities of buying and merchandising.

Marketing mix: also known as the 4 Ps or 7 Ps. It refers to the integrated implementation of Product, Price, etc., to achieve sales and profits. A marketing mix is the tactical implementation of a marketing strategy.

Marketing plan: the planned marketing activity of a brand proposed for a defined period of time.

Marketing research: the wider process of gathering market information – both secondary and primary.

Marketing strategy: the long-term plan designed to utilise a brand's resources to maximise sales and profits in markets. Ansoff's matrix provides strategic options for planning to grow sales of products in markets.

Massification: the mass consumption and adoption of a product or service.

Masstige: refers to the cool status associated with accessing and owning trendy branded products that are at relatively low prices. It is literally a combination of the words 'mass' and 'prestige'. It arises from the lower entry price points of products sold by status/prestige (often luxury) brands.

Media: different types of communication vehicles ranging from print (newspapers, magazines, books) to broadcast (TV, radio, cinema) and new media (Internet).

Merchandising: the operational role responsible for maximising margin through effective planning and management of stock. It is a highly numerate role.

Mergers and acquisitions: refers to the strategic process of one organisation buying and assimilating another. In some markets it provides the only way to grow sales and profits, especially if a market is saturated.

Message: a concise marketing communication that is delivered by using audio/ visual).

Mission statement: refers to the (officially written and circulated) rationale or purpose of an organisation and its activities. It is closely linked to the organisation's generic strategy and as such provides direction and vision for all the staff.

Multi-brand group: a conglomerate that owns and operates multiple brands within a sector. Examples include LVMH, which operates Christian Dior, Lanvin, Louis Vuitton and Pucci, among others. In the UK, Arcadia is a multi-brand retailer group that owns Topshop, Miss Selfridge, Wallis, Dorothy Perkins and Burton, among others.

Multi-channel distribution: the distribution of products to customers using a combination of third-party channels such as agents, licensing, wholesaling, franchising and direct retailing channels.

Mystery shopping: retailers and brands sometimes employ professional companies to evaluate the shopping experience and service provision by posing as customers. The intention is to improve the overall retail provision and customer experience.

Need: something that stimulates action with the intention of achieving satisfaction. Marketers seek to identify, target and satisfy a range of physiological and psychological needs in consumers through the creation and provision of products and services.

Net profit: profit obtained after operating costs but before taxes. It is also known as pre-tax profit.

New/Win/Free: key words used in sales promotion to incentivise consumers to buy products or services.

Observational research: a form of social research that involves the direct observation of subjects in their natural setting. A typical fashion application would be competitive shopping where an individual from a product-buying or merchandising team will visit competitors' stores specifically to observe new products, product ranging, pricing, sales promotions, and window and store presentations. Such on-the-ground research is critical to effective operational management decision-making in buying and merchandising.

Once it's gone, it's gone: a marketing approach that limits the supply of products in a fast-changing market. It is intended to create a perception of exclusivity in mass markets. Zara is a good example of a fashion retailer that limits the replenishment of styles to motivate consumers to buy products as they arrive in stores.

Online: the term means operating via the Internet.

On-pack sales promotions: sales promotions (incentives) which are located on or in the packaging of a product.

On-trend: fashion retailing term to refer to any fast-moving trend defined by style, colour or fabric that emerges within a season. There can be several trends emerging and running concurrently at any point in a season.

Open-ended questions: questions that seek to elicit responses that are deeper, more complex and more detailed than the limited answers to closed questions. Such questions are designed to encourage full answers using the subject's own knowledge and/or feelings.

Open-to-buy (OTB): the available budget for a fashion retailer to spend on stock during a specified period (usually week/season).

Opinion leader: an individual to whom others look for direction and whose views are valued. It is typically associated with an individual who sets a trend.

Opportunity cost: the cost of a lost opportunity when you pursue one course of action instead of another. It typically relates to a comparison between one investment and the potential for another. For example, a decision to undertake a risky diversification should be measured against the potential earnings from a safer market-penetration strategy.

Own label/brand: a retailer's own range of products. Increasingly the term relates to the products of retailer brands. The term own-brand is more commonly used as more retailers use branding to differentiate themselves.

PDI: personal disposable income: how much an individual has left to spend.

Pen portrait (customer profile): a written description of a target customer, which includes details of demographics, attitudes, personality and a typical lifestyle. These more detailed insights into the target customer help to direct decisions about the marketing mix. The information should be based on robust market research.

Penetration pricing: a pricing strategy which uses a low RSP to achieve an increased market share.

Perceived risk: risk that is believed to exist or may exist. It is an important consideration for marketers as customers perceive greater risk of dissatisfaction the higher the price they have to pay. This typically results in customers undertaking more research prior to purchasing expensive products or services.

Perceptual map: also known as a positioning map (see chapter 3).

Personal selling: refers to the use of trained salespeople to sell products.

Planning: the process of organising activities, finances and events for future implementation

PLC/IPO (Public Limited Company/Initial Public Offer): refers to the conversion of a company into a publicly owned one through the sale of shares (also known as company stock). It is normally undertaken to raise financial capital for investment in further business activities.

POP (proof of purchase): consumers may be asked to retain receipts, labels or possibly packaging in order to claim a prize, discount or other offer, usually at a later date. The need to save these this can encourage consumer loyalty and ultimately increased or more frequent purchasing. Often used as a key element of sales promotion campaigns. (POP can also refer to point of purchase.)

PR (public relations): the specific marketing function that seeks to promote an organisation and its products and activities by generating publicity.

Press day: a day in which retailers and brands promote their new seasons collections to the media (normally the fashion press). There are three main press days in a year, falling in April, July and November.

Press release (news release): a short and concisely written summary of the main features of an event such as a new season's collection, product or store launch. It is typically aimed at fashion journalists and may feature in a press pack. Press releases can take hard copy of digital formats.

Price: an amount of money agreed between a seller and buyer for the sale and purchase of a product or service. Selling price can refer to any transaction in a supply chain. Retail price refers to the price paid by a consumer.

Price architecture: a series of selling prices within the whole price range.

Price elasticity of demand *see* elasticity of demand

Price point: a specific selling price.

Primary data: data which are collected specifically for an original research project.

Prime contractor: when a fashion brand or supplier uses several factories, the major factory used to produce the garment is often known as the prime rather than the secondary contractor.

Product: a generic term that refers to something tangible which is designed, manufactured and sold by a brand and delivers a number of benefits to consumers who are willing to pay for them.

Product benefits: the reason a customer is willing to buy a product or service is to obtain the various benefits that it provides. Marketers need to convey the benefits of products clearly to customers.

Promotion: refers to the process of communication and persuasion used by an organisation in the marketing of its products and activities.

Promotional mix: the specific mix of promotional tools and techniques used by an organisation to achieve promotional aims and objectives.

Promotional pricing: prices are often reduced in fashion businesses on either a permanent or temporary basis. Permanent price reductions are generally applied to consistently poorly performing styles, with the aim of accelerating the rate of sale and ultimately clearing a problem. Temporary price reductions are often applied to running lines during sales and promotional periods to stimulate demand and ultimately net profitability. Temporary price reductions can usefully be used to lower stock levels of overstocked products.

Psychographics: a form of segmentation based on consumers' lifestyles.

Psychological pricing: often a specific fashion price point may be created to give a perception of value. For example, £99.99 is often perceived by consumers as being much cheaper than £100 even though only a 1p saving is made. Sometimes prices are deliberately set at a higher-than-expected level, with some consumers being fooled into believing that the product is of better quality than it really is. Consumers' perception of what constitutes reasonable price value varies dramatically according to their level of product and market understanding and their own financial circumstances.

Publicity: communication about an organisation and its activities (including products) generated through the media via third parties – normally journalists. Publicity is normally achieved by fashion brands through PR activities.

Pure play: a term used to refer to an internet-only trading company.

Push and pull strategies: marketing promotion strategies that have different objectives and operational methods. A pull strategy is concerned with attracting or 'pulling' a customer to a brand through advertising and other image-based communications. The aim is to persuade customers actively to seek out a brand and its products. A push strategy involves incentivising retailers and stockists to carry and sell stock. The brand's intention is to make the stock as widely available to customers as possible.

Qualitative research: a form of research that involves the use of unstructured exploratory techniques (such as group discussions and in-depth interviews) and that are based on statistically small samples which are used in order to understand a problem more fully.

Quantitative research: a form of research that involves the collection of (statistically) large samples of quantitative data and usually some form of statistical analysis. Quantitative research is often used to substantiate the findings from qualitative research.

Random sample: refers to a type of sample, known as a probability sample, where all potential respondents in a population of interest have an equal, known and non-zero chance of being selected.

Range: the scope and scale of any fashion product or service offer. It generally consists of a specified and predetermined number of products, colours, styles, sizes and prices. Often whole ranges or specific parts of a fashion range are given a theme name, for example, 'Out of Africa'. Good range planning makes product selection easier for the customer.

Recall: refers to the recollection of a communication by consumers.

Reference group: a group of people to which an individual (consumer) refers when making a purchase decision.

Relationship marketing: the opposite approach to transactional marketing. A relationship marketing strategy is one which aims to secure long-term business through genuine customer loyalty (as opposed to incentivised repeat purchasing).

Retailer: a business that sells directly to consumers. Mostly commonly associated with shops but also includes catalogue and internet-based selling to consumers.

Retailer brand: also known as own brand and has been referred to as retailer own label (own label for short). This is discussed in some detail in chapter 8. Essentially it is a retailer's own 'named' product. It might take the retailer's name (if the retailer has some brand status) or operate as a separate name such as Per Una at M&S.

Reverse auction: a type of auction in which the main objective is to achieve a low purchase price as sellers compete to obtain business. A reverse auction is more commonly understood by consumers as a competition in which a person guesses the lowest value of goods or services in order to win them. The lowest unique bidder is the winner. Reverse auctions have become much more accessible to consumers through the Internet, although their increased popularity as competitions has resulted in more phone/text-facilitated reverse auctions.

RSP (retail selling price): sometimes also referred as the RRP (recommended retail price), MSRP (manufacturer's suggested retail price), SRP (suggested retail price) or list price. Although it is now illegal to fix retail prices, retailers and brands often print price lists showing the RSP. By setting this as a benchmark, the idea is to maintain a high-price integrity for the brand, to try and stop it being discounted irrationally. It can also act as a reference price for consumers. However, it can also be used as a method of psychological consumer deception, by creating the perception of a higher product value than is actually the case. In some European countries, the creation and manipulation of a 'bogus' high 'recommended' RSP is illegal.

RTW (ready-to-wear): most commonly refers to the luxury/designer level fashion sector that is showcased twice a year at the international fashion weeks. The shows run in a consistent sequence: New York, London, Milan and Paris. Paris is considered to be the most important fashion week with approximately 100 luxury or designer fashion brands showing.

Runway show: also known as a catwalk show. It is any kind of show where models display fashion garments and accessories by parading down a raised platform for the benefit of an audience. Fashion weeks feature either ready-to-wear or couture fashion collections and are mostly attended by the fashion press and buyers.

Sales: a measure of the numbers of products sold either by volume (numbers of units) or by financial value over a specified period (usually week/month/season/year).

Sales density: the concentration of sales in a specific selling space, usually expressed as the sales generated per square metre of trading floor space over a year.

Sales promotions: refers to all forms of incentive-based promotions that are intended to induce trial and increase volume sales. Sales promotions are more directly linked to sales performance than advertising and PR. Fashion is not a sophisticated user of sales promotions compared with FMCG brands, and fashion retailers tend to rely mostly on price-discounting to drive sales.

Sample: a first or early example of a proposed garment or product produced by a manufacturer, which is normally sent to the fashion buyer for evaluation, approval and sealing. Press samples are either specifically made or are the first off production and couriered ahead of shipment of the bulk order.

SBU (strategic business unit): a brand or company that sits within a portfolio of companies owned by a conglomerate. Lanvin could be considered an SBU of LVMH and Top Shop an SBU of Arcadia Group.

Season: a period of time during which fashion products are sold, usually spring/summer (Feb.–July) and autumn/winter (Aug.–Jan.).

Second life: a virtual world in which 'residents' (signed-up, paying members) interact with each other within the 'world' by using avatars. Individuals can customise their avatar in any way they choose and buy land to set up home or run a business. Certain brands see virtual worlds as good vehicles for brand communication, since the residents tend to fit the innovator or early-adopter demographic profiles.

Secondary data/research: refers to knowledge and information that already exists and does not require a marketer to commission new (primary) research.

Secondary research/data: refers to research that already exists. It is also known as 'desk research' due to the sedentary nature of poring over literature. Secondary research is so called since it refers to published research that originated for some other reason but subsequently assists further research purposes.

Segmentation (market segmentation): refers to the process of dividing markets into groups of consumers who are similar to each other, but sufficiently different from other consumers to become a market. This is discussed in chapter 3.

Sell-through: refers to the percentage of a product sold from a total order or 'buy'. It is normally used in the context of the percentage sold at full price compared with that sold at mark-down and terminal stock (unsold).

Semantic Differential Scale (Osgood Scale): refers to a type of categorical, non-comparative scale with two opposing adjectives separated by a sequence of unlabelled categories, for example Good 1 2 3 4 5 6 7 Poor.

Semiotics is the theory of signs and symbols in language and the meanings they convey. In research it is used to identify and evaluate the true meaning behind consumers' linguistic responses, to decode their cultural frames of reference and behaviours. It employs specialist techniques to overcome the problems of conditioned or expected responses (social group norms) and provides a deeper understanding of consumers' motivations.

Share of voice: refers to the proportion of all promotion achieved by a brand within a specific sector.

Shopping: the act of browsing, selecting and purchasing products and services. As consumers have become wealthier and more informed, so retailers and brands have enhanced the shopping experiences offered.

Shopping centre: generally an idea of the 1970s, where an older historic shopping area has a modern, multi-floor, enclosed shopping precinct built adjacent to it. In some instances they were also built as freestanding entities on land adjacent to towns, and more recently larger regional shopping centres such as Lakeside, Bluewater and the Metro Centre have been built adjacent to convenient motorways in remoter but car-friendly locations. (Brent Cross was Britain's first purpose-built enclosed shopping centre, opened in 1976.)

SKU (stock-keeping unit): refers to a product in a particular style in a particular colour and of a specific size. It is essentially a unit of stock.

Slogan: a short memorable phrase or statement that is intended to sum up a marketing proposition and easily be recalled by customers. It is most commonly used in advertising. A strapline is sometimes used to reference a slogan that is associated with a specific brand.

Social class: a largely outdated concept that segments a population according to education and occupation. In the past, assumptions were made about the relationship between income levels and occupation. These no longer have the same relevance, as the 'middle class' in the UK has expanded and absorbed many so-called working-class people. Reliance on social class alone to define a target market would be naive.

Social networking: the practice of communicating socially through organised web environments on the Internet. Examples include Facebook, Bebo and MySpace.

Spiff: A financial incentive placed on the sale of a specific product. It is normally operated in the premium fashion clothing market where sales staff work on commission. A spiff will be placed on a slow-selling product style or colour so that the salesperson will receive a fixed amount of money per product sold. It is a very effective sales promotion linked to personal selling.

Stock cover: a KPI indicating how many weeks' worth of stock a retailer has left at the current rate of sale. If cover is very low, then the retailer is selling stock quickly and needs to buy more.

Stock turn: a KPI referring to the number of times that a stockholding is sold out in a specified period – usually a year.

Strategy: a long-term plan that utilises resources to achieve objectives.

Style: an individual mode of expression or 'look'. It typically refers to the design of a fashion product or the way in which an individual combines clothing and accessories to create an outfit.

Subculture: a group of people with a culture (whether distinct or hidden) that differentiates them from the larger culture to which they belong. In a fashion context, subcultures often adopted fashion styles to demonstrate their belonging, for example, the punks and their ripped and distressed clothing styles.

Subliminal advertising: refers to the covert communication of messages by brands to consumers.

Supermarket: a larger, self-service retailer selling a wide variety of fast-moving food and non-food products.

Supplier: any external organisation that produces fashion products or delivers associated services. They are generally financially separate and independent from the purchasing organisation.

Supply chain: refers to the network of businesses and logistics concerned with moving products from manufacturers to consumers.

Survey: refers to the process of gathering marketing research data about customers and markets.

SWOT (strengths, weaknesses, opportunities and threats): used as a planning tool to understand the internal situation of an organisation and to inform the development of a strategy. SWOT is normally used in conjunction with the PEST tool.

Target market: a group of customers who are targeted by an organisation with a marketing mix.

Telemarketing: when telephone contact is used in connection with any form of marketing activity. Usually it is mostly in the context of selling and research activities and processes.

Terminal stock: old stock which is left over at the end of a fashion season.

Test marketing (trial line): the design, manufacture and sale of a small number of a product or style to assess consumers' demand.

Trade barriers/tariffs: trade barriers are sometimes used by countries against one another to try and protect their indigenous business or industrial activities. Such protectionism can take the form of special import taxes or duties, annual import level quotas or (often unreasonable) legal or quasi-legal product or service specifications – or a combination of these. The World Trade Organisation is opposed to trade barriers.

Trade fair: a specialist exhibition or static show where manufacturers or service providers pay to display their products and service offers to business buyers. It is not open to the general public and normally has a specialist theme or product offer. They are generally bi-annual. Première Vision for Fabrics and Prêt-à-Porter for ready-made garments are both international shows held in Paris.

Trade promotion: any form of B2B sales promotional activity aimed at encouraging the initial stocking or ongoing sales of a product/service by a retailer.

Turnover: a term used to denote a level of sales achieved over a specific period. Annualised retail sales are sometimes referred to as annual turnover. The terms are interchangeable but turnover is more usually applied to the sales of a manufacturing business.

USP (unique selling proposition): sometimes referred to as unique selling point, the term refers to a unique package of product benefits that positively distinguishes the offer of one fashion business from another. Few fashion businesses are able to rely on a single selling point or benefit to keep customers from switching to competitors. The term has evolved to become emotional selling proposition (ESP).

Value: the perceived or actual 'worth' of something compared with its financial cost. A consumer evaluates the benefits offered by a product or brand compared with the price they will have to pay. Sometimes the term 'value' is also used to reference low prices.

Value chain: a term defined by Michael Porter, the famous business writer, which in essence suggests that the value chain is based on the organisation as a series of processes that each creates value. For example, the manufacturing (or service) organisation is a system, made up of subsystems each with inputs, transformation processes and outputs. Inputs, transformation processes and outputs involve the acquisition and consumption of resources – money, labour, materials, equipment, buildings, land, administration and management. How value chain activities are carried out determines costs and affects profits and ultimately net profitability.

Value retailing: a mode of retailing that obviously and regularly offers product and/or services below the average market price(s).

Variety retailer: a large-store-space retailer that sells a wide range of clothing, household and sometimes food products, but not high-ticket items such as furniture, carpets and electrical goods.

Viral marketing: planned and innovative campaigns which rely on consumer interest, enthusiasm and word of mouth to generate circulation around the Internet or other network.

Visual merchandising: the retailing function that is responsible for in-store and window presentation. It is sometimes referred to as display.

Warehouse: a large, housed facility for holding stock. Most large fashion retailers have moved over to DCs, which do not store stock for any length of time but simply receive it and then dispatch it to store in the correct quantities and packaging. DCs tend to be more efficient and cost-effective than warehouses.

Website: a visual presence on the Internet that is owned and managed by a person or company. In fashion business these tend to be either promotional or transactional.

Wholesale: this is a method of distribution where a brand sells its products to retailers as a means of accessing a consumer market. The brand sells its products at a price lower than the agreed or recommended RSP in order to allow a profit margin for the retailer. In other words, the price paid to the retailer is not that charged by the brand. Although the brand therefore receives a lower selling price (than it would by distributing through its own stores), wholesaling provides some real advantages, which include accessing a location where no new retail site is available.

World Trade Organisation (WTO): a group of countries that come together to agree terms for international trade. Talks have replaced the old General Agreement on Tariffs and Trade (GATT).

references

Anderson, C. (2006), *The Long Tail: How Endless Choice is Creating Unlimited Demand*, London: Random House Business Books.

Angeloni, U. (2001), *The Boutonnière: Style in One's Lapel*, New York: Universe.

Armstrong, G. and Kotler, P. (2004), *Marketing: An Introduction*, Upper Saddle River, NJ: Prentice Hall.

Benady, D. (2004), *Marketing Week*.

Cameron, M. A., Baker, J., Peterson, M. and Braunsberger, K. (2003), 'The Effects of Music, Wait-Length Evaluation, and Mood on a Low-Cost Wait Experience', *Journal of Business Research*, 56(6): 421–30.

Charles-Roux, E. (1981), *Chanel and Her World*, London and Chittenden: Weidenfeld & Nicholson.

Clifton, R. (2003), *The Future of Brands*, New York: New York University Press.

Clifton, R. (2003), 'Fashion 2003 – Luxury in a Cool Climate', *International Herald Tribune* Conference Report (www.wgsn.com).

Ford, T. (2001), 'Fashion 2001 – The Business and The Brand', *International Herald Tribune* Conference Report (www.wgsn.com).

Forth, I. (2004), in J. Doonar, 'French Connection', *Brand Strategy* (October): 10.

Friedman, V. (2006), London Fashion Week, *Financial Times*, 15 September.

Gobé, M. (2001), *Emotional Branding: The New Paradigm for Connecting Brands to People*, New York: Allworth.

Jackson, T. (2005), 'Modern Luxury – Dubai 2005', *International Herald Tribune* Conference Report (www.wgsn.com).

Jackson, T. (2007), 'Supreme Luxury – Moscow 2007', *International Herald Tribune* Conference Report (www.wgsn.com).

Jackson, T. and Shaw, D. (2001), *Mastering Fashion Buying & Merchandising Management*, Basingstoke: Palgrave Macmillan.

Kapferer, J-N. (1992), *Strategic Brand Management: New Approaches to Creating and Evaluating Brand Equity Long Term*, London: Kogan Page.

Klein, N. (2000), *No Logo, No Space, No Choice, No Jobs: Taking Aim at the Brand Bullies*, London: Flamingo.

Kotler, P. (1974), 'Atmospherics as Marketing Tool', *Journal of Retailing*, 49(4): 48–64.

Kotler, P. and Armstrong, G. (2006), *Principles of Marketing*, 11th edn, Harlow: Pearson/ Prentice Hall.

Kotler, P., Wong, V., Saunders, J., Armstrong, G. and Burk Wood, M., (2001), *Principles of Marketing*, 3rd edn, Harlow: Financial Times/Prentice Hall.

Levitt, T. (1960) 'Marketing Myopia', *Harvard Business Review*, July–August.

Levitt, T. (1962) *Innovation in Marketing: New Perspectives for Growth and Profit*, New York: McGraw-Hill.

Lynch, D. and Kordis, P. L. (1998), *Strategy of the Dolphin Scoring a Win in a Chaotic World*, New York: William Morrow.

Maslow, A. H. (1943), 'A Theory of Human Motivation', *Psychological Review*, 50: 370–96.

McDonald, I. (2005), 'French Connection: General Retail Broker's Report', London: Numis Securities.

Menkes, S. (2001), 'Fashion 2001 – The Business and the Brand', *International Herald Tribune* Conference Report (www.wgsn.com).

MINTEL (2004) 'Health and Beauty Retailing – UK', Mintel marketing report, March, London: Mintel International.

National Statistics, www.statistics.gov.uk/methods_quality/ns_sec/ (accessed 9 April 2008).

Nielsen, A. C., *Retail Pocket Book 2007*, Oxford, NTC.

Nielsen/NetRatings (2006), www.nielsen-netratings.com/pr/pr_080305_UK_pdf (accessed 8 June 2008).

Olins, W.(2003), *Wally Olins on Brand*, London: Thames & Hudson.

Perreault, W. D. Jr, Cannon, J. P. and McCarthy, E. J. (2008), *Essentials of Marketing: A Marketing Strategy Planning Approach*, Boston: McGraw-Hill/Irwin.

Pinault, F. (2006), ' Luxury 2006', *International Herald Tribune* Conference Report (www. wgsn.com).

Porter, M. E. (1980), *Competitive Strategy*, New York: The Free Press.

Radice, V. (2002b), 'Fashion 2002 – Luxury Unlimited', *International Herald Tribune* Conference Report (www.wgsn.com).

Randall, G. (1997), *Branding*, London: Kogan Page.

Rogers, E. M. (1995), *Diffusion of Innovations*, 4th edn, New York: The Free Press.

Sishy, I. (2004), *Interview with Giorgio Armani*, New York: Royal Academy and Guggenheim Museum Publications.

Talmage, P. A., *Dictionary of Market Research*, http://www.fieldshare.net/search_dictionary. php (accessed 22 September 2008).

Tech Tribe Report (2006), 'Face "The Youth Marketing Agency"', May.

UK Institute of Public Relations, www.cipr.co.uk/direct/careers.asp?v1=whatis (accessed 14 May 2008).

Warren, E. (1996), *Long-Range Planning: The Executive Viewpoint*, Upper Saddle River, NJ : Prentice-Hall.

WF (Worldpanel Fashion) (2007), 'Report on UK Fashion Clothing', April, London: Taylor Nelson Sofres.

Wipperfürth, A. (2005), *Brand Hijack: Marketing without Marketing*, New York: Portfolio.

Yamaguchi, Y. (2007), 'European Luxury Goods', *UBS Investment Research*, 22 January.

Zeithaml, V. (2000), *Services Marketing: Integrating Customer Focus across the Firm*, Boston and London: Irwin/McGraw-Hill.

index

customers (*continued*)
  as research focus   25–6
  retention of focus   263
  'smart'   16
  see also consumers
cut, make and trim (CMT)   33, 206

Dahl, Sophie   191
Daily Mail   28
Daimler-Chrysler   37
data analysis, poor   49
data collection   45–6
  and analysis   29, 30, 40
  methods   40–2, 42, 49
  process   42
data mugging   23
data transmission, speed of   302
databases
  and direct marketing   179
  of fashion journalists   193
Davies, George   265
Davy, Chelsy   290
DDB (agency)   253
De Sole, Domenico   295
de-cluttering   228
Dean, James   97
Debenhams   82, 187, 214, 250, 264, 309
  Designers at Debenhams 250
decision-making   4, 24–5, 32, 33, 55,
  122, 150
decoding   159
deductions, wrong   49
demand
  changes in   103
  elasticity of   126, Fig. 5.1
  identifying   xvi
democratisation of luxury   126
demographics   10, 25, 48, 55–6, Fig. 3.2
  changes in   18, 301
department stores   147, 215, 218, 220,
  226, 275
  and concessions   115, 223–4
  window displays   228
depth interviews   41–2
design
  departments, in-house   104, 318
  development   107
  and pricing   130–1
  protection   104
  store   275
  uniqueness of   77
design-led approach   3
design-to-stores supply chain   89

designer brands   57, 92–3, 104
designers   35, 36
  British   190
  graduate   180
  high mark-downs   129
  as owners   294–5
  as retailers   104, 318
  star   269, Table 8.7
  successful   269, Table 8.7
Desperate Housewives   18
'detect and alert' systems   111
developing nations, clothing manufacture
  in   145
Diageo   187
Diane von Furstenberg   248
dichotomous questions   43
Dickens, Charles   63
Diet Coke   287
differential advantage   77, 175
differentiated marketing   75–6, 83–4,
  296
differentiation   297, 298, 320
diffusion labels   133
digital natives/immigrants   15
digital technology   166, 275–7, 302
Dior, Christian   93
direct and indirect forces   300–1
direct marketing   151, 156, 157, 160, 172,
  178–9
direct rating test   174
direct response advertising   151
directly operated store (DOS)   270,
  285–6
discount retailers   20, 59, 218, 221
discounting   48, 62, 87–8, 106, 107, 125,
  131, 134
  business problems related to   140–1
  categories of   290
  detrimental effects of   134, 140
  level of discount   181
  level of   139, 152
  phased   141
  product failures   106, 110
  regulations on   154
  slow-moving lines   32, 129, 131
  temporary and permanent   138–40
Disney Corporation   37, 210
display
  quality of   227
  range and depth   101
  schemes, brand-funded   183–4
  techniques, rules of   201
disposable income, increase in   18